LIBRARY OF NEW TESTAMENT STUDIES

641

Formerly the Journal for the Study of the New Testament Supplement series

Editor
Chris Keith

Editorial Board
Dale C. Allison, John M. G. Barclay, Lynn H. Cohick, R. Alan Culpepper, Craig A. Evans, Robert Fowler, Simon J. Gathercole, Juan Hernández Jr., John S. Kloppenborg, Michael Labahn, Matthew V. Novenson, Love L. Sechrest, Robert Wall, Catrin H. Williams, Brittany E. Wilson

Religious Experience and the Creation of Scripture

Examining Inspiration in Luke-Acts and Galatians

Mark Wreford

LONDON • NEW YORK • OXFORD • NEW DELHI • SYDNEY

T&T CLARK
Bloomsbury Publishing Plc
50 Bedford Square, London, WC1B 3DP, UK
1385 Broadway, New York, NY 10018, USA
29 Earlsfort Terrace, Dublin 2, Ireland

BLOOMSBURY, T&T CLARK and the T&T Clark logo are trademarks of
Bloomsbury Publishing Plc

First published in Great Britain 2021
This paperback edition published 2022

Copyright © Mark Wreford, 2021

Mark Wreford has asserted his right under the Copyright, Designs and Patents Act, 1988,
to be identified as Author of this work.

For legal purposes the Acknowledgements on p. xi constitute an extension
of this copyright page.

All rights reserved. No part of this publication may be reproduced or transmitted
in any form or by any means, electronic or mechanical, including photocopying,
recording, or any information storage or retrieval system, without prior
permission in writing from the publishers.

Bloomsbury Publishing Plc does not have any control over, or responsibility
for, any third-party websites referred to or in this book. All internet addresses given in
this book were correct at the time of going to press. The author and publisher regret any
inconvenience caused if addresses have changed or sites have ceased to exist, but can
accept no responsibility for any such changes.

A catalogue record for this book is available from the British Library.

A catalog record for this book is available from the Library of Congress.

ISBN: HB: 978-0-5676-9663-2
PB: 978-0-5676-9869-8
ePDF: 978-0-5676-9664-9
ePUB: 978-0-5676-9666-3

Series: Library of New Testament Studies, 2345678X, volume 286

Typeset by Newgen KnowledgeWorks Pvt. Ltd., Chennai, India

To find out more about our authors and books visit www.bloomsbury.com
and sign up for our newsletters.

For Ellie

Contents

Acknowledgements		xi
List of abbreviations		xiii
Introduction		1
Aims of the study and methodology		5
Section 1 Approaching Religious Experience: Theoretical Foundations		9
1 Religious Experience and New Testament Research		11
1.1. Religious experience in biblical studies research		12
1.1.1. *Religionsgeschichtliche Schule*		13
1.1.2. Lacuna in RE research		15
1.1.3. The recovery of RE as a theme in biblical studies		16
1.1.4. Recent contributions		21
1.2. Religious experience in religious studies research		25
1.2.1. William James		26
1.2.2. RE as a *sui generis* phenomenon		27
1.2.3. RE as a cultural construct		28
1.2.4. RE and non-linguistic meaning		29
1.3. Religious experience: A review		30
2 Approaching Religious Experience		31
2.1. Accessing subjective experience through texts		32
2.1.1. 'Hermeneutical perspicuity': Can we see through the text?		32
2.1.2. Historical analogy: Can we understand the experiences?		34
2.1.3. Hermeneutical charity: Must we accept the text's claims?		36
2.2. Experience and language		36
2.2.1. Models of affective understanding		41
2.3. Religious experience and theology		44
2.3.1. Phenomenology and bracketing		45
2.3.2. Methodological naturalism		46

	2.3.3.	Methodological pluralism	48
	2.3.4.	Exegetical focus	49
2.4.	Defining religious experience		50
	2.4.1.	'Felt impacts'	51
	2.4.2.	'Trans-empirical realities'	51
	2.4.3.	'Within the culturally patterned life'	52
	2.4.4.	'Of an individual or group'	52
	2.4.5.	Summary	53
2.5.	Defining Scripture		53
	2.5.1.	The creation of Scripture	54
	2.5.2.	Scripture, RE and inspiration	55
	2.5.3.	Scripture and canonicity	56
2.6.	Applying the approach		59

Section 2 Religious Experience and the Creation of Scripture in Luke-Acts and Galatians — 61

3 Experience and Speech at Pentecost — 63

3.1.	The theophany of the Spirit at Pentecost		66
	3.1.1.	The setting of Pentecost in Luke's narrative of fulfilment	66
	3.1.2.	Pentecost imagery	69
	3.1.3.	Hellenistic examples of ecstasy	70
	3.1.4.	The Sinai theophany	73
	3.1.5.	Theophanic imagery and the experience of the Spirit's outpouring	76
3.2.	Tongues-speech as revelatory		79
	3.2.1.	Tongues-speech as RE	79
	3.2.2.	Tongues-speech as Spirit-revealing utterance	82
	3.2.3.	Glossolalic function	83
	3.2.4.	Xenolalic content	85
	3.2.5.	Divine and human agency in tongues-speech	89
3.3.	Revelatory preaching: Peter's speech		92
	3.3.1.	The form and impact of Peter's speech	92
	3.3.2.	The content of Peter's speech	95
3.4.	Religious experience, inspired exegesis and revelation		97

4	From Experience to Writing: The Inclusion of the Gentiles and the Lukan *Doppelwerk*		101
	4.1. The inclusion of the Gentiles: Acts 10–15		102
		4.1.1. Narrative setting	102
		4.1.2. A collection of REs	104
	4.2. From religious experience to report		105
		4.2.1. Peter's RE	106
		4.2.2. Peter's epistemological journey	107
		4.2.3. Peter's defence speech (Acts 11:1–18)	110
		4.2.4. Peter's Jerusalem contribution (Acts 15:7–11)	113
	4.3. From report to decision: Critical communal reception		114
		4.3.1. The critical role of the community	115
		4.3.2. James's judgement	116
		4.3.3. From decision to inspired writing: The Apostolic Decree	117
	4.4. Writing about writing: Luke-Acts in light of the prologue and the inclusion of the Gentiles		121
		4.4.1. The prologue (Luke 1:1–4)	122
		4.4.2. The inclusion of the Gentiles as exemplar	126
		4.4.3. Luke-Acts as Scripture	130
5	From Experience to Epistle: Paul's Letter to the Galatians		133
	5.1. Religious experience in Galatians		134
		5.1.1. Patterns of RE in Galatians	135
	5.2. Revelatory beginnings		136
		5.2.1. God's revelation of the gospel of Jesus Christ to Paul	136
		5.2.2. The Galatians' beginning with the Spirit	146
	5.3. Participatory lives		154
		5.3.1. Paul's Christ-life	154
		5.3.2. The Galatians' Christ-formation	157
	5.4. Ethical empowerment		159
		5.4.1. Summary	161
	5.5. Religious experience and the creation of Galatians		162
		5.5.1. Paul's purpose in writing: Galatians as defence speech	162
		5.5.2. Inspired content: Paul's gospel	164

5.5.3.	Galatians' wider relevance	166
5.5.4.	Galatians as Scripture	168

Conclusion: Religious Experience and the Creation of Scripture — 171

Bibliography — 177
Index of References — 199
Index of Names and Subjects — 204

Acknowledgements

This work is a revised version of my PhD thesis, which was funded by the Midlands3Cities Doctoral Training Partnership. I am grateful for both the opportunity to complete the research and further grants to undertake trips to Israel and Pompeii.

I am especially grateful to my *Doktorvater*, Professor Roland Deines. Without him, this research project would not have appeared. More than that, though, I am deeply grateful for his friendship. Professor Deines has provided a model of insightful scholarship and Christian hospitality to which I continue to aspire.

I am also deeply grateful to my examiners, Professor Graham Twelftree and Doctor Peter Watts, whose robust and thorough engagement with my work has greatly improved it. I would also like to register my thanks to my reviewer and those who read parts of this manuscript before publication: Tim Murray, King-Ho Leung, Mark Button, and Peter Wreford. Any remaining errors are, of course, entirely mine.

Finally, I would like to thank my wife, Ellie, and children, Caleb, Luke and Simeon. Without your unfailing support I could not have attempted this work and you have borne the unseen costs of its completion.

Soli Deo Gloria

Abbreviations

Abbreviations in this work follow *The SBL Handbook of Style: For Biblical Studies and Related Disciplines*, 2nd edn. Atlanta, GA: SBL, 2014. Abbreviations not found there are listed below.

Aposteldekret	*Aposteldekret und antikes Vereinswesen*. Edited by Markus Öhler. Tübingen: Mohr Siebeck, 2009
BBS	*Behavioral and Brain Sciences*
BHGNT	*Baylor Handbook on the Greek New Testament*
CogEmo	*Cognition and Emotion*
Edwards	Edwards, Mark J., ed. *Galatians, Ephesians, Philippians*. ACCS. Downers Grove: InterVarsity, 1999
Epiphanies	*Epiphanies of the Divine in the Septuagint and the New Testament*. Edited by Roland Deines and Mark Wreford. Tübingen: Mohr Siebeck, forthcoming
ET	English Translation
Experientia I	*Experientia I: Inquiry for Religious Experience in Early Judaism and Christianity*. Edited by Frances Flannery, Colleen Shantz and Rodney A. Werline. SymS 40. Atlanta, GA: SBL, 2008
Experientia II	*Experientia II: Linking Text and Experience*. Edited by Colleen Shantz and Rodney A. Werline. Atlanta: SBL, 2012
Heritage	*Jesus and the Heritage of Israel: Luke's Narrative Claim upon Israel's Legacy*. Edited by David P. Moessner. Harrisburg: Trinity Press International, 1999
HistHumS	*History of the Human Sciences*
IJPR	*International Journal for the Philosophy of Religion*
IVPNTC	*Inter-Varsity Press New Testament Commentary* Series
JAbPsy	*Journal of Abnormal Psychology*
JExpPsy	*Journal of Experimental Psychology: Human Perception and Performance*
JSHJ	*Journal for the Study of the Historical Jesus*
JSPS	*Journal for the Society of Pentecostal Studies*
MusTheo	*Music Theory Spectrum*
PCS	*Pentecost Commentary Series*
PNTC	*Pillar New Testament Commentary*
PsyBul	*Psychological Bulletin*
RE	Religious Experience
TCogSci	*Trends in Cognitive Sciences*
TSAC	*The Spirit and Church*
WesTJ	*Wesleyan Theological Journal*
ZECNT	*Zondervan Exegetical Commentary on the New Testament*

Introduction

This study is concerned with the relationship between religious experiences (REs) and the creation of the texts which became New Testament Scripture. It explores the possibility that certain REs were understood as revelatory and consequently inspired the writing of NT texts. This idea has been proposed by several scholars,[1] and most extensively in Roland Deines's argument that Matthew and Paul understood themselves to be writing Scripture.[2] However, these treatments remain mostly suggestive, and the thesis has not yet been thoroughly explored. Indeed, the processes by which these texts were treated as scriptural by the earliest Christian community and came to be canonized are often subject to scholarly scrutiny[3] but the connection is rarely made with the writers' experiences of God. This means that the academic discourse rarely reaches to questions of the relationship between RE and notions of inspiration: what role did REs have in causing the writers to write? And what did they think they were doing when they were writing? This study addresses both questions.

First, it reflects on the importance of the REs of a writer and their audience for the understanding of the writing itself. Because many NT texts make prominent claims about encounters with God, this is in some ways an obvious point. Nevertheless, the widespread presupposition of naturalist explanatory models means that this element

---

[1] Cf. N. T. Wright, 'How Can the Bible be Authoritative', *Vox Evangelica* 21 (1991): 7–32; D. Moody Smith, 'When Did the Gospels Become Scripture?' *JBL* 119 (2000): 3–20; Francis Watson, 'Gospel and Scripture: Rethinking Canonical Unity', *TynBul* 52 (2001): 161–82 (167); Martin Hüneburg, 'Das Matthausevangelium als heilige Schrift. Vom Anspruch eines Textes', *Quatember* 71 (2007): 144–55. Cf. also Serge Ruzer, 'Did the New Testament Authors Aspire to Make Their Compositions Part of Scripture? The Case of the Johannine Prologue', in *Oriental Studies and Interfaith Dialogue*, ed. Máté Hidvégi (Budapest: L'Harmattan, 2018), 347–61, who concludes that John did not intend his text to become Scripture.
[2] Roland Deines, 'Did Matthew Know He Was Writing Scripture?: Part 1', *EJT* 22 (2013): 101–9, and 'Did Matthew Know He Was Writing Scripture?: Part 2', *EJT* 23 (2014): 3–12; 'Revelatory Experiences as the Beginning of Scripture: Paul's Letters and the Prophets in the Hebrew Bible', in *From Author to Copyist: Essays on the Composition, Redaction, and Transmission of the Hebrew Bible*, ed. Cana Werman (Winona Lake, IN: Eisenbrauns, 2015), 275–307.
[3] See e.g. Lee Martin McDonald, *The Formation of the Biblical Canon*, 2 vols (London: Bloomsbury, 2017). Cf. also the concise summary and extensive bibliography in Jörg Frey, 'Einführung', in *Qumran und der biblische Kanon*, ed. Michael Becker and Jörg Frey, Biblisch-theologische Studien 92 (Neukirchen-Vluyn: Neukirchener Verlag, 2009), 1–63.

is often missing in historical analyses of the NT.[4] The publication of two edited volumes by the *Experientia* SBL group evidence a growing interest in this topic, and the contributions to these volumes have examined the ways in which Second Temple Jewish writings including the NT texts have been experientially shaped, and how they themselves seek to shape ongoing REs. I will contribute to this discussion by offering a definition of RE in the NT and arguing that experiences which fit within this definition are presented as key elements in shaping the NT texts by considering Luke-Acts and Galatians as indicative examples of a broader pattern. Thus, my work emphasizes the simple but often forgotten truth that the NT texts claim to exist because of REs which inculcated a felt need for communication. Consequently, they cannot be properly understood without this element, even if other motivations may also have contributed to the decision to write.

Second, this study reflects on the scriptural status of these texts. This question is usually asked only after the initial production and reception of the text in its immediate target audience, but I will argue that potential scripturality can be seen as a part of that initial process.[5] Writing about Qumran, Sidnie White Crawford summarizes a set of criteria for assessing the claim that a text was authoritative for a faith community: a text can be considered as having been authoritative for the community if it (a) is quoted or alluded to authoritatively or generates its own commentary; (b) 'claims for itself divine authority, for example by attribution to Moses'; and (c) is copied multiple times.[6] That the majority of the writings ultimately included in the NT canon were cited authoritatively and copied multiple times from a relatively early point in their reception history can hardly be disputed. The general assumption, however, is that the authoritative status which they appear to have had from a relatively early stage in their reception history and which ultimately manifested itself in their canonization reflects later developments,[7] rather than the intentions of their creators. That is, it was a function of communities converging on this kind of interpretation of them, in a similar manner to the way that some suggest Jesus did not claim to be God but came to

---

[4] Cf. the analysis of Robert L. Webb, 'The Historical Enterprise and Historical Jesus Research', in *Key Events in the Life of the Historical Jesus*, ed. Darrell L. Bock and Robert L. Webb, WUNT I.247 (Tübingen: Mohr Siebeck, 2009), 9–93 (40–7). Webb identifies 'ontological naturalistic history' and 'methodological naturalistic history' as approaches common in contemporary biblical studies which proceed on the basis of presuppositions which demand the setting aside of faith commitments. Cf. similarly Roland Deines, 'God's Role in History as a Methodological Problem for Exegesis', in *Acts of God in History*, WUNT I.317 (Tübingen: Mohr Siebeck, 2013), 1–26. See further §2.3.2. Cf. also the similar arguments in relation to the consideration of miracles in Craig S. Keener, *Miracles: The Credibility of the New Testament Accounts* (Grand Rapids, MI: Baker Academic, 2011), 83–208; and Graham H. Twelftree, *Jesus the Miracle Worker: A Historical and Theological Study* (Downers Grove, IL: IVP, 1999), 17–53.

[5] So similarly Roland Deines, 'The Term and Concept of Scripture', in *What Is Bible?*, ed. Karin Finsterbusch and Armin Lange, CBET 67 (Leuven: Peeters, 2012), 235–81 (271–8).

[6] Sidnie White Crawford, *Rewriting Scripture in Second Temple Times* (Grand Rapids, MI: Eerdmans, 2008), 8–9. Crawford presents these criteria as 'fairly well agreed' in the field (8), citing VanderKam and Flint in support.

[7] For an indicative example, see D. A. Carson, Leon Morris and Douglas Moo, *An Introduction to the New Testament* (Grand Rapids, MI: Zondervan, 1992), 231: 'The abiding religious significance, in the sense of canonical, authoritative documents, was the product of later decision rather than the intention at the time of writing.'

be venerated as such after his death.⁸ My research focuses on the question of whether the NT writers did in fact intend to claim this kind of religious authority for their writings on the basis that they convey revelatory content derived from REs.

This means that I am not considering the role of RE in shaping the communal reception of texts. Although the label 'Scripture' is usually reserved for texts which have particular authority for a faith community over time, it is possible for an author to try to claim this kind of status and for scholars to analyse such claims separately from analysing their success in gaining acceptance.⁹ Indeed, in communities well acquainted with authoritative writings such claims may even perhaps be expected, and it is not uncommon to encounter them in Second Temple Jewish texts, including those on which Crawford bases her analysis.¹⁰ What makes the NT writings different from the rewritten Scriptures at Qumran or the apocalyptic literature of the Second Temple period is the events in which they discern God's activity: they present themselves primarily as responses to God's revelation in Jesus Christ and subsequently his ongoing presence through the Spirit. For their authors, then, writing meant engaging with God's ongoing activity after the model of the Old Testament writings,¹¹ and this could explain any absence of explicit claims to scriptural authority: the authority of the OT writings is a function of their being received as an authentic witness to God's interactions with his people rather than a result of their explicitly stating this point.

I will develop this claim by considering Luke-Acts and Galatians. Luke's writings present a good starting point because his narrative of Christian origins reflects at length on the ways in which the first believers perceived themselves to be bearing inspired witness to God's action in Christ. Further, he offers his own reflection on the importance of his writing in his statement of purpose in the prologue to the *Doppelwerk* (Luke 1:1-4). This makes it possible to examine the relation between Luke's presentation of inspired witness and his own understanding of his writing.

Within Luke-Acts, the Pentecost narrative is of particular importance. In it, Luke depicts a RE which issues in the inspired recitation of the story of 'God's mighty deeds' (2:11) by the gathered believers, and makes possible Peter's scriptural witness to Christ (2:14-35), which Luke presents as the same kind of 'utterance' (2:4, 14). This story acts as a fulcrum as Luke's narrative pivots from depicting the activity of Jesus Christ who uniquely bears the Spirit (Luke 3:22) to focus on the witness (see esp. Acts 1:8; 2:32; 10:39-44) of Jesus' disciples in the power of the same Spirit. In the later narrative of the inclusion of the Gentiles (Acts 10-11, 15), Luke develops this theme by focusing on Peter's witness to the outpouring of the Spirit on Cornelius. Peter's witness evokes the same reaction as immediate REs – such as miracles – have earlier in the *Doppelwerk* and ultimately leads to the writing of the Apostolic Decree, a letter which explicitly claims that the Holy Spirit has validated the decision it communicates (Acts 15:28).

---

⁸ For an overview of some of the critical issues, cf. the contributions to Michael F. Bird, ed., *How God Became Jesus* (Grand Rapids, MI: Zondervan, 2014).
⁹ See §2.5.
¹⁰ See e.g. *Baruch*, 1 Maccabees, *1 Enoch*, *4 Ezra* and the so-called rewritten Scripture texts at Qumran (*Jubilees*, 11QTemple, 1QpHab), as well as Josephus's attempts to situate himself in relation to e.g. Jeremiah (*War* 5:391-3) and Ezekiel (*War* 5:19-20).
¹¹ I use OT to designate traditions present across the Hebrew Bible and LXX.

Together, the narratives of Pentecost and the inclusion of the Gentiles tell a story of inspired witness to God's activity which crystallizes in writing. Initially, Luke links the disciples' Spirit-filling with their ability to adequately convey the revelatory significance of the life, death and resurrection of Jesus Christ. This develops into Peter's capacity to discern God's revelation in the ongoing work of the Spirit and witness to that in ways which shape the community's knowledge of God. Further, these stories reflect on Luke's understanding of his own action in writing: he deliberately adopts a biblical style to tell Theophilus 'the truth' (Luke 1:3) about Jesus Christ, and situates his story in relation to the established Scripture of the OT as a story of 'fulfilment.' Luke-Acts, then, is a textual witness to the activity of God in Christ and through the Spirit, which makes an implicit claim to scriptural authority on the basis of its capacity to convey revelatory content. This, in turn, suggests that Luke saw himself as inspired to write.

While Paul does not offer a statement of purpose in the same way as Luke, Galatians does include an autobiographical reflection on God's revelation of Christ to him (Gal 1:15–16), as well as an account of the Galatians' encounter with the Spirit through his own ministry (Gal 3:1–5). Indeed, his retelling of the Galatians' conversion even suggests that Paul understood his own ministry in a similar manner to the way Luke presents the earliest disciples' witness to Christ: the ongoing impact of Christ in his life made him capable of revealing the gospel to the Galatians. However, Paul refers to his and the Galatians' foundational REs to ground an argument that his addressees have not been adequately formed by their encounter with his gospel. In this defensive letter, he attempts to address this lack by 'repreaching' the gospel to an audience from whom he is currently absent. Doing this textualizes his ministry, which represents a significant risk: it could 'flatten' his gospel proclamation, removing the richness of his all-encompassing embodied performance when present with the community. On the other hand, Paul's description of his encounter with Christ in terms of Jeremiah's call (Gal 1:15) suggests a point of comparison in their activity as writers. That Paul conceived of his activity in writing in this way is implied both by the claim of the Epistle itself to lasting normativity for the Galatians' religious life (see e.g. Gal 5:5, 22–23) and the development of the articulation of his gospel in similar terms in later letters to the Romans and the Corinthians. In the letter to the Galatians, Paul attempts to reconvey to his addressees the gospel message which brought about faith in them when they first heard it in order to form Christ in them (Gal 4:20). This, in turn, suggests that he saw himself as inspired to write a text which could proclaim the gospel to an audience from which he was absent.

On my account, both Luke and Paul wrote texts which make a particular authority claim on their reading communities – namely, that they are conveying divinely inspired content and should be read accordingly. This, combined with their intentional situation of their texts in relation to the established Scripture of the OT, suggests that they intended to write texts that would have scriptural status. Though Paul's letter to the Galatians and Luke's *Doppelwerk* are very different texts, reflecting their authors' differing intentions and the different contexts they were written to address, both writers claim to witness to REs in which the God of Israel has revealed himself in a new way. Thus, the questions of what caused them to write and how they perceived their own actions in writing are linked. For both Luke and Paul, the intention to write texts which claim scriptural authority arose in response to the discernment of God's revelatory activity. After the model of the OT writings which form the responsive textual 'deposit' of God's revelatory interactions with his people, they were both 'inspired' to write by these events and present themselves as people qualified to retell and respond to them in a way which conveys their true meaning – a task which they both associate with the work of the Spirit.[12] In this sense, they both intended to write Scripture in response to new REs, and perceived themselves to be inspired to do so.

Aims of the study and methodology

In analysing the role of REs in causing the NT writers to write and informing their understanding of what they were doing, I employ a historical-critical approach that focuses on the final form of the text. I take the texts included in the NT canon as products of their respective authors' intention to encapsulate in their writings a message which is meant to reflect upon a RE based on a revelatory event. Consequently, it is possible the texts can evidence both the impact of specific REs on their authors and illuminate their authors' self-understanding as writers. My aim is to systematically explore these possible impacts in Luke-Acts and Galatians as prototypical examples of a broader trend of the impact of RE which could be visible in other NT writings. However, the contested nature of RE makes a more extensive methodological comment necessary. In this section I will prefigure conclusions reached in Chapters 1 and 2, as well as summarizing the approach of the remaining chapters: more detailed argumentation and bibliographical references can be found in those chapters.

In Chapter 1, I set the study within a history of relevant research, focusing on treatments of RE. This is useful because the NT attests a range of phenomena which were perceived as having religious significance and the particular experiences which were taken as revelatory and prompted the writing of the NT texts sit within this broad category. I begin by considering treatments of RE in biblical studies, outlining the early contributions of the *religionsgeschichtliche Schule* and the neglect of the topic under the influence of the so-called 'Bultmann School'. I then identify three important contributors to the retrieval of RE in biblical studies – James D. G. Dunn, Larry W. Hurtado and Luke Timothy Johnson. From Dunn, Hurtado, and Johnson, I take three points of confluence: (1) accounts of RE can offer access to the experiences they describe; (2) REs can be a source of creative religious expression; and (3) it is important to approach accounts of RE on the assumption that they are not *necessarily* mistaken. In the remainder of Chapter 1, I bring these points brought into conversation with indicative examples of contemporary biblical studies approaches to RE and a brief summary from the side of religious studies. This allows me to identify methodological challenges to each of the three points outlined above, as well as the lack of an inductive definition of RE as questions to be addressed in Chapter 2.

---

[12] For Luke, see esp. Acts 1:8; 2:1–42. For Paul, see 1 Cor 2:1–5; 1 Thess 1:5. This sense might also be visible in the reference to power in Gal 3:4.

In Chapter 2, I offer a constructive proposal for the analysis of RE in the NT, developing my methodology more fully. First, I defend the claim that accounts of RE can offer insight into the experiences they describe, arguing that a sensitive reading of the NT texts can enable historical reconstruction of events 'behind' the text (§2.1). Second, I address the suggestion that REs are separable into medically explicable phenomena and culturally derived interpretations. Against this constructivist understanding of RE, I give an account of the role of experience in shaping religious understanding which emphasizes its irreducible qualitative contribution (§2.2). Third, I address the historiographical implications of my focus on RE. As the standard approach in the field is methodologically naturalistic, I draw on phenomenology of religion to articulate an alternative approach which focuses on insider perspectives but suspends judgement on the reality of their truth claims (§2.3). In the remainder of Chapter 2, I present my own inductive definition of RE in the NT (§2.4) and outline an approach to the creation of Scripture (§2.5), before giving an overview of how the approach will be applied to Luke-Acts and Galatians (§2.6).

The next three chapters are predominantly exegetical, applying the approach developed in the first section. In Chapters 3 and 4 I focus on Luke-Acts, claiming that Luke's depiction of inspired witness in the narratives of Pentecost and the inclusion of the Gentiles allows his readers to understand his own account in a similar way as an inspired writing, or in other words, as a witness to a revelatory action of the divine worthy to be preserved and communicated in a writing that has the potential to serve in a scriptural way for its intended audience. To achieve this, I analyse the presentation of Spirit-influenced speech at Pentecost (Acts 2) in Chapter 3. I argue that Luke establishes the possibility that human speech – both tongues-speech and Peter's scriptural sermon – can convey revelatory content by witnessing to God's activity in Christ. In Chapter 4, I examine the way this develops in Luke's depiction of Peter's witness to the outpouring of the Spirit on the Gentiles (Acts 10–11). At the Jerusalem convocation (Acts 15) Peter's spoken witness conveys revelatory content which shapes communal decision making and leads to the production of the Apostolic Decree. This letter makes an explicit claim of inspiration for the content it communicates (Acts 15:28). I conclude by arguing that Luke's own statement of purpose (Luke 1:1–4) should be read in light of these narratives, which suggest that Luke-Acts is intended as an inspired witness to God's activity in Christ and his ongoing influence through the Spirit that implicitly claims scriptural authority for its audience.

In Chapter 5, I develop my argument by arguing that the understanding of Scripture-writing visible in Luke-Acts is also implicitly present in Paul's presentation of his writing to the Galatians. Paul witnesses to his and the Galatians' initial REs (Gal 1:10–11, 15–16 and 3:1–5) – which I term revelatory beginnings – to ground his attempt to recall his gospel message to his addressees. Indeed, the key purpose of the letter is to allow Paul to convey this revelatory content in his absence. Further, the allusion to prophetic call narratives in the Apostle's autobiographical account of God's revelation of Christ to him suggests the possibility that he saw his own writing analogously to OT prophetic writings insofar as his letter represents an extension of his embodied ministry. I conclude by arguing that Paul intended the letter to the

Galatians to function with scriptural authority for its addressees because it conveys the revelatory content of his gospel.

In my conclusion, I return to my central questions and argue first that in Luke-Acts and Galatians REs are presented as the reason for the existence of the texts and that they appear to have shaped what is written. Second, I claim that both Luke and Paul understood themselves to be creating new scriptural writings on the basis of their relationship to new REs.

Section 1

Approaching Religious Experience: Theoretical Foundations

1

Religious Experience and New Testament Research

In this study, I will argue that religious experiences (REs) which were perceived as divine revelatory actions inspired the writing of at least some of the texts which became New Testament Scripture, and that the eventual inclusion of these texts in the NT canon in part reflects their writers' intention to produce scriptural texts. Analysing this dual claim will require a rigorous engagement with RE, and in this chapter I will situate my work within a history of research on RE. An exhaustive consideration of all relevant material is not necessary in light of several recent publications, including my own.[1] Instead, I will outline older approaches to RE (§1.1.1) and its subsequent neglect (§1.1.2), before focusing on its retrieval by James D. G. Dunn, Larry W. Hurtado and Luke Timothy Johnson (§1.1.3). I will suggest three points of confluence in their research and bring these into conversation with four indicative recent approaches (§1.1.4) and religious studies treatments of RE (§1.2). At the end of this chapter (§1.3), I will identify four theoretical questions which must be addressed when considering RE as a historical phenomenon and possible cause in the creation of the writings which came to make up the NT. In Chapter 2, I will then suggest a constructive approach which can address these questions to serve as a theoretical groundwork for my exegetical test cases.

---

[1] Cf. Roland Deines and Mark Wreford, 'Epiphanies of the Divine in the Septuagint and the New Testament: Mutual Perspectives', in *Epiphanies of the Divine in the Septuagint and the New Testament*, ed. Roland Deines and Mark Wreford (Tübingen: Mohr Siebeck, forthcoming); Jörg Frey and John R. Levison, 'The Origins of Early Christian Pneumatology: On the Rediscovery and Reshaping of the History of Religions Quest', in *The Holy Spirit, Inspiration, and the Cultures of Antiquity*, ed. Jörg Frey and John R. Levison, Ekstasis 5 (Berlin: De Gruyter, 2014), 1–38; Mark Batluck, 'Religious Experience in New Testament Research', *CurBR* 9 (2010): 339–63; Clint Tibbs, *Religious Experience of the Pneuma: Communication with the Spirit World in 1 Corinthians 12 and 14*, WUNT II.230 (Tübingen: Mohr Siebeck, 2007), 77–111; Larry W. Hurtado, 'Religious Experience and Religious Innovation in the New Testament', *JR* 80 (2000): 183–205. More broadly, cf. Martin Jay, *Songs of Experience: Modern American and European Variations on a Universal Theme* (Los Angeles: University of California, 2005), 78–131.

1.1. Religious experience in biblical studies research

Moule notes that 'almost wherever one starts, the discussion of Christian experience leads without much delay to some question about the Spirit of God'.[2] This has two implications for this review: first, it explains why material treating the Spirit will figure prominently in a survey of research into RE; second, it already gestures towards the theological implications of considering the possible historical role played by REs in the processes which led to the creation of the NT texts. REs are inherently bound up with theological claims about reality and divine revelation.[3] This makes it potentially problematic to consider such experiences within the scholarly field of biblical studies, which arose as a historical discipline in opposition to theology.[4] As Luke Timothy Johnson notes, 'Scholars' openness to RE is entangled in their theories about the way reality is structured',[5] and assumptions about the structure of reality inform understandings of the nature of history and the historiographical task.[6] Consequently, attitudes to RE in biblical studies often reflect theological presuppositions. However, Hengel argues that 'we cannot talk theologically of God's disclosure of himself in Jesus and the apostolic testimony without at the same time grasping the form and content of this communication by means of historical research'.[7] Studying the potential REs that motivated the NT authors to write and shaped the writings they produced is one way to try to grasp the 'form and content' of their inspiration.

Reflection on experience has been an important resource for Christian theology since at least Augustine,[8] but during the Reformation the question of how to treat claimed immediate revelatory experiences of God came to the fore. In 1525, radical reformers such as Andreas Karlstadt and Thomas Müntzer appealed to RE-derived knowledge of God's will to justify violent political action.[9] In response,

---

[2] Charles F. D. Moule, *The Holy Spirit* (London: Mowbray, 1978), 7.
[3] For an overview of the discussion surrounding experience as a theological source, cf. Ben Quash, 'Revelation', and Ellen T. Charry, 'Experience', in *The Oxford Handbook of Systematic Theology*, ed. John Webster, Kathryn Tanner and Iain Torrance (Oxford: Oxford University Press, 2007), 325–44 and 413–31, respectively.
[4] The division between 'dogmatic' and 'biblical' theology is often traced back to Johann Philip Gabler's 1787 address available in J. Sandys-Wunsch and L. Eldredge, trans. and eds, 'J. P. Gabler and the Distinction between Biblical and Dogmatic Theology: Translation, Commentary, and Discussion of His Originality', *SJT* 33 (1980): 133–58. Cf. discussion in C. Kavin Rowe and Richard B. Hays, 'Biblical Studies', in *Oxford Handbook of Systematic Theology*, ed. John Webster, Kathryn Tanner and Iain Torrance (Oxford: Oxford University Press, 2007), 436–55.
[5] Luke Timothy Johnson, *Religious Experience in Earliest Christianity: A Missing Dimension in New Testament Studies* (Minneapolis, MN: Fortress, 1998), 53.
[6] Cf. Roland Deines, 'God's Role in History as a Methodological Problem for Exegesis', in *Acts of God in History*, ed. Christoph Ochs and Peter Watts (Tübingen: Mohr Siebeck, 2013), 1–26; and ch. 2: 'Worldviews and Historiographical Decision Making', in Jonathan Rowlands, *The Metaphysics of Historical Jesus Research: An Argument for Increasing the Plurality of Metaphysical Frameworks within Historical Jesus Research* (PhD thesis, University of Nottingham, 2020), 87–126.
[7] Martin Hengel, *Acts and the History of Earliest Christianity* (Philadelphia, PA: Fortress, 1979), 136.
[8] See e.g. St. Augustine, *Confessions*, trans. Henry Chadwick (Oxford: Oxford University Press, 1991). Cf. Charles Taylor, *Sources of the Self: The Making of the Modern Identity* (Cambridge: Harvard University, 1989), 132, who argues that Augustine helps make reflection on experience 'a step on [the] road back to God' for Christian theology.
[9] Cf. Anthony C. Thiselton, *The Holy Spirit: In Biblical Teaching, through the Centuries, and Today* (London: SPCK, 2015), 259–62.

Martin Luther, who saw the Holy Spirit as 'the fullest gift to *all, including the most "ordinary," Christians*',[10] denounced their attitude as *Schwärmerei* ('enthusiasm'). In doing so, Luther was critiquing what he saw as an insufficient recognition of human sinfulness: in 'baptizing' their subjective feelings as revelatory, Karlstadt and others had consumed 'the Holy Spirit, feathers and all',[11] resulting in an inappropriate treatment of human feelings as theological data. However, as Zahl notes, the result was that 'enthusiasm' came to function as a polemic label for 'subjectivistic, chaotic, emotional, and irrational'[12] religious phenomena. In this sense, it was used to discredit later movements, such as the Pietist revivalists, who drew on experience as a theological resource in the aftermath of the Reformation.[13]

Nevertheless, the Pietist emphasis on experience distinctively shaped theological reflection in the eighteenth century. Awakening preacher Jonathan Edwards focused on religious affections,[14] and John Wesley's commitment to 'experimental theology' shaped the so-called Wesleyan Quadrilateral, which raised experience to a theological source alongside Scripture, reason, and tradition.[15] Pietism also influentially coincided with the Enlightenment elevation of reason, as well as romanticism, in the work of Friedrich Schleiermacher. Accepting that the erosion of scriptural authority by historical criticism meant religion needed to be placed on a new foundation, Schleiermacher argued that it could best be grounded in feeling – a category intended to stand alongside reason (thinking) and morality (action) as naming an irreducible anthropological element. For Schleiermacher, this feeling – famously most truly apprehended as the 'feeling of absolute dependence'[16] – is only ever noticeable in particular REs of an 'other'. Thus, Nimmo argues that Schleiermacher aims to allow 'the lived experience of the Christian to form and inform the dogmatic presentation'.[17] However, this emphasis on feeling ultimately helped underwrite the development of German liberal theology in the nineteenth century, and thus formed the context in which the *religionsgeschichtliche Schule* emerged.

1.1.1. *Religionsgeschichtliche Schule*

At the end of the 'long nineteenth Century' the *religionsgeschichtliche Schule* sought, like Schleiermacher, to focus on the lived experience of religion. Of particular importance was Hermann Gunkel's seminal monograph, *Die Wirkungen des heiligen Geistes nach*

---

[10] Thiselton, *Holy Spirit*, 255; italics original.
[11] Martin Luther, *Against the Heavenly Prophets in the Matter of Images and Sacraments*, trans. Conrad Bergendorff and Bernhard Erling, Luther's Works 40 (Philadelphia: Muhlenberg, 1958), 83.
[12] Simeon Zahl, 'Experience', in *The Oxford Handbook of Nineteenth Century Christian Thought*, ed. Joel Rasmussen, Judith Wolfe and Johannes Zachhuber (Oxford: Oxford University Press, 2017), 177–95 (179).
[13] Cf. W. R. Ward, *The Protestant Evangelical Awakening* (Cambridge: Cambridge University Press, 1992).
[14] Jonathan Edwards, *The Religious Affections* (1746 repr., New York: Dover, 2013).
[15] See Albert C. Outler, 'The Wesleyan Quadrilateral in Wesley', *WesTJ* 20 (1985): 7–18.
[16] Friedrich D. E. Schleiermacher, *The Christian Faith*, trans. and ed. H. R. Mackintosh and J. S. Stewart (Edinburgh: T&T Clark, 1999), 16.
[17] Paul T. Nimmo, 'Introduction to the Third Edition', in Schleiermacher, *The Christian Faith* (Edinburgh: T&T Clark, 2016), ix–xiii (x). Cf. similarly, Zahl, 'Experience', 182.

der populären Anschauung der apostolischen Zeit und der Lehre des Apostels Paulus.[18] Gunkel begins by analysing 'the popular views of the Spirit', taken from the synoptics and Acts as representative of the views of the earliest Christian community, and concludes with an examination of Paul's teaching on the Spirit.

As Turner notes, Gunkel's work 'is really a *historian's* attack on the idealism of liberal theology, which tended to reduce "Spirit" to the rational development of ideas'.[19] It was groundbreaking and provocative because Gunkel claimed that the earliest Christian community were not speaking about a doctrine when they spoke about the Holy Spirit, but 'the supernatural power of God which works miracles in and through the person'.[20] Moreover, Gunkel argued that these experiences were accessible to critical study. He asked 'what type of phenomena the communities and Paul regarded as pneumatic', with the ultimate aim of 'liv[ing] the pneumatic's inner states after him', in order to 'define the concept of an activity of the Spirit and thus that of the Spirit himself'.[21] For Gunkel then, the term 'Spirit' was an explanatory label applied to an experiential phenomenon:

> The primitive community was not at all concerned with a doctrine of the Holy Spirit and his activities ... Rather, at issue are quite concrete facts, obvious to all, which were the object of daily experience and without further reflection were directly experienced as effected by the Spirit ... [Excepting occasionally in Paul] we find in our sources absolutely no doctrinal statements regarding the Spirit, though we find a host of descriptions of the Spirit's activities.[22]

Although he does not address it, Gunkel's claim that 'Spirit' was a descriptive label applied to unusual experiences intuitively interpreted acutely raises the issue of the relationship between REs and the language used to express them. As Turner puts it, the question was, 'Did the primitive church have a *theology* of the Spirit (or was "Spirit" just an "explanation" offered for dramatic supernatural events or charismata)?'[23] Gunkel argued the latter and claimed that understanding these explanations could allow an interpreter to access the subjective experiences of the 'pneumatics' writing them. The argument that doctrinal developments were secondary to RE found later echoes in the work of Adolf Deissmann, who described Christianity as primarily a religious movement centred on worship and experience,[24] and Albert Schweitzer, who argued that mystical participation in Christ was of primary importance to Paul.[25]

---

[18] Hermann Gunkel, *Die Wirkungen des heiligen Geistes nach der populären Anschauung der apostolischen Zeit und der Lehre des Apostels Paulus* (Göttingen: Vandenhoeck und Ruprecht, 1888). ET, *The Influence of the Holy Spirit: The Popular View of the Apostolic Age and the Teaching of the Apostle Paul* (Philadelphia, PA: Fortress, 1979).

[19] Max Turner, *Power from on High: The Spirit in Israel's Restoration and Witness in Luke-Acts*, Journal of Pentecostal Theology Supplement Series 9 (Sheffield: Sheffield Academic, 1996), 23.

[20] Gunkel, *Influence*, 35.

[21] Gunkel, *Influence*, 3, 9.

[22] Gunkel, *Influence*, 13–14.

[23] Turner, *Power*, 35.

[24] Adolf Deissmann, *Paul: A Study in Social and Religious History* (New York: Harper & Bros, 1911); Adolf Deissmann, *The Religion of Jesus and the Faith of Paul* (London: Hodder & Stoughton, 1923).

[25] Albert Schweitzer, *Die Mystik des Apostels Paulus* (Tübingen: Mohr Siebeck, 1930).

Another innovative feature of Gunkel's work was his argument that earliest Christianity needed to be considered in its Jewish context rather than primarily in light of the Hebrew Bible: 'The assumption of Jewish influence always carries much greater probability than does the assumption of the influence of the Old Testament.'[26] This raises the question of how REs relate to their received framework – the historical milieux within which they occur. This element of Gunkel's work initially prompted a search for appropriate intertexts: Paul Volz critiqued Gunkel's depiction of Judaism as inaccurate to the sources, primarily constructed as a non-pneumatic foil to his charismatic presentation of Christianity,[27] and Hans Leisegang argued that Hellenistic – particularly Greek mystic and mantic – sources offered better comparative material for early Christian experience than early Jewish sources.[28]

In 1926, two influential critical responses appeared. Friedrich Büchsel rejected Leisegang's comparison of the NT texts with Greek mysticism and mantic prophecy and sought to demonstrate continuity in the conceptions of the Spirit across the NT (contra Gunkel),[29] and Heinrich von Baer argued that for Luke the Spirit was defined by relation to Israelite salvation history.[30] Nevertheless, all parties took as axiomatic Gunkel's argument that the Spirit was best examined through its 'symptoms' – through an examination of reports of RE which took seriously claims to particular and extraordinary experiences. The discussion centred on which sources offered the best context within which to interpret these reports. A significant difference between Leisegang and his later critics, though, is that he looked for parallel patterns of experience in Hellenistic sources, whereas Büchsel and von Baer argued that literary parallels should be allowed to shape an understanding of the experiences being described. These approaches to the question of how RE relates to a received framework point in opposite directions: following Gunkel, Leisegang claimed insight into experience and used that to shape his evaluation of disparate literary sources, emphasizing similarities; Büchsel and von Baer were more cautious in allowing literary evidence to shape speculative reconstructions of experience, magnifying differences.

1.1.2. Lacuna in RE research

After the First World War, there was a dramatic shift in German theological scholarship with the rise of dialectical theology. This had significant implications for the study of RE,[31] particularly through the dominance of the 'Bultmann school' in NT

---

[26] Gunkel, *Influence*, 13.
[27] Paul Volz, *Der Geist Gottes und die verwandten Erscheinungen im Alten Testament und im anschliessenden Judentum* (Tübingen: Mohr, 1910).
[28] Hans Leisegang, *Der heilige Geist: Das Wesen und Werden der mystisch-intuitiven Erkenntnis in der Philosophie und Religion der Griechen* (Leipzig: Teubner, 1919); Hans Leisegang, *Pneuma Hagion: Der Ursprung des Geistbegriffs der synoptischen Evangelien aus der griechischen Mystik* (Leipzig: Hinrichs, 1922).
[29] Friedrich Büchsel, *Der Geist Gottes im Neuen Testament* (Gütersloh: Bertelsmann, 1926).
[30] Heinrich von Baer, *Der Heilige Geist in den Lukasschriften* (Stuttgart: Kohlhammer, 1926).
[31] Cf. Gerd Lüdemann and Alf Özen, 'Religionsgeschichtliche Schule', *TRE* 28 (1997): 618–24 (622–4), on the effect of dialectical theology on the generation of scholars taught by members of the *religionsgeschichtliche Schule*.

research.³² Although Bultmann's focus on discerning the existential importance of the text for the reader privileged lived experience in one sense, Batluck notes that 'by their emphasis on the metaphysical, crisis theologians lost sight of the earthly and experiential dimension of the biblical texts, gravitating instead to research on the theological formulations of these authors'.³³ Indeed, in an early letter to leading liberal theologian Adolf von Harnack, Barth claimed that 'so-called "religious experience" is as different from the awakening of faith by God as earth is from heaven'.³⁴ Here, Barth was critiquing liberal theology for over-optimistic projection in a manner similar to Luther's critique of *Schwärmerei*. Barth saw a historical focus on lived religion – including RE – as unhelpful in light of dialectical theology's 'definitive conclusion that Christian faith was not a religion, but rather the end of all human religion'.³⁵ Rather, as he argued in the second edition of his Romans commentary, revelation is not accessible to historical study: in Jesus' resurrection 'the Holy Spirit touches the old world of the flesh, but touches it as a tangent touches a circle, that is, without touching it'.³⁶ Consequently, as Frey and Levison note, 'The experiences of ancient communities and New Testament authors were considered not only inaccessible but also theologically irrelevant and uninteresting.'³⁷

1.1.3. The recovery of RE as a theme in biblical studies

While there was some interest in RE in the interim,³⁸ it was another change in theological climate which ultimately led to a wider retrieval of RE as a significant *topos* of NT research: the rise of Pentecostal and charismatic Christianity. James Dunn's influential *Baptism in the Spirit* was explicitly intended to address Pentecostal claims regarding Spirit baptism,³⁹ and he was critical of the tendency to discount RE as 'too subjective and mystical in favour of a faith which is essentially an affirmation of biblical propositions'.⁴⁰ *Baptism in the Spirit* was followed in 1975 by *Jesus and the Spirit*, which was 'written out of the conviction that religious experience is a vitally important dimension of man's experience of reality'.⁴¹ Dunn took RE as 'the core

---

[32] For the use of this label see Andreas Lindemann, 'Bultmannschule', in *Jesus Handbuch*, ed. J. Schröter and Christine Jacobi (Tübingen: Mohr Siebeck, 2017), 402–10.

[33] Batluck, 'Religious Experience', 343; so also, Frey and Levison, 'Origins', 18–23.

[34] Karl Barth, 'Fifteen Answers to Professor von Harnack', in *The Beginnings of Dialectic Theology*, ed. James M. Robinson (Richmond: John Knox, 1968), I:167.

[35] Ulrich Luz, 'Paul as Mystic', in *The Holy Spirit and Christian Origins: Essays in Honour of James D. G. Dunn*, ed. Graham N. Stanton et al. (Grand Rapids, MI: Eerdmans, 2004), 131–43 (131).

[36] Karl Barth, *The Epistle to the Romans*, trans. Edwyn C. Hoskyns (London: Oxford University Press, 1933), 30.

[37] Frey and Levison, 'Origins', 20.

[38] See e.g. Percy G. S. Hopwood, *The Religious Experience of the Primitive Church: The Period Prior to the Influence of Paul* (New York: Scribner's, 1937); and Eduard Schweizer, 'πνεῦμα', *TDNT*, VI: 332-451 (396): 'Long before the Spirit was a theme of doctrine, He was a fact in the experience of the community.' Cf. Tibbs, *Religious Experience*, 90–4; Frey and Levison, 'Origins', 28–9.

[39] James D. G. Dunn, *Baptism in the Spirit: A Re-examination of the New Testament Teaching on the Gift of the Spirit in Relation to Pentecostalism Today*, SBT 15 (London: SCM, 1970), 1–4.

[40] Dunn, *Baptism*, 226.

[41] James D. G. Dunn, *Jesus and the Spirit: A Study of the Religious and Charismatic Experience of Jesus and the First Christians as Reflected in the New Testament* (London: SCM, 1975), ix.

of religion' and argued that this should be allowed to shape inquiry into Christian origins: 'It must be important therefore to inquire closely into the religious experience which launched this new religion: what were those recognitions of God's activity which constituted a new faith of such dynamic and durable vitality?'[42] He set out to analyse early Christian RE to determine what, if anything, was distinctive about it. The study is ordered chronologically, working from Jesus' experience through that of the earliest community to Paul's experiential theology and on to the remaining letters and the Johannine material. Dunn tells a declension narrative: Jesus was intensely charismatic and inspired the early community in this direction, but as the fire of the first generations faded it gave way to a more hierarchical community with more rigid doctrinal expression.[43] In part, this is because Dunn located the essence of Christian RE in its eschatological orientation, which he took to have been shaped by intense initial experiences but to have shifted to address the perceived 'delay' of the parousia.

Though he does not cite him Dunn's construal of RE is similar to William James's,[44] and he addresses the question of the accessibility of experience by asserting that 'any attempt to understand religious phenomena must take into account the explanations which others offer for their own experience'.[45] He also distinguishes between non-linguistic experience and linguistic description of experience: 'Personal experience, if it is accessible at all, is accessible only as conceptualized experience.'[46] An example can help demonstrate the point: Dunn argues that the predominant correlate of Jesus' unique self-understanding in his RE was 'a sense of sonship' reflected in the abba prayer recorded in Mark 14:36:[47] the prayer-language (abba) reflects a conceptual framework (sonship) which was rooted in Jesus' experience (feeling of sonship).

Considering the relationship between REs and received frameworks, Dunn cautions against 'discounting *the creative force of religious experience*'.[48] He argues both that whatever 'titles and concepts [Jesus] took over from the Old Testament did not shape his experience of God, but were as much, if not much more, shaped and interpreted by it',[49] and that Paul's 'writings bear eloquent and passionate testimony to the creative power of his own religious experience'.[50]

Dunn's work was hugely generative, and in the wake of the publication of *Jesus and the Spirit*, Batluck identifies four strands of RE research: '1) mystical/revelatory religious experience, 2) religious experience as an effect of the Holy Spirit, 3) religious experience in historical Jesus studies, and 4) religious experience as a broad category.'[51] Though Batluck's overview does not consider either the religious studies engagement with RE which has informed biblical research[52] or the Pentecostal response to

---

[42] Dunn, *Jesus*, 1.
[43] Dunn, *Jesus*, 357–8.
[44] See §1.2.1 on William James.
[45] Dunn, *Jesus*, 3.
[46] Dunn, *Jesus*, 11.
[47] Dunn, *Jesus*, 24–6.
[48] Dunn, *Jesus*, 4; italics original.
[49] Dunn, *Jesus*, 91.
[50] Dunn, *Jesus*, 4.
[51] Batluck, 'Religious Experience', 345.
[52] See §1.2 on Religious Experience in Religious Studies Research.

Dunn,[53] his final section identifies Larry Hurtado and Luke Timothy Johnson as key contributors to this scholarly discussion. I will consider each of them in turn, before identifying three points of commonality in the approaches of Dunn, Hurtado and Johnson which will inform my argument, and considering more recent contributions.

In his first monograph published in 1988, *One God, One Lord*, Hurtado argued that RE was an important force in the innovative development of beliefs about Jesus in earliest Christianity.[54] He initially compares the treatment of Jesus by the earliest Christians with the veneration of other angelic and intermediary figures in Jewish mysticism, arguing that the use of devotional[55] language towards Jesus marked a distinctive 'mutation', because Jesus was venerated at a level beyond any other intermediary figure.[56] He then raises the historical question of what might prompt such a mutation – what might bring a monotheistic Jew to express a devotion to Jesus similar to their devotion to God? In response, Hurtado points to the REs of the earliest Christians, both of Jesus' earthly ministry and of claimed resurrection appearances.[57] Much of Hurtado's later work extends themes already present in this early volume. Of particular importance to my study is his development of the argument that RE can be a historical cause of innovation in religious belief and practice in the 2000 article 'Religious Experience and Religious Innovation'[58] and the more recent return to a similar theme in 'Revelatory Experience and Religious Innovation in Earliest Christianity'.[59]

In the former article, Hurtado defends the claim 'that powerful religious experiences can themselves contribute significantly, sometimes crucially, to religious innovations and are not limited to serving as "legitimizing devices" for previously formed beliefs and practices'.[60] Hurtado draws primarily on social scientific research to support this claim, though he questions the tendency in that discipline to "explain away" REs as meaning constructs built on top of medically explicable phenomena.[61] Hurtado presents RE as always experienced in relation to an existing framework but occasionally capable of reformulating or reconfiguring the religious commitments of the experiencer, and makes a persuasive argument that it is possible that RE could cause someone to change their patterns of religious belief and behaviour. Consequently, he

---

[53] For an overview, cf. William P. Atkinson, *Baptism in the Spirit: Luke-Acts and the Dunn Debate* (Eugene: Pickwick, 2011).

[54] Larry W. Hurtado, *One God, One Lord: Early Christian Devotion and Ancient Jewish Monotheism* (London: SCM, 1988), esp. 114–22.

[55] Larry W. Hurtado defines 'devotion' as a 'portmanteau word for the beliefs and related religious actions that constituted the expressions of religious reverence of early Christians' (*Lord Jesus Christ: Devotion to Jesus in Earliest Christianity* (Grand Rapids, MI: Eerdmans, 2003), 3).

[56] Hurtado, *One God*, 93–124.

[57] Hurtado, *One God*, 114–22.

[58] Larry W. Hurtado, 'Religious Experience and Religious Innovation in the New Testament'. *JR* 80 (2000): 183–205.

[59] Larry W. Hurtado, 'Revelatory Experiences and Religious Innovation in Earliest Christianity'. *ExpTim* 125 (2014): 469–82; cf. also his recent consideration of Christian Origins: Larry W. Hurtado, *Why on Earth Did Anyone Become a Christian in the First Three Centuries?* (Milwaukee, WI: Marquette University, 2016).

[60] Hurtado, 'Innovation', 190.

[61] Hurtado, 'Innovation', 189.

is particularly interested in the cognitive content of 'revelatory' REs: he presents RE as capable of confronting the recipient with new theological realities which prompt further reflection.

A minor limitation of Hurtado's work stems from his use of insights drawn from social-scientific scholars such as Rodney Stark. In his classic article, 'A Taxonomy of Religious Experience',[62] Stark follows William James[63] in privileging more unusual REs. This is reflected in Stark's labelling of the most 'extreme' mystical experiences 'revelatory', which implies an unambiguously positive correlation between intensity and intimacy that sits awkwardly with the accounts of RE in the NT. Adopting this framework, Hurtado does not develop a particularly nuanced account of the relationship between RE and language, but simply assumes the ability to infer the nature of the cognitive content of certain outstanding experiences from the nature of the theological changes they prompt. Though this represents a legitimate approach to the topic, it fails to reckon with the difficulty of assessing the impact of non-linguistic experience and could obscure less dramatic REs which nevertheless shaped NT texts.[64]

Johnson's key contribution to the discussion of RE in the NT can be found in a short monograph based on his 1997 Stone Lectures at Princeton Theological Seminary in which he argues for a new approach to the religion of early Christianity that 'is neither history in the strict sense of the term, nor is it theology'.[65] Johnson wants to reclaim the idea of 'religion', and advocates a phenomenological approach which he describes as 'a way of seeing ... that begins with the assumption that religious language and religious experience are actually about something and deserving of attention in their own right'.[66] Though he does not engage Dunn's work, Johnson argues along similar lines, advocating a sensitive rereading of accounts of RE against the backdrop of the 'spirit-filled' ancient world in which the NT writers lived. Self-consciously attempting to retrieve elements of the *religionsgeschichtliche Schule*, Johnson's approach is intended to counter reductive accounts[67] which reduce the particularity of the REs reported in the NT to part of a developmental schema, be it theological or historical.

Johnson begins two chapters of theoretical argument by claiming that the NT is full of experiential language which 'does not serve primarily to state propositions about reality ... so much as to express, refer to, and argue from human experiences',[68] and particularly experiences of power. Similarly to Gunkel, Johnson defines *pneuma* as 'precisely, active power ... In this sense, the symbol "Holy Spirit" serves as the linguistic expression of the experience of power'.[69] This power is unusual: it '"goes

---

[62] Rodney Stark, 'A Taxonomy of Religious Experience'. *JSSR* 5 (1965): 97–116.
[63] See §1.2.1 on William James.
[64] Cf. Mark Wreford, 'Diagnosing Religious Experience in Romans 8', *TynBul* 68 (2017), 203–22, for an example of a less extreme case in which the theological innovation is a qualitatively altered understanding of a prior theological commitment that might nevertheless qualify as revelatory.
[65] Johnson, *Experience*, vii. Cf. also Luke Timothy Johnson, *Scripture and Discernment: Decision Making in the Church* (Nashville, TN: Abingdon, 1983).
[66] Johnson, *Experience*, 182.
[67] I intend 'reductionism' in the positive sense of explanation in terms of an alternative framework which offers a simpler account of complex phenomena. Cf. e.g. Robert Segal, 'In Defense of Reductionism', *JAAR* 51 (1983): 97–127.
[68] Johnson, *Experience*, 4.
[69] Johnson, *Experience*, 8.

beyond" the subject's available categories of comparison' and can consequently be labelled 'transcendent'.[70] This bold claim allows Johnson to argue that accounts of RE must be read charitably if they are to be understood on their own terms, insofar as they claim to report something irreducible to other explanatory frameworks. To this end, Johnson advocates a phenomenological approach, by which he means 'a critical inquiry into consciousness and its contents taking with equal seriousness the *noesis* (or knowing subject) and the *noema* (or subject known) in all their delicate interplay'.[71] He applies this approach to case studies of baptism, tongues-speech and ritual meals in his final three chapters.

Johnson's study raises three points. First, he consistently attempts to defer the question of whether the *noemae* of RE are real or not. He critiques the 'insistence that the past must be just like "what we see in Europe every day" [as] a rejection of the "other" on the historical plane cognate to the rejection of "the Other" that religious language itself insists on speaking of', but claims that it is possible to 'bracket' 'judgement concerning the extramental existence or non-existence of such states of consciousness'.[72] This is a fine balancing act and it means that Johnson's account of RE requires an openness to the *possibility* that God exists and was really encountered by the New Testament authors.[73] However, it is not necessary to concede the validity of any given truth claim to consider it charitably.

Second, Johnson's heuristic definition of RE is a modification of Joachim Wach's[74] into a four-part description: 'Religious experience is a response to that which is perceived as ultimate, involving the whole person, characterized by a peculiar intensity, and issuing in action.'[75] It is interesting that, despite Johnson's emphasis on the importance of the particular accounts of RE in the NT, he uses an abstract definition 'as a means of pointing to the sort of reality we mean'.[76] More importantly, it is not clear that all REs reported in the NT fit within the reach of this definition. For example, are angels and demons 'perceived as *ultimate*'?

Third, Johnson works both from reports of RE and from a speculative historical reconstruction of communal organization, for which he analyses the RE that might have been generated by the likely manner in which baptisms were conducted. At this point Johnson's approach is helpfully more holistic than either Dunn's or Hurtado's which focus solely on linguistic evidence: even where they consider changes in behaviour, these are reported, whereas Johnson works from a speculative reconstruction of initiation rituals. By considering examples of ritually mediated REs (baptism; ritual

---

[70] Johnson, *Experience*, 58.
[71] Johnson, *Experience*, 43; italics original.
[72] Johnson, *Experience*, 42, 44.
[73] Christopher Mount, '"Jesus is Lord": Religious Experience and the Religion of Paul' (paper presented at the annual meeting of the SBL, Washington, DC, 18 November 2006), infers that Johnson's argument requires more than simply an openness to this possibility. This is not necessarily the case, however, given that Johnson restricts his comments to the understanding of the biblical authors.
[74] See §1.2.2.
[75] Johnson, *Experience*, 63. Wach's original definition is less concise, but follows the same basic pattern (see Joachim Wach, *Types of Religious Experience Christian and Non-Christian* (Chicago: University of Chicago, 1951), 32–3).
[76] Johnson, *Experience*, 60.

meals), Johnson also highlights the emphasis on immediate RE in the scholarly discussion introduced so far.

In conclusion, Dunn, Hurtado and Johnson have each contributed distinctively to the retrieval of RE as a legitimate *topos* in NT research, and there are three points of confluence in their approaches which will inform my study. First, each of them recognizes the gap between report and experience, but asserts that textual reports of RE can offer genuine access to underlying experiences when carefully examined. On the other hand, none goes so far as to suggest that it is possible to gain objective access to the subjective experiences of the NT authors in ways which would allow readers to inhabit them in the manner that Gunkel had suggested.

Second, each of them argues that RE can be a source of creative religious expression. They claim that the effects of REs can be traced by examining the ways in which the new expressions they give rise to relate to historically accessible religious traditions. However, they do not, on the whole, consider the ways in which tradition itself may have shaped REs, nor the relationship between non-linguistic RE and cognitive content.

Third, all three argue that it is important to approach reports of RE under the assumption that they could possibly be accurate. While each argues that they are considering the perceptions of the NT authors,[77] the notion that RE should be treated seriously in its own right presupposes the possibility that it need not necessarily be reduced to a medically explicable experience and a theologically derived interpretation.

Throughout, these scholars inhabit a tension between history and theology: each analyses historical data, but wants to ask broadly theological questions (e.g. how did Jesus understand his relationship to God? How can we understand the development of Christology? How did baptism transform individuals?). Fundamentally, to paraphrase Hengel, each attempts to grasp the form and content of theological realities by means of historical research. My work will build on and extend their insights. First, I will give a theoretical defence of each of these three points of confluence against common critiques in Chapter 2. Second, I will address a desideratum in the discussion so far by expounding an inductively derived definition of RE. Third, I will argue that one way in which the kinds of experience examined by Dunn, Hurtado and Johnson shaped religious traditions was by contributing to the creation of Scriptures.

1.1.4. Recent contributions

Since its retrieval as a topos in biblical research in the work of Dunn, RE has continued to gain attention. In this section, I will survey four recent contributions as indicative examples of approaches to RE taken in the contemporary discussion. These range from Clint Tibbs's claim of insight into experiences described in the text to John Levison's assertion that such experiences are essentially inaccessible and therefore of limited interest. More suggestive are the balanced approaches advocated by Troels Engberg-Pedersen and Colleen Shantz, and I will consider each in turn.

---

[77] Cf. Samuel V. Adams, *The Reality of God and Historical Method: Apocalyptic Theology in Conversation with N. T. Wright*, New Explorations in Theology (Downers Grove, IL: IVP, 2015), for a theological examination of the limits of this kind of approach.

Clint Tibbs focuses on 1 Corinthians 12 and 14 and argues at the end of his review of scholarship on these chapters that 'what seems to be lacking in much of this study is a deeper understanding of the experiences that underlie these terms'.[78] While aware of constructivist critiques of RE – the claim that 'different religious and cultural groups might interpret the selfsame phenomena as coming from either good or evil spirits'[79] because interpretations of RE reflect the context in which they arise – he argues that it remains possible to explore what might be a distinctively Christian experience of the Spirit on the basis that the earliest Christians themselves sought to discern between various spiritual influences. Similarly to Gunkel, Tibbs sees his study as a historical corrective to theologically informed accounts of the Spirit in the NT insofar as he takes earliest Christian RE to be contradictory to later Nicene doctrine because of the variety of spirits attested in NT accounts of RE.[80] Methodologically, Tibbs's approach recalls Leisegang's: he claims insight into the RE underlying the experiential language of the NT, and seeks to situate this experience among other depictions of spirit communication in that period. However, Tibbs's claimed insight occasionally leads him to read texts in ways that obscure elements of their content. For example, he argues,

> If the Mesopotamian and Greco-Roman evidence for prophetic amnesia suggests that this phenomenon was typical of communicating with spirits via human mediums, this might, at least, imply that such was the case in OT texts that refer to indwelling spirits communicating with an audience, *despite the fact that the OT texts do not detail the phenomenon of amnesia in contexts of inspiration.*[81]

Accordingly, Tibbs's approach appears to overestimate the availability of experience, to the extent that he allows an assumed understanding of REs to shape the interpretation of texts in a manner which potentially obscures important differences.

Levison's major work *Filled with the Spirit*[82] develops earlier material[83] to offer an analysis of passages in Israelite, early Jewish and early Christian literature related to Spirit-filling. He argues that REs themselves are basically inaccessible: 'How ever could we verify statements about "spirit" [sic] in the lives of ancient figures?'[84] Rather, he is particularly concerned with tracing points of comparison across literary corpora to illuminate the target text by identifying influential conceptual trends which transcend any particular text. This is a self-conscious and critical reappropriation of elements of the *religionsgeschichtliche Schule*, but Levison describes his aim as 'contextualisation' rather than 'genealogical explanation', differentiating himself from classic *religionsgeschichtlich* approaches at this point.[85] This method is most obvious in *The Spirit in First Century Judaism*, where each chapter is structured around isolating the

---

[78] Tibbs, *Religious Experience*, 54.
[79] Tibbs, *Religious Experience*, 55.
[80] Cf. Tibbs, *Religious Experience*, 108–11, 269–83.
[81] Tibbs, *Religious Experience*, 141–2; italics mine.
[82] John R. Levison, *Filled with the Spirit* (Grand Rapids, MI: Eerdmans, 2009).
[83] Most importantly, John R. Levison, *The Spirit in First Century Judaism*, AGJU 29 (Leiden: Brill, 1997).
[84] Levison, *Filled*, 48 n.14.
[85] Cf. Frey and Levison, 'Origins', 33–4.

'exegetical movements' authors are making, before identifying 'relevant milieux' which provide an illuminating context for these developments.[86] For example, Levison argues that Philo's explanation of inspiration in his retelling of the Balaam story (exegetical movement) relies heavily on Hellenistic conceptions of inspiration (relevant milieu).

Levison's work challenges the idea of a focus on RE in considering the development of biblical interpretation in the first century as he argues that 'the writings of first century biblical interpreters, therefore, exhibit enormous creativity and diversity with respect to the *effects* and the *nature* of the spirit [sic], depending upon their contextual needs'.[87] This need not necessarily remove the possibility that RE was a contributing factor to a writer's 'contextual needs', but Levison is referring primarily to the manner in which Jewish interpreters sought to retell biblical narratives in ways that made sense to their contemporary readers. Accordingly, his argument implies that a robust examination of conceptual resources across diverse corpora of literature, combined with an understanding of the issues faced by writers in attempting to communicate old concepts to new audiences, can broadly account for innovative depictions of the Spirit. In *Filled with the Spirit* Levison extends this argument, claiming that early Christian language should only very rarely be attributed to the impact of RE because (a) experiential language in the NT is far less prevalent than Gunkel assumed; and (b) early Christian claims regarding the Spirit were not particularly unique.[88] He presents his study as a critique of Gunkel's focus on the Spirit's effects, and goes beyond asserting the inaccessibility of subjective RE to arguing that it is a mistaken emphasis. This argument partly relies on Levison's broader claim that the Spirit of life and the Holy Spirit should not be differentiated and leads him later to argue that 'inspired' early Christian exegesis should be seen as a 'studied mode of interpreting the Scriptures in light of Jesus'.[89] Though this may be correct, it does not adequately explain what might prompt such a rereading. The 'inspired' interpretation of Scripture in Acts, for example, appears to reflect what the believers perceived as a decisively new salvation-historical situation on the basis of Jesus' death and resurrection (appearances), and their infilling with the Spirit. To neglect this dimension of their understanding is to downplay an element which gives their inspired interpretation much of its impetus, and thus it fails to account adequately for the argument that RE can be a driving force in religious innovation.

Where Tibbs appears to overestimate the possibility of insight into experiences described in ancient texts and Levison argues that they are basically inaccessible, Engberg-Pedersen offers a more nuanced approach. In a 2008 article on Paul's RE, he argues that 'just because [Paul's] reference to his own religious experiences serves certain functions and the experiences themselves always came in interpreted form, we should not conclude that there was nothing to be interpreted and to serve those functions'.[90] Echoing Gunkel's critique of the idealism of liberal theology, this false

---

[86] Cf. Levison, *First Century Judaism*, 4–6, for a brief description of this method.
[87] Levison, *First Century Judaism*, 240; italics original.
[88] Levison, *Filled*, 227–9.
[89] Levison, *Filled*, 360.
[90] Troels Engberg-Pedersen, 'The Construction of Religious Experience in Paul', in *Experientia I*, 147–58 (150). This is developed in Troels Engberg-Pedersen, *Cosmology and Self in the Apostle Paul: The Material Spirit* (Oxford: Oxford University Press, 2010).

conclusion is labelled the 'idealist fallacy', against which Engberg-Pedersen insists on the '"realist" claim that ... something happened'.[91] However, the article begins with a very brief consideration of the arguments against considering RE claiming that the vast majority of them are well-founded. Consequently, Engberg-Pedersen argues that research on RE must remember

> Paul's religious experiences did in fact come in interpreted form. He did focus on issues of ethnicity in relation to his understanding of the Christ event. He did use the reference to his own religious experience for the various rhetorical purposes suggested. And, in particular, he was not concerned to relate his own religious experiences for their own sake, but always as part of a relationship with others. Still, he did have them.[92]

This approach recognizes the theoretical limits of the accessibility of subjective experiences, but insists that it is still possible to reasonably conclude that Paul did have REs, and that it is possible to speak about them on the basis of the accounts he has provided. On the other hand, it leaves little room for non-linguistic experience to push back against the interpretive framework within which it is necessarily embedded, and it is not clear on this account whether Engberg-Pedersen avoids construing RE as solely a confirmatory phenomenon.

The most significant recent contributions to the study of RE in biblical studies – including Engberg-Pedersen's treatment of Paul's RE – have come in the form of two edited volumes in 2008 and 2012.[93] In the introduction to the former, Frances Flannery explains that the volumes reflect the insight that 'the texts that are the sources of scholarship on early Judaism and early Christianity often have as their *raison d'être* some religious experience of the author and/or of the community ... What we *can* do is to take seriously the textual *articulation* of religious experience in antiquity'.[94] The most significant theoretical contribution comes in the introduction to the second volume by Shantz,[95] which offers a concise summary of her own argument in *Paul in Ecstasy*.[96]

Shantz begins by noting that 'for many years, [assuming] the possibility of accessing subjective experience has been considered a theoretical misstep at best and apologetics disguised as analysis at worst',[97] before attempting to address various critiques which fit broadly into these two categories. First, she considers the argument that subjective experience is inaccessible to critical study, which she combines with the claim that theological appeals to RE constitute special pleading because they cannot be critically assessed. Against this, she points to theoretical approaches 'which are providing more

---

[91] Engberg-Pedersen, 'Construction', 150.
[92] Engberg-Pedersen, 'Construction', 150.
[93] *Experientia I*; *Experientia II*.
[94] Frances Flannery with Nicolae Roddy, Colleen Shantz and Rodney A. Werline, 'Introduction: Religious Experience Past and Present', in *Experientia I*, 1–10 (2); italics original.
[95] Colleen Shantz, 'Opening the Black Box: New Prospects for Analyzing Religious Experience', in *Experientia II*, 1–15.
[96] Colleen Shantz, *Paul in Ecstasy: The Neurobiology of the Apostle's Life and Thought* (Cambridge: Cambridge University Press, 2009).
[97] Shantz, 'Black Box', 1.

transparent means to access experience', including Bourdieu's concept of *habitus*, and the insights of Cognitive Science of Religion into patterns of human behaviour.[98] Second, she engages the problem of reductionism. While accepting that 'constructivist critique is well taken as a response to "veridical experience" or proof of divinity', she contests 'the idea that language both creates and exhausts experience'.[99] This creates space to ask both what kinds of experience might prompt someone to create the texts that have been preserved in the NT and what experiences a text might be intended to produce in its readers.

Shantz concludes by reflecting on the category of RE, arguing that 'rather than treating "religious experience" as a compound term, we treat it as a noun modified by an adjective'.[100] With this in mind, she cites Melford Spiro's definition of religion as 'culturally patterned interaction with culturally postulated superhuman beings',[101] and argues that a focus on experience allows 'non-logocentric' ways of knowing, and the role of the body in shaping this interaction to come into view. In this way, Shantz develops an approach to RE which fits with the emphases of the approaches to RE of Dunn, Hurtado and Johnson. Where Tibbs argues for a level of insight into experiences that allows him to critique the textual presentation of them and Levison suggests that experience is basically inaccessible, the contributions of Engberg-Pedersen and Shantz suggest a more nuanced approach. Shantz in particular balances a critical awareness of the importance of interpretation of experience with an assertion of its holistic role in shaping cognitive commitments. That she does this in conversation with a sociologist of religion reflects a strength of the *Experientia* volumes: their engagement with religious studies approaches to RE. It is to this area that I will now turn my attention, in order to survey that discussion and identify key conversation partners.[102]

1.2. Religious experience in religious studies research

At the same time as the *religionsgeschichtliche Schule* was an ascendant influence in biblical studies at the turn of the twentieth century, religious studies research turned its attention to RE. Most famously this took the form of psychologist and philosopher

---

[98] Shantz, 'Black Box', 5.
[99] Shantz, 'Black Box', 7–8.
[100] Shantz, 'Black Box', 11.
[101] Melford E. Spiro, 'Religion: Problems of Definition and Explanation', in *Anthropological Approaches to the Study of Religion*, ed. Michael Banton (London: Tavistock, 1966), 85–126 (96).
[102] It would also be possible to consider RE from a theological perspective. There are two reasons for not doing so: (1) RE is relevant to discussions of revelation which sit close to the heart of theological inquiry (at the very least since Barth made God's speaking the starting point of his dogmatics), meaning it would be impossible to cover sufficient material; and (2) while theological questions inform RE research within biblical studies, the interest is in historical claims of human experience of God and not on how to speak faithfully about such experience within a faith community. For theological discussion of relevant themes, cf. Nicholas Lash, *Easter in Ordinary* (Notre Dame: University of Notre Dame, 1986); Nicholas Wolterstorff, *Divine Discourse: Philosophical Reflections on the Claim That God Speaks* (Cambridge: Cambridge University Press, 1995); and the contributions to R. Douglas Geivett and Paul K. Moser, eds, *The Testimony of the Spirit: New Essays* (Oxford: Oxford University Press, 2017).

William James's Gifford Lectures, published in 1902 as *The Varieties of Religious Experience*.[103] James's study proved hugely influential[104] until the impact of the linguistic turn prompted a re-evaluation both of his work and approaches to RE. The resulting constructivist approach to RE remains regnant in the field, but recent developments have suggested weaknesses. This is significant for my research insofar as biblical scholars including Hurtado, Johnson and the recent contributors to the *Experientia* volumes have looked to scholars of religion to provide theoretical resources for the examination of RE. To this end, I will offer an overview of the development of the religious studies discussion beginning with William James in order to contextualize conversation partners engaged in my constructive proposal in Chapter 2.

1.2.1. William James

In *The Varieties of Religious Experience*, James employs a comparative method similar to the *religionsgeschichtliche Schule* to examine an array of written accounts of RE. He aimed to offer a taxonomy of RE, taking it to be a universal feature of human life. In a similar manner to both Gunkel and Dunn, James took RE to be the core of religion, as can be seen in his definition of the latter as '*the feelings, acts, and experiences of individual men in their solitude, so far as they apprehend themselves to stand in relation to whatever they may consider the divine*'.[105] James's individualist definition emphasizes the subjective nature of RE. In his lectures treating mysticism – which he presents as the 'highest' form of RE – he argues that 'mystical states ... usually are, and have the right to be, absolutely authoritative over the individuals to whom they come ... [but] no authority emanates from them which should make it a duty for those who stand outside of them to accept their revelations uncritically'.[106]

While the subjective emphasis prevents RE from acting as a tendentious ground for sweeping theological claims, James also argues that the very existence of RE has consequences for everyone – regardless of whether or not they have had one. He begins his lectures on mysticism by stating that 'the subject of [mystical experience] immediately says that it defies expression ... Although so similar to states of feeling, mystical states seem to those who experience them to be also states of knowledge'.[107] In this way, he balances the apparent ineffability of mystical experience with its claimed cognitive content. This in turn suggests to him that

> [Mystical experiences] open out the possibility of other orders of truth, in which, so far as anything in us vitally responds to them, we may freely continue to have

---

[103] William James, *The Varieties of Religious Experience: A Study in Human Nature* (1902 repr., Abingdon: Routledge, 2008). Cf. discussion in Charles Taylor, *Varieties of Religion Today: William James Revisited* (Cambridge: Harvard University, 2002); Wayne Proudfoot, ed., *William James and a Science of Religions: Reexperiencing the Varieties of Religious Experience* (New York: Columbia University, 2004).
[104] Cf. Jay, *Songs*, 78–131.
[105] James, *Varieties*, 26; italics original.
[106] James, *Varieties*, 297.
[107] James, *Varieties*, 267.

faith ... The existence of mystical states absolutely overthrows the pretension of non-mystical states to be the sole and ultimate dictators of what we may believe.[108]

Accordingly, for James, any description of reality which seeks to take seriously accounts of RE must remain open to the *possibility* that the truth claims in those accounts are accurate. This prefigures Johnson's later argument that RE must be taken seriously on its own terms, rather than being reduced to an 'epiphenomenon' of historical developments.[109]

James also sought to articulate an epistemological approach which could remain open to RE, while acknowledging its subjectivity and the attendant limitations of its truth claims due to their unverifiability. He opposed reductionism, arguing that meaning should be an integral part of holistic descriptions of reality: for example, the attribution of Paul's 'vision on the road to Damascus [to] a discharging lesion of the occipital cortex' did not take into account the meaning which James saw as in some way *inherent* in the experience itself.[110] Indeed, James rejected this approach to 'explaining away' religious phenomena, labelling it 'medical materialism'.[111] In so doing, he articulated an approach that has similarities with the claims of Dunn, Hurtado and Johnson that RE itself should be taken seriously as a historical cause in the growth of Christianity and the development of its literature.

1.2.2. RE as a *sui generis* phenomenon

James's argument that RE was the core of religion initially proved persuasive and his approach was adopted and extended, with the result that religious studies research on RE grew while the rise of dialectical theology led to its neglect in biblical studies. During this period, Lutheran theologian Rudolf Otto combined the influences of James and Schleiermacher,[112] and argued that encounters with the 'numinous' – his term for the transcendent 'Other', unrelated to the Kantian *noumenal* – underpinned all particular religious expressions.[113] Otto pushed Schleiermacher's description of feeling as an epistemological category and James's argument that feeling was the 'core' of religion to an extreme conclusion: where they had sought to find a unifying point in diverse experiences, Otto argued for a foundational *type* of experience and used it to explain diverse accounts of religion. Otto presented the experience of the numinous as irreducible and universal, but also as unique (*sui generis*). This account made it possible to privilege both religion as the expression of such experience and the 'insider' perspective of those who had had REs, as they could not be challenged or explained on the basis of alternate frameworks.

---

[108] James, *Varieties*, 297, 299.
[109] Cf. Johnson, *Experience*, 24–6.
[110] James, *Varieties*, 21.
[111] James, *Varieties*, 14–17.
[112] See Rudolf Otto, 'How Schleiermacher Rediscovered the *Sensus Numinis*', in *Religious Essays: A Supplement to 'The Idea of the Holy'* (London: Oxford University Press, 1931). Cf. Jay, *Songs*, 111–14.
[113] See Rudolf Otto, *The Idea of the Holy*, 2nd edn (Oxford: Oxford University Press, 1957), 25–30, for the terminology.

The idea of a unique type of experience of 'the holy' or 'the sacred' underlying all religious expressions was taken up in the 'Chicago School', associated with the comparative approach to religion developed by Joachim Wach[114] and his successor, Mircea Eliade.[115] Wach argued for a *religionswissenschaftlich* (science of religions) approach to religion, employing a social-scientific methodology to describe and compare particular religious expressions and suggested that new experiences of the numinous underwrite the creation of new religious movements. His analysis anticipated, though for different reasons, both Hurtado's later argument and the social scientific research he draws on to make it.

Eliade focused less on the social and institutional aspects of religion and more on its literature. He argued that experience of 'the sacred' was fundamental to religious expression, and devoted his research to attempting to trace the impact of experiences of 'the sacred' in the diverse mythological literatures of varied communities. Both Wach and Eliade assumed, like Otto, that they had particular insight into a unique, universal type of experience, and that from this vantage point they could trace its impact in diverse religious contexts.

1.2.3. RE as a cultural construct

Thanks to Wach and Eliade, RE remained a significant area of religious studies research. However, as Ann Taves, a leading scholar of religion, notes, 'In the wake of the general linguistic turn within the humanities ... this entire approach was called into question.'[116] The notion of a *sui generis* type of experience that was distinctively religious was rejected on the basis that there is no 'pristine' experience. Rather, all experience is in fact linguistically constructed, meaning that RE is itself a cultural construct. In Shantz's terms, this meant a rejection of the treatment of RE as a compound noun, in favour of understanding it as a noun modified by an adjective.

A classic expression of this position is Wayne Proudfoot's *Religious Experience*,[117] which argues that religion is a complex phenomenon that scholars can profitably reduce to its simpler constituent parts: the religious description (adjective) can and should be separated from the scientifically explicable experience (noun). To support his argument, Proudfoot drew on research that appeared to demonstrate that even the most basic emotional experiences were separable into physiological responses and culturally constructed objects.[118] This account of RE privileged the explanatory

---

[114] See Joachim Wach, *Sociology of Religion* (London: Kegan Paul, 1947). For an appropriation of Wach within biblical studies, cf. Johnson, *Experience*, 60-8.

[115] See Mircea Eliade, *The Sacred and the Profane: The Nature of Religion* (San Diego, CA: Harcourt Brace, 1959); Mircea Eliade, *Patterns in Comparative Religion* (London: Sheed and Ward, 1958).

[116] Ann Taves, *Religious Experience Reconsidered: A Building-Block Approach to the Study of Religion and Other Special Things* (Princeton, NJ: Princeton University, 2009), 5.

[117] Wayne Proudfoot, *Religious Experience* (Berkeley: University of California), 1985. Cf. also Robert H. Sharf, 'Experience', in *Critical Terms for Religious Studies*, ed. Mark C. Taylor (Chicago: University of Chicago, 1998), 94-116.

[118] Cf. Proudfoot, *Religious Experience*, 98-102, drawing particularly on Stanley Schachter and Jerome E. Singer, 'Cognitive, Social and Physiological Determinants of Emotional State', *Psychological Review* 69 (1962): 379-99.

perspective of the scholar, and generated significant criticism of previous approaches. As an indicative example, Russell McCutcheon argues that taking religion as essentially the product of a *sui generis* experience obscures the sociopolitical status of both the experience being analysed and the scholar analysing it.[119]

This constructivist account of RE came to dominate religious studies research into the topic which consequently focused on the processes by which certain experiences gain religious status, and how claims of RE are used in religious discourse. The implications of these developments for biblical studies are visible in the critiques addressed by Engberg-Pedersen and Shantz and noted above (§1.1.4).

1.2.4. RE and non-linguistic meaning

The cultural constructivist critique of *sui generis* treatments of RE is appropriate and helpful, but it goes too far when used to suggest that experience is completely reducible to language. Indeed, Zahl has noted that 'even the most "constructivist" recent psychological accounts of affective processes reject the sort of simplistic social and cultural constructivism adopted by Lindbeck and Proudfoot',[120] and which Shantz critiques.

For the purposes of this study, there are two developments in recent research which will inform my approach to RE. First, affective neuroscientist Elaine Fox points out that 'in spite of several attempts, no study has been able to fully replicate the effects' of the psychological research on which Proudfoot relies to demonstrate the separability of physiology and object in emotional responses.[121] Clearly, this suggests that the theory is open to question, problematizing the assertion that emotional experience is necessarily and exclusively culturally constructed. Second, and similarly, developments in neuroscientific research have led philosopher of religion Jason Blum to argue that 'affect plays a necessary and central physiological role in establishing consciousness'.[122] This in turn 'suggests that certain kinds of awareness are nonlinguistic, and that even those experiences that are thoroughly pervaded by language likely include nonlinguistic components'.[123] I will draw on these lines of research to develop my constructive approach in the next chapter.

---

[119] Russell T. McCutcheon, *The Discipline of Religion: Structure, Meaning, Rhetoric* (London: Routledge, 2003), 206. Cf. similarly Robert Segal, 'Reductionism in the Study of Religion', in *Religion and Reductionism: Essays on Eliade, Segal, and the Challenge of the Social Sciences for the Study of Religion*, ed. Thomas A. Idinopulos and Edward A. Yonan (Leiden: Brill, 1994), 4–14; and Edward A. Yonan, 'Clarifying the Strengths and Limits of Reductionism in the Discipline of Religion', in *Religion and Reductionism: Essays on Eliade, Segal, and the Challenge of the Social Sciences for the Study of Religion*, ed. Thomas A. Idinopulos and Edward A. Yonan (Leiden: Brill, 1994), 43–8.

[120] Simeon Zahl, 'On the Affective Salience of Doctrines', *Modern Theology* 31 (2015): 428–44 (430 n.9).

[121] Elaine Fox, *Emotion Science: Cognitive and Neuroscientific Approaches to Understanding Human Emotions* (New York: Palgrave Macmillan, 2008), 150–1.

[122] Jason N. Blum, 'The Science of Consciousness and Mystical Experience: An Argument for Radical Empiricism', *JAAR* 82 (2014): 150–73 (161).

[123] Blum, 'Consciousness', 162.

1.3. Religious experience: A review

From the above review, it is clear that there remain theoretical questions regarding the possibility of approaching RE within New Testament studies. These run along three lines. First, RE is often still viewed only as a subjective phenomenon which is consequently unavailable to critical study. This raises the question of whether and how subjective experience can become accessible to critical study. Second, the relationship between RE and religious language has been contested, raising the question of whether and how REs can shape language. Third, claims to RE are frequently used to support claims to knowledge of God. Taking seriously truth claims related to REs implies an openness to the possibility of a transcendent reality, even for a historiographical approach which seeks to engage them critically. In the following chapter, I will articulate a constructive proposal for approaching RE which attempts to address these questions.

One further issue related to this study is the question of how REs can be identified in biblical texts. As Batluck notes, 'Early Christian studies has yet to propose an inductively substantiated definition for religious experience.'[124] This is a significant issue, as Johnson rightly argues that definitions serve 'heuristic and diagnostic' purposes, functioning 'as a means of pointing to the sort of reality we mean and enabling us to distinguish among its cognates'.[125] I will argue for a heuristic definition for exegetical purposes, refining and elaborating that offered in my earlier analysis of Romans 8.[126]

---

[124] Batluck, 'Religious Experience', 354.
[125] Johnson, *Experience*, 60.
[126] Wreford, 'Diagnosing', 221–2.

2

Approaching Religious Experience

In the previous chapter I situated this study in relation to existing research into religious experience (RE) and concluded by pointing to four outstanding methodological issues: (1) the availability of subjective experience to critical study; (2) the relationship between RE and religious language; (3) the appropriateness of RE as a historical category; and (4) the definition of RE particularly in the NT texts. In this chapter, I will address these points, outlining a constructive proposal for the treatment of RE which I will use to analyse Luke-Acts and Galatians in the second section of the study.

In the first instance, it is necessary to defend the claim that the linguistic traces left by people – in this case, the NT texts – can legitimately be seen as giving insight into subjective experiences in ways which allow us to talk meaningfully about them (§2.1). At a general level, this claim has been problematized by the focus on philosophy of language in the latter part of the twentieth century rooted in the writings of Ludwig Wittgenstein and Ferdinand de Saussure and known as the 'linguistic turn'.[1] More specifically, claims of RE are sometimes considered to be inherently dubious on the basis that they are unlike the experiences of the scholars examining the texts.

Second, constructivist accounts of RE similarly argue that experience is inescapably shaped by language. On such accounts, RE can only ever be 'confirmatory' in character and can profitably be explained by reference to its sociopolitical functions. This runs counter to my claim that the texts of the NT include innovative expressions of religious language made partly in response to REs which are not entirely explicable by reference to the linguistic contexts within which they emerged. To support this construal, I will identify an alternate way of understanding the relationship between experience and language, drawing on phenomenology of religion (§2.2).

Third, constructivist accounts of RE arose at least in part as a helpful critique of the special pleading of *sui generis* accounts of RE. This raises the question of whether the category itself can be useful outside of a theologically committed framework. To address this issue, I will argue for a historiographical approach which privileges insider perspectives, but defers judgement regarding their truth claims (§2.3).

---

[1] The seminal publication is Richard Rorty, ed., *The Linguistic Turn: Recent Essays in Philosophical Method* (Chicago: University of Chicago, 1967). The relevance of the linguistic turn for biblical studies is explored in Anthony C. Thiselton, *New Horizons in Hermeneutics: The Theory and Practice of Transforming Biblical Reading* (1992 repr., Grand Rapids, MI: Zondervan, 2012), esp. 80–148.

It will also be necessary to define important terms for my argument and I have already suggested that the discussion of RE within biblical studies would benefit from an inductive definition which avoids special pleading but offers 'heuristic and diagnostic'[2] benefits for exegesis (§2.4). Beyond these questions, which were introduced in the previous chapter, I will also offer an understanding of Scripture (§2.5) and outline how the approach will be applied to Luke-Acts and Galatians as exemplary NT texts in which a prototypical pattern of relationship between RE and claims to scriptural status is visible (§2.6).

2.1. Accessing subjective experience through texts

Since Gunkel's attempt to 'live the pneumatic's inner states after him',[3] what Flannery terms the 'beneficial but dead-ended insight of deconstructionism and post-structuralism' has cautioned against 'claiming an understanding of any other person's subjective experience'.[4] Flannery points here to the importance of postmodern theory in shaping historical approaches to subjective experience, and appears to accept an engagement with the 'textual *articulation*' of experience as the limit of critical study.[5] Against this acceptance, Dunn argues that 'a sympathetic study of the language with which Jesus and the first Christians articulated their religious experience should therefore enable us to gain some insight into their self-understanding and evaluation of their experience'.[6] In other words, a sensitive reading should make it possible for 'us to enter *at least some way* into the experience of others'.[7] To enable this, Dunn presupposes that the biblical authors want their readership to come close to the original experience and relies on the possibility of discerning authorial intent through a text (what I will call 'hermeneutical perspicuity'; §2.1.1), historical insight into analogous experiences ('the principle of analogy'; §2.1.2) and a 'sympathetic' approach ('hermeneutical charity'; §2.1.3). In light of theoretical critiques which have problematized this approach, I will defend each point in turn.

2.1.1. 'Hermeneutical perspicuity': Can we see through the text?

The textual accounts of REs found in the NT claim to witness to specific experiences that occurred in the lives of those reporting them. Thus, they generally aim to

---

[2] Luke Timothy Johnson, *Religious Experience in Earliest Christianity: A Missing Dimension in New Testament Studies* (Minneapolis, MN: Fortress Press, 1998), 60.
[3] Hermann Gunkel, *The Influence of the Holy Spirit: The Popular View of the Apostolic Age and the Teaching of the Apostle Paul* (Philadelphia, PA: Fortress, 1979), 3.
[4] Flannery, 'Introduction', in *Experientia 1*, 1–10 (1–2); italics original, citing Foucault, Derrida and Geertz. See esp. Clifford Geertz, *The Interpretation of Cultures* (New York: Basic, 1973), 3–30, 87–125.
[5] Flannery, 'Introduction', 2; italics original.
[6] James D. G. Dunn, *Jesus and the Spirit: A Study of the Religious and Charismatic Experience of Jesus and the First Christians as Reflected in the New Testament* (London: SCM, 1975), 3.
[7] Dunn, *Jesus*, 3; italics mine.

communicate something of the experience and its significance, even if it also appears that certain NT texts were also intended to achieve a particular affect in their readers which might ultimately bring them into contact with the reality described.[8] Consequently, there is a hermeneutical distance between the texts and the experiences of the authors. Jaques Derrida famously magnifies this difference, asserting that 'the intention which animates utterance will never be completely present in itself and its content'.[9] On the other hand, Derrida's assertion need not undermine the possibility of successful textual communication allowing insight into the experiences and intentions of authors. According to James K. A. Smith, the insight of deconstructionism is that although perfect communication is impossible, adequate understanding may be achieved: 'What Derrida's account of language and interpretation gives us is not a sense of the *impossibility* of communication but rather a sense of the *risk* of communication.'[10] A textual account of subjective experience is not identical to the experience itself, but it exists to communicate something of the experience – and this remains the case for biblical texts even where an individual author cannot be straightforwardly assumed insofar as they exist only because someone(s) intended to produce something meaningful to others. Assuming that the act of communication is successful, it should be possible for a sensitive reader to understand something of the experience to which the text bears witness.[11] For this reason, even though Gunkel goes too far in assuming that the author is 'fully present' to him in a way which would enable him to relive their experiences, it is not necessary to assume that the author is 'completely absent' in a way which would render their experiences entirely inaccessible to the reader. Rather, it is possible that 'the author is *really* present, but not fully present'[12] to the reader through the text. On this account, misunderstanding is a *possible*, but not *necessary* effect of the distance between reader, text, and author. In this sense, we can see 'through' the text. Our vision is not perfect, but it is adequate to permit discussion of the experiences which the texts witness to and the question of whether any given reading is adequate must be settled on a case-by-case basis, decided by whether it offers a coherent, compelling account of the text's witness, which is in principle compatible with the text's history of impact and reception.[13]

---

[8] See e.g. John 20:31: 'But these things are written *so that you may come to believe* that Jesus is the Messiah, the Son of God, and that *through believing you may have life in his name*.' Cf. Robin Griffith-Jones, 'Transformation by a Text: The Gospel of John', in *Experientia I*, 105–23.
[9] Jacques Derrida, 'Signature Event Context', in *Margins of Philosophy* (Chicago: University of Chicago, 1982), 309–30 (327).
[10] James K. A. Smith, *The Fall of Interpretation: Philosophical Foundations for an Incarnational Hermeneutic* (Grand Rapids, MI: Baker Academic, 2012), 219; italics original.
[11] Cf. Kevin J. Vanhoozer, *Is There a Meaning in This Text?* (Grand Rapids, MI: Zondervan, 1998), 139: 'It is a kind of interpretation neither absolute nor arbitrary, that yields *adequate* knowledge – adequate for the purpose of understanding' (italics original).
[12] Smith, *Fall of Interpretation*, 217; italics original.
[13] In this way, my approach remains valid in the face of recent critiques of the importance of authorial intent for the interpretation of NT texts, e.g. Edwin K. Broadhead, *The Gospel of Matthew on the Landscape of Antiquity* (WUNT 378, Tübingen: Mohr Siebeck, 2017).

2.1.2. Historical analogy: Can we understand the experiences?

The REs reported in the NT are separated from us not only by hermeneutical distance but also historical. To address this, Dunn argues that the principle of analogy[14] can allow a sensitive reader to understand elements of others' experiences insofar as they attempt to communicate them:

> It is impossible to enter [fully] into someone else's experience ... Nevertheless, our own experience and the knowledge which we have of human experience in general does enable us to enter at least some way into the experience of others and even to appreciate sympathetically something of experiences otherwise strange to us.[15]

This basic point is assumed in all historical reconstruction, but the applicability of the principle of analogy to *religious* forms of experience is contested for two reasons. First, contemporary REs have generally not been treated as sufficiently credible and accessible to enable the formation of analogies. This argument has generally been tacit: claims of unusual experience are doubted because they are not analogous with the experiences of scholars, or the majority of people they tend to observe.[16] This has been increasingly called into question in recent research in part by what Frey and Levison describe as 'the growing influence of [Pentecostal and charismatic] forms of Christianity ... with their focus upon claims to human experience of the divine'.[17] Similarly, recent treatments of miracles have shown that readings which a priori reject their possibility rely on an outdated and unsustainable set of theoretical assumptions and inappropriately dismiss a vast array of relevant data.[18] While this affirms the availability of contemporary – and other historical, non-biblical – experiences with which to form analogies to the REs reported in the NT, advances in neuroscience have also afforded new insights into human experience which can offer helpful new lines along which to interrogate NT accounts of RE.[19] Accordingly, this first concern has been comprehensively answered, and I will assume that accounts of RE need not a priori be dismissed as inaccurate or in need of alternative explanation simply on the basis that they describe unusual experiences.

---

[14] For a classic articulation, see Ernst Troeltsch, 'Historical and Dogmatic Method in Theology', in *Religion in History*, ed. J. L. Adams and W. F. Bense (Minneapolis, MN: Fortress, 1991), 11–32.

[15] Dunn, *Jesus*, 3. Cf. Flannery, 'Introduction', 2.

[16] Cf. Jack Levison, *Inspired: The Holy Spirit and the Mind of Faith* (Grand Rapids, MI: Eerdmans, 2013), who includes explicit accounts of the way in which encounters with contemporary RE have shaped his approach to the sources (15–17; 71–3).

[17] Jörg Frey and John R. Levison, 'The Origins of Early Christian Pneumatology: On the Rediscovery and Reshaping of the History of Religions Quest', in *The Holy Spirit, Inspiration, and the Cultures of Antiquity*, ed. Jörg Frey and John R. Levison (Berlin: De Gruyter, 2014), 1.

[18] See Craig S. Keener, *Miracles: The Credibility of the New Testament Accounts* (Grand Rapids, MI: Baker Academic, 2011). Keener addresses theoretical issues (83–208) before adducing extensive non-biblical parallels to the miracles recorded in the NT (209–600). Cf. Luke Timothy Johnson, *Miracles: God's Presence and Power in Creation* (Louisville, KY: Westminster John Knox, 2018), 21–77.

[19] Cf. Blum, 'The Science of Consciousness and Mystical Experience: An Argument for Radical Empiricism', *JAAR* 82 (2014): 150–73; Colleen Shantz, *Paul in Ecstasy: The Neurobiology of the Apostle's Life and Thought* (Cambridge: Cambridge University Press, 2009), 67–109.

Second, accounts of RE sometimes claim they were unique, or ineffable.[20] Admitting such a claim would clearly put the experience described beyond the reach of analogous understanding, and consequently beyond the reach of analogical historical description. On the one hand, the majority of accounts of RE in the NT are in fact intended to make experiences accessible to others with the intention of shaping their religious beliefs and behaviours, meaning that a claim of uniqueness does not generally appear to be intended – with 2 Corinthians 12:1–4 an exceptional example which proves the rule.

Hurtado's argument that RE can be a significant factor in religious innovation presupposes that RE cannot in every case be entirely explained on the basis of pre-existing cultural phenomena, however.[21] This suggests that something new was learned by the recipient of the RE. According to Jonathan Z. Smith, such a claim to have derived new knowledge from experience is itself problematic: 'There is no primordium – it is all history. There is no "other" – it is all what we see in Europe every day.'[22] This leads Smith to argue against Hurtado's suggestion that REs can provide new knowledge: rather, experience itself is culturally constructed and meaning is only worked out by reference to conceptual frameworks which are reshaped gradually over time. The suggestion is, as Johnson puts it, that 'history dissolves all claims to revelation and thereby deprives Christianity of any special claim to uniqueness ... [It] is dissolved into a loose arrangement of competing political and ideological claims within the Jewish version of Hellenistic culture.'[23]

However, it is possible that Smith's understanding of the principle of analogy fails to account for the epistemological structure of experience. Hermeneutic theorist Hans-Georg Gadamer claims that 'the negativity of experience has a curiously productive meaning. It is not simply that we see through a deception and hence make a correction, but we acquire a [more] comprehensive knowledge.'[24] Here, Gadamer is arguing that experiencing something unexpected forces one to notice one's own historically situated horizon and its limits – to recognize 'that the "in-itself" is [actually] a "for-me"'.[25] Accordingly, learning something new not only adds to our knowledge but also teaches us its limits, leading to the anticipation of new experiences which bring new knowledge. This is of particular importance for an examination of the NT insofar as 'distinctive of biblical mentality is a pronounced openness toward the dimension of the Other; indeed, manifestations of the Other are expected'.[26] Accordingly, Smith's account of the principle of analogy gives an unhelpful account of the role of experience

---

[20] This is generally true of mystical experience, which Blum defines in part by its deviation from what is 'normal': 'a report of an encounter between a mystic and ultimacy that is more intimate than that afforded by religious practice as performed by the larger, general religious community' (*Zen and the Unspeakable God: Comparative Interpretations of Mystical Experience* (University Park: Pennsylvania State University, 2015), Kindle edition, loc. 157).

[21] Hurtado, 'Religious Experience and Religious Innovation in the New Testament'. *JR* 80 (2000): 183–205.

[22] Jonathan Z. Smith, *Imagining Religion: From Babylon to Jamestown* (Chicago: University of Chicago, 1982), xiii.

[23] Johnson, *Experience*, 35.

[24] Hans-Georg Gadamer, *Truth and Method* (1960 repr., London: Bloomsbury, 2013), 362.

[25] Gadamer, *Truth and Method*, 482.

[26] Klaus Berger, *Identity and Experience in the New Testament* (Minneapolis, MN: Fortress, 2003), 12.

in shaping belief. It is both anachronistic to the worldview of the NT authors and inappropriately flattens the variety and particularity of the NT sources by bringing 'all of history ... to the level of the observer'.[27] Instead, a 'sympathetic' engagement with the NT sensitive to its 'otherness' as well as its similarity can understand *to a certain extent* the experiences which the texts attempt to relate, even when they are presented as innovative and unusual.

2.1.3. Hermeneutical charity: Must we accept the text's claims?

So far, I have argued for a 'sensitive' reading similar to the 'sympathetic study', Dunn advocates. This raises the question of how far the texts' claims must be respected in order to produce readings which do not obscure the experiences to which they witness. There are two sides to this question: first, how should the perspective of the scholar interact with the horizon of the text? Second, how should we treat the faith claims which arise from the experiences witnessed to in the text and form part of the text? This second question will require further discussion below (§2.3). However, it is helpful at this point to note that RE should not be seen as constituting what philosopher William P. Alston describes as 'veridical experience of the presence and/or activity of God'.[28] Faith claims based on RE are as suspect as any others, if not more so: they are not necessarily accurate and experiencers may even be mistaken in their perceptions, descriptions and evaluations of their experiences.

Nonetheless, regardless of whether the faith claims made on the basis of these experiences are correct, it remains the case that the experiences themselves may have played an important role in the historical processes that resulted in the creation of the NT texts. Except where the evidence suggests otherwise,[29] texts which claim to witness to particular experiences need not be a priori explained on other bases. Consequently, in answer to the first question, a comprehensive historical description of the origins of the texts should attempt to take their possible experiential shaping into account. I will now consider the relationship between experience and language to suggest how this might be done.

2.2. Experience and language

Despite theoretical reservations regarding the availability of subjective experience through the critical study of textual accounts, I have argued that it is possible to come to some kind of understanding of the experiences to which the NT texts bear witness. However, the linguistic turn has also given rise to strong constructivist understandings of the relationship between experience and language that have challenged the claim that

---

[27] Johnson, *Experience*, 30.
[28] William P. Alston, 'Religious Experience', in *Routledge Encyclopedia of Philosophy*, ed. Edward Craig (London: Routledge, 1998), VIII: 250–5 (250).
[29] That is, in cases in which there are good reasons to suggest alternate explanations for the presence of accounts of RE in the texts, including deceitful employment of RE claims in order to strengthen an otherwise unpersuasive case.

RE can generate innovative linguistic expression. For example, Steven Katz offers an indicative constructivist account of the relationship between RE and religious language when he argues that 'the Hindu mystic does not have an experience of x which he then describes in the, to him, familiar language and symbols of Hinduism, but rather *he has a Hindu experience*'.[30] The implication is that the cultural construct (Hinduism) is determinative for *both* the meaning of the experience *and* its character: were this mystic located in a different tradition he would not have 'the same' experience but describe it in different terms; rather, he would have a different experience. This, in turn, suggests that RE is inherently 'conservative' in character: while it may be possible for RE understood in this way to precipitate a 'radical hermeneutic approach' to a received tradition,[31] it is not possible for it to include new content which generate religious innovations. However, drawing on social-scientific research which points to a positive correlation between revelatory experiences and new religious movements,[32] Hurtado claims that RE was instrumental in the development of early Christianity: 'It is simplistic to regard religious experiences as only derivative from prior beliefs and to fail to see that religious experiences can modify beliefs and/or generate new ones, in some cases resulting in significant innovations.'[33] If Hurtado is correct, a strong constructivist account of RE in the NT will be inadequate.

However, Hurtado does not consider the gap between experience and language. In fact, he distinguishes between the experience itself and its cognitive content in a similar manner to Katz:

> What makes certain experiences 'revelatory' (at least in the circles shaped by biblical traditions) is not so much the *physiological effects or some dramatic phenomena*, but instead the recipient's *perception of new cognitive content* and, as in Paul's case, the accompanying sense that some divine commission is conveyed.[34]

On this account, the experience is separable into 'physiological effects and dramatic phenomena' and 'cognitive content', and the latter is what is important.

Hurtado is correct that the NT focuses on the theological significance of particular REs rather than their often peculiar character, but the separation here could obscure the role of the experience itself in shaping insights which arise from it. Though she does not engage Hurtado, Shantz argues that approaching RE in this way can be 'cognicentric'.[35]

---

[30] Steven T. Katz, 'The "Conservative" Character of Mysticism', in *Mysticism and Religious Traditions*, ed. Steven T. Katz (Oxford: Oxford University Press, 1983), 3–60 (4); italics mine.
[31] Katz, '"Conservative" Character', 30–1.
[32] See e.g. Rodney Stark, 'Normal Revelations: A Rational Model of "Mystical" Experiences', *Religion and the Social Order* 1 (1991): 239–51. For an introductory discussion of the development of religious groups including a consideration of the role of RE, cf. Ingur Furseth and Pål Repstad, *An Introduction to the Sociology of Religion* (London: Routledge, 2016), 133–50.
[33] Larry W. Hurtado, 'Revelatory Experiences and Religious Innovation in Earliest Christianity', *ExpTim* 125 (2014): 472.
[34] Hurtado, 'Revelatory Experiences', 471; italics mine.
[35] The term is from Michael J. Harner, *The Way of the Shaman* (San Francisco, CA: Harper and Row, 1990), xx. For a discussion of four types of cognicentrism, cf. Jorge N. Ferrer, *Participation and the Mystery: Transpersonal Essays in Psychology, Education, and Religion* (New York: SUNY, 2017), 97–8.

She argues that rather than attempting to discern the impact of experiences on the texts, 'even those who recognize elements of religious experience attempt to explain them as theological deductions wrapped up in "mystical' language".[36] This is not how RE is presented in the NT. Even where Paul claims to have received his gospel in a RE (Gal 1:11-12), this came through God's 'revelation of his Son in me' (Gal 1:15-16) which appears to refer to a visionary experience (cf. 1 Cor 15:3-8), and emphasizes the personal nature of the experience. Paul did more than perceive new cognitive content: he encountered Christ in a transformative, embodied experience.

For this reason, even Taves's recent attempt to develop 'attribution theory' as a refined constructivist approach in light of neuroscientific advances is ill suited to draw out the role of experience in shaping innovative understanding in the NT. Though she accepts the possibility of mystical experiences remaining 'the same' across cultures, Taves insists that 'meaning and significance will still be hashed out in the old-fashioned way between people who make claims regarding the meaning or significance (or lack thereof) of such experiences'.[37] Consequently, even though altering the religious tradition of the 'Hindu mystic' in Katz's example to make them a Jewish one may not totally alter the *character* of the experience in the way that hard constructivist accounts had previously argued, it would change its 'inherent' meaning.

This argument depends on Taves's account of the relationship between experience and representation. She considers the way that young (prelinguistic) children learn to interpret the world around them through visual data, and their own existence through bodily feedback as they move. For these children, to experience something means to make a mental representation of these external realities. This suggests to her that experience – consciousness of something – 'is better understood as embodied behaviour, where ... behaviour is broadly construed to include linguistic and mental events as well as overt actions'.[38] In arguing that experience itself refers to an 'embodied behaviour', Taves intends to '[break] down the rigid dichotomy between experience and representation',[39] and so between the 'first-person' experience of, for example, drinking coffee and the 'third-person' representation or description of that experience. This is because even something as mundane as the experience of drinking coffee can only be understood insofar as it can be represented – even when it is only represented mentally by the person doing the drinking. Thus, even if the 'sameness' of two REs could be scientifically established, their meaning would be entirely determined by the cultural concepts available to the persons experiencing them because they could not be understood apart from some kind of representation – whether mental or expressed.

However, the claim that the inherent character of experience is entirely constructed has never been without serious critique. At the most basic level, philosopher of religion Sallie King argues that the experience of drinking coffee demonstrates the limits of the

---

[36] Shantz, *Ecstasy*, 33.

[37] Ann Taves, *Religious Experience Reconsidered: A Building-Block Approach to the Study of Religion and Other Special Things* (Princeton, NJ: Princeton University, 2009), 83–4; cf. 118–19.

[38] Taves, *Reconsidered*, 64.

[39] Taves, *Reconsidered*, 68. For critique, cf. John R. Searle, 'Putting Consciousness Back in the Brain: Reply to Benett and Hacker *Philosophical Foundations of Neuroscience*', in *Neuroscience and Philosophy: Brain, Mind, and Language*, ed. Daniel Robinson (New York: Columbia, 2007), 97–125.

power of cultural frameworks to construct experience. Her argument is worth quoting at length:

> Think about one's own experience of tasting coffee, or anything else for that matter. Certainly one may be predisposed to like coffee depending upon what one has heard and witnessed with respect to coffee. One may eagerly seek out an opportunity to acquire such experience or try to avoid it. Being told that coffee is bitter would predispose one to find bitterness in the taste. But there, I claim, is where the conditioning power of the 'coffee tradition' ends. It cannot cause the subject to have the total experience s/he has of coffee. Why? The main reason is that the taste of coffee is ineffable … Likewise mysticism: the experience itself occurs within a context, a religious tradition, an individual's own personal history and concerns, etc. But as with [drinking coffee] … these things do not exhaust the content of experiences which occur within such contexts.[40]

This intuitive insight that experience exceeds what can be said about it opens the possibility of meaningful, non-linguistic experience.

More broadly, neuroscientific research into basic affective responses[41] suggests that 'some emotions seem to appear in all cultures, as well as across many animal species'.[42] Though the identification of so-called 'basic' emotions such as these has not gone unchallenged,[43] Fox points out that 'in spite of several attempts, no study has been able to fully replicate the effects' of psychological experiments intended to demonstrate the separability of the physiological effects of emotions and their linguistic content which would support a hard constructivist understanding of emotion.[44] The presence of 'basic' affective experiences appears to point to an important source of non-linguistic meaning which can have a dramatic and discernible impact on understanding. Cognitive psychologists Clore and Schiller describe this impact as follows: 'Affective appraisals occur automatically and unconsciously, generating feelings that vary in pleasantness and activation … making some things depressing and awful but others

---

[40] Sallie B. King, 'Two Epistemological Models for the Interpretation of Mysticism', *JAAR* 56 (1988): 257–79 (264, 6). Cf. similarly, Troels Engberg-Pedersen, 'The Construction of Religious Experience in Paul', in *Experientia I*, 149–50; Shantz, *Ecstasy*, 74. For critique, cf. Daniel C. Dennett, 'Quining Qualia', in *Consciousness in Modern Science*, ed. A. Marcel and E. Bisiach (Oxford: Oxford University Press, 1988), 42–78.

[41] Cf. Elaine Fox, *Emotion Science: Cognitive and Neuroscientific Approaches to Understanding Human Emotions* (New York: Palgrave Macmillan, 2008), 17: 'The term *affect* is probably best reserved for the entire topic of emotions, feelings and moods together, even though it is often used interchangeably with *emotion*' (italics original).

[42] Fox, *Emotion Science*, 84.

[43] See Paul Ekman, 'An Argument for Basic Emotions', *CogEmo* 6 (1992): 169–200; David Matsumoto and Paul Ekman, 'Basic Emotions', in *The Oxford Handbook to Emotion and the Affective Sciences*, ed. David Sander and Klaus R. Scherer (Oxford: Oxford University Press, 2009), 69–72; Christine Wilson-Mendenhall and Lawrence W. Barsalo, 'A Fundamental Role for Conceptual Processing in Emotion', in *The Emotions Handbook*, ed. Lisa Feldman Barrett, Michael Lewis and Jeannette M. Haviland-Jones (New York: Guildford, 4 2016), 547–63.

[44] Fox, *Emotion Science*, 150–1.

exciting and wonderful.'[45] Thus, non-linguistic affective experience can decisively impact behaviour and even cognitive perception. Accordingly, it appears that it may offer a useful analogue for considering the ways RE and religious language might interrelate. The question is whether it is possible to approach REs in a way which preserves their subjectivity and non-linguistic character in a descriptive historical account of their impact on the NT texts.

Phenomenology of religion offers one such approach. As an alternative to 'approaches that construe religion in historical and/or socio-cultural terms, and seek to explain it as a naturalistic phenomenon,'[46] such as Taves's attribution theory, it argues that the appropriate emphasis on historical context present in constructivist approaches to RE need not preclude the possibility of focusing on experiences themselves. Blum characterizes the difference between phenomenology of religion and constructivist approaches as a difference between 'explaining' and 'interpreting'. That is, whereas constructivist accounts employ social-scientific tools to demonstrate causal relationships between social, cultural or economic phenomena and religious expressions (explaining) even where they are associated with unusual (but medically explicable) phenomena, a phenomenological approach is more interested in describing religion as experienced by the believing subject (interpreting).[47] To support the validity of an interpretive approach to accounts of RE, Blum – similarly to Johnson[48] – asserts the importance of considering religion on its own terms to comprehensive historical understanding.

The suggestion of a 'religious' approach to ancient texts is not straightforward. Constructivist emphasis on the determinative role played by particular cultural frameworks could suggest that each 'religion' should be considered on its own terms, and not grouped into a distinct domain. Earlier phenomenologists of religion, such as Eliade, claimed that grouping was possible on the basis of their having comprehended the 'essence' underlying every particular religious expression.[49] For Blum, however, treating religion as an 'irreducible' category means only accepting that 'religious' approaches to historical data can legitimately stand alongside economic, political or sociological. For religion to be considered irreducible, 'all that is required is simply that "religion" refer to some domain of human experience and culture that is sufficiently significant or "real enough" to merit attention as a particular domain of inquiry'.[50] Treated in this way, a phenomenological approach to description need not

---

[45] Gerald L. Clore and Alexander J. Schiller, 'New Light on the Affect-Cognition Connection', in *The Emotions Handbook*, ed. Lisa Feldman Barrett, Michael Lewis and Jeannette M. Haviland-Jones (New York: Guildford, ⁴2016), 532–46 (532).

[46] Jason N. Blum, 'Retrieving Phenomenology of Religion as a Method for Religious Studies', *JAAR* 80 (2012): 1025–48 (1026). Cf. James K. A. Smith, 'Liberating Religion from Theology: Marion and Heidegger on the Possibility of a Phenomenology of Religion', *IJPR* 46 (1999): 17–33.

[47] Cf. Blum, 'Retrieving Phenomenology', 1029–30; so similarly, Johnson, *Experience*, 57: 'The task of phenomenology ... is to observe and describe behavior and its discernible functions rather than to draw ontological conclusions.'

[48] Johnson, *Experience*, 4–37.

[49] See e.g. Mircea Eliade, *Sacred and Profane: The Nature of Religion*, trans. Willard R. Trask (San Diego, CA: Harcourt Brace, 1959), 232. This is similar to how Gunkel's attempt to 'live the pneumatic's inner states after him' (*Influence*, 3) stands at the fountainhead of the *religionsgeschichtliche Schule*: Gunkel claims first-person insight into the third-person reports of RE in the text.

[50] Blum, 'Retrieving Phenomenology', 1034–8 (1035).

undermine the validity of explanatory/constructivist approaches. Rather, a descriptive account of the role of RE in the formation of the NT texts can further understanding by complementing other approaches and contributing to a more complete historical understanding.

This approach is better suited to developing Hurtado's argument that powerful REs were a driving force in fomenting religious innovation in the early Christian community. However, close analysis of the NT will also require a nuanced development of the analogy between affective experience and the manner in which new REs can give rise to new religious expressions. The models elaborated in Mark Wynn's *Emotional Experience and Religious Understanding*[51] offer one framework for this, and I will introduce them now.

2.2.1. Models of affective understanding

Above I noted that affective appraisals can decisively shape perceptions, and thereby contribute to the reconsideration of cognitive commitments. Though not all REs mentioned in the NT have this kind of impact, at least some of them can be understood in similar terms insofar as they were taken to be revelatory because they reshaped the perceptions of those who had them. Philosopher of religion Mark Wynn focuses on the same connection when he argues that experience can shape understanding decisively and irreducibly: 'Emotional feelings can themselves carry intellectual content ... [and] in some cases, this content may not be otherwise available, in which case feeling's role may be not just constructive, but indispensable.'[52] Wynn continues to identify four comparative models: (a) an intuitive affective response may offer a starting point for conceptual understanding (affectively toned perception); (b) feeling can qualitatively alter a prior conceptual understanding (affectively deepened understanding); (c) feeling can provide a framework which shapes what we value, determining how we interrogate the world around us (affective salience); and (d) feeling may intuitively point towards a resolution which goes beyond presently observable data (affective anticipation). I will briefly introduce each model to aid my later analysis of Luke-Acts and Galatians.

(a) Affectively toned perception

This model concerns 'primitive' affective responses, which are similar to basic emotions. An affectively toned perception occurs when features of reality are grasped intuitively, rather than on the basis of conceptual inference. For Wynn, this kind of perception 'is particularly radical because it involves the idea of an entirely non-conceptual grasp of the world's character.'[53] He draws on John Deigh, a philosopher of emotion, to explain the model: 'Something that looks dangerous is something that one can infer

---

[51] Mark Wynn, *Emotional Experience and Religious Understanding* (Cambridge: Cambridge University Press, 2005).
[52] Wynn, *Emotional Experience*, xi.
[53] Wynn, *Emotional Experience*, 94.

is dangerous from the way it looks, whereas one need make no inference to see that something looks scary.'[54]

Any affectively toned perceptions the NT authors had are not available for scrutiny but it is possible that their writings may reflect the impact of this kind of experience, and it might be possible to analyse this by considering the relationship between affectively toned perception and cognition. This can be straightforwardly competitive. Deigh notes that although the appearance of scariness can persist in spite of inferential knowledge to the contrary, as in the case of irrational fears, children usually grow out of fears as their affective responses are appropriately educated and governed by reason.[55] However, Wynn argues that the direct apprehension of a feature of reality can interact with reason in another way, being imaginatively combined with constructed conceptual categories to develop the significance of a basic experience.[56] The resulting understanding would be cognitively constructed, but it remains dependent on the impact of the original perception: 'While primal affects in this case no longer offer a direct (concept-independent) awareness of the character of the world, nonetheless the resulting state of mind depends for its content (depends for its sense of what the world is like) on the contribution of a primal, affectively toned sensitivity.'[57] In such a case, the understanding which arises would manifest the irreducible impact of the basic perception through its linguistic expression.

In applying this model to RE, Wynn draws on Jonathan Edwards's description of 'that idea which the saint has of the loveliness of God, and that sensation, that kind of delight he has in that view'.[58] For Edwards, the believer's *idea* of God's loveliness – their theological understanding – is wrapped up with their *sense* of his loveliness: if the *sense* were lacking, it would qualitatively alter the *idea*. Thus, the cognitive content of the believer's *understanding* of God is dependent on an irreducibly experiential *sense* of God. In my consideration of Galatians, I will argue that Paul's encounter with Christ can be understood as this kind of affectively toned perception: when God revealed Christ 'in him', Paul had a distinctive *sense* of God's glory centred on the distinctive *idea* of the crucified, raised, glorified Christ.[59]

(b) Affectively deepened understanding

Wynn's next model concerns the way in which affective experience may build upon prior conceptual understanding to qualitatively alter it – that is, how feeling can bring about a new understanding of an already available concept. I have argued that something like this process might be visible in the way Paul describes the Spirit of

---

[54] John Deigh, 'Cognitivism in the Theory of Emotions', *Ethics* 104 (1994): 824–54 (842).
[55] Deigh, 'Cognitivism', 851.
[56] Wynn, *Emotional Experience*, 94–6.
[57] Wynn, *Emotional Experience*, 96.
[58] Jonathan Edwards, *The Religious Affections* (1746 repr., New York: Dover, 2013), 136.
[59] Cf. §5.2.1 on Paul's revelatory beginning. Cf. also Volker Rabens's account of the relationship between knowing the gospel and encountering Christ in Paul (*The Holy Spirit and Ethics in Paul: Transformation and Empowering for Religious-Ethical Life*, WUNT II.283 (Tübingen: Mohr Siebeck, 2013²), 178–90).

adoption in Romans 8: there, he appeals to a shared experience of God's grace which deepened an available conceptual understanding of God as Father.[60]

An important feature of this model is that it implies a readiness for particular action which was not present before. Wynn draws on philosopher of emotion Peter Goldie's example of seeing a gorilla in a zoo and noticing that the cage door is open, but not initially *understanding the significance* of these connected facts.[61] Though the danger of proximity to the animal is already known, the emotional reaction of fear deepens that understanding when the implications of the situation are properly realized. This new understanding prompts a new stance: 'Now, in feeling fear towards the gorilla you are emotionally engaged with the world, and, typically, you are poised for action in a new way – poised for action out of the emotion.'[62] Though limited, this example establishes the possibility of an affective response shaping embodied actions in ways that are not reducible to cognitive inference. As I will argue below (§5.4), it is possible that a similar understanding may underlie Paul's account of the fruit of the Spirit. This list, which offers the Galatians an example with which to compare themselves, suggests that being 'guided by the Spirit' (5:25) should have a noticeable impact on embodied actions.

(c) Affective salience

Wynn's third model is concerned with affective salience – the way in which emotional feeling structures a construal of the meaning of the world around us.[63] At its most basic, this argument is very simple: emotions help humans pick out the features of importance in any given situation. In this model, affects function similarly to a paradigm. For Wynn, this means that emotions can shape reflective understanding: 'By lighting up features of our environment, emotional feelings can help to train our attention on certain matters rather than others ... [and] arous[e] certain concerns.'[64] For example, anger may prompt a thorough search for a person's wrongdoing, shaping the conclusion not necessarily through prejudice but by guiding attention to particular questions and evidence which would otherwise have gone unnoticed. Such a model might shape religious understanding by providing questions and assumptions for inquiry, prompting a paradigm shift in religious understanding. In Chapter 4, I will argue that the Luke's story of Gentile inclusion (Acts 10–11, 15) details a paradigm shift on the basis of a series of REs which are presented as having an affective impact on Peter that leads him to attend to evidence differently.

---

[60] Cf. Mark Wreford, 'Diagnosing Religious Experience in Romans 8', *TynBul* 68 (2017): 212–14.
[61] Peter Goldie, *The Emotions: A Philosophical Exploration* (Oxford: Oxford University Press, 2000), 61.
[62] Goldie, *Emotions*, 61.
[63] Cf. the definition in Adam T. Biggs et al., 'Semantic and Affective Salience: The Role of Meaning and Preference in Attentional Capture and Disengagement', *JExpPsy* 38 (2012): 531–41: the 'personal affective valence of a stimulus ... i.e., the positive, negative, or neutral feelings evoked in the observer by a particular object of consciousness' (538).
[64] Wynn, *Emotional Experience*, 104.

(d) Affective anticipation

Wynn's final model considers how affective experience can offer non-conceptual access to information not available elsewhere. Wynn points to the late philosopher of mind Geoffrey Maddell's musical example: 'Hearing the dominant seventh evokes a desire, and sometimes something akin to a longing, for its resolution.'[65] Here, an affective perception of the tension in the music prompts an expectation of its resolution, despite the fact that the resolution itself has not been directly perceived: 'On account of its felt recognition of the tension, the mind is cast forward, in desire, to an anticipated moment of "resolution".'[66] In this way, the affective appreciation of the tension itself offers some form of knowledge as a part of its inherent intentionality: the listener has some sense of what is required to resolve the current tension. Something similar may be visible in Paul's account of the 'groaning' (στενάζω and cognates; see Rom 8:23, 26; 2 Cor 5:2, 4) which marks his addressees' present experience. Particularly in Romans 8, this experience of the Spirit is associated with the tension of living in hope which has not yet been seen (24–25). This eschatological reality can, however, be deemed certain and its character can be at least partially grasped on the basis of the experience of the tension itself (18–21).

In summary, Wynn's four models offer a variety of approaches to RE which can inform a reading of the NT, allowing an understanding of how experience may have shaped reflection which goes beyond a consideration of what the particular cognitive content of any RE may have been. Accordingly, they offer a useful conceptual resource with which to interrogate accounts of RE within the NT. This, in turn, will enable a robust extension of Hurtado's argument that RE should be accepted as a possible historical cause within a wider approach to the texts which is informed by phenomenology of religion.

2.3. Religious experience and theology

So far, I have argued for an approach to the NT texts which attempts to uncover the intention and experience of the writer, and a phenomenological interpretive approach which focuses on their experience. Both of these suggestions raise the question of how far the faith-based truth claims that the writers of the NT make on the basis of these experiences must be followed. As Hurtado has established, there is good reason to accept the claim that certain experiences had historical impact. However, recognizing that these experiences held special significance both for those who had them and for those willing to credit their claims as true raises the question of how metaphysical truth claims about the trans-empirical realities[67] whose activity is discerned in REs should be treated.

This is a significant question because the study of RE has previously been associated with 'special pleading', particularly when REs have been taken as offering

---

[65] Geoffrey Maddell, 'What Music Teaches about Emotion', *Philosophy* 71 (1996): 63–82 (76).
[66] Wynn, *Emotional Experience*, 106.
[67] For this terminology, cf. Anthony C. Thiselton, *The Hermeneutics of Doctrine* (Grand Rapids, MI: Eerdmans, 2007), 377.

veridical knowledge of God which cannot be critically examined. This has led to the claim that phenomenology of religion is in fact theology in disguise rather than a critical, descriptive approach to historical data,[68] and a similar criticism has been made of Johnson's attempt to employ a phenomenological approach within biblical studies.[69] Both Blum and Johnson attempt to answer these critiques by deferring judgement regarding the accuracy of truth claims based on REs by employing the phenomenological notion of 'bracketing'. In this section, I will defend this approach and address its historiographical and exegetical implications.

2.3.1. Phenomenology and bracketing

The roots of phenomenology as a philosophical movement can be traced back to Edmund Husserl, who claimed philosophers needed to 'get back to the things themselves'.[70] To achieve this, he argued for a 'phenomenological ἐποχή' in which '*we put out of action the general positing which belongs to the essence of the natural attitude* ... [This is] "phenomenological" ἐποχή which also *completely shuts me off from any judgement about spatiotemporal factual being*'.[71] Thus, for Husserl, getting back to the things themselves means suspending presuppositions to focus on experience itself, as consciousness of an object: 'Gaining access to experience phenomenologically means getting back to it without any of the baggage of theorisation, which thrives on a multitude of unperceived presuppositions'.[72] It is important to note, however, that Husserl's aim is not to apprehend 'objective' truth by removing subjective concerns, in the manner associated with historical positivism.[73] Rather, he argues that 'it is not now a matter of excluding all prejudices that cloud the pure objectivity of research ... [but] the world as matter of fact is excluded, but not the world as *Eidos* [i.e. as it appears to consciousness]'.[74] The focus is on what appears to the knowing subject, and particular attention is paid to the points at which this appearance challenges theoretical presuppositions.

When applied to the study of textual accounts of RE, this has two implications. First, it means allowing an emphasis on the emic, or insider, perspective.[75] Practically, Blum

---

[68] Cf. e.g. Robert Sharf, 'Experience', in *Critical Terms for Religious Studies*, ed. Mark C. Taylor (Chicago: University of Chicago, 1998), 95: 'By emphasizing the experiential dimension of religion – a dimension inaccessible to strictly objective modes of inquiry – the theologian could forestall scientific critique.'

[69] See Christopher Mount, 'Jesus Is Lord: Religious Experience and the Religion of Paul', paper presented at the annual meeting of the SBL, Washington, DC, 18 November 2006.

[70] Edmund Husserl, *Logical Investigations*, trans. J. N. Findlay (London: Routledge, 1970), I:168.

[71] Edmund Husserl, *The Essential Husserl: Basic Writings in Transcendental Phenomenology*, ed. Donn Welton (Indianapolis: Indiana University, 1999), 65; italics original.

[72] Natalie Depraz, 'The Philosophical Challenge', in *On Becoming Aware: A Pragmatics of Experiencing*, ed. Natalie Depraz, Francisco J. Varela and Pierre Vermersch (Amsterdam: John Benjamins, 2002), 169–203 (174).

[73] Arguably, this kind of objectivity remains the goal of Frey and Levison, 'Origins', 37, who seek to obviate individual biases through the knowledge of the group.

[74] Husserl, *Basic Writings*, 65–6.

[75] Cf. David M. Fetterman, 'Emic/Etic Perspective', in *The Sage Encyclopedia of Qualitative Research Methods: A-L*, ed. Lisa M. Given (Newbury Park, CA: Sage, 2008), 249: 'Emic perceptions are shared views of cultural knowledge from the insider's "normative" perspective. An etic perspective is the external social scientific perspective on reality.'

argues that this means presuppositions regarding the existence or non-existence of God must be suspended 'in order to disclose meanings as constructed and experienced from the perspective of religious consciousness'.[76] The aim of this process is to allow the historical 'other' to come clearly into view, even where their beliefs are incompatible with researchers'.

Second, however, it does not mean *sharing* the subject's view.[77] While emic perspectives are given priority, verifying truth claims and evaluating their accuracy in describing reality is not an aim of this descriptive process. Blum makes a helpful comparison with psychoanalysis: 'The actual existence of the characters, events, and places in the dream … is irrelevant. It is, rather, the meaning that is derived from the dream … that the psychoanalyst and the literature student seek to disclose. Interpretation of meaning neither requires nor implies reality.'[78] Similarly, Johnson argues that using this approach makes it possible to 'tak[e] with equal seriousness the *noesis* (or knowing subject) and the *noema* (or subject known) in all their delicate interplay while bracketing (holding in suspension) judgments concerning the extramental existence or non-existence of such states of consciousness'.[79] A phenomenological approach to RE defers the question of God's reality. In doing so, it allows RE itself to be foregrounded, taking seriously its reality in human consciousness and including it as a possible cause within historical description. This makes experience visible in a manner which allows for an interpretation – as opposed to a reductive explanation – of its significance for the authors of the NT texts. Taking this approach will, however, require a consideration of historiographical presuppositions.

2.3.2. Methodological naturalism

On the one hand, taking a phenomenological approach to RE means suspending the question of God's (non-)existence. On the other, a naturalist worldview which presupposes that God does not exist or interact with the world represents a conceptual framework which can distort interpretations of RE. Insofar as it permits only 'natural' causation into historical description, it clashes with the emic perspective of the NT authors. Here, it is helpful to recall the hermeneutic approach outlined above (§2.1). Similarly to Husserl, Gadamer argues that understanding begins 'when something addresses us … We now know what this requires, namely, the fundamental suspension of our own prejudices'.[80] However, Gadamer also points out that prejudices cannot be recognized without an experience of distance: 'Temporal

---

[76] Blum, 'Retrieving Phenomenology', 1032.
[77] Cf. the parallel discussion in Brian M. Howell and Jenell Williams Paris, *Introducing Cultural Anthropology: A Christian Perspective* (Grand Rapids, MI: Baker Academic, 2011), 4–15: 'The anthropological perspective … refers to the attempt by the anthropologist to explain a cultural context from the *inside*, understanding the motives, actions, and beliefs of others in their own terms. This does not mean anthropologists are trying to become different kinds of people, to "*go native*"' (13; italics original).
[78] Blum, 'Retrieving Phenomenology', 1032.
[79] Johnson, *Experience*, 44; italics original.
[80] Hans-Georg Gadamer, *Truth and Method*, trans. Joel Weinsheimer and Donald G. Marshall (1960 repr., London: Bloomsbury, 2013), 310.

distance [is] a positive and productive condition enabling understanding ... It will make conscious the prejudices governing our own understanding.'[81] On this account, accurate interpretation implies the temporary suspension of presuppositions, which are themselves identified through an encounter with the text in its otherness. Moreover, this goes some way to answering potential critiques of the possibility of suspending presuppositions: the aim is not modernist objectivity purified of bias, but openness to the perspective of the text achieved through a sensitivity to the challenge it presents to existing presuppositions.

The openness of the NT authors to the influence of trans-empirical realities offers a distinct challenge to a naturalist worldview which presupposes the possibility of offering a complete historical description of the causal connections between events without reference to such realities. This kind of historiographical approach is particularly associated with Ernst Troeltsch, the German liberal theologian whose principle of correlation argues that all historical events must be explicable as part of 'a current in which everything is interconnected and each single event is related to all others'.[82] This approach to history – dubbed 'ontological naturalistic' by Webb[83] – remains dominant in historical-critical biblical study.[84] Though this approach remains useful, it will be necessary to take a different historiographical approach which does not clash with the epistemological commitments of the NT authors[85] at this point. Here, Webb's concept of 'critical theistic history' might be useful. It is '*open* to the possibility of theistic [i.e. trans-empirical] causation' precisely because it allows a focus on particular events to supersede the claims of the 'scientific' worldview of the scholar, but retains an emphasis on the critical role of the scholar in assessing historical claims.[86] Similarly, Deines attempts to articulate foundational elements of a 'theological historiography'[87] which

---

[81] Gadamer, *Truth and Method*, 308–9.

[82] Troeltsch, 'Dogmatic Method', 14.

[83] See Robert L. Webb, 'The Historical Enterprise and Historical Jesus Research', in *Key Events in the Life of the Historical Jesus*, ed. Darrell L. Bock and Robert L. Webb (Tübingen: Mohr Siebeck, 2009), 40–7. Webb also identifies 'methodological naturalistic history' as an approach which proceeds on the same assumptions when dealing with biblical history by temporarily setting aside personal faith commitments.

[84] For an example, cf. James H. Charlesworth, 'A Review of Darrell L. Bock and Robert L. Webb (eds), *Key Events in the Life of the Historical Jesus*', *JSHJ* 11 (2013): 203–23.

[85] For recent accounts of biblical epistemologies that emphasize the role of God in the act of knowing, cf. Dru Johnson, *Biblical Knowing: A Scriptural Epistemology of Error* (Eugene, OR: Wipf and Stock, 2013), esp. 149–80; and Ian W. Scott, *Paul's Way of Knowing: Story, Experience, and the Spirit* (Grand Rapids, MI: Baker Academic, 2009), esp. 143–58.

[86] Webb, 'Historical Enterprise', 47; cf. 40 n.82: 'In the naturalistic approach, science is dominant and so is determinant for how cause and effect operates in history. In the theistic approach, event in history is dominant and so cause and effect may not always function according to science.' For critique, cf. Stephen J. Patterson, 'Is the Christ of Faith also the Jesus of History?' in *Debating Christian Theism*, ed. J. P. Moreland, Chad Meister and Khaldoun A. Sweis (Oxford: Oxford University Press, 2013), 447–57 (448–9).

[87] This is different from theological exegesis/interpretation: theological exegesis means interpreting Scripture with the church for the sake of deepening contemporary theological understanding (cf. e.g. Daniel J. Treier, *Introducing Theological Interpretation of Scripture: Recovering a Christian Practice* (Nottingham: Apollos, 2008)); theological historiography means writing history under the assumption that God exists.

could navigate between fideism and scepticism, by allowing for the critical inclusion of trans-empirical realities as historical causes.[88] These arguments parallel Christian philosopher Alvin Plantinga's 'reformed epistemology', which defends the role of 'properly basic' beliefs that cannot be justified but must be held in order to navigate the world.[89] For Plantinga, these commitments are not properly available for critical scrutiny and defence, but represent paradigms within which other judgements are made. Thus, insofar as they are both 'properly basic', both naturalist and theological paradigms can be assumed with equal legitimacy when approaching evidence. The openness of the NT authors to trans-empirical realities clashes more strongly with naturalist historiographical presuppositions than theological historiographical presuppositions: for that reason, this framework is useful. In later chapters, I will assume the basic validity and usefulness of this kind of historiographical framework for the descriptive task of accounting for the importance of RE to the creation of Scripture from the perspective of particular NT authors.

However, the purpose of situating my approach in relation to theological historiography is solely to demonstrate that it sits within the range of possibilities open to historical-critical biblical study. It is not necessary to subscribe to the description of 'extramental reality' on which Webb, Deines and Plantinga base their studies to employ their structural insights for the purpose of interpreting accounts of RE in the NT: that is a theological question beyond the scope of this study. Rather, I will employ this framework heuristically insofar as it takes me closer to the perspective of the NT authors, and aim to be sensitive to challenge by their texts where it does not. In this way, I will maintain a phenomenological approach even where I draw on the potential resources of theological historiography. This is possible because phenomenological description demands a sensitive suspension of (dis)beliefs challenged by the source material for the sake of accurate interpretation, whereas theology is an exploration of existence within a framework of faith commitment.

2.3.3. Methodological pluralism

Thus far, I have argued that a phenomenological approach entails a focus on the experience and understanding of the subject with two implications. First, judgements regarding the extramental reality of what is experienced are deferred. Second, the privileging of emic perspectives necessitates a re-evaluation of standard historiographical presuppositions in historical-critical biblical study insofar as they clash with those of the NT authors. However, the conceptual resources I draw on to address these points – both in phenomenology of religion and in theological historiography and epistemology – are uniformly intended to be employed within a methodologically pluralist context.[90] Thus, this approach is intended as complementary

---

[88] Roland Deines, 'God's Role in History as a Methodological Problem for Exegesis', in *Acts of God in History*, ed. Christoph Ochs and Peter Watts (Tübingen: Mohr Siebeck, 2013), esp. 20–6.

[89] See e.g. Alvin Plantinga, *Warranted Christian Belief* (Oxford: Oxford University Press, 2000).

[90] Cf. indicatively the explicit articulations of this point in Blum, 'Retrieving Phenomenology', 1034; Deines, 'God's Role', 26.

2.3.4. Exegetical focus

Within the limits of a focus on the way RE informs the intentions of the NT authors in the creation of their texts, my exegetical study will consider the logical structures and connections within reported experiences and their interaction with other knowledge. This demands a broadly literary-historical engagement with the texts. I will focus predominantly on the final form of Luke-Acts and Galatians, asking how they attest to the influence of RE in the process of their creation. This means that the facticity of accounts of RE is significant for, but not central to my study.

Luke-Acts and Galatians stand in different relations to RE, and this can help illustrate the point. In his epistle, Paul offers a first-hand account of God's revelation of Christ to him and of his missionary proclamation to the Galatians. This means there is a close connection between RE and text, allowing the assumption that Paul's account was likely accurate to his own and his addressees' understanding (cf. §5.2.2). Luke-Acts, however, offers a narrative of Christian origins, whose date is contested.[91] If the writings are dated to the 70s–80s, this would support my argument insofar as an early date would strengthen the possibility that the 'we-passages' attest the author's own involvement,[92] with this putting him in contact with both Paul and the Jerusalem church during Paul's imprisonment.[93] This, in turn, would suggest that his story was composed in a context where eyewitnesses to the events described remained prominent members of the community and so speak in favour of the basic historicity of the narrative.[94] If, however, Luke-Acts was composed later in reliance on traditions,[95] this would not undermine my analysis. Regardless of date and historicity, the narrative of Luke-Acts includes depictions of early claims to inspired witness which would still reflect on Luke's own statement of purpose. As a result, both questions surrounding historicity and source-critical attempts to isolate early traditions are significant for, but not central to my study. It is possible that such approaches could enable a more precise

---

[91] For an overview of the discussion, cf. Craig S. Keener, *Acts: An Exegetical Commentary*, 4 vols (Grand Rapids, MI: Baker Academic, 2012–15), I:383–401.

[92] 'Luke would have been open to sharp criticism should he have been unable to validate the eyewitness testimony if called upon to do so. But that Luke's authorial audience would have heard the "we" passages in just this way [as implying his own involvement] is equally clear' (Mikeal C. Parsons, *Acts*, PCNT (Grand Rapids, MI: Baker Academic, 2008), 240). For a reading of the use of the first person purely as a literary device, cf. Richard I. Pervo, *Acts*, Hermeneia (Minneapolis, MN: Fortress, 2009), 392–6.

[93] The use of the first-person plural is concentrated in four passages: 16:10–17; 20:5–15; 21:1–18; 27:1–28:16. These suggest both that the writer accompanied Paul on missionary journeys and that he accompanied him to Jerusalem where they met with the leaders of the Jerusalem church (21:17–18). If the writer remained in Jerusalem for at least some of the period of Paul's imprisonment before his eventual voyage to Rome, he would have had ample opportunity to speak to those involved in it.

[94] So e.g. Martin Hengel, 'The Lukan Prologue and Its Eyewitnesses: The Apostles, Peter, and the Women', in *Earliest Christian History: History, Literature, and Theology*, ed. Michael F. Bird and Jason Maston, WUNT II.320 (Tübingen: Mohr Siebeck, 2012), 533–88.

[95] So e.g. Parsons, *Acts*, 16–17; Richard I. Pervo, *Dating Acts: Between the Evangelists and the Apologists* (Santa Rosa, CA: Polebridge, 2006), 149–99.

reconstruction of experiences underlying the texts, but the importance of RE for the intended purpose of the final text is at least as visible in the way it shaped the final form and effected Luke's self-understanding as a writer.

The differences between Luke-Acts and Galatians also highlight the importance of defining terms. Any definition of RE will need to be broad enough to encompass both the signs and wonders described at least second-hand by Luke and Paul's accounts of the experience of God revealing Christ to him (Gal 1:15–16) and of him and the Galatians receiving the Spirit (Gal 4:4). Similarly, in considering the possibility that these texts were intended to be scriptural, it will be necessary to consider how this category can include both Luke's narrative of Christian origins for Theophilus and Paul's feisty letter of self-defence to a young congregation. I will address these points in turn in the next two sections.

2.4. Defining religious experience

Describing RE in a way which suspends the imposition of an anachronistic epistemological framework and privileges insider perspectives will require a definition as a 'means of pointing to the sort of reality we mean and enabling us to distinguish among its cognates'.[96] I suggest that RE can be defined as *the felt impacts of trans-empirical realities within the culturally patterned life of an individual or group*.[97]

This definition is intended to be diagnostic: it represents a 'dragnet' which can be passed through the texts of the NT with a view to identifying accounts of RE. This is necessary partly because of the relative neglect of RE, but also because of the tendency to rely on definitions and taxonomies which obscure at least some passages which seem to me to witness to the impact of trans-empirical realities.[98]

Further, this definition is intended to work from the text up, being descriptive rather than prescriptive. It should consequently be able to include the variety of experiences which are presented as having special religious significance in the NT, and this is why it is important to leave the definition open to a broad variety of experiences other than

---

[96] Johnson, *Experience*, 60.
[97] Cf. the slightly different earlier version in Wreford, 'Diagnosing', 221: '*The felt impact of trans-empirical elements within the culturally patterned life of an individual or group*.' The changes are (1) the pluralization of 'impact' to 'impacts'. This serves to emphasize the variety of experiences, and avoid the connotation of either a shared mystic object or certain theological accounts of revelation (see e.g. Karl Barth, *The Epistle to the Romans*, trans. Edwyn C. Hoskyns (London: Oxford University Press, 1933), 30, who speaks about the objective impact of God's self-revelation on the world). (2) The substitution of 'realities' for 'elements'. This serves to emphasize both the reality of non-discursive elements for those having REs and the openness of the observer to this perspective.
[98] For example, cf. Johnson, *Experience*, 60. Similarly, in 'Innovation', Hurtado draws heavily on Rodney Stark whose taxonomy of REs situates them along a sliding scale from most frequent and encouraged to least frequent and encouraged. To this, it would be appropriate to add 'least intimate to most intimate', as Stark claims that 'an important dimension along which these encounters can be ordered is the sense of intimacy between the two "persons" involved' ('A Taxonomy of Religious Experience', *JSSR* 5 (1965): 97–116). This is problematic because the communication of cognitive content is not straightforwardly correlated with intimacy in the NT.

those at the mystical extremes which tend to be the focus of definitions in religious studies literature.[99]

Though it is intended to be descriptive, this definition is also intended as an analytical tool. For it to work as a useful category to capture diverse experiences described in the NT corpus, it will necessarily be abstracted from the language of the NT writings themselves. At the same time, it should avoid the imposition of an anachronistic epistemological framework. This is in keeping with the phenomenological interpretive approach outlined above which is intentionally sensitive to insider perspectives in order to interpret their claims. This point also highlights a significant intended limit for the definition: it is not offered as a general definition of RE which could be applied beyond the boundaries of the NT without revision. I will now elaborate and defend the definition, considering its individual elements in turn.

2.4.1. 'Felt impacts'

Taking the first word on its own, the multivalence of the term 'felt' makes it particularly useful for this definition. First, it emphasizes the importance of affective experience, insofar as 'feeling' is both a technical term in that discourse[100] and more colloquially connotes a sense of understanding which reaches beyond propositional knowledge. Second, 'felt' can imply a certain subjectivity to any understanding associated with it: feeling is a subjective phenomenon, and arguments based on feeling are often subject to worthy critique for being similarly subjective. Third, the term can suggest a depth of emotional resonance.

The key drawback of employing 'felt' derives from its usage by Schleiermacher.[101] His suggestion that religion can be grounded in a 'feeling of absolute dependence' was an attempt to establish religious piety as having its basis in a realm of knowledge distinct from reason and moral action after Kant. This sense is not intended in my definition.

The second word, 'impacts', refers to noticeable effects trans-empirical realities have according to the NT authors which are, however, not verifiable insofar as the experiences are not repeatable on demand. In combination with 'felt', it is intended to gesture towards the broad range of these effects.

2.4.2. 'Trans-empirical realities'

'Trans-empirical realities' is intended to denote realities which can be experienced but are beyond empirical verifiability. In the first instance, though some NT texts witness to claimed encounters with God, there are many other spiritual entities which appear to have been experienced by the NT authors, such as angels, demons, principalities,

---

[99] Cf. e.g. Blum, *Unspeakable God*, loc. 162–3.
[100] Cf. Fox, *Emotion Science*, 16–17; esp. Table 1.1.
[101] Cf. Friedrich D. E. Schleiermacher, *The Christian Faith*, trans. and ed., H. R. Mackintosh and J. S. Stewart (Edinburgh: T&T Clark, 1999), 16–25.

powers, 'elements of the world' and so on.[102] Thus, 'trans-empirical realities' is an attempt to include both divine reality and the populous *Geisterwelt* assumed in the NT texts in a way which does not diminish its variety.

It is also important to distinguish between 'mundane' experience and 'special' experiences. Within the NT, it is generally the object of RE which confers special status on the experience from an emic perspective – an experience of the Spirit is special because the Spirit is special. It is not necessary to accept such claims, but an adequate description must take account of the way that these experiences apparently have a shared quality ('specialness') which divides them from experiences of everyday phenomena. Designating these phenomena 'realities' does not represent a metaphysical claim, nor an inappropriate acceptance of the truth claims of the text: rather, it allows for an interpretation of the text which more closely mirrors the attitude of the author.

2.4.3. 'Within the culturally patterned life'

In the first instance, 'within' is intended as a way of recognizing that REs are had by particular people in particular times and places. This remains the case regardless of whether the content of the experience leads the experiencer to claim that they were removed from the world during the experience or to see in its theological significance an exceeding of temporal-spatial horizons. To describe these experiences in human language, experiencers must remain within time and space.

More importantly, these experiences occur within 'culturally patterned lives'. This is perhaps the most delicate segment of the definition as it attempts to balance a phenomenological approach with the constructivist insight that experience is always described within a received framework and understandings of its meaning are therefore reliant on the concepts available therein. Nonetheless, it is not the case that 'cultural patterning' is all that exists of the experience: conceptual representation does not exhaust meaning. Consequently, while these experiences occur *within culturally-patterned lives*, insofar as the impact of a trans-empirical reality interacts in all known instances in the NT with the received framework of the experiencer, they *exceed cultural patterning* insofar as they are irreducible to conceptual representation. Thus 'life' is an essential part of this formula. REs are complex, irreducible phenomena which occur as part of the lives of people who have culturally patterned worldviews. They are not conceptually explicable phenomena, wholly derived from cultural patterns.

2.4.4. 'Of an individual or group'

The final element of the definition reflects the variety of experiences witnessed to in the NT, which includes REs that apparently happened to more than one person at the

---

[102] Cf. Guy Williams, *The Spirit World in the Letters of Paul the Apostle: A Critical Examination of the Role of Spiritual Beings in the Authentic Pauline Epistles*, FRLANT 231 (Göttingen: Vandenhoeck und Ruprecht, 2009).

same time. In this way, it not only reflects an emphasis on particular experiences but also avoids the individualist tendency inherent in Jamesian approaches to RE.[103] Such a focus would be anachronistic to the NT period, during which there was substantially less focus on the individual than in contemporary Western culture.[104] In looking beyond the individual to the way that their RE can interact with that of the group, I am following Gorman's suggestion that the gospel is personal, but not private:[105] the same can be said, mutatis mutandis, of the REs to which the NT texts witness. It is also the case that unusual phenomena such as altered states of consciousness can be group-based rather than purely individual,[106] which means that a descriptive definition of RE in the NT texts must be equipped to recognize experiences which are not limited to individuals.

2.4.5. Summary

Having elaborated the various elements of a definition of RE, it is worth restating it: REs are *the felt impacts of trans-empirical realities within the culturally patterned life of an individual or group*. It is important to note that this definition is intended to be heuristic in two senses: it is both experimental and exploratory. It is experimental insofar as it is based on observation of textual accounts of RE. It is exploratory insofar as it remains under constant revision in the course of its application to the text. In this dual sense, it is an empirical definition. The aim of this study is to examine how experiences captured by this definition have shaped the texts of the NT, and whether they contributed to a sense for the authors that what they were writing should have special religious significance for its intended audience – that is, whether it was intended to function scripturally. This second point will require a discussion of Scripture.

2.5. Defining Scripture

The aim of this study is to develop and explore the suggestion that the biblical authors were aware that they were writing Scripture. I claim that the way these writings are situated in relation to new REs can help illuminate that discussion. In this section, I will introduce the discussion I am engaging, and explain what it means for an NT writer to be 'inspired' to 'write Scripture'.

---

[103] Cf. Taylor, *Varieties of Religion Today: William James Revisited* (Cambridge: Harvard University Press, 2002), 23–5: '[James] has trouble getting beyond a certain individualism' (23).

[104] For an overview, cf. Ben C. Dunson, 'The Individual and Community in Twentieth- and Twenty-First-Century Pauline Scholarship', *CurBR* 9 (2010): 63–97.

[105] Michael J. Gorman, *Cruciformity: Paul's Narrative Spirituality of the Cross* (Grand Rapids, MI: Eerdmans, 2001), 36–8.

[106] Cf. e.g. Bruce J. Malina and John J. Pilch, *A Social-Science Commentary on the Book of Acts* (Minneapolis: Fortress, 2008), 27–8, where they take the experience at Pentecost as an example of 'Group Trance'.

2.5.1. The creation of Scripture

In examining the role of REs in the creation of Scripture I am drawing on and developing Deines's work, making it helpful to describe his account of how Scripture develops. In the first instance, he argues that *'what becomes Scripture at a later point was initially received and experienced as a word of God'*.[107] This argument is developed by reference to the prophetic reception of 'the word of the Lord' in the OT, by figures such as Samuel (1 Sam 15:10), Elijah (1 Kgs 17:2, 8; 21:17, 28), Isaiah (Isa 38:4) and Jeremiah (1:4, 11, 13, etc.).[108] For Deines, the importance of this formula suggests that perceived revelations stand at the beginning of the textual traditions which developed into the prophetic literature incorporated in the Hebrew Bible and LXX: 'The problem is not so much that the biblical texts are ambiguous about this point but, rather, that historical scholarship is somehow oblivious to these claims about a revelatory experience as the prime cause for the prophetic words to be collected and eventually written down.'[109] This point stands even when the instability of even the NT textual traditions is taken into account.[110] As Sandra Heinen notes, 'Any interpretation of the Bible's content – as that of any other text – is likely to be based on the premise that someone must have intended to produce something meaningful and that there is therefore some meaning "in" the text which is worth decoding.'[111] This remains the case even where the ensuing textual tradition has obscured any original prophet or writer: Deines is here gesturing towards the impulse which produces the textual tradition in the first place.

Elsewhere, Deines points out that a model of God's prior personal communication with Scripture writers to inspire them appears to have been assumed by Philo and Josephus in their treatment of scriptural texts,[112] and argues that such a framework was available for development by the NT writers. Indeed, Eva Mroczek's recent re-evaluation of the literary imagination in the Second Temple period points in a similar direction when she argues for an 'imagined library of sacred writing [that] was vast and its catalog somewhat vague, with no established list or particular number of works that it could accommodate', and an openness to the possibility of both further discoveries and further 'inspiration' insofar as figures like Enoch continued to write in the heavens.[113] In such a context, it is inherently plausible that the NT writers could have imagined their own texts as contributing to a corpus of 'scriptural' literature, and

---

[107] Roland Deines, 'The Term and Concept of Scripture', in *What Is Bible?*, ed. Karin Finsterbusch and Armin Lange, CBET 67 (Leuven: Peeters, 2012), 235–81 (271); italics original.

[108] See Roland Deines, 'Revelatory Experiences as the Beginning of Scripture: Paul's Letters and the Prophets in the Hebrew Bible', in *From Author to Copyist: Essays on the Composition, Redaction, and Transmission of the Hebrew Bible*, ed. Cana Werman (Winona Lake, IN: Eisenbrauns, 2015), 276, for a fuller list and comment.

[109] Deines, 'Paul's Letters', 276.

[110] Cf. Matthew D. C. Larsen, 'Accidental Publication, Unfinished Texts and the Traditional Goals of New Testament Textual Criticism', *JSNT* 39 (2017): 362–87.

[111] Sandra Heinen, 'Exegesis without Authorial Intention? On the Role of the "Author Construct" in Text Interpretation', in *Biblical Exegesis without Authorial Intention: Interdisciplinary Approaches to Authorship and Meaning*, ed. Clarissa Breu (Leiden: Brill, 2019), 7–24 (16).

[112] Deines, 'Scripture', 267–71.

[113] Eva Mroczek, *The Literary Imagination in Jewish Antiquity* (Oxford: Oxford University Press, 2016), 155.

Deines highlights Paul's claims in 1 Thessalonians that his gospel message 'came to you not in word only, but also in power and in the Holy Spirit and with full conviction' (1:5), and that 'you accepted it not as a human word but as what it really is, God's word, which is also at work in you believers' (2:13). He argues the claim that God's word became manifest in his own preaching of the gospel 'means [Paul] attributes to his preaching the same spiritual and religious quality as that of the biblical prophets, who are regularly described as communicators of God's word to his people'.[114] By focusing on the way that Paul situates his message, and implicitly his writing, in relation to the experience of receiving God's word, Deines suggests that the text itself was intended to have religious significance: it is presented as a response to revelatory events which can convey their significance by acting as a 'deposit' of a revelation from God centred on Jesus. In this sense, Paul's writing arguably represents a distinctive 'mutation' to the perpetual extension of sacred physical writings 'that does not assume that revealed writing is entirely graspable or entirely known, but exists beyond the horizons of available text' depicted by Mroczek[115] – in parallel to Hurtado's diagnosis of such a mutation in early Christian devotion to Jesus. On this model, a writer intended to write Scripture when *they intended to write a text which functioned with religious authority to shape the lives of those in the intended audience on the basis of conveying theological insight*. In the NT, it is possible these writings are distinctive insofar as they present their theological insights as being *derived from perceived revelatory events*, already suggesting an important role for RE in determining the character of these texts.

2.5.2. Scripture, RE and inspiration

This understanding of how scriptural writings might be created emphasizes that the texts produced stand in two relations. As theologian John Webster puts it,

> The term 'Holy Scripture' refers primarily to a set of texts, but importantly and secondarily to its divine origin and its use by the church. Thus the content of the term can only be thoroughly mapped by seeing this set of texts in connection with purposive divine action in its interaction with an assemblage of creaturely events, communities, agents, practices, and attitudes.[116]

Here, Webster points to a set of relationships to define Scripture: on the one hand, it relates to God as a part of his revelation; on the other, it relates to the faith community as an authoritative theological 'source'. Similarly, although, as a theologian, Webster is interrogating the role played by a stable collection of texts for one particular faith community (the OT and NT for Christians), his analysis of the relationships in which Scripture is situated is useful for historical analysis. In the first instance, as Judith Newman notes, 'Scripture is distinguished from other literature for any given

---

[114] Deines, 'Paul's Letters', 299.
[115] Mroczek, *Literary Imagination*, 88.
[116] John Webster, *Holy Scripture: A Dogmatic Sketch* (Cambridge: Cambridge University Press, 2003), 1.

community to the degree that the former is understood to have, ultimately, a divine origin'.[117] Second, though, Deines points out that, 'in antiquity, every message or piece of knowledge which was intended to outlive its progenitor needed a support group willing and able to provide the required means to preserve the message and pass it on to a future generation'.[118] Thus, scriptural texts are perceived to be sufficiently important that they should be preserved by a community, and without such reception would not have the chance to become Scripture.

The reception of a text as conveying revelatory content is vital if it is to achieve scriptural status, but it is not my focus here. It might be possible to consider the ways in which RE could have influenced the reception processes which culminated in canonization, but this is beyond the scope of my study. In theological terms, this means I am considering 'the influence of the Holy Spirit on the writers of the Bible' rather than 'that influence of the Holy Spirit on the minds of believers that causes them to believe firmly that the Christian message, or some aspect of it, [i.e. the claim that Scripture is inspired or revelatory] is true'.[119] For this reason, I will focus on the claims the NT texts make on their readers. In examining the intentions of the writers for their own works and embedded in the texts themselves, I will also examine their self-presentation. If they claim to be particularly capable of writing a scriptural text, this implies a claim that the writer's own actions stand in special relation to God's activity in the world. This is the sense I intend when discussing 'inspiration'. Thus, a writer can be said to be inspired when *the writer presents him- or herself as especially qualified to write a text which can convey theological insight derived from perceived revelations*.

2.5.3. Scripture and canonicity

The core of my argument is that the writing activities of those in the NT were intended to produce Scripture and that this is visible in their relation to new REs. In those REs, members of the earliest community discerned new theological insights – they came to understand God differently as a result of those events. This, in turn, prompted them to write. Specifically, it prompted them to write Scripture – authoritative texts which could convey the revelations they perceived through these new REs. This account of the origins of biblical texts challenges what Michael Kruger identifies as a scholarly consensus that the canonicity of the biblical texts is 'extrinsic' – namely the 'idea that the New Testament canon was not a natural development within early Christianity, but a later artificial development that is out of sync with Christianity's original purpose'.[120] Against this consensus, Kruger argues that 'the phenomenon of canon was one that arose early and naturally within the first few stages of Christianity'[121] partly on the basis

---

[117] Judith H. Newman, *Before the Bible: The Liturgical Body and the Formation of Scriptures in Early Judaism* (Oxford: Oxford University Press, 2018), 14.
[118] Deines, 'Scripture', 274.
[119] Stephen T. Davis, 'An Ontology of the Spirit', in *The Testimony of the Spirit*, ed. R. Douglas Geivett and Paul K. Moser (Oxford: Oxford University Press, 2017), 54–65 (59); italics removed.
[120] Michael J. Kruger, *The Question of Canon: Challenging the Status Quo in the New Testament Debate* (Nottingham: Apollos, 2013), 17.
[121] Kruger, *Question of Canon*, 210.

that 'the first-century environment was conducive to the production of such books'.[122] Deines develops a similar argument when he suggests that canonicity could be construed as a recognition of scriptural status intended by the initial author. As Deines notes in his discussion of Matthew, the communication of insights in scriptural form 'does not infer, however, that the intended audience would immediately and automatically receive it as God's word. And even if they did, it does not follow that its status as a message from God would endure past its immediate context.'[123] Notwithstanding this appropriate caution, it is plausible to assume that a text whose message was accepted as revelatory by its initial addressees could come to be used in the group's worship and thus ritualized and sacralized, with the body of texts which could legitimately serve such functions ultimately requiring communal assent and becoming fixed. On this account, canonization – first the informal fixing of a static body of texts which remains open to new ones, and later the formal closing of the canon with its codification in lists – is an outgrowth of a process which began with RE.

In this way, the research questions outlined in the introduction come together here. First, it is important to examine how REs have shaped the text itself such that it may have been perceived as revelatory by its initial addressees. Second, the role of RE in shaping the writing can inform an understanding of what the author thought she or he was doing. Though I will not argue that Paul or Luke had a 'NT canon' in mind, I will claim that they intended their texts to have a scriptural function and that they perceived themselves to be especially capable to convey revelatory content in an authoritative writing on the basis of close connection to REs, such that their text should inform the community's religious belief and praxis in a similar manner to the way that established Scriptures were treated.

Claims to inspiration and scriptural authority were by no means unusual in the period the NT texts were written. At this point, there was a stable core of authoritative scripture accepted across the pluralistic Second Temple Jewish context,[124] even if the 'canon' remained open.[125] The fluidity of the environment presented an opportunity for writers who sought to claim religious authority, as Deines notes: 'In a religious community within a cultural climate that has a tradition of venerating written documents as authoritative and as a (secondary) medium of God's communication with his people, every new "author" who wanted to present a message as divinely authorised had to decide if he wanted to communicate his God-given insights as potential Scripture or not.'[126] Indeed, several writings from this period appear intent on claiming scriptural status. As Newman notes, 'Even after the presumed end of prophecy claimed by Josephus and others, many other texts circulated that claimed

---

[122] Kruger, *Question of Canon*, 77. Cf. Mroczek, *Literary Imagination*, which supports the suggestion that such books could readily be produced even as she argues that this undermines the possibility of strong canonical boundaries in the Second Temple Period.

[123] Roland Deines, 'Did Matthew Know He Was Writing Scripture?' *EJT* 22 (2013): 4.

[124] Cf. Stephen G. Dempster, 'The Old Testament Canon, Josephus, and Cognitive Environment', in *The Enduring Authority of the Christian Scriptures*, ed. D. A. Carson (London: Apollos, 2016), 321–61.

[125] Cf. Timothy H. Lim, *The Formation of the Jewish Canon* (New Haven, CT: Yale University, 2013), esp. 156–66.

[126] Deines, 'Did Matthew Know', 4.

revelatory status.'[127] The so-called 're-written Scriptures' at Qumran such as *Jubilees* and 11QTemple[a] attempted to derive authority from their relationship to texts which were established as Scripture, with the dual effect of solidifying the status of the source text and claiming scriptural status for the textualized reinterpretations.[128] In these texts, the revelation of the divine was mediated through established Scriptures.[129] According to Schniedewind, this trend is already visible in the work of the Chronicler, and is part of a trajectory in which the locus of inspiration moves from the 'prophet' – who delivers a divine message rooted in his own experience, which is written down and preserved by a hearing community who accept the claims made about the message – to the 'exegete', whose inspiration is mediated by existing texts, and whose claim to scriptural authority focuses on interpretation.[130]

On the other hand, Hall also identifies several early Jewish and Christian texts, such as 1 Maccabees, *4 Ezra* and the Enoch library, that claim to relate 'revealed history',[131] explaining the meaning of historical events from a 'revelatory' perspective. The Enoch library and *4 Ezra* in particular make a claim to authoritative, scriptural status which is rooted in the close connection between their content and REs.[132] That not all of these texts became scriptural emphasizes the role of communal reception in the creation of Scripture. Nonetheless, it does not mean that the texts do not attempt to claim religious authority.[133]

In the Second Temple period, then, texts could claim scriptural status. The NT texts appear to have been similarly intended to be authoritative for their readers and hearers. Though they do not expound the significance of old texts for a new context, they innovatively offer new theological contributions on the basis of what were perceived to be new revelations. However, I will argue that the NT texts situate themselves in relation to God's action in recent history partly by situating themselves in relation to

---

[127] Newman, *Before the Bible*, 14.

[128] Cf. George J. Brooke, 'Between Authority and Canon: The Significance of Reworking the Bible for Understanding the Canonical Process', in *Reworking the Bible: Apocryphal and Related Texts at Qumran*, ed. Esther Chazon, Devorah Dimant and Ruth Anne Clements, STDJ (Leiden: Brill, 2005), 85–104, who argues that rewritten Scripture simultaneously 'canonizes' its source and 'sacralizes' itself.

[129] Cf. similarly James L. Kugel's argument that the increasing prominence of Scripture allowed scriptural interpreters to 'take over part of the ancient prophet's role' (*The Bible as It Was* (Cambridge: Belknap, 1997), 17).

[130] William M. Schniedewind, *The Word of God in Transition: From Prophet to Exegete in the Second Temple Period*, JSOTSup 197 (Sheffield: Sheffield Academic, 1995), see esp. 238–49. James L. Kugel traces a similar shift and correlates it with historical changes in the understanding of the self (*The Great Shift: Encountering God in Biblical Times* (New York: Houghton Mifflin Harcourt, 2017), see esp. 338–44).

[131] Robert G. Hall cites as examples a diverse collection of texts including Josephus's *Jewish War*, *Jubilees*, *Liber Antiquitatum Biblicarum*, Judith, *1 Enoch*, *4 Ezra*, *Shepherd of Hermas* and Luke-Acts (*Revealed Histories: Techniques for Ancient Jewish and Christian Historiography*, JSPSup 6 (Sheffield: JSOT, 1991)).

[132] See *1 Enoch* 104–5 and *4 Ezra* 14.

[133] Josephus's *Jewish War* is perhaps the exception among Hall's examples, and this may be partly due to the dual audience Hall identifies: 'Josephus wrote the *Jewish War* under imperial patronage to persuade Jews to revolt no more against Rome and to persuade Romans to retaliate no further against Jews' (*Revealed Histories*, 29). Nevertheless, Josephus does appear to link himself to Ezekiel (*War*, 5:19–20) and Jeremiah (*War*, 5:391–3) to add authority to his account.

REs and that this is intended as a claim to inspiration and scriptural status. It is here that I see the connection between RE and the creation of Scripture.

2.6. Applying the approach

In Section 1, I have situated my research within a *Forschungsgeschichte* (Chapter 1) and articulated a constructive approach to RE in order to interrogate its relationship to claims of scriptural status in the NT (Chapter 2). In the following chapters, I will apply this approach to the question of how RE appears to have influenced the creation of Scripture by examining Luke-Acts and Galatians.

Luke-Acts (Chapters 3-4) is of particular significance for my argument because Luke's narrative of Christian origins offers extended reflection on the ways in which the first believers perceived themselves to be empowered by the Spirit to witness to God's activity in Christ. In his description of Pentecost, Luke offers an intriguing account of the relationship between language and RE. This allows the passage to act as a fulcrum around which the narrative pivots from focusing on Christ to depicting the impact of the Spirit in the missional activity of the disciples. This is further developed in the account of the decision to admit Gentiles into the earliest Christian communities. Here, Luke depicts a process in which RE plays a significant role in shaping Peter's witness to the work of the Spirit which itself comes to play a key role at the Jerusalem convocation. At this meeting, James makes the decision to write a letter. This is clearly intended to be an authoritative missive to be read in the congregation it is sent to, and it also includes an explicit claim to inspiration for the content it communicates, and thus, implicitly for the writing itself. Further, Luke begins his *Doppelwerk* by reflecting on the function and purpose of his writings in ways which offer insight into his own intentions (Luke 1:1-4), making it possible to examine to some extent how his presentation of RE interacts with his stated intentions for his writing(s). Specifically, he depicts a situation in which believers can offer inspired witness to Christ in writing, implicitly claiming scriptural status for his own text.

Similarly, Galatians stands out as a useful testing ground to establish the wider relevance of the pattern visible in Luke-Acts because it contains Paul's autobiographical account of his own encounter with the risen Christ (1:12-16). Indeed, RE is foundational to Paul's letter insofar as he roots his argument in his own revelation and the Galatians' encounter with his embodied gospel proclamation (3:1-5) and appears to be using the letter itself to confront them again with this revelatory message. As a letter of defence, Galatians is a proxy-speech which textualizes statements perhaps more naturally made in person and which are intended to carry particular authority, and this already suggests Paul intends it to function similarly to the Scriptures on whose authority he draws in writing it. That various elements of Paul's expression in Galatians are picked up elsewhere in ways that suggest his expression here can be seen as a textual crystallization of normative elements in his thought only strengthens this claim.

The purpose of focusing on Luke-Acts and Galatians, then, is to establish the possibility of a broader pattern among the NT texts. I will treat Luke-Acts first because the pattern is more fully developed in that writing. However, I will argue that, despite the significant differences between the writings, the same emphases are also present in Galatians. Accordingly, these two texts serve as paradigmatic examples, with the intention that any pattern of relationship between RE and the writers' intention to produce a scriptural text visible here could be used to examine other NT texts. To that end, I will begin by looking at Luke's account of Pentecost in the next chapter.

Section 2

Religious Experience and the Creation of Scripture in Luke-Acts and Galatians

3

Experience and Speech at Pentecost

Over the course of the next two chapters, I will build on the theoretical foundations of Section 1 to argue that Luke's[1] two-volume account of Christian origins was intended as a scriptural text by examining its treatment of religious experience (RE). Luke presents human speech as revelatory by connecting it with God's action in history and, in doing so, creates space to present spoken witness to God's action as inspired. This in turn clears the way to establish writing – as a form of communication derivative from speech – as a medium which can be authoritative and inspired on the basis of a close relation to RE. In light of Luke's own expression of purpose at the beginning of the Gospel, I will suggest that Luke intended his own work to be seen as such a writing.

This chapter focuses on the first part of that argument, considering Luke's understanding of the connection between RE and speech by examining his depiction of the outpouring of the Spirit at Pentecost. According to Luke's portrayal in Acts 2, human speech functions as part of God's revelation in two ways. First, the outpouring of the Holy Spirit is depicted as resulting in a form of tongues-speech which is uniquely described within the NT. I will argue that in Luke's depiction this speech event forms part of God's historical action: it is presented as a RE for both the speakers and the gathered crowd who hear their own languages, acting as an external manifestation of the Spirit's presence and thus forming part of a theophany of the Spirit (§3.1). Through this connection, human speech becomes a phenomenon in which divine reality can be

---

[1] It is not necessary for my argument to consider the authorship of the Third Gospel and Acts. In the following I will refer to the author of the work as Luke rather than e.g. 'the *auctor ad Theophilum*' (cf. Heidrun Gunkel, *Der Heilige Geist bei Lukas*, WUNT II.389 (Tübingen: Mohr Siebeck, 2015)) or 'Lukas' (cf. Daniel Lynwood Smith and Zachary Lundin Kostopoulos, 'Biography, History, and the Genre of Luke-Acts', *NTS* 63 (2017): 390–410), following the majority of commentators (cf. i.a. William S. Kurz, *Acts of the Apostles*, CCSS (Grand Rapids, MI: Baker Academic, 2013); David Peterson, *The Acts of the Apostles*, PNTC (Grand Rapids, MI: Eerdmans, 2009); C. K. Barrett, *A Critical and Exegetical Commentary on the Acts of the Apostles*, 2 vols (Edinburgh: T&T Clark, 1994–8)). While I recognize the fluidity of textual traditions in the ancient world (cf. Matthew D. C. Larsen, 'Accidental Publication, Unfinished Texts and the Traditional Goals of New Testament Textual Criticism', *JSNT* 39 (2017): 362–87, the dismissal of the idea of an original author as useful for engaging the text of Matthew in favour of viewing the text as 'Living Tradition' by Broadhead would go too far in this case because the Third Gospel and Acts explicitly present themselves as the work of a particular author (see §4.4.1; Edwin K. Broadhead, *The Gospel of Matthew on the Landscape of Antiquity*. WUNT 378 (Tübingen: Mohr Siebeck), 316).

noticeably present in a new way in Luke's narrative. In this sense, the speech itself is revelatory (§3.2).

Second, Luke extends the implications of this unique speech event to Peter's sermon by presenting that reasoned discourse as the same kind of 'utterance' (Acts 2:14; ἀποφθέγγομαι). This demonstrates that Peter's sermon itself should be understood as a revelatory witness to Christ (§3.3) and that, for Luke, both tongues-speech and 'plain speech' discourse which witnesses to Christ can make divine reality noticeably present to their hearers. In this way, Peter's speech is integral to the revelation of the divine at Pentecost as Luke depicts it. I will conclude this chapter by noting hints in Peter's sermon that suggest implications for the status of Luke's own writing (§3.4) which look forward to Chapter 4.

Before turning to the text, however, it will be helpful to outline relevant exegetical presuppositions. Although it is beyond the scope of this study to consider the geographical provenance and date of Acts,[2] my argument assumes the narrative unity of Luke and Acts, and considers Luke's intention for the two volumes as a whole. While narrative unity broadly remains a scholarly consensus, it is not unchallenged. That the two books were written by the same author is almost universally accepted,[3] but the nature of the *literary* connection between them has been contested on two fronts. First, the consensus that these two documents are telling one story simply because they come from the same pen[4] has been challenged by Parsons and Pervo on the basis of generic, narrative and theological differences between the works.[5] Second, the lack of evidence for a unified reading of Luke and Acts in the early reception history of these texts has been used to question the historicity of readings which treat the two documents as a literary unity.[6]

Both objections can be addressed. In the first instance, Parsons and Pervo consider five possible kinds of literary unity – authorial, canonical, generic, narrative and theological – disputing the final three. From the outset, their critique is framed as one of nuance rather than rejection: they prefer to see Luke and Acts as 'independent but interrelated works'.[7] In a later article, Pervo explains that this means seeing Acts as

---

[2] See the discussions in Craig S. Keener, *Acts: An Exegetical Commentary*, 4 vols (Grand Rapids, MI: Baker Academic, 2012–15), I:383–401, 423–34; and Ben Witherington III, *The Acts of the Apostles: A Socio-Rhetorical Commentary* (Grand Rapids, MI: Eerdmans, 1998), 51–65. Cf. also §2.3.4 where I note that while an early date for Luke-Acts could aid my argument in some ways, it is not vital for its success.

[3] Patricia Walters, *The Assumed Authorial Unity of Luke and Acts: A Reassessment of the Evidence* (Cambridge: Cambridge University Press, 2009), is an exception to the consensus.

[4] This thesis was influentially advanced by Henry J. Cadbury, *The Making of Luke-Acts* (New York: Macmillan, 1927), 8–9, and most extensively defended by Robert C. Tannehill, *The Narrative Unity of Luke-Acts: A Literary Interpretation*, 2 vols (Minneapolis: Fortress, 1986–90).

[5] Mikeal C. Parsons and Richard I. Pervo, *Rethinking the Unity of Luke and Acts* (Minneapolis, MN: Fortress, 1990). Similarly, Todd C. Penner is sceptical of claims of narrative unity as 'theologizing' ('Contextualizing Acts', in *Contextualizing Acts: Lukan Narrative and Greco-Roman Discourse*, ed. Todd C. Penner and Caroline Vander Stichele, SBLSymS 20 (Leiden: Brill, 2004), 1–22 (9)).

[6] See Andrew Gregory, *The Reception of Luke and Acts in the Period before Irenaeus*, WUNT II.169 (Tübingen: Mohr Siebeck, 2003); Andrew Gregory, 'The Reception of Luke and Acts and the Unity of Luke-Acts', *JSNT* 29 (2007): 459–72. Cf. C. Kavin Rowe, 'Literary Unity and Reception History: Reading Luke-Acts as Luke and Acts', *JSNT* 29 (2007): 449–57.

[7] Parsons and Pervo, *Rethinking*, 126.

a 'sequel rather than a second volume'.[8] This appears to entail 'not presum[ing] that the author planned and executed his books in advance'.[9] However, it must at least be considered an open possibility that a close reading could lead to the conclusion that the 'careful attention to structure'[10] Pervo discerns in the composition of Acts could have been applied to the two volumes as a whole, especially if 'the significant omission or holding over of narrative detail from the first volume to the second'[11] is visible. This is indeed the case in Luke's treatment of 'clean and unclean' and the initiation of the Gentile mission, which are both removed from Luke's synoptic source material and reserved until Peter's encounter with Cornelius in Acts 10. Generic unity has proven more difficult to address,[12] but cannot disprove literary unity by itself anyway: the argument is essentially cumulative. While the same is true for theological unity to an extent, the widespread acknowledgement that key themes persist across the volumes suggests that any difference is a matter of nuance rather than necessarily entailing literary disunity. Accordingly, though the critique of Parsons and Pervo has rightly drawn attention to the individual integrity of both the Third Gospel and Acts, it has not mounted a significant critique against the usefulness of considering the possible development of core themes across the two volumes.

Rowe sees the second objection, which questions the 'historicity' of readings that presume a literary unity on the basis that there is no manuscript evidence that Luke and Acts were ever 'issued' or initially read together, as a development of Parsons's and Pervo's canonical category.[13] However, the scope of this argument is challenged by Johnson who argues that 'as important as reception history is, it cannot be prescriptive for all interpretation', and especially interpretations which seek to examine Luke's literary and theological voice.[14] For such an approach, it is both valid and necessary to attempt to follow the tendency of the text itself in order to draw out the logical connections embedded therein.

Summarizing the debate, Bock claims 'that too much is being made of this difference when all sides acknowledge the existence of a literary linkage',[15] and it is possible to discern something of an emerging consensus which reflects this: it is valid to approach Acts both as an intentional continuation of the story begun in Luke and on its own terms.[16] Bock suggests that the former approach is 'most important for doing biblical

---

[8] Richard I. Pervo, 'Israel's Heritage and Claims upon the Genre(s) of Luke and Acts: The Problems of a History', in *Heritage*, 127–43 (142).
[9] Richard I. Pervo, *Dating Acts: Between the Evangelists and the Apologists* (Santa Rosa, CA: Polebridge, 2006), 20.
[10] Pervo, *Acts*, 20.
[11] Loveday Alexander, 'Reading Luke-Acts from Back to Front', in *The Unity of Luke-Acts*, ed. Jos Verheyden, BETL 142 (Leuven: Peeters, 1999), 419–46 (421).
[12] Cf. Smith and Kostopoulos, 'Genre'; Sean A. Adams, *The Genre of Acts and Collected Biography*, SNTSMS 156 (Cambridge: Cambridge University Press, 2013); T. E. Phillips, 'The Genre of Acts: Moving toward a Consensus?' *CurBR* 4 (2006): 365–96.
[13] Rowe, 'Literary Unity', 132 n.3.
[14] Luke Timothy Johnson, 'Literary Criticism of Luke-Acts: Is Reception-History Pertinent?' *JSNT* 28 (2005): 159–62.
[15] Darrell L. Bock, *A Theology of Luke's Gospel and Acts*, Biblical Theology of the New Testament (Grand Rapids, MI: Zondervan, 2011), 59.
[16] So e.g. Gregory, 'Reception', 466–70; Marcus Bockmuehl, 'Why Not Let Acts Be Acts?' *JSNT* 28 (2005): 163–6.

theology', whereas the latter makes possible readings which reflect the historical emphases implicit in the early canonical separation of Luke and Acts.[17] As my project is more concerned with Luke's narrative and theological claims – specifically the ways in which he relates his own work to claimed early encounters with divine reality – I will follow Bock, who argues for a nuanced reading of Luke and Acts as a literary unity where it can illuminate specific themes. One key theme that runs through the work is that of fulfilment. That Luke relates his Pentecost account to this theme speaks of its central importance to the development of his narrative, and I will begin my examination here.

3.1. The theophany of the Spirit at Pentecost

Though the Pentecost account has long fired the Christian imagination, Luke's description of the events is notably brief. The unusual phenomena are dealt with in four verses (Acts 2:1–4), before the focus shifts to the responses of outsiders (2:5–13). The historicity of any possible event underlying this account has long been debated, but it is not my primary focus here. As I have argued above (§2.3.4), historicity is not irrelevant to my argument, but nor is it central to it. It is more important for my purposes to consider (a) the way in which Luke describes the link between human speech and RE in this foundational passage, and (b) how this theological understanding embedded in his narrative reflects on the claims of his own writing. To this end, I will argue first that the significance of Pentecost for Luke's story of fulfilment means that its depiction has implications for his work as a whole (§3.1.1). Second, I will consider how he emphasizes the presence of the divine, arguing that the imagery Luke uses is suggestive of a particularly potent theophany. I will then build on these suggestions to argue that the tongues-speech at Pentecost can best be understood as revelatory speech (§3.2), insofar as it forms a part of the theophanic manifestation of the Spirit, before turning my attention to Peter's sermon (§3.3).

3.1.1. The setting of Pentecost in Luke's narrative of fulfilment

The importance of Acts 2 for the Lukan *Doppelwerk* has long been recognized, and Luke himself marks the importance of the events contained in the chapter with the introduction of fulfilment language – συμπληροῦσθαι[18] – in its Septuagint-inspired[19] first sentence. The term signals the multifaceted significance of Acts 2, situating the account: (1) as the fulfilment of the risen Jesus' twice-repeated promise of the Holy Spirit (Luke 24:49; Acts 1:8); (2) in relation to Scripture as a surprising fulfilment of the

---

[17] Bock, *Theology*, 60.
[18] Cf. David Peterson, 'The Motif of Fulfilment and the Purpose of Luke-Acts', in *The Book of Acts in Its Ancient Literary Setting*, ed. Bruce W. Winter and Andrew D. Clarke (Grand Rapids, MI: Eerdmans, 1993), 83–104, esp. 85–7, where Peterson considers 'the language of fulfilment', beginning with πληρόω and cognates, and including πίμπλημι, τελέω and cognates, and terms referring to God's will and its completion (βουλή, θέλημα, δεῖ, ἔδει) and Scripture (γράφω and cognates).
[19] Cf. Gen 25:24; Lev 8:33; Jer 25:12.

prophecy of LXX Joel 3:1–5; and (3) as a divine action within the salvation-historical story of fulfilment told in Luke-Acts (cf. Luke 1:1).[20]

First, the events of Pentecost are anticipated in both Luke 24:46–49 and Acts 1:5–8.[21] In both passages, Jesus promises the outpouring of the Spirit in his final words to his disciples before his ascension. The second iteration of the promise appears to form the agenda for the narrative which follows,[22] and in Acts 2:1 the fulfilment of Jesus' programmatic pronouncement begins. This is a foundational moment as the outpouring of the Spirit at Pentecost enables its continuing fulfilment in the ensuing Christian mission to Jerusalem (Acts 2–7), Judea (8–9) and the ends of the earth (10–28).

Second, the events of Pentecost are situated within a scriptural framework. At the beginning of Peter's sermon, which Luke uses to provide an interpretation of the events, they are presented as the fulfilment of LXX Joel 3:1–5 (MT 2:28–32). The quotation is placed after the event as part of its interpretation but logically precedes it insofar as the events are presented as fulfilling existing Scripture (Acts 2:14). The text cited – which I will consider in greater detail below (§3.3.2) – declares the arrival of an eschatological context in which all will be filled with the Spirit and consequently prophesy.[23] Thus, this citation can be read as a way of locating space within an existing scriptural framework for new revelatory experiences through which people could come to a saving knowledge of God.[24] However, it is also significant that Joel is a prophetic book. It is a text which claims to be a product of prophecy and so to be able to offer a divine perspective on historical events.[25]

As Deines notes, 'In the time of [the NT authors] the message of the prophets is accessed *in written form* as Scripture, which means that the notion that the "word of God" is actually a written word can be taken as the rule rather than the exception.'[26] Consequently, it is conceivable that Luke uses this citation to suggest that the experiences in which he sees the fulfilment of this prophetic text could themselves be expected to give rise to a text which presents an authoritative perspective on the history

---

[20] William S. Kurz also suggests a 'double entendre: that the deeper meaning of the Jewish Pentecost is fulfilled in the events of Acts 2' ('Promise and Fulfillment in Hellenistic Jewish Narrative and in Luke and Acts', in *Heritage*, 147–70 (149 n.7)).

[21] Turner is right (contra Robert P. Menzies, *Empowered for Witness: The Spirit in Luke-Acts* (London: T&T Clark, 2004), 172) to see 'power' (Luke 24:49) as 'a referential term for the Spirit' in this case (*Power from on High: The Spirit in Israel's Restoration and Witness in Luke-Acts* (Sheffield: Sheffield Academic, 1996), 254).

[22] Cf. Joseph A. Fitzmyer, *The Acts of the Apostles*, AB 31 (New York: Doubleday, 1998), 200, as representative of a wide consensus.

[23] See esp. 2:18, where Luke appears to have added 'and they will prophesy' (καὶ προφητεύσουσιν) to the citation to emphasize this feature. See further §3.3.2.

[24] Acts 2:37–38 makes clear that Peter's inspired proclamation was of soteriological importance to those present.

[25] Cf. Donald Stuart, who argues that Joel offers 'a variation on a perspective on history and a way of portraying key events in that history long known to orthodox Israelites' (*Hosea—Jonah*, WBC 31 (Texas: Thomas Nelson, 1988), 227).

[26] Roland Deines, 'Revelatory Experiences as the Beginning of Scripture: Paul's Letters and the Prophets in the Hebrew Bible', in *From Author to Copyist: Essays on the Composition, Redaction, and Transmission of the Hebrew Bible*, ed. Cana Werman (Winona Lake, IN: Eisenbrauns, 2015), 300; italics original.

of God's action towards his people. That is to say, it is possible that the prevalence of prophetic texts could have shaped the expectations of the early Christian religious milieu in both their content *and* their form. Although it is uncontroversial to suggest that the content of scriptural texts shaped religious expectations, the second point is more obscure. If, however, it is granted that the content of a text such as Joel's may have shaped Jewish religious expectation in this period,[27] it is at least possible that where REs reshaped faith commitments, this might have been expected to crystallize in a written form similar to that of the scriptural texts which created conceptual space for the experiences.[28] This is especially the case for the kinds of revelatory experiences Hurtado considers. He argues that these 'communicate something new or revised, sometimes something that is valid or relevant for others and not simply the recipient, and so issu[e] in a sense of calling to disseminate the revelation'.[29] Assuming a context in which these REs were seen as the fulfilment of existing prophetic Scriptures, perhaps the most obvious form for this dissemination to take might have been in writing as 'new Scriptures'.

Third, the use of συμπληροῦσθαι to denote the arrival of the day of Pentecost emphasizes its salvation-historical significance within the schema of fulfilment which runs through Luke-Acts.[30] The phrase Luke uses to locate this event temporally occurs only once elsewhere in the *Doppelwerk* in Luke 9:51.[31] There, it marks Jesus' turn to Jerusalem by referring to the 'completion of the days for him to be taken up' (ἐν τῷ συμπληροῦσθαι τὰς ἡμέρας τῆς ἀναλήμψεως αὐτοῦ). This is a decisive point in Luke's narrative, beginning Jesus' journey towards Jerusalem and ultimately leading to his passion, resurrection and – uniquely among the Synoptics – ascension. The outpouring of the Spirit is similarly closely associated with Jesus' passion, resurrection and ascension to the right hand of the Father (Acts 2:22–24; 31–33), and likewise marks a decisive moment in Luke's account of salvation history. Through the parallel, redactional[32] phrasings at these significant points in his Gospel and Acts, Luke signals

---

[27] In the present context, cf. e.g. Menzies and Turner who trace the ways in which Second Temple Jewish Literature evidences particular forms of religious expectation on the basis of the Jewish Scriptures (*Empowered*, 48–101; *Power*, 86–137), though Joel itself is not prominent in this regard (Turner, *Power*, 130–1).

[28] Cf. Michael J. Kruger, *Question of Canon: Challenging the Status Quo in the New Testament Debate* (Nottingham: Apollos, 2013), 71–8.

[29] Larry W. Hurtado, 'Revelatory Experiences and Religious Innovation in Earliest Christianity', *ExpTim* 125 (2014): 470–1.

[30] For discussion of the theme of fulfilment in Luke-Acts, cf. Peterson, 'Fulfilment'; Kurz, 'Promise'; Darrell L. Bock, 'Scripture and the Realisation of God's Promises', in *Witness to the Gospel: The Theology of Acts*, ed. I. Howard Marshall and David Peterson (Grand Rapids, MI: Eerdmans, 1998), 41–62; Charles H. Talbert, 'Promise and Fulfillment in Luke-Acts', in *Luke-Acts: New Perspectives from the Society of Biblical Literature Seminar*, ed. Charles H. Talbert (New York: Crossroads, 1984), 91–103. Cf. more broadly, John T. Squires, *The Plan of God in Luke-Acts*, SNTSMS 76 (Cambridge: Cambridge University Press, 1993).

[31] Elsewhere in the NT, the verb συμπληροῦσθαι occurs only in Luke 8:23 in reference to the filling of a boat with water, but this is not relevant.

[32] Cf. Gerd Lüdemann, *Early Christianity According to the Traditions in Acts: A Commentary* (Minneapolis, MN: Fortress, 1989), 38; Kurz, 'Promise', 149.

the 'fulfilment character' of what follows.³³ Further, both Luke 9:51 and Acts 2:1 are part of Luke's narrative 'concerning the deeds which have been fulfilled among us' (περὶ τῶν πεπληροφορημένων ἐν ἡμῖν πραγμάτων; Luke 1:1). As Talbert notes, 'To have heard Luke-Acts read as a continuous whole would have been to hear it as a narrative of fulfilment'³⁴ of which Pentecost is a vitally important part. Indeed, later in Acts, Luke has Peter refer to the events of Pentecost as a 'beginning' (ἀρχῇ; 11:15) as he explains the opening of the way of salvation to the Gentiles – the third geographic strand of Jesus' programmatic pronouncement.³⁵ This clearly suggests that for Luke, Pentecost marks a significant new beginning in his story of God's interactions with his people.³⁶

The importance of this episode suggests its content reflects on the claims of Luke's wider narrative. As Frein notes, Luke's own writing is presented as a record of God's fulfilment of 'both the words of the great prophets of Israel's past and those of recent prophets (especially Jesus) who appear in Luke's narrative'.³⁷ Though Luke presents Jesus as more than a prophet (cf. esp. Luke 24:19–27), Frein's comment demonstrates that Luke's description of Pentecost draws attention to the way he presents his own writing as a record of God's recent actions which stand in continuity with scripturally informed expectations.³⁸ Consequently, when Luke depicts divine reality as becoming present at Pentecost, this has implications for the status of his own writing. To develop this point, I will suggest that Luke's depiction of the outpouring of the Spirit implies that he understood Pentecost as a theophany of the Spirit with significant implications for the relationship between human speech and divine reality.

3.1.2. Pentecost imagery

In Acts 2:1–4, Luke describes the outpouring of the Spirit:

καὶ ἐγένετο ἄφνω ἐκ τοῦ οὐρανοῦ ἦχος ὥσπερ φερομένης πνοῆς βιαίας καὶ ἐπλήρωσεν ὅλον τὸν οἶκον οὗ ἦσαν καθήμενοι καὶ ὤφθησαν αὐτοῖς διαμεριζόμεναι γλῶσσαι ὡσεὶ πυρὸς καὶ ἐκάθισεν ἐφ' ἕνα ἕκαστον αὐτῶν, καὶ ἐπλήσθησαν πάντες πνεύματος ἁγίου καὶ ἤρξαντο λαλεῖν ἑτέραις γλώσσαις καθὼς τὸ πνεῦμα ἐδίδου ἀποφθέγγεσθαι αὐτοῖς.³⁹

---

[33] Cf. Jürgen Roloff, *Die Apostelgeschichte* (Göttingen: Vandenhoeck und Ruprecht, 1981), 40: the phrase 'das Folgende als ein Geschehen auszeichnen, das Erfüllungscharakter hat' (ET: 'marks the following as an event that has fulfilment character').
[34] Charles H. Talbert, *Reading Acts: A Literary and Theological Commentary on the Acts of the Apostles* (Macon, GA: Smyth & Helwys, 2005), xv; cf. similarly Joel B. Green, *The Gospel According to Luke*, NICNT (Grand Rapids, MI: Eerdmans, 1997), 8–12.
[35] See §4.2.3.
[36] With e.g. Bock, *Theology*, 144; contra Turner, *Power*, 353.
[37] Brigid C. Frein, 'Narrative Predictions, Old Testament Prophecies and Luke's Sense of Fulfilment', *NTS* 40 (1994): 22–37 (36–7).
[38] On scriptural worldview, cf. Roland Deines, 'Jesus and Scripture: Scripture and the Self-Understanding of Jesus', in *All That the Prophets Have Declared*, ed. Matthew Malcolm (Milton Keynes: Paternoster, 2015), 39–70.
[39] When the day of Pentecost had come, they were all together in one place. And suddenly from heaven there came a sound like the rush of a violent wind, and it filled the entire house where they were sitting. Divided tongues, as of fire, appeared among them, and a tongue rested on each of them. All

Here, he mentions three phenomena that mark the coming of the Spirit: 'a sound out of heaven like that of a rush of violent wind which filled the whole house where they were sat' (2:2), 'divided tongues as of fire' which appeared and 'sat' on each one of them (2:3) and the infilling of all present with 'Holy Spirit' (2:4) which caused them to speak in tongues. As is widely recognized, this picture language marks the outpouring of the Spirit as an episode in which the divine becomes noticeably present. The phenomena described here were widely used to signify divine presence in ancient literature: Pervo notes that 'the signs accompanying the revelation are those of the classic HB epiphany',[40] and van der Horst introduces the relevant section of his collection of Hellenistic parallels to Acts by asserting that 'wind and especially fire (often on the head) are frequently regarded as signs of divine presence'.[41] However, this already hints that the specific intertexts Luke is engaging – and, thus, the significance of his terminology – are contested.

Levison has recently argued that Luke's combination of fire, filling and intoxication motifs should be seen as situating the account within a milieu of ecstatic Greco-Roman experience.[42] This, he claims, can better explain Luke's choice of imagery than a comparison with OT texts, such as the tower of Babel (Gen 11) and the giving of the Law at Sinai (Ex 19) which have long been regarded as possible intertexts.[43] The connection with Babel is primarily conceptual – the argument usually turns on the suggestive use of συγχέω to denote confusion in Acts 2:6 and LXX Genesis 11:7 and the importance of multiple languages in both passages – meaning this potential intertext does not go very far towards explaining the imagery used to depict the outpouring of the Spirit. Accordingly, though I will explore this connection below (§3.2.4), I will focus initially on the other two options – ecstatic Hellenistic experience (§3.1.3), and the Sinai theophany (§3.1.4) – before examining the role of experience in shaping Luke's choice (§3.1.5).

3.1.3. Hellenistic examples of ecstasy

In *Filled with the Spirit*, Levison argues that 'if the story of Sinai lies in the background of Pentecost, it does so quiescently, by way of subtle allusion rather than the shout of clear correspondence'.[44] Rather than reading the three phenomena – sound of wind, tongues

of them were filled with the Holy Spirit and began to speak in other languages, as the Spirit gave them ability (NRSV).

[40] Pervo, *Acts*, 61; cf. Keener, *Acts*, I:801–4.
[41] Pieter van der Horst, 'Hellenistic Parallels to the Acts of the Apostles (2.1–47)', *JSNT* (1985): 49–60 (49). It is worth remembering that despite later artistic depictions of the event, Acts 2:1–4 actually does not say that the fire rested *on the heads* of those present; the parallels that van der Horst lists are of varying strength.
[42] Cf. John R. Levison, *Filled with the Spirit* (Grand Rapids, MI: Eerdmans, 2009), 325–65, and the more nuanced revision of a similar argument in Heidrun Gunkel, Rainer Hirsch-Luipold and John R. Levison, 'Plutarch and Pentecost: An Exploration in Interdisciplinary Collaboration', in *The Holy Spirit, Inspiration, and the Cultures of Antiquity*, ed. Jörg Frey and John R. Levison, Ekstasis 5 (Berlin: De Gruyter, 2014), 63–94.
[43] Cf. Frances Martin, ed., *Acts*. ACCS (Downers Grove, IL: IVP, 2006), 19–20: 'The [church] Fathers are sensitive to Luke's allusive theology of a new Sinai ... They are aware that Luke is alluding to the undoing of Babel in the gift of tongues.'
[44] Levison, *Filled*, 325–6.

of fire, speaking in tongues – that mark the outpouring of the Spirit together, he groups the reports of fire and filling (2:3 and 4) with the later charge of drunkenness (2:13) as tropes related to Hellenistic depictions of enthusiasm and ecstatic speech. Taking the 'association between fire and infilling ... [as] part and parcel of a widespread and commonplace Greco-Roman conception about inspiration', he claims that this forms the dominant context for Luke's account.[45] To support these claims, Levison appeals primarily to Plutarch as a key source for Greco-Roman attitudes towards ecstasy and Philo as an example of Jewish interaction with these ideas. There are four parallels which Levison identifies between Acts 2 and Greco-Roman conceptions: (1) the language of filling with Spirit; (2) the presence of fire; (3) the appearance of intoxication; (4) 'the presence of a sober, rational interpretation of the religious tradition'.[46]

First, Levison links filling with πνεῦμα with ecstasy, defined as the 'eviction' of the mind[47] to argue that 'Luke situates the experience of Pentecost in a robust cultural setting that saw filling with a *pneuma* as the precipitating factor in enthusiasm'.[48] Although both writers are concerned to depict a certain kind of 'intensity', Luke's Pentecost narrative appears to contrast quite strongly with Plutarch's careful and considered depiction of possible filling with πνεῦμα. Plutarch is particularly concerned to avoid the impression that the divine interacts with human bodies: in On the Obsolescence of Oracles, a reinterpreted stoic πνεῦμα – identified with the physical πνεῦμα known at Delphi – acts as a kind of buffer, fitting the body for the revelation of divine things and maintaining a certain distance between divine and human. Thus, although Plutarch does have Lamprias speak positively of the possibility of the body being filled (432F–433B), this is 'less in terms of spiritual content than physiological preparation'.[49] As Gunkel et al. note, this actually contrasts with Luke's perception of 'the spirit [sic] as a divine actor and thus a carrier of the divine message – a concept that Plutarch is trying to avoid'.[50]

Second, Levison argues that 'Luke adopts the image of fire only in relation to filling by the spirit [sic] ... Fire is not a free-floating element of Pentecost that in some general way evokes God's presence'.[51] In this sense, he sees fire and filling as closely associated, and suggests that this mirrors a similarly close connection in hellenistic discussions of inspiration, which is visible in Lucan's depiction of Pythia's ecstatic inspiration when Apollos 'dart[s] flame into her vitals'.[52] For Gunkel et al., 'it is this association of filling and fire that allows the experience of Pentecost to be situated in a Greco-Roman literary

---

[45] Levison, *Filled*, 331, referring back to his examination of the Greco-Roman sources of this position in 154–77.
[46] Gunkel et al., 'Pentecost', 90. In *Filled*, Levison focuses on 'Fire, filling, and intoxication' (326–35) before turning his attention to 'Speaking in tongues' and 'Inspired interpretation of Scripture' (336–61). The same basic structure underlies §4 in Gunkel et al., 'Pentecost'.
[47] Levison, *Filled*, 327, citing Philo, *Heir*, 2.264.
[48] Levison, *Filled*, 328.
[49] Gunkel et al., 'Pentecost', 82. Cf. 86: 'This point of view [the idea that the divine plays vocal chords like an instrument], according to Plutarch, would have the damaging effect of entangling a god in human affairs in such a physical way that the god's majesty would be compromised.'
[50] Gunkel et al., 'Pentecost', 83.
[51] Levison, *Filled*, 329.
[52] *On the Civil War*, 5.120.

context, in which inspiration was depicted as a fiery experience'.[53] It is not entirely clear how useful these parallels are, however. Levison overstates his case when he claims that 'these three dimensions of the Pentecost experience [fire, filling, and intoxication] find only the most slender foothold in Luke's scriptures'.[54] In fact, wind and fire are important features of OT theophanies,[55] and it is likely that this is more prominently echoed in Luke's Pentecost account than Levison initially allows.[56] An important point here is that Levison rarely mentions the sound of the wind,[57] preferring to link fire and filling with the later charge of drunkenness: in Luke's narrative, however, the charge of drunkenness is a later response (2:13, 15) to the short initial theophany (2:1-4).

However, while Levison treats his first two points independently, they are essentially cumulative with his third. He is attempting to demonstrate linguistic links in order to identify a milieu on which Luke can be seen to be drawing by using this terminology and this comes to the fore in his treatment of drunkenness. Gunkel et al. highlight Plutarch's comparison of filling with πνεῦμα and drunkenness:

> It is likely that by warmth and diffusion it opens up certain passages through which impressions of the future are transmitted, just as wine, when its fumes rise to the head, reveals many unusual movements and also words stored away and unperceived. 'For Bacchic rout and frenzied mind contain much prophecy', according to Euripides, when the soul becomes hot and fiery, and throws aside the caution that human intelligence lays upon it, and thus often diverts and extinguishes the inspiration.[58]

Levison also points to Philo's description of ecstatic bodies as 'flushed and fiery' (ἐνερευθὲς εἶναι καὶ πεπυρωμένον) with the result that 'many of the foolish are deceived and suppose that the sober are drunk'.[59] According to Levison, Luke's rebuttal of a similar charge implies he accepts that the behaviour of those on whom the Spirit has been poured can look like drunkenness to outsiders. On this basis, Levison argues that 'Luke allows the residue of ecstasy to linger, the resonance of enthusiasm to permeate

---

[53] Gunkel et al., 'Pentecost', 84.
[54] Levison, *Filled*, 334.
[55] Outside of fire, filling is in fact present in the OT as Levison's *Filled* itself demonstrates, though he argues it does not have the kinds of implications seen at Pentecost. However, *Filled* suffers from a lexically determined approach: as James B. Shelton notes, Levison does not consider 'Hebrew parallels of ecstatic prophecy' ('Delphi and Jerusalem: Two Spirits or Holy Spirit? A Review of John R. Levison's *Filled with the Spirit*', *Pneuma* 33 (2011): 47-58 [53]).

Intoxication is rarer, but in association with eschatological judgement not unheard of (Isa 29:9; cf. Ps 75:8; Jer 25:15; 51:7; in the NT, cf. Rev 14:10; 16:19). Luke's account of John the Baptist's prophecy that Jesus would 'baptise with the Holy Spirit and with fire' (Luke 3:16) and the eschatological emphasis in the emendation to the quotation of Joel (Acts 2:17) suggest that such a thought may not be completely removed from the present narrative.
[56] This seems to be reflected in the more nuanced evaluation of Gunkel et al., 'Pentecost', 66-72.
[57] Levison refers to the sound of the wind, but only to demonstrate the 'chaos' implied in Luke's description (*Filled*, 328-9). Cf. Shelton's critique of the assertion that the scene is chaotic ('Delphi', 53-4).
[58] Plutarch, *Def. orac.*, 432E (Babbitt, LCL).
[59] *Drunkenness*, 147.

the events of Pentecost' reflecting 'a latent appreciation for mildly illicit Greco-Roman conceptions of inspiration'.[60]

The parallels Levison cites can perhaps illuminate the charge of drunkenness in Acts 2:13, but their significance should not be overstated. Whereas Acts 2 describes tongues of fire which denote the presence of the divine and come to rest on people, Philo describes the altered external appearance of an inspired person and Plutarch uses the physiological effects of drunkenness as an analogy to explain the impact of spirit-filling. Moreover, Plutarch continues to consider the possibility that ecstatic inspiration might be an effect of dryness or even cooling, and elsewhere speaks about Bacchic 'wineless drunkenness and joyousness' brought on by ivy without any mention of heat.[61] It is also significant that van der Horst cites a range of parallels which support a connection between the appearances of drunkenness and ecstasy without relying on the connection between 'fire, filling, and intoxication' which Levison develops.[62]

The fourth and final parallel suggested by Gunkel et al. between Plutarch and Luke is 'the presence of a sober, rational interpretation of the religious tradition'.[63] This appears to be based on Plutarch's discussion of the way in which the 'physical carrier of the message shapes the appearance of the message',[64] but the suggested parallel is entirely lacking. Both the Pythia and the inspired believers in Acts produce intelligible speech, but any similarity ends there: Plutarch intends to remove any implication that the god is responsible for the wording of the Pythia's oracle whereas Luke asserts that the Spirit is intimately involved in empowering speech beyond the natural capabilities of the tongues-speakers.

Consequently, Levison's proposed Hellenistic background could help explain the accusation of drunkenness, though it is not necessary given the broader association evidenced in van der Horst's collection of parallels. It is less successful, however, at explaining Luke's choice of imagery to depict the outpouring of the Spirit. This in turn suggests that Luke's primary intention was not to draw connections with contemporary Hellenistic understandings of ecstasy. I will now turn my attention to the intertextual links with the Sinai theophany. If this can be established as Luke's primary intertext, that will have implications for the intended resonance of his imagery in this passage.

3.1.4. The Sinai theophany

Despite Levison's argument that its influence is quiescent if present, the Sinai theophany in Exodus 19:16-19 offers another possible source for Luke's imagery. In this passage, God appears to Moses for the Israelites to witness (19:9b-15, 20-25), and gives him the 10 commandments (20:1-17). The suggestion that this was a key intertext for Luke in shaping his account is supported by the identification of distinctive linguistic parallels between LXX Exodus 19:16-19 and Acts 2, noted in bold:

---

[60] Levison, *Filled*, 332, 335.
[61] Cf. *Def. orac.*, 432F-33B; *Quaest. rom.*, 291B.
[62] Van der Horst, 'Hellenistic Parallels', 54-5.
[63] Gunkel et al., 'Pentecost', 90.
[64] Gunkel et al., 'Pentecost', 86.

ἐγένετο δὲ τῇ ἡμέρᾳ τῇ τρίτῃ γενηθέντος πρὸς ὄρθρον καὶ ἐγίνοντο **φωναὶ** καὶ ἀστραπαὶ καὶ νεφέλη γνοφώδης ἐπ' ὄρους Σινα, **φωνὴ** τῆς σάλπιγγος **ἤχει** μέγα· καὶ ἐπτοήθη πᾶς ὁ λαὸς ὁ ἐν τῇ παρεμβολῇ. καὶ ἐξήγαγεν Μωυσῆς τὸν λαὸν εἰς συνάντησιν τοῦ θεοῦ ἐκ τῆς παρεμβολῆς, καὶ παρέστησαν ὑπὸ τὸ ὄρος. τὸ δὲ ὄρος τὸ Σινα ἐκαπνίζετο ὅλον διὰ τὸ **καταβεβηκέναι ἐπ' αὐτὸ τὸν θεὸν ἐν πυρί**, καὶ ἀνέβαινεν ὁ καπνὸς ὡς καπνὸς καμίνου, καὶ ἐξέστη πᾶς ὁ λαὸς σφόδρα. ἐγίνοντο δὲ αἱ φωναὶ τῆς σάλπιγγος προβαίνουσαι ἰσχυρότεραι σφόδρα· Μωυσῆς ἐλάλει, ὁ δὲ θεὸς ἀπεκρίνατο αὐτῷ **φωνῇ** (Exod 19:16–19).[65]

First, sounds which signal divine presence are described in both stories with cognates of ἠχέω (Acts 2:2; Exod 16:16).[66] Second, fire appears as a marker of God's presence (Acts 2:3; Exod 16:18). Third, in both cases people's attention is caught by a φωνή (Acts 2:6; Exod 16:16, 19).

In the retelling of this event in LXX Deuteronomy 4, God's voice becomes even more closely associated with fire and a further linguistic link is also established as both passages describe the phenomena as coming 'from heaven': **ἐκ τοῦ οὐρανοῦ** ἀκουστὴ ἐγένετο **ἡ φωνὴ** αὐτοῦ παιδεῦσαί σε, καὶ ἐπὶ τῆς γῆς ἔδειξέν σοι τὸ **πῦρ** αὐτοῦ τὸ μέγα, καὶ **τὰ ῥήματα αὐτοῦ ἤκουσας ἐκ μέσου τοῦ πυρός** (4:36; cf. 11–12).[67]

The Sinai theophany is also retold in Philo's *On the Decalogue* 33–46, and this version includes further linguistic and conceptual links with Acts 2. In *Decalogue* 46, Philo reworks the deuteronomic claim that God's words were heard 'from the midst of the fire' (4:36) to suggest that 'the flame became articulate speech' which spoke in a 'language (διάλεκτον) familiar to the audience'. There are both linguistic and conceptual parallels between Philo and Luke here. Philo introduces the term διάλεκτος, which occurs in Acts 2:6 and 8, and his emphasis on the comprehensibility of God's voice to his people mirrors the 'overcomprehensibility'[68] at the heart of Luke's Pentecost narrative.[69] Philo also emphasizes the cosmic scope of Sinai, developing a reference to the all-covering smoke which attended the heavenly fire (καπνός; Exod 19:18; *Decalogue* 44) to assert the universal significance of the revelation:

---

[65] And it happened on the third day, when it was toward dawn, **sounds** and lightning and dark cloud were occurring on the mount Sina; the **sound** of a trumpet was **ringing loudly**, and all the people in the camp were terrified. And Moyses led the people out from the camp for a meeting with God, and they stood near, below the mountain. Now the mountain Sina was smoking in its entirety, **because God had come down upon it in fire**, and the smoke was rising up like the smoke of a furnace. And all the people were very astonished. Now the sounds of the trumpet, increasing, became much stronger. Moyses was speaking and God answered him with **sound**. (NETS)

[66] This point is strengthened by the sparse usage of such terminology in the NT, and especially the parallel usage of Heb 12:19 also in reference to Sinai; elsewhere only Luke 4:37 of a 'report' about Jesus, 21:25 for the 'roaring' of eschatological waves; and 1 Cor 13:1 to describe the 'sound' of a clanging cymbal.

[67] '**From the sky** his **voice** became audible to discipline you, and on earth he showed you his great **fire**, and **you heard his words coming from the midst of the fire**' (NETS).

[68] Cf. Michael Welker, *God the Spirit* (Minneapolis, MN: Fortress, 1994), 250–3.

[69] Cf. similarly Gunkel et al., who see here 'a conviction much like the relationship between tongues as of fire and the comprehensible recitation of God's praiseworthy acts in Acts 2' ('Pentecost', 70).

Πάντα δ' ὡς εἰκὸς τὰ περὶ τὸν τόπον ἐθαυματουργεῖτο ... πυρὸς οὐρανίου φορᾷ **καπνῷ** βαθεῖ τὰ ἐν κύκλῳ συσκιάζοντος· ἔδει γὰρ θεοῦ δυνάμεως ἀφικνουμένης μηδὲν τῶν τοῦ κόσμου μερῶν ἡσυχάζειν, ἀλλὰ πάντα πρὸς ὑπηρεσίαν συγκεκινῆσθαι (*Decalogue* 44).⁷⁰

This universal emphasis is made even more explicit when he says elsewhere that the trumpet blast of God's voice delivering the law reached to 'the ends of the universe' (*Spec. Laws* 2.189). In Luke's Pentecost narrative, similar terminology and imagery is present in the passage quoted from Joel (Acts 2:19; LXX Joel 3:3). However, for Luke, the cosmic significance of the Spirit's outpouring is eschatological.⁷¹

Philo's expanded rendering of the Sinai theophany demonstrates the plasticity and fecundity of the original story during this period and has several features in common with Luke's account of Pentecost. It must, though, be balanced against Josephus's much more restrained retelling. Josephus divests the passage of its religious significance, presents the unusual phenomena as thoroughly natural and includes a plea to the reader to use their reason to interpret the tale.⁷² Moreover, any allusions Luke intends to the Sinai theophany appear in a much more restrained form than Philo's expansive rendering, and Menzies has challenged the idea that it is specifically the Sinai theophany that lies in the background of Acts 2. Rather, he argues that Luke's linguistic parallels suggest an allusion to theophany 'in general'.⁷³ That there are significant elements of the Pentecost story which are not derived from the Sinai theophany supports this suggestion. The presence of the Holy Spirit, the recitation of God's praiseworthy acts and speaking in other languages are highlighted as significant differences by Gunkel et al.⁷⁴ To this, we could add the sound of wind: although wind is an element of other OT theophanies, it is not present in the Sinai theophany.⁷⁵ Clearly, these are significant differences which undermine any suggestion of strict literary dependence.

However, literary dependence and 'intertextual echoes'⁷⁶ are not the same thing, and Luke's Pentecost narrative is presented primarily as a depiction of a new RE rather than a retelling of the Sinai theophany. If there are echoes, it is in order to establish the possible way in which a new RE stands in relation to Sinai. Notwithstanding the differences between the passages, Turner identifies six elements of structural correspondence shared by Acts and Philo's rendering of the Sinai theophany:

---

⁷⁰ 'It was natural that the place should be the scene of all that was wonderful ... the rush of heaven-sent fire which shrouded all around in **dense smoke**. For when the power of God arrives, needs must be that no part of the world should remain inactive, but all move together to do Him service' (Colson, LCL).
⁷¹ The clearest evidence for this is the redactional alteration of the citation to begin with 'in the last days' (2:17); cf. §3.3.2.
⁷² *Ant.*, 3.5.2 (79–82).
⁷³ Menzies, *Empowered*, 196; cf. similarly Gunkel et al., 'Pentecost', 68; Gerhard Schneider, *Die Apostelgeschichte*, 2 vols, HThK (Freiburg: Herder, 1980), 1:246-7; Hans Conzelmann, *A Commentary on the Acts of the Apostles*, ed. Eldon Jay Epp with Christopher R. Matthews, trans. James Limburg et al., Hermeneia (Philadelphia, PA: Fortress, 1987), 16.
⁷⁴ Gunkel et al., 'Pentecost', 68.
⁷⁵ For wind as a theophanic element, cf. Exod 15:8, 10; 1 Kgs 19:11–12; Ps 18:1; Job 38:1.
⁷⁶ Cf. Richard B. Hays, *Echoes of Scripture in the Letters of Paul* (New Haven, CT: Yale, 1989), 18–19.

Both Philo and Luke (i) envisage a holy theophany before the assembled people of God; (ii) in each case we have to do with a redemptive-historical event on earth … (iii) in each this sign or wonder involves a miraculous sound, and a rush of something 'like' fire from heaven descending to the people, and dividing to reach all, and (iv) in each case this results in a miraculous form of speech, spreading and so coming to be heard by a multiplicity … in their own language … (v) each involves an important 'gift' given to God's people and (vi) this gift comes to Israel as the consequence of Israel's leader … ascending to God.[77]

On this basis, Turner argues that it is hard to believe that 'the Pentecost account would not "remind" a reader of Jewish Sinai traditions',[78] and this is persuasive, especially if the paramount importance of the giving of the law is recalled.[79] Accordingly, it appears Luke recalls this significant originary event in an attempt to convey the significance discerned in the disciples' early RE raising the question of what kind of experience may have prompted Luke to allude to the Sinai theophany to depict it.

3.1.5. Theophanic imagery and the experience of the Spirit's outpouring

Having examined the likely intertextual sources of Luke's imagery, it is possible to consider the ways in which experience may have shaped their use. In the first instance, as the Sinai theophany provides the primary intertext for the imagery employed in Luke's account of Pentecost, it is reasonable to infer that he intends to portray the outpouring of the Spirit as a theophanic event, an occurrence in which the divine becomes temporarily personally present within the world in a particularly noticeable way.[80]

However, the metaphorical imagery Luke uses to depict the outpouring of the Spirit also suggests something about how the Spirit is present. Marshall notes that Luke uses the language analogically (*like* fire; *like* wind) and argues that this 'indicate[s] that we have to do with a supernatural occurrence',[81] which cannot be directly described. Marshall is right – as the description of the sound of the wind coming 'from heaven'

---

[77] Turner, *Power*, 284–5.
[78] Turner, *Power*, 285.
[79] For the impact of this theophany on lived RE, cf. Brian C. Howell, 'The Divine Voice as Metaphor and Action', in *Epiphanies*; James L. Kugel, *Great Shift: Encountering God in Biblical Times* (New York: Houghton Mifflin Harcourt, 2017), 177–86. As Sejin Park demonstrates, Pentecost itself acquires an association with the giving of the law, becoming a festival of covenant renewal (*Pentecost and Sinai. The Festival of Weeks as a Celebration of the Sinai Event*, LHBOTS (London: T&T Clark, 2008)). The pre-Lucan sources for this association are references to covenant renewal celebrations in *Jubilees* 1.1–2 and 6.17–22, and the *Community Rule* (1QS 1–3). Despite some suggestive linguistic connections (cf. Gunkel et al., 'Plutarch', 70–2) Marshall notes the loud silence of Philo and Josephus ('The Significance of Pentecost', *SJT* 30 (1977): 349), and Turner argues that this association 'was not yet fully established in official Judaism', adding that 'hard evidence for mainline views is only forthcoming from the time of R. Jose ben Halafta [2nd century AD]' (*Power*, 281).
[80] Cf. the definition of epiphany in Stefan Krauter, 'Heavenly Support in 2 Maccabees 15: Biblical Memories, a Vision, and a Sword', in *Epiphanies*: 'The temporary full personal presence of a god in this world, in contrast to the idea of steady presence (e.g. in a cult statue) on the one hand and the notion of total withdrawnness on the other.'
[81] I. Howard Marshall, *Acts*, TNTC (Nottingham: IVP, 1980), 68; cf. Witherington, *Acts*, 132.

(Acts 2:2) demonstrates – but his claim must be balanced against the way Luke's description intentionally flirts with physicality. Luke describes the way the divided tongues like fire 'sat, one on each of them' (ἐκάθισεν ἐφ' ἕνα ἕκαστον αὐτῶν; 2:3). This suggests an almost physical interaction, in which a visual manifestation that looked like tongues of fire actually seemed to settle on each person present.[82] This emphasis is consistent with Luke's description of the descent of the Spirit on Jesus at his baptism[83] in 'bodily form like a dove' (σωματικῷ εἴδει ὡς περιστερὰν; Luke 3:22). The language is analogical, but in both cases the emphasis is on an apparently convincing physical appearance.[84] Further, this nuance is peculiarly Lukan among the Synoptics (cf. Mark 1:10; Matt 3:16). Thus, although a supernatural occurrence is implied, Luke goes out of his way to emphasize the tangible – perhaps, even, historical – nature of the event. At both Jesus' baptism and Pentecost the Spirit descends, making divine reality present in a tangible way at salient moments in Luke's narrative.

This tendency is striking in Luke's context. Malina and Pilch rightly observe that the distinction of 'the imperceptible realm of God from the concrete and measurable realm of human beings' is anachronistic to the NT authors, but their claim that 'it was quite natural for God (and gods) to interact with humans, and vice versa' goes too far.[85] In fact, Levison's comparison of Luke's depiction with Plutarch's careful description of the physiological 'buffering' role of the πνεῦμα suggests that great care was usually taken to preserve gods' transcendence when depicting an interaction with creation, and Schaper notes a similar tendency in the LXX interpretation of the Sinai theophany.[86] Luke's descriptions of the bestowals of the Spirit on Jesus and his disciples are different: they emphasize the tangible reality of the Spirit by creating analogies with physical things. Schnabel's suggestion that Luke's description of the wind makes 'a comparison of the actual phenomenon with meteorological experiences that Luke's readers were familiar with'[87] is helpful here: the emphasis is certainly on divine activity, but it is divine activity which occurs and is graspable within the world.

Luke's willingness to depict divine reality through physical forms – as a dove, as the sound of a wind, as fire – prepares the ground for a more audacious move: he lists the tongues-speech of the believers at Pentecost as a manifestation of the Spirit's presence alongside the twin analogies of wind and fire. In doing so, he highlights the experiential

---

[82] Cf. Glen Menzies, 'Pre-Lucan Occurrences of the Phrase "Tongue[s] of Fire"', *JSPS* 22 (2000): 27–60. Menzies's search does not reveal any particularly close parallels, potentially hinting at genuine visionary experience underlying this innovative usage.

[83] Cf. Parsons who links the ekphrastic language of Pentecost with Luke's emphasis on the 'bodily form' of the dove in Luke 3:22 (*Acts*, PCNT (Grand Rapids, MI: Baker Academic), 38), and Johnson who argues for a parallelism between Jesus' baptism and the outpouring of the Spirit on the disciples (*Acts*, 47).

[84] Cf. John Nolland, *Luke 1:1–9:20*, WBC 35A (Waco, TX: Thomas Nelson, 1989), 161. Nolland notes that Luke resolves Mark's ambiguous language 'in terms of visual form', and points out that 'Luke has almost totally reformulated his Markan source' in his account of Jesus' baptism (160), which further emphasizes Luke's redactional role here.

[85] Bruce J. Malina and John J. Pilch, *A Social-Science Commentary on the Book of Acts* (Minneapolis: Fortress, 2008), 6.

[86] Cf. Joachim Schaper, 'God's Presence amongst the Israelites According to LXX Exodus and LXX Deuteronomy', in *Epiphanies*.

[87] Eckhard J. Schnabel, *Acts*, ZECNT (Grand Rapids, MI: Zondervan, 2014), 114.

roots of his imagery. David Moffitt recognizes this and argues that the disciples saw their experience as an encounter with the glory of the Lord.[88] Peter's sermon clarifies the relationship between God, Jesus and the Spirit (Acts 2:32–33): God raises Jesus up, exalts him to his right hand and gives him the promise of the Spirit (cf. Luke 24:49; Acts 1:4); from his exalted position, Jesus pours out the Spirit, which, Peter suggests, refers primarily to 'this that you both see and hear' in this instance.

In this depiction, Jesus' divinity is emphasized: he stands with God and pours out the Spirit on the disciples, who are empowered by the Spirit to bring salvation to those around them through their prophetic witness to Christ.[89] The outpouring of the Spirit manifests this new reality to God's people and Moffitt interprets the theophanic imagery in light of OT references to the presence of God in the tabernacle. He argues that the link Luke makes between the outpouring of the Spirit and Jesus' exaltation creates a connection with his salvific sacrifice: 'The experience of the gift of the Spirit's outpouring led Jesus' early followers to assume that he had done something to make them pure in some new and amazing way.'[90] This interpretation finds support in Gäckle's argument that the application of cultic imagery to the Christian community in the NT itself derives in part from the experience of God's presence in their midst,[91] and, as Moffitt notes, a connection between 'cleansing' and reception of the Spirit becomes particularly visible in the story of Cornelius (Acts 10:1–48). It does not, however, appear to be the controlling thought in Luke's description of Pentecost.

Here, the focus is rather on the establishment of a new kind of relationship between God and the disciples. Turner argues for a 'loose correspondence' between Pentecost and Sinai which presents the Pentecost 'as part of the fulfilment and *renewal* of Israel's covenant' but not as 'the *beginning* of the New Age or Salvation for the disciples'.[92] Though he is correct to note the correspondence, Pentecost does represent a new beginning. In fact, Luke has Peter refer to it precisely as 'the beginning' in Acts 11:15. As Luke presents it, then, after Jesus' death his disciples understood themselves to be in relationship with God in a new way on the basis of experiences in which they detected the influence of his Spirit. It appears that the experience of this new reality was sufficiently decisive as to evoke the memory of the foundational theophany of God to Moses on Sinai after he had led the people out of Egypt. Thus, the imagery of wind and fire alerts the reader to the fact that with the arrival of the Spirit, the God of Israel who has been active in Israel's history and in the life of Jesus Christ has become present again.

For this reason, the most significant thing that happens at Pentecost is that the Spirit is poured out. In the felt impact of the Spirit's presence, the disciples discerned a new reality which had significant repercussions for their relationship with God,

---

[88] David M. Moffitt, 'Atonement at the Right Hand: The Sacrificial Significance of Jesus' Exaltation in Acts', *NTS* 62 (2016): 549–68.
[89] Cf. Johnson on the prophetic portrayal of the disciples (*The Acts of the Apostles*. SP 5 (Collegeville, PA: Liturgical Press, 1992), 12–14).
[90] Moffitt, 'Atonement', 562.
[91] Volker Gäckle, 'The New Temple and New Priesthood in the New Testament: The Divine Presence in the Community of Believers', in *Epiphanies*.
[92] Turner, *Power*, 289, 353; italics original.

and Luke reflects this in echoing the foundational theophany of YHWH to Moses at Sinai in his portrayal of their first Spirit-filling. The tongues-speech which followed was a manifestation of this, meaning that it comes third in a series of theophanic phenomena manifesting this divine presence together with wind and fire, and is the only one available to a wider public. The proclamation in tongues at Pentecost is clearly performed under the inspiration of 'the Spirit' which 'gave them utterance' (τὸ πνεῦμα ἐδίδου ἀποφθέγγεσθαι αὐτοῖς; Acts 2:4) and represents a paradigm-shifting fulfilment of Jesus' promise in 1:8 that the disciples will be empowered to witness. In the next section, I will argue that this suggests that Luke is depicting the human speech itself as revelatory. In doing this, Luke is developing a depiction of inspired witness, and I will later argue (§4.4) that this reflects on his intentions for his own writing.

3.2. Tongues-speech as revelatory

In the previous section, I argued that the events of Pentecost represent a theophany of the Spirit which is foundational for the remainder of Luke's story. With the outpouring of the Spirit, the focus of the story moves to the disciples' witness to Christ, in which the Spirit enables them to retell the story of Jesus' life, death, and resurrection to bring about salvation, and I will now consider the implications for the unusual speech-act which forms part of Luke's narrative of the outpouring of the Spirit. Tongues-speech is integral to the manifestation of the Spirit at Pentecost, and this makes human speech a part of the theophanic event as Luke presents it. I will first consider the experience of speaking in tongues, before examining in turn how this phenomenon's form, Spirit-bestowed 'utterance' (ἀποφθέγγεσθαι; Acts 2:4), and content, 'God's mighty deeds' (μεγαλεῖα τοῦ θεοῦ; 2:11), present it as a Spirit revealing utterance which combines inspired innovation and scriptural continuity.

3.2.1. Tongues-speech as RE

In Chapter 2, I defined REs as *the felt impacts of trans-empirical realities within the culturally patterned life of an individual or group*. On Luke's account, the tongues-speech at Pentecost fits within this definition, even though he gives no indication of how tongues-speech was subjectively perceived by any of the speakers – except, perhaps, Peter. In Acts 2:4, Luke reports that those on whom the Spirit was poured out 'began to speak in other languages as the Spirit gave them utterance'. This describes the felt impact of a trans-empirical reality. Indeed, Malina and Pilch even see sufficient evidence in the narrative to describe it as a report of a 'group trance experience of the promised Spirit of God',[93] although this is based on a flawed assumption that tongues-speech is necessarily associated with trance states (see §3.2.5).

The tongues-speech at Pentecost is not merely a RE for the speakers, though. It is presented as a public-facing phenomenon which provokes amazement in a watching

---

[93] Malina and Pilch, *Acts*, 27.

crowd. Insofar as the tongues-speech stands alongside the wind-like sound and the fire-like vision as a third marker of the Spirit's theophanic presence, hearing it can also be understood as a RE. This is certainly the implication when Peter tells the crowd that Jesus has received the promise of the Spirit from the Father and poured it out, resulting in 'this that you both see and hear' (Acts 2:33). This means Luke presents tongues-speech both as an experience had by the disciples and as a sign (cf. 2:19)[94] to the gathered outsiders.

Here, the parallelism Luke develops between the outpouring of the Spirit at Pentecost with Jesus' baptism is worth highlighting, as it offers a way to understand the disciples' filling. In Luke 3:21–4:1 when Jesus has been baptized and is praying, 'heaven was opened and the Holy Spirit descended upon him in bodily form like a dove', and a 'voice from heaven' (φωνὴν ἐξ οὐρανοῦ) declares him to be 'my beloved son' (3:21–22). This is followed by a genealogy which traces Jesus' lineage back to Adam (3:23–38), before Jesus is described as 'full of the Holy Spirit' (πλήρης πνεύματος ἁγίου; 4:1). After being tempted (4:1–13), he delivers his first, programmatic sermon 'in the power of the Spirit' (ἐν τῇ δυνάμει τοῦ πνεύματος; 4:14), claiming Isaiah's prophecy is fulfilled in him (4:14–21). Luke introduces the story of Jesus' baptism by situating it both world-historically (3:1–2) and salvation-historically by quoting Isaiah 40:3–5 (3:4–6) to show that 'it signifies the beginning of a new period that is characterized by the salvific work of God in history'.[95] In Luke's telling, this centres on Jesus receiving the Spirit: this is what allows him to present himself as the 'anointed one' (4:18) in fulfilment of Isaiah 61:1–2 in his sermon.

Acts 2 includes several echoes of Jesus' anointing. The disciples receive the Spirit while gathered (2:1), presumably to pray (cf. 1:14). They encounter the Spirit in almost physical form (2:2–3) and are 'all filled with Holy Spirit' (ἐπλήσθησαν πάντες πνεύματος ἁγίου; 2:4). Immediately after this, Luke inserts a list of nations (2:9–11) which can be understood as a parallel to Jesus' genealogy, as both emphasize the universal scope of salvation.[96] Further, the initial experience of Spirit filling is challenged (2:13), but answered by reference to the fulfilment of Scripture in a prototypical sermon

---

[94] Contra e.g. Witherington, who sees the reference to signs and wonders in 2:19 as entirely eschatological because the 'wonders' are absent from the narrative (*Acts*, 143). By contrast, Menzies separates the signs from the wonders, arguing that 'the miracles in Luke-Acts are precursors of those cosmic signs which shall signal the Day of the Lord' (*Empowered*, 186). This better recognizes the significance of the event itself in the inauguration of a new age.

[95] David W. Pao, *Acts and the Isaianic New Exodus*, WUNT II.130 (1998 repr., Grand Rapids, MI: Baker Academic, 2002), 44. Cf. Conzelmann's influential construal of Luke's account of salvation history as 'divided up into three epochs: the time of Israel, the time of Jesus (as the centre), and the time of the church' (*Acts*, xlv), which has been taken up and defended by Gunkel (*Heilige Geist*, esp. 9–12, 266–70). Conzelmann's schema is critiqued by Nolland, ('Salvation-History and Eschatology', in *Witness to the Gospel: The Theology of Acts*, ed. I. Howard Marshall and David Peterson (Grand Rapids, MI: Eerdmans, 1998], 63–81). It is not necessary to follow Conzelmann rigidly to discern in Pentecost a 'new beginning', however: Darrell L. Bock, *A Theology of Luke's Gospel and Acts* (Grand Rapids, MI: Zondervan, 2011), 389–90, argues for a basic two-part, 'promise and fulfilment' structure of salvation history, but allows Jesus' ministry to form a distinct period within the 'fulfilment'. For a critique of the argument that Pentecost represents a new beginning, cf. Turner, *Power*, 353.

[96] So e.g. Parsons, *Acts*, 39–40.

(2:14–36). In the Third Gospel, Jesus receives the Spirit at his baptism in a decisive way which permeates his actions throughout the rest of the narrative and changes salvation history.[97] The implication is that the same is true, though in a limited way, of the disciples in Acts: they are filled with the Spirit in a way which permeates their speech at a significant new beginning in salvation history. An important difference between Jesus and the disciples, though, is that Luke presents Jesus as more than a prophet. As the anointed one, Jesus does not merely prophesy, but fulfils Scripture – partly by pouring out the Spirit after his exaltation. This brings about a further theophany, and the disciples' speech is brought *within* this theophany, becoming an embodied site in which God can be noticeably present within history. Whereas Jesus fulfils Scripture in the power of the Spirit, the disciples are empowered by his outpouring of the Spirit to witness to Christ (cf. Acts 1:8).

Luke not only describes felt impacts of the Spirit on the speakers and hearers at Pentecost but also situates them in relation to culturally patterned frameworks. Acts 2:6 clarifies that what the disciples say in tongues is spoken in human languages, known to the crowd which has gathered around the speakers: they are 'their native languages' (τῇ ἰδίᾳ διαλέκτῳ).[98] Uniquely on this occasion in the NT, speaking in tongues produces intelligible speech, and consequently interacts here both with the culturally patterned frameworks of the languages themselves and the expectations of the language speakers. The odd relation of the tongues-speech at Pentecost to existing languages is what causes the crowd's amazement. Despite being immediately intelligible to those who hear it, it demands interpretation (2:12). Ultimately, this results in a reinterpretation of the received scriptural framework; after all, tongues-speech is an unlikely phenomenon in which to identify the fulfilment of Joel's prophecy. Nonetheless, in Peter's sermon (2:14–36), the Pentecost event is interpreted in relation to Scripture as exactly that. Here, the emphasis is on the speakers, who are depicted as prophets on the basis of their tongues-speech (esp. 2:18).

Finally, the RE is both personal (individual humans speak) and communal: the Spirit is poured out on 'all' those present (2:1, 4)[99] and they are heard by a 'multitude' of 'devout Jews from every nation' (2:5–6). Thus, Luke presents tongues-speech as a RE and I will now argue that his presentation of the disciples' speech raises the possibility that though it was given to them by the Spirit they could have intended what they said to be revelatory.

---

[97] Cf. Gunkel, *Heilige Geist*, 69–75.
[98] On Luke's account as depicting xenolalia i.e. the speaking of unlearned human languages, cf. Max Turner, 'Early Christian Experience and Theology of "Tongues": A New Testament Perspective', in *Speaking in Tongues: Multi-Disciplinary Perspectives*, ed. Mark J. Cartledge (Milton Keynes: Paternoster, 2006), 1–33 (4): 'This sense is virtually demanded co-textually.'
[99] I take 'all' to refer to the whole community of 120. So similarly i.a., Schnabel, *Acts*, 113; Gunkel, *Heilige Geist*, 142; Ernst Haenchen, *The Acts of the Apostles: A Commentary*, trans. B. Noble et al. (Oxford: Blackwell, 1971), 167 n.4. The fact that more than twelve languages are spoken makes it difficult to hold to the interpretation that 'all' in 2:1 refers to the twelve disciples (see e.g. Nelson P. Estrada, *From Followers to Leaders: The Apostles in the Ritual of Status Transformation in Acts 1–2*, JSNTSup 255 (London: T&T Clark, 2004), 204–8), and the opening up of the promise in 2:38–39 makes it unnecessary within the narrative.

3.2.2. Tongues-speech as Spirit-revealing utterance

On three occasions in Acts, Luke reports a group's first encounter with the Spirit as being marked by tongues-speech.[100] In each case he describes the inspired activity as 'speaking in tongues' using the verb λαλέω and the noun γλῶσσα in the dative plural. Uniquely in 2:4, though, he modifies this noun with the adjective ἕτερος ('other'), making clear that at Pentecost those filled with the Spirit spoke in a plurality of discernible languages. The terminology of amazement which pervades the passage (συγχέω; 2:6; ἐξίστημι; 2:7, 12; θαυμάζω; 2:7; διαπορέω; 2:12) emphasizes the apparent strangeness of the occurrence. The occasion of the amazement is made clear: hearers are being addressed 'in our own native tongues' (τῇ ἰδίᾳ διαλέκτῳ ἡμῶν ἐν ᾗ ἐγεννήθημεν; 2:8) by people who could not be expected to know them, and despite the fact that those present sufficiently shared a *lingua franca* for Peter's single-language address to be adequate to the task of interpreting the event to the crowd. As Welker puts it, 'The miracle of the baptism in the Spirit lies not in what is difficult to understand or incomprehensible, but in a totally unexpected comprehensibility and in an unbelievable, universal capacity to understand.'[101]

The apparent uniqueness of the account of Pentecost has raised the question of what kind of experience might underlie the account, and whether a tale of early ecstatic glossolalia has been reinterpreted or exaggerated in order to serve Luke's theological purposes in this passage by emphasizing the universal proclamation of the gospel.[102] The judgement that 'it is implausible that these (or any) spirit-filled people were speaking foreign languages'[103] is probably too sweeping in light of accounts of xenolalia external to the NT.[104] However, the designation of what is said as 'tongues-speech' – a form which consistently appears to denote unintelligible glossolalia elsewhere in the NT[105] – suggests that despite the uniqueness of this speech event, it can still be considered in a similar manner to other accounts of glossolalic speech. With this argument, I am suggesting that Luke is here depicting the first outpouring of the Spirit in a way which reflects on the disciples' witness – and ultimately his own

---

[100] Elsewhere in 10:46 Cornelius and his household (see §4.1.2) and in 19:6 the Ephesian disciples.
[101] Welker, *God the Spirit*, 230–1. I do not, however, intend to subscribe to Pesch's assertion that Pentecost is a 'miracle of languages *and* of hearing' (*Die Apostelgeschichte*, EKK (Göttingen: Patmos, 2014), I:104) on which Welker draws, in any strong sense. The miracle is a speaking miracle: what makes the speaking miraculous is its intelligibility in the various native tongues of the crowd; only in this sense should it be considered a 'hearing miracle' (with e.g. John B. Polhill, *Acts*, NAC 26 (Nashville, TN: Broadman, 1992), 99–100; Max Turner, *The Holy Spirit and Spiritual Gifts: Then and Now* (Carlisle: Paternoster, 1996), 218; contra e.g. Pervo, *Acts*, 64; Jenny Everts, 'Tongues or Languages? Contextual Consistency in the Translation of Acts 2', *JPT* 4 (1994): 71–80).
[102] So, influentially, Conzelmann, *Acts*, 15, cf. 160.
[103] Malina and Pilch, *Acts*, 28.
[104] For an overview of relevant evidence, cf. Keener, *Acts*, I:816–21. It is particularly worth noting that xenolalia – the speaking of unlearned foreign languages – is not unknown outside of the Bible or the Christian tradition, and instances have been cited for mediums; see J. Gwyn Griffiths, 'Some Claims of Xenoglossy in the Ancient Languages', *Numen* 33 (1986): 141–69. The lack of reliable evidence for this phenomenon makes it unlikely, however, that all NT references to tongues-speech should be read as references to xenolalia (so Christopher Forbes, *Prophecy and Inspired Speech in Early Christianity and Its Hellenistic Environment*, WUNT II.75 (Tübingen: Mohr, 1995), 72–4).
[105] Acts 10:46; 19:6; 1 Cor 12:10, 28, 30; 13:1, 8; 14:1–27, 39.

written text – and links the human expression with divine revelation through this specific RE. To develop this argument, there are three points of interest regarding the way in which this RE communicates: (1) the glossolalic function of the speech; (2) the xenolalic content of the speech; and (3) the relationship between divine and human agency in the production of the speech. I will consider each in turn to examine how Luke relates this speech to the presence of the Spirit.

3.2.3. Glossolalic function

In his study of the OT prophets, Heschel claims that 'as a witness, the prophet is more than a messenger. As a messenger, his task is to deliver the word; as a witness, he must bear testimony that the word is divine.'[106] The tongues-speech at Pentecost seems to serve a similar double function as a prophetic witness: while it declares a message in intelligible speech (it delivers a word), this is proclaimed in tongues-speech. Consequently, it is reasonable to assume that Luke intends the tongues-speech at Pentecost to function in a similar manner to glossolalia in other contexts, which means, in part, acting as evidence of God's involvement through the Spirit (cf. 10:46; 11:15; 15:8; 19:6).[107] The reported reaction of the crowd bears this point out: despite the fact that the tongues-speech at Pentecost has an immediately intelligible content, its meaning remains ambiguous and its first hearers are 'confused' and 'amazed' (συνεχύθη and ἐθαύμαζον; Acts 2:6, 7). This raises the question of how tongues-speech might be understood as communication in this instance: how might its glossolalic form be understood to contribute to a specific function within the narrative?

David Hilborn argues that questions 'about the capacity of ... glossolalia to communicate meaningful information are anticipated'[108] in Paul's limitation of the ecclesial use of glossolalia to contexts in which it is 'put into words, i.e. render[ed] in articulate intelligible speech'[109] in 1 Corinthians 14. Despite the differences between Luke's depiction of tongues-speech in Acts 2 and Paul's analysis, Hilborn draws on speech act theory, implicature and relevance theory to consider how glossolalic speech might communicate something which can be interpreted ('put into words') without including meaningful cognitive content that can be translated in a manner which is helpful for my analysis of how Luke intends to depict the function of the tongues-speech in Acts 2.

---

[106] Abraham J. Heschel, *The Prophets* (1962 repr., New York: HarperPerennial, 2001), 26–7.
[107] Cf. Graham H. Twelftree, *People of the Spirit: Exploring Luke's View of the Church* (Grand Rapids, MI: Baker Academic, 2009), 90, 94.
[108] David Hilborn, 'Glossolalia as Communication: A Linguistic-Pragmatic Perspective', in *Speaking in Tongues: Multi-Disciplinary Perspectives*, ed. Mark J. Cartledge (Milton Keynes: Paternoster, 2006), 111–46 (113).
[109] Anthony C. Thiselton, *The First Epistle to the Corinthians*, NIGTC (Grand Rapids, MI: Eerdmans, 2000), 1098. Thiselton's reading of διερμηνεύω ('interpreted') here is broader than that advocated by Forbes, *Inspired Speech*, 65–72; the broader reading is useful in capturing elements of communication which are not straightforwardly linguistic. On the other hand, this should not be taken to diminish the communicative possibilities of tongues-speech: Turner rightly points out that Paul makes 'an immediate parallel (not merely an illustration) between *glossais lalein* and the *heteroglossoi* (foreign languages) of Isaiah 28:11' (*Spiritual Gifts*, 223).

Speech act theory, as influentially developed by the philosopher of language J. L. Austin, separates the *locutionary* act *of* speaking from the *illocutionary* act achieved *in* speaking and the *perlocutionary* effect achieved *by* speaking. For example, Austin argues that it is analytically useful to 'distinguish the locutionary act "he said that ..." from the illocutionary act "he argued that ..." and the perlocutionary act "he convinced me that ..."'.[110] Hilborn uses this distinction to argue that glossolalia may have *illocutionary* and *perlocutionary* dimensions, even if its *locutionary* form lacks cognitive content.[111] Specifically, he highlights illocutionary acts categorized as 'expressives': speech acts which 'at once denote and realise the psychological state of the speaker' including lament, apology, thanks and ejaculations like 'Hurrah' and 'Ouch' which 'function as Expressive illocutionary acts without propositional content'.[112] Hilborn argues that if glossolalia is this kind of speech act, it might meaningfully express a feeling without having cognitive content: 'If speech is recast as a tool and mode of action ... and if it can be used to perform meaningful expressions of *feeling* and *emotion* without propositional reference ... glossolalia could yet be seen as communicating a range of expressive illocutions.'[113]

To identify more precisely the way that the expressive illocutions of glossolalic speech might successfully achieve a specific, and possibly intended, impact in the hearer – a perlocutionary effect – Hilborn considers how successful communication relies on the hearer comprehending 'not only what is *said* ... but also what is *meant*, or "implicated"'.[114] So, although glossolalia does not offer cognitive content (there is no 'what' that is 'said'), it 'typically compensates for these communicative deficits by increasing the affective intensity of worship'.[115] On this account, the *speech act itself* can function as a means of pointing to an affective reality, interpreted by the hearer insofar as it makes specific presuppositions manifest to them. In this way, encountering a glossolalic speech act can be a RE for the hearer if, for example, it triggers an affectively toned perception, affectively deepens understanding or perhaps points affectively towards a resolution in a similar manner to the 'wordless groans' (στεναγμοῖς ἀλαλήτοις) of the Spirit mentioned in Romans 8:26.[116]

There are, however, two important differences between the tongues-speech described in 1 Corinthians 14 and that depicted in Acts 2. First, Luke describes xenolalia rather than glossolalia, and I will consider this below (§3.2.4). Second, at Pentecost, the

---

[110] J. L. Austin, *How to Do Things with Words* (Oxford: Oxford University Press, 1962), 102.

[111] Cf. similarly James K. A. Smith who argues that 'tongues-speech is a kind of speech act which can be illuminated by the categories of speech act theory, but at the same time ... in order for tongues-speech to even "count" as a speech act will require a certain retooling of some basic assumptions' (*Thinking in Tongues: Pentecostal Contributions to Christian Theology* (Grand Rapids, MI: Eerdmans, 2010), 145).

[112] Hilborn, 'Glossolalia', 120. Cf. John R. Searle, *Expression and Meaning: Studies in the Theory of Speech Acts* (Cambridge: Cambridge University Press, 1979), 12–16.

[113] Hilborn, 'Glossolalia', 120–1; italics original.

[114] Hilborn, 'Glossolalia', 123.

[115] Hilborn, 'Glossolalia', 130. Cf. also Turner, *Holy Spirit*, 310; Frank D. Macchia, 'Sighs Too Deep for Words: Toward a Theology of Glossolalia', *JPT* 1 (1992): 47–73. The implication is that glossolalia is a 'restricted code' which can function to identify a separate micro-community; cf. Douglas Davies, 'Social Groups, Liturgy and Glossolalia', *Churchman* 90 (1976): 193–205.

[116] See §2.2.1.

context is not congregational, meaning that the tongues-speech must be interpreted by reference to different, and likely not shared, presuppositions regarding its status. Both the initial reaction to the phenomenon itself – it raises a question (Acts 2:12) – and the immediate contest over its interpretation (2:13–14) are evidence of this. Still, the tongues-speech at Pentecost need not be fulfilling an entirely different function to that at Corinth: Paul attributes tongues-speech the character of a 'sign' (σημεῖον; 1 Cor 14:22) precisely because of its ambiguity to outsiders, and it seems to operate similarly in Luke's narrative. In the citation of LXX Joel 3:1–5, attention is drawn to the promise of prophetic activity through the addition of an essentially redundant repetition of 'and they will prophesy' (Acts 2:18), before the promise of cosmic portents in the heavens is balanced with a parallel promise of 'signs on the earth below' (σημεῖα ἐπὶ τῆς γῆς; 2:19). It is well known that the themes of Spirit-inspired witness[117] and 'signs and wonders'[118] run throughout the book of Acts, but Menzies is surely correct to argue that this first, 'special form of Spirit-inspired prophetic speech serves as a unique sign that "the last days" have arrived'.[119] In this case, the Pentecost tongues-speech would share the character of a sign: it would be a manifestation of God's presence, which requires appropriate interpretation if it is to be rightly understood.

Moreover, the affective impact of the tongues-speech at Pentecost was, at least partly, that it 'amazed' (ἐθαύμαζον; 2:7) its hearers. Elsewhere in Acts, this term is employed to express Moses's astonishment in response to God's theophanic presence in the burning bush (7:31), the Israelites' amazement at a miraculous sign (3:12) and the disciples' witness (4:13) and in an OT citation regarding God's action within history on behalf of his people (13:41).[120] Its occurrence here implies that the tongues-speech at Pentecost confronts the hearer with a controversial claim about divine presence in its very existence. In this way, the tongues-speech at Pentecost appears to retain the glossolalic function of a sign elsewhere attributed to tongues-speech: it both communicates a message and witnesses to the divine source of that message through its potential affective illocutionary impact.[121]

3.2.4. Xenolalic content

As already noted, the tongues-speech at Pentecost is unique in the NT because it is delivered in 'other' human languages.[122] Despite its glossolalic function as a sign, it is a different kind of sign than that described in 1 Corinthians 14:21–25. There, Paul

---

[117] Cf. Acts 3:15 (cf. 3:12); 4:33; 5:32; 14:3; 15:8; 23:11; 22:15; 26:16, 22.
[118] Acts 4:13, 31; 5:32; 6:10; 9:31; 13:9, 52.
[119] Robert P. Menzies, *Speaking in Tongues: Jesus and the Apostolic Church as Models for the Church Today* (Cleveland, OH: CPT, 2016), 22.
[120] The term has a similar valence in several occurrences in Luke's Gospel (1:21, 63; 2:18, 33; 4:22; 8:25; 9:43; 11:14; 20:26) and particularly in association with resurrection (24:12, 41), though there are a couple of occurrences with a slightly different emphasis (7:9; 11:38).
[121] This analysis may suggest a nuance to Johnson's otherwise helpful suggestion that the event *rather than* the tongues-speech is interpreted in Peter's sermon (*Acts*, 54). While Johnson is right that the tongues-speech does not require *translation* it nonetheless requires *interpretation* if its full significance is to be rightly understood.
[122] The suggestion that διάλεκτος means dialects (e.g. Levison, *Filled*, 323) cannot be seriously defended, as it runs counter to the text. As Polhill points out, τῇ ἰδίᾳ διαλέκτῳ ('their own languages/ dialects'; 2:6, 8) is used synonymously with ἡμετέραις γλώσσαις ('our own languages/

describes unintelligible tongues-speech as a sign for unbelievers, before immediately calling for its use to be limited in their presence in favour of prophecy (14:23–25) in order that they not simply hear tongues-speakers 'raving' (μαίνεσθε; 14:23).[123] He supports his understanding of tongues-speech as a sign of judgement by quoting Isaiah 28:11, suggesting that unbelievers cannot understand tongues-speech and so are confronted by the reality of their exclusion from the people of God.[124]

In Acts 2, though, outsiders encounter tongues-speech which presents them with an intelligible message. This suggests that this tongues-speech stands in a different relation to outsiders, possibly subverting the implication of judgement latent in Paul's citation of Isaiah. Rather, the tongues-speech at Pentecost represents an initial opening of the possibility of salvation to a global audience (cf. Acts 2:5–11, 37–41). On the other hand, the reaction of the crowd is multifaceted, including both positive amazement and negative confusion which gives rise to an accusation of drunkenness. Despite the fact that tongues-speech still produces the kind of reaction Paul presumably sought to avoid,[125] Luke emphasizes that a significant number of people responded favourably to the events, being 'cut to the heart' (κατενύγησαν τὴν καρδίαν; Acts 2:37; cf. 1 Cor 14:25) by Peter's sermon.

In light of this, the possible link with the 'confusion' (σύγχυσις) of languages at Babel (Gen 11) is worth revisiting. The linguistic echo is sufficiently slender that the connection has been challenged and as Barrett rightly points out, 'Luke does not say that confusion (σύγχυσις) was ended; it was now caused by an unexpected ability to understand what was said.'[126] However, this need not remove the possibility of an intertextual link between Babel and Pentecost. The story of Babel can be seen as including both threat and promise: it highlights God's judgement against 'a self-serving unity that resists God's scattering activity', but also opens the possibility of a recovery of God's intention for humanity to fill the world (Gen 1:28).[127] This raises the possibility of a relationship other than 'reversal' between Babel and Pentecost. On

---

tongues'; 2:11), and both expressions are clarified through the list of nations whose languages are audible (*Acts*, 100).

[123] Throughout, I have rendered μαίνομαι with 'raving'. This is a more restrictive translation than e.g. Tibbs's (*Religious Experience of the Pneuma: Communication with the Spirit World in 1 Corinthians 12 and 14* (Tübingen: Mohr Siebeck, 2007), 254–5), but it has the benefit of reflecting the apparent emphasis on speech present in the NT usage of the term (see §3.3.1). In Hellenistic usage, cognate terms are used for female followers of Dionysius and divine inspiration. Here, then, 'raving' means speaking in a frenzy, and particularly in a religious context.

[124] This represents what has emerged as a consensus reading of a difficult passage; cf. Thiselton, *1 Corinthians*, 1122–6; Karl O. Sandnes, 'Prophecy – a Sign for Believers (1 Cor 14,20-25)', *Bib* 77 (1996): 1–15; Wayne Grudem, '1 Cor. 14:20–25: Prophecy and Tongues as Signs of God's Attitude', *WTJ* 41 (1979): 381–96. For an alternative rendering, cf. Bruce C. Johanson, 'Tongues, a Sign for Unbelievers?: A Structural and Exegetical Study on 1 Corinthians XIV.20-25', *NTS* 25 (1979): 180–203. Within the NT, it is possible to see echoes of this role of the Spirit in John 16:15.

[125] The comparison is strengthened if μαίνεσθε (1 Cor 14:23) has religious significance, given the possible spiritual significance of the charge of 'drunkenness' (cf. John 10:20).

[126] Barrett, *Acts*, I:119.

[127] Walter Brueggemann, *Genesis*, Interpretation (Atlanta: John Knox, 1982), 98–9, drawing on a 'dialectic between unity and scattering', which reaches back to Gen 10:18. Cf. Gordon J. Wenham, *Genesis 1–15*, WBC 1 (Waco, TX: Thomas Nelson, 1987), 242: 'Whereas God wanted man to fill the earth, he seeks to congregate in one town, Babel.'

this basis – allied with the fact that Luke's list of nations potentially draws on the table of nations in Genesis 10[128] – Pentecostal theologian Frank Macchia argues that it is possible to see in Luke's depiction of Pentecost both a reversal of the threat of Babel and a figurative reading of possibilities latent in it: 'At Pentecost, the peoples of the world do not come together to build a temple ... Instead, the tongues that glorify God come down from heaven as holy flames that touch human reality and enter speech.'[129] The global relevance of Pentecost highlighted by the list of nations offers a 'fulfilment' of Babel insofar as it affirms the scattering of the people by not denying their languages, but simultaneously asserts a united understanding. In this way, Luke appears to suggest that this instance of xenolalia has a theological resonance by the mere fact of its occurrence.

However, Luke also describes its intelligible content: the speakers proclaimed τὰ μεγαλεῖα τοῦ θεοῦ ('God's mighty deeds'; Acts 2:11). This phrase echoes the LXX, where the term μεγαλεῖα occurs fifteen times.[130] LXX Deuteronomy 11:2 demands that the current generation of Israelites themselves recognize τὰ μεγαλεῖα of God rather than leaving this task to their children, because they have seen both 'the discipline' (τὴν παιδείαν) of the Lord and 'his signs and his wonders' (καὶ τὰ σημεῖα αὐτοῦ καὶ τὰ τέρατα αὐτοῦ), meaning specifically their deliverance from Egypt. This positive sense is taken up in 3 Maccabees 7:22, which refers to τὰ μεγαλεῖα God performed for the 'salvation' (σωτηρίᾳ) of his people, enabling them to return to Jerusalem with property restored to them. Similarly, in LXX Psalm 70:19 God's μεγαλεῖα are the concrete manifestation of his 'righteousness' (δικαιοσύνην; 70:15), 'salvation' (σωτηρίαν; 70:15) and 'wonders' (θαυμάσια; 70:17).[131] The majority of occurrences of the term are in Sirach, and there is a slightly different emphasis in Sirach 17, where knowledge of 'the greatness of the works' of God (τὸ μεγαλεῖον τῶν ἔργων; 17:8) is granted to the first human beings: a knowledge of the greatness of God's works is a part of their intimate

---

[128] See James M. Scott's extensive account of the significance of the table of nations in Genesis 10, its substantial biblical reception history and impact on both the structure of Acts and particularly 2:9–11 ('Luke's Geographical Horizon', in *The Book of Acts in Its Graeco-Roman Setting*, ed. David W. J. Gill and Conrad Gempf (Grand Rapids: Eerdmans, 1994), 483–544). For an alternate construal, cf. Gary Gilbert, 'The List of Nations in Acts 2: Roman Propaganda and the Lukan Response', *JBL* 121 (2002): 497–529.

[129] Frank D. Macchia, 'Babel and the Tongues of Pentecost: Reversal or Fulfilment?' in *Speaking in Tongues: Multi-Disciplinary Perspectives*, ed. Mark J. Cartledge (Milton Keynes: Paternoster, 2006), 34–51 (44). Cf. the similar interpretation of Cyril of Jerusalem, *Catechetical Lecture* 17.17 (Edwards):

> The multitude of those listening was confounded; it was a second confusion, *in contrast to the first evil confusion* at Babylon. In that former confusion of tongues *there was a division of purpose*, for the intention was impious. Here there was a *restoration and union of minds* since the object of their zeal was righteous. Through what occasioned the fall came the recovery. (italics mine)

[130] Deut 11:2; Tobit 11:15; 2 Macc 3:34; 7:17; 3 Macc 7:22; LXX Ps 70:19 (MT 71:19); Odes 9:49; Sirach 17:8, 10, 13; 18:4; 36:7 (NRSV 36:10); Sirach 42:21; 43:15; 45:24. Tobit 11:15 speaks about τὰ μεγαλεῖα which happened to Tobit in Media, and Sirach 45:24 speaks about the μεγαλεῖον of the priesthood. These, along with Polybius, 3.87.5 are less directly relevant to the usage in Acts 2:11. Odes 9:49 is part of a lightly reworked version of Mary's *Magnificat* where μεγαλεῖα replaces μεγάλα in Luke 1:49.

[131] Cf. 1QS I.21 for this sense also.

relationship with him (17:10, 12–13). This phrase is also used in a parallelism in Sirach 18:4 where the context is again creation, establishing a connection between God's works and μεγαλεῖα.

There is also a threatening side to the knowledge of God's μεγαλεῖα. In Sirach 36:7, as part of a plea that God would 'renew signs and other wonders' (ἐγκαίνισον σημεῖα καὶ ἀλλοίωσον θαυμάσια; 36:5) by pouring out judgement on the nations in a show of his glory (36:3–4), the writer asks that God would remember his covenant and that his μεγαλειά would be recounted (καὶ ἐκδιηγησάσθωσαν τὰ μεγαλειά σου). The implication is that God's μεγαλειά are his judgemental acts towards the nations which either God's people will retell as new evidence of his covenant faithfulness or their enemies will be forced to recount. Similarly, in 2 Maccabees 3:34, God's epiphanic 'flogging' of Heliodorus for attempting to rob his temple should cause him to report 'the greatness of God's power' (τὸ μεγαλεῖον τοῦ θεοῦ κράτος). In 2 Macccabees 7:17, the fifth martyred brother also warns that 'the greatness of his power' (τὸ μεγαλεῖον αὐτοῦ κράτος) will torture those killing him because God has not forsaken his people (7:16).

In the LXX, then, μεγαλεῖα primarily refers to the story of God's covenant faithfulness to his people, which is rooted in the past but remains open to new action on their behalf with the emphasis generally on judgement. These two elements coalesce in Acts 2. The disciples encounter, recognize and recount God's μεγαλεῖα in the outpouring of the Spirit at Pentecost, and it is *in this recounting itself* that the power of God is made manifest to the nations – though this is not an act of judgement but of grace, even if it is presented as an eschatological event.[132]

The question of exactly what the tongues-speakers said at Pentecost remains open. In his *TDNT* entry, Grundmann argues that in Acts 2:11 'τὰ μεγαλεῖα are the mighty acts of God which relate to, and consist in, the story of Christ, and which form the content of NT proclamation … the reference is probably to the mighty acts of God which are contained in his epiphany in Christ'.[133] Consequently, one implication of Luke's presentation is that the Spirit enables the events of the recent past to be rightly understood in their salvation-historical perspective.[134] However, even though the epiphany of God in Christ is clearly its central element, Luke's broader story of fulfilment reaches back into the OT and forward into the outpouring of the Spirit and the proclaiming of the gospel to the ends of the earth. As an element of this story,

---

[132] This is suggested by Luke's addition of ἐσχάταις ἡμέραις to the first line of his citation from Joel in Acts 2:17; cf. Witherington, *Acts*, 140: 'The working of the Spirit is seen as the sign that the eschatological age has begun.' However, it is not that 'die verheissene Endereignisse sind Gegenwart' (G. Stählin, *Die Apostelgeschichte*, NTD 5 (Göttingen: Vandenhoeck und Ruprecht, 1962), 42), but rather 'die letzte Epoche vor der Aufrichtung des eschatologischen Reiches' (Roloff, *Apostelgeschichte*, 53) (ET: 'the promised end time events are present' but rather 'the last epoch before the establishment of the eschatological Kingdom').

[133] W. Grundmann, 'μέγας', *TDNT*, IV: 529–44 (541).

[134] Cf. Ulrich Luck, 'Kerygma, Tradition und Geschichte Jesu bei Lukas', *ZTK* 57 (1960): 51–66 (65): 'Daraus ergibt sich für [Luke] gerade unter theologischem Gesichtspunkt die Frage nach der Vergangenheit, in der sich die πράγματα ereignet haben, die sich ihm durch den Geist als μεγαλεῖα τοῦ θεοῦ erschließen' (ET: 'For [Luke], this raises from a theological perspective the question of the past in which the πράγματα occurred, which the Spirit reveals to him as μεγαλεῖα τοῦ θεοῦ').

then, the recounting of God's μεγαλεῖα in the tongues-speech at Pentecost is likely to reach back to the OT, with the possible implication that it could be understood as an inspired interpretation of Scripture.[135] It also, however, reaches into the present of the tongues-speakers' experience:[136] they perceived that the same power which was at work in Christ's resurrection was now being poured out on them as Jesus had promised, and their speech was intended to convey this understanding.

In this way, this recounting of God's μεγαλεῖα remains open to his ongoing action: as xenolalic speech, it retells the story of divine history 'until today', while at the same time forming a new part of that story. Its hearers are confronted by a witness to Christ which is itself part of Luke's ongoing story of fulfilment insofar as it makes manifest the power of the outpoured Spirit. In presenting this as part of his narrative, Luke offers a paradigmatic example of empowered witness to Christ. The revelatory speech of the disciples retells of the story of God's fulfilment of his purposes within Luke's textual retelling of that same story. Further, this occurs in response to the outpouring of the Spirit and in a manner which makes the theophanic presence of the Spirit manifest. Within his narrative, then, Luke opens up the possibility of revelatory human speech, and this is closely linked with RE. In the next section, I will consider the relationship between divine and human agency in the production of the tongues-speech to argue that Luke suggests that the disciples themselves intended to say something revelatory.

3.2.5. Divine and human agency in tongues-speech

So far, I have considered the glossolalic function of the tongues-speech at Pentecost as a sign with an affective valence that confronts hearers with a claim about its divine origins, and the xenolalic content of the speech which retells the story of God's mighty acts in a way that is open to new and surprising acts and in fact constitutes such an act itself. This already demonstrates the capacity of the tongues-speech to be revelatory in a way which allows this speech event to act as a paradigmatic example in Luke's narrative. One final point to consider is the way in which tongues-speech is produced. It is here that the experiential shaping of Luke's account is most likely to be evident, as he is describing a phenomenon probably experienced or observed by both his sources and readers given its apparent prevalence in the early Christian community. This remains the case whether or not the depiction of an original outpouring of the Spirit is entirely accurate.

In Acts 2:4, Luke writes that ἐπλήσθησαν πάντες πνεύματος ἁγίου καὶ ἤρξαντο λαλεῖν ἑτέραις γλώσσαις καθὼς τὸ πνεῦμα ἐδίδου ἀποφθέγγεσθαι αὐτοῖς ('they were all filled with Holy Spirit and began to speak in other languages as the Spirit was giving to utter to them'). The main verbs of the three clauses (underlined) balance the depiction of divine and human agency. First, Luke says that all 'were filled' with Holy Spirit. Despite the fact that 'all' is the subject of this verb, it is a divine passive: God – or,

---

[135] Cf. Levison, *Filled*, 347–51, who comes to a similar conclusion for a different reason.
[136] Cf. Grundmann's later comment that occurrences of the cognate verbal form μεγαλύνω in Acts 10:46 and 19:17 suggest 'acclamations on the proclamation or experience of mighty divine acts' points in this direction ('μέγας', 543).

Jesus at God's right hand (2:33) – is filling 'all' with the Holy Spirit. This is important because tongues-speech is reliant on a prior filling of the Spirit: ἐπλήσθησαν is aorist, denoting a completed action upon which the further clauses follow. God is ultimately depicted as the author of the event, emphasizing its theophanic character. Similarly, the final clause of the verse says that the Spirit 'was giving' (ἐδίδου) the ability 'to utter to them' (ἀποφθέγγεσθαι αὐτοῖς). This implies that for as long as they were speaking the disciples perceived themselves to be compelled and enabled by the Spirit.

However, in the middle clause, 'all' is the subject of 'began' (ἤρξαντο). This makes 'all' the subject of 'beginning to speak', and clearly attributes the actual act of speaking to those present. This undermines a straightforward attribution of the speech to God. Rather, Luke suggests that God's revelatory presence in tongues-speech would not be possible without the tongues-speakers' willing and active engagement of their lungs, tongues and lips in response to the felt impact of the Spirit. In Luke 12:12, a subtle difference between Luke and the other Synoptics (Matt 10:19–20; Mark 13:11) points in a similar direction. Luke presents the Spirit as 'teaching' believers what to say, rather than speaking 'in them' (ἐν ὑμῖν; Matt 10:20).[137] There as here, the speech is the believers' own: it is Spirit-empowered, but it is not reducible to an activity of the divine.

Despite the nuanced balance between divine and human agency implied in Luke's choice of language, the Pentecost tongues-speech is frequently labelled ecstatic.[138] In the absence of a readily agreed definition of ecstasy,[139] it is generally assumed that this must be produced without human agency – it is produced by the possession of the human person by an external, trans-empirical influence in ways which diminish and remove human agency. Such an understanding would remove the possibility that the human speaker could be involved in the production of the speech in a way that could make it difficult for the tongues-speech at Pentecost to function as a prototypical example of inspired witness for Luke's narrative. Philo describes ecstatic utterance as a result of the eviction of reason from the mind by the arrival of a divine Spirit,[140] and such a view of ecstasy is not uncommon in Hellenistic sources.[141] It is not clear, though, that it corresponds to Luke's depiction of tongues-speech, in which the Spirit has control of human speech without removing human agency.

Luke's account is different from ecstatic speech in which the believer's bodies became 'instruments'[142] which the Spirit played. It is possible, though, that Philo's discussion of inspiration may offer a different model which is more closely analogous.

---

[137] Cf. Steve Walton, 'Whose Spirit? The Promise and the Promiser in Luke 12:12', in *The Spirit and Christ in the New Testament and Christian Theology*, ed. I. Howard Marshall, Volker Rabens and Cornelis Bennema (Grand Rapids, MI: Eerdmans, 2012), 35–51.

[138] Cf. e.g. Craig A. Evans, 'The Prophetic Setting of the Pentecost Sermon', in *Luke and Scripture: The Function of Sacred Tradition in Luke-Acts*, ed. Craig A. Evans and James A. Sanders (Minneapolis, MN: Fortress, 1993), 212–24; James D. G. Dunn, *Jesus and the Spirit: A Study of the Religious and Charismatic Experience of Jesus and the First Christians as Reflected in the New Testament* (London: SCM, 1975), 148–52; Haenchen, *Acts*, 175.

[139] Cf. Jack Levison, *Inspired: The Holy Spirit and the Mind of Faith* (Grand Rapids, MI: Eerdmans, 2013), 9–11.

[140] Philo, *Heir*, 264–5.

[141] See Cicero, *Div.* 1, 32, 70–1; Plutarch, *Def. orac.* 417C, 432C–F; and Apuleius, *Metam.*, 8:27.

[142] Cf. *Def. orac.* 414D, as a negative suggestion. Cf. also *Pyth. orac.*

Helmut Burkhardt argues that Philo's description of Scripture as the result of Mosaic prophecy refers to three types of inspiration as follows: '1. Oracles which are given by God himself, 2. Oracles which are comprised of human question and divine answer, 3. Oracles which are given by the prophet themselves'.[143] Of these, the first corresponds to ecstatic utterance in which 'the prophet functions only as interpreter'.[144] The second refers to passages which include question and answer between a human and God, and is not relevant here. Burkhardt argues that the third type can be 'drawn throughout with the colours of enthusiasm' but that 'in it the personality of the prophet is not (as in the first form) turned off, but rather comes to the fore'.[145] This comes closer to the kind of balance Luke implies, and Burkhardt continues to show how thinking about this type of inspiration allows Philo to speak about Scripture simultaneously as divinely inspired *and* as the product of Moses's own wisdom and insight.[146] Where Luke's account differs is the description of filling: it is being filled by the Holy Spirit that prompts the disciples to start speaking, and the speech act itself depends on the ongoing work of the Spirit.

Luke's account of tongues-speech in Acts 2 thus appears to differ from ancient discussions of inspiration. Although research into contemporary tongues-speech cannot provide a completely secure analogue for the practice described in Acts 2:4, it might support an account of tongues-speech which follows Luke's own emphases. While it has been argued that tongues-speaking is strongly correlated with trance states,[147] further psychological research has shown that neither trance states[148] nor psychological deficiency[149] correlate with tongues-speech. In fact, rather than being linked exclusively with a loss of 'personality' it appears that tongues-speech is a phenomenon over which speakers can exhibit control. It is possible that the tongues-speech at Pentecost was similar: having been filled with the Spirit, the disciples opened their mouths intending to express something of their encounter with the divine. What actually came out of their mouths was Spirit-empowered speech in other languages.

---

[143] Helmut Burkhardt, 'Inspiration der Schrift durch weisheitliche Personalinspiration: Zur Inspirationslehre Philos von Alexandrien', *TZ* 47 (1991): 214–25 (218–19), citing *Moses* 2, 188. German original: '1. Orakel, die von Gott selbst gegeben sind, 2. Orakel, die durch menschliche Frage und göttliche Antwort entstehen, 3. Orakel, die vom Propheten selbst gegeben werden'.

[144] Burkhardt, 'Inspiration', 219. German original: 'der Prophet nur als Dolmetscher fungiert'.

[145] Burkhardt, 'Inspiration', 219. German original: 'durchaus mit den Farben des Enthusiasmus gezeichnet werden' but that 'in ihr die Persönlichkeit des Propheten nicht (wie bei der ersten Form) ausgeschaltet wird, sondern ausdrücklich zum Zuge kommt'.

[146] Burkhardt, 'Inspiration', 219–21.

[147] Cf. Felicitas Goodman, *Speaking in Tongues: A Cross-Cultural Study of Glossolalia* (Chicago: University of Chicago Press, 1972), 8: 'The glossolalist speaks the way he does because his speech behaviour is modified by the way the body acts in the particular mental state often termed trance'.

[148] See N. P. Spanos and E. C. Hewitt, 'Glossolalia: Test of the Trance and Psychopathology Hypotheses', *JAbPsy* 88 (1979): 427–34.

[149] See W. K. Kay and L. J. Francis, 'Personality, Mental Health and Glossolalia', *Pneuma* 17 (1995): 253–63. For an overview of psychological research into tongues-speech, cf. William K. Kay, 'The Mind, Behaviour and Glossolalia: A Psychological Perspective', in *Speaking in Tongues: Multi-Disciplinary Perspectives*, ed. Mark J. Cartledge (Milton Keynes: Paternoster, 2006), 111–46 (113). Cf. also the critique of 'psychopathological' accounts of revelation in Rodney Stark, 'A Theory of Revelations', *JSSR* 38 (1999): 287–308.

Nevertheless, it functioned as a speech act with an affective impact and thus potentially even achieved the purpose the speakers intended. This account coheres with Luke's claim that at Pentecost, God's action and human speech coincide.

The result is that in Luke's telling this RE was the beginning of a new period in the fulfilment of God's purposes in which the disciples had become capable of intentionally revelatory speech. At Pentecost, he depicts the Spirit as making divine reality present in tongues-speech, and, consequently, as making the human speech of those on whom the Spirit has been poured out revelatory.[150] The implication is that the disciples can choose to offer a revelatory witness to Christ through the power of the Spirit which has been poured out on them. In the next section, I will argue that Luke intends the unusual tongues-speech at Pentecost to be seen as prototypical rather than unique by examining his presentation of Peter's sermon as a similar kind of utterance.

3.3. Revelatory preaching: Peter's speech

In this section, I will first examine the form (ἀπεφθέγξατο; Acts 2:14) and impact (2:37–42) of Peter's speech (§3.3.1), before considering its content (2:14–36; §3.3.2). In the final section, I will draw conclusions for the chapter and suggest some implications for the relationship between RE, inspired exegesis and revelation (§3.4) in Luke's thought and these will act as a bridge to the discussion of Luke's own writing in Chapter 4.

3.3.1. The form and impact of Peter's speech

Like the Pentecost event itself, Peter's speech is a significant part of Luke's narrative of fulfilment.[151] It is the first speech that witnesses to Jesus in fulfilment of his programmatic pronouncement in Acts 1:8.[152] Jesus tells the disciples that they will be his 'witnesses' (μάρτυρες) in Jerusalem, and Luke goes out of his way to point out that this is happening in Peter's sermon when he has him say 'this Jesus God raised up, and of that all of us are witnesses (μάρτυρες)' (2:32).

Further, Luke uses the verb 'to utter' (ἀποφθέγγομαι) to denote the act of speaking. The term only occurs twice elsewhere in the NT, both in Acts: in Acts 2:4, where it refers to the 'utterance' given by the Spirit, and in Acts 26:25. The latter occurrence depicts Paul's response to an accusation of madness from Festus. Paul claims to be 'uttering sober truth' (σωφροσύνης ῥήματα ἀποφθέγγομαι), rather than 'raving' (μαίνομαι). Levison starts from the opposition between 'raving' and 'uttering sober truth' in 26:25 and argues that Luke intends to diminish the appearance of ecstasy in his report of Pentecost,[153] but this interpretation is not compelling. Rather, Luke

---

[150] Contra Jacob Jervell, *The Theology of the Acts of the Apostles* (Cambridge: Cambridge University Press, 1996), 50–1.
[151] Following the conventions of ancient historiography, Luke is likely solely responsible for the composition of this speech.
[152] So e.g. Schnabel, *Acts*, 126; Pervo, *Acts*, 74; Darrell L Bock, *Acts*, BECNT (Grand Rapids, MI: Baker Academic, 2007), 111.
[153] Levison, *Filled*, 357–61.

appears to use ἀποφθέγγομαι to denote loud,[154] inspired witness to Christ in fulfilment of a pronouncement of Jesus in each of these three cases. The Spirit-bestowed utterance in tongues at Pentecost is clearly loud (it attracts the attention of a crowd) and makes manifest the outpouring of the Spirit in fulfilment of Jesus' pronouncement (1:8). In proclaiming God's mighty deeds, I have argued that it retells the story of salvation in a way which brings present events within its scope and presents a revelatory challenge to the gathered crowd in its character as a sign. It does this by witnessing to Christ's resurrection, insofar as Luke presents the outpouring directly as a result of his exaltation (2:33).

Luke's depiction of Paul's defence in his trial with Agrippa and Festus follows a similar pattern. Paul's stance is that of an orator (26:1), and his mode of speech provokes Festus's own 'loud' interruption to charge him with 'raving' (μαίνομαι), allowing the assumption that Paul's speech was loud. He also witnesses to God's mighty deeds by telling the story of Christ (26:22–23) and drawing his own recent history into that story (26:12–21). Finally, Paul's speech fulfils Jesus' pronouncement that the Spirit would inspire witness in court (Luke 12:11–12). Luke also creates a suggestive contrast here, by using ἀποφθέγγομαι to describe Paul's mode of speech in direct opposition to the charge that he is 'raving' (μαίνομαι). Like ἀποφθέγγομαι, μαίνομαι is rare in the NT: it occurs only three times elsewhere. Of particular interest is its appearance in 1 Corinthians 14:23 in the midst of Paul's discussion of tongues-speech.[155] Here, Paul argues that outsiders who encounter a church filled with glossolalic speakers will say that its members are 'raving' (μαίνεσθε). To avoid this, believers should instead prophesy, in order that 'an unbeliever or outsider who enters is reproved by all and called to account by all' (14:24). In this alternative scenario, 'the secrets of the their heart are disclosed' (τὰ κρυπτὰ τῆς καρδίας αὐτοῦ φανερὰ γίνεται; 14:25) and they will worship God. This is pertinent to Luke's description of Paul's trial appearance. Paul's claim that he is uttering truth is followed by an appeal which reproves Agrippa on the basis of his knowledge of Scripture (Acts 26:27) that is both intended and interpreted as an ultimately unsuccessful challenge that Agrippa should 'become a Christian' (26:28). Rather than raving, then, Paul's defence speech reproves and challenges its primary addressee, Agrippa.

Peter's sermon in Acts 2 can fit within this pattern. First, it is loud: Peter addresses a large crowd by lifting up his voice (2:14). Second, as noted above, Peter's sermon is a prototypical plain-speech witness to Christ in fulfilment of the programmatic pronouncement in 1:8. Third, like the Pentecost tongues-speech and Paul's apology, Peter's speech retells the story of God's action to bring about salvation (cf. 2:21, 40). It also includes present events, taking the outpouring of the Spirit as its starting point. In form, then, Peter's sermon is presented as an inspired witness of the same kind as the tongues-speech which attended the outpouring of the Spirit.

Further, as Stanton notes, one of the apologetic strategies employed is precisely 'to remind the audience of the wonders and signs in the ministry of Jesus in order

---

[154] Cf. J. Behm, 'ἀποφθέγγομαι', TDNT, I:447.
[155] Elsewhere in John 10:20 accusing Jesus of demon possession, and Acts 12:15 of Rhoda when she claims Peter has returned.

to show that the events of Pentecost – and also the raising of Jesus from the dead – should not have caught them completely by surprise',[156] because they are a continuation of what Jesus began. The implication is that Peter's sermon conveys insight into the divine plan fulfilled in those events. This supports Peterson's claim that 'samples of apostolic preaching have an important function in Luke's narrative, illustrating how opportunities were taken to testify to the person and work of Christ in a variety of situations. As such, they are part of the unique revelation of God.'[157] In this sense, Peter's sermon is presented as a revelatory speech.

That Peter's speech is a Spirit-empowered witness is reinforced by a key difference between the three speech acts denoted with ἀποφθέγγομαι: their respective impacts. The tongues-speech provokes a split reaction because of its ambiguity: some in the crowd are amazed; others are confused and attribute the event to drunkenness. Paul's witness to Agrippa is clear, but ultimately unsuccessful.[158] Peter's sermon, however, unambiguously reproves those who hear it (Acts 2:22–23), and has a profound emotional impact, 'cutting them to the heart' (κατενύγησαν τὴν καρδίαν; Acts 2:37)[159] and prompting the hearers to ask how they might be saved.[160] Elsewhere in Acts, Luke attributes preparation of the heart to receive the gospel message (16:14) and the impact of the message itself (15:9) to the God who knows hearts (15:8). Thus, although on one level this description of the impact of the sermon demonstrates the persuasiveness of Peter's speech,[161] it simultaneously points to the way that the Spirit has worked through his words. In this way, the effect of Peter's sermon matches its form: human and divine agency combine to produce speech which has a profound impact on its hearers because it conveys revelatory content. The implication is that Peter is aware of this possibility and intends to achieve it.

Two final points deserve attention. First, Luke's account likely reflects assumptions made by his sources, meaning that the account itself is shaped by their RE – even if not by his own. Thus, it appears that the consistent experience of the power of the Spirit in this early community convinced them that they were now capable of speaking in a revelatory way, and Luke is reflecting this: through the presence of the Spirit, Peter – and the others who come after him in the rest of Acts – can reveal Christ, insofar as they share in and extend the ministry of Jesus by witnessing to his life, death and resurrection. Second, and more striking, is the possibility that Luke saw his own action in writing in similar terms – as an inspired witness to Christ which

---

[156] Graham N. Stanton, *Jesus of Nazareth in New Testament Preaching*, SNTSMS 27 (Cambridge: Cambridge University Press, 1974), 16.

[157] Peterson, *Acts*, 144.

[158] As a legal defence, it seems to be successful on one level insofar as it secures 'another declaration of Paul's innocence' (Fitzmyer, *Acts*, 763). However, this is clearly not the main point.

[159] Cf. Witherington on the LXX usage of the verb, where it is used to convey a range of deep, negative emotions including anger, being humbled or stung and remorse (*Acts*, 153 n.89).

[160] The impact of Peter's sermon is similar to that envisaged in Paul's advocation of prophecy over tongues-speech in 1 Cor 14:24–25: outsiders will find themselves 'reproved by all, called to account by all' (ἐλέγχεται ὑπὸ πάντων, ἀνακρίνεται ὑπὸ πάντων) and have 'the secrets of their hearts made open' (τὰ κρυπτὰ τῆς καρδίας αὐτοῦ φανερὰ γίνεται) with the result that they will bow down and worship God. The difference in the impacts of the tongues-speech and Peter's sermon suggests that Acts 2 supports a similar understanding.

[161] So e.g. Pervo, *Acts*, 84; Witherington, *Acts*, 153; Bock, *Acts*, 140.

could convey revelatory content to its readers and hearers. The content of Peter's speech situates the experience of Pentecost in relation to established Scripture, and in so doing raises the possibility that Luke could even have thought of the text he was producing as scriptural. I will explore the content of Peter's speech in the next section (§3.3.2), and develop the argument that Luke saw his writing as scriptural more fully in the following chapter.

3.3.2. The content of Peter's speech

Peter's sermon is a scripturally based witness to Christ.[162] In retelling the events of Jesus' life, death and resurrection, however, it can also be seen as a rehearsal of God's mighty acts which situates itself in relation to the tongues-speech at Pentecost. This is mainly done through the quotation of Joel. The differences between Luke's version and the wording of the LXX are well known and noted in the table below.[163]

LXX Joel 3:1–5	Acts 2:17–21
3:1: Καὶ ἔσται μετὰ ταῦτα καὶ ἐκχεῶ ἀπὸ τοῦ πνεύματός μου ἐπὶ πᾶσαν σάρκα, καὶ προφητεύσουσιν οἱ υἱοὶ ὑμῶν καὶ αἱ θυγατέρες ὑμῶν καὶ οἱ πρεσβύτεροι ὑμῶν ἐνύπνια ἐνυπνιασθήσονται, καὶ οἱ νεανίσκοι ὑμῶν ὁράσεις ὄψονται	2:17: καὶ ἔσται <u>ἐν ταῖς ἐσχάταις ἡμέραις</u>, **λέγει ὁ θεός**, ἐκχεῶ ἀπὸ τοῦ πνεύματός μου ἐπὶ πᾶσαν σάρκα, καὶ προφητεύσουσιν οἱ υἱοὶ ὑμῶν καὶ αἱ θυγατέρες ὑμῶν *καὶ οἱ νεανίσκοι ὑμῶν ὁράσεις ὄψονται καὶ οἱ πρεσβύτεροι ὑμῶν ἐνυπνίοις ἐνυπνιασθήσονται·*
3:2: καὶ ἐπὶ τοὺς δούλους καὶ ἐπὶ τὰς δούλας ἐν ταῖς ἡμέραις ἐκείναις ἐκχεῶ ἀπὸ τοῦ πνεύματός μου.	2:18: καὶ **γε** ἐπὶ τοὺς δούλους **μου** καὶ ἐπὶ τὰς δούλας **μου** ἐν ταῖς ἡμέραις ἐκείναις ἐκχεῶ ἀπὸ τοῦ πνεύματός μου, **καὶ προφητεύσουσιν**
3:3: καὶ δώσω τέρατα ἐν τῷ οὐρανῷ καὶ ἐπὶ τῆς γῆς, αἷμα καὶ πῦρ καὶ ἀτμίδα καπνοῦ	2:19: καὶ δώσω τέρατα ἐν τῷ οὐρανῷ **ἄνω** καὶ **σημεῖα** ἐπὶ τῆς γῆς **κάτω**, αἷμα καὶ πῦρ καὶ ἀτμίδα καπνοῦ

---

[162] Although the speech is a Lukan composition, this need not mean it is entirely alien to Peter's manner of presenting the gospel: 'True, the speeches interspersed through Acts also serve to develop Luke's own theological ideas, but as a rule he does this by use of older traditions, and often attempts to give an appropriate characterisation of individual speakers' (Hengel, *Acts*, 61). Cf. the discussion in Keener, *Acts*, I:271–319.

[163] In the table, <u>alterations are underlined</u>, **additions are in bold** and *reordered phrases are in italics*.

LXX Joel 3:1–5	Acts 2:17–21
3:4: ὁ ἥλιος μεταστραφήσεται εἰς σκότος καὶ ἡ σελήνη εἰς αἷμα πρὶν ἐλθεῖν ἡμέραν κυρίου τὴν μεγάλην καὶ ἐπιφανῆ	2:20: ὁ ἥλιος μεταστραφήσεται εἰς σκότος καὶ ἡ σελήνη εἰς αἷμα, πρὶν ἐλθεῖν ἡμέραν κυρίου τὴν μεγάλην καὶ ἐπιφανῆ.
3:5: καὶ ἔσται πᾶς, ὃς ἂν ἐπικαλέσηται τὸ ὄνομα κυρίου, σωθήσεται· ὅτι ἐν τῷ ὄρει Σιων καὶ ἐν Ιερουσαλημ ἔσται ἀνασῳζόμενος, καθότι εἶπεν κύριος, καὶ εὐαγγελιζόμενοι, οὓς κύριος προσκέκληται	2:21: καὶ ἔσται πᾶς ὃς ἂν ἐπικαλέσηται τὸ ὄνομα κυρίου σωθήσεται· [2:39: ὅσους ἂν προσκαλέσηται κύριος ὁ θεὸς ἡμῶν]

Several of these emendations reflect emphases which run throughout Acts, including the balancing of 'wonders (τέρατα) in the heavens above' with 'signs (σημεῖα) on the earth below' (2:19).[164] Similarly, the reordering of the young men seeing visions and the old men dreaming dreams to give priority to the former (2:17) is appropriate given the prominence of visionary activity in Luke's story.[165] This suggests the differences may well reflect Luke's intent. In this case, the addition of the basically redundant 'and they will prophesy' in 2:18 places heavy emphasis on prophetic speech.

In the first instance, this designation applies to the tongues-speech of the believers upon whom the Spirit is poured out. Secondarily, however, it also suggests Peter's own speech should be seen as prophetic. When Peter addresses the puzzled crowds, he does so as someone upon whom the Spirit has just been poured out (2:17; cf. 2:4).[166] As Peterson rightly argues, then, 'Peter's extensive and carefully argued speech has a prophetic character and is as much a Spirit-inspired utterance as the speaking in other languages'.[167] When Peter says 'this is that', not only the tongues-speech but also his own prophetic sermon, and the disciples' empowered witness as Luke will continue to depict it in the remainder of Acts are included within this horizon.

In this way, Peter's sermon forms a parallel to Jesus' programmatic sermon in Luke 4. There, Jesus takes up Isaiah's prophetic expectation and declares it fulfilled in his person on the basis of a prior Spirit-empowerment in ways developed in the rest of the Third Gospel narrative. Here, the exalted Jesus pours out the Spirit (Acts 2:33) and empowers Peter to take up Joel's prophetic expectation and declare it fulfilled in his and the other believers' inspired speech in ways developed in the rest of Acts. Jesus was

---

[164] Cf. Acts 2:22, 43; 4:30; 5:12; 6:8; 7:36; 14:3; 15:12.
[165] E.g. at key moments like Paul's conversion in Acts 9; the sending of Peter to Cornelius in Acts 10; the appearance of a 'Macedonian man' to Paul and subsequent alteration of his missionary travel plans in Acts 16.
[166] There is an important association between Spirit-filling and public speaking, which is made more explicit elsewhere in the early chapters of Acts (3:12–26; 4:8–17, 31; 6:8, 15–7:55) but is nonetheless present here.
[167] Peterson, *Acts*, 139.

uniquely Spirit-empowered (Luke 3:22) in the way that his words and deeds revealed and embodied God's action in history in fulfilment of Scripture (Luke 4:21), but his outpouring of the Spirit makes it possible for the disciples' speech to be revelatory on the basis of their ongoing relationship to him. It is, after all, the Spirit of Jesus (Acts 16:7) who inspires the disciples.

The sermon also shares its basic content with the tongues-speech which declared God's mighty deeds. Although it is 'plain speech' – delivered in a *lingua franca*, in a recognisably non-ecstatic mode – the sermon refers to God's 'definite plan and foreknowledge' of the Christ-event (Acts 2:23). This makes clear that Luke intends this speech to function as a summary statement of God's mighty deeds spelled out at greater length in his first volume.[168] Moreover, Luke has Peter begin by interpreting the events of Pentecost through the prophecy of LXX Joel 3:1–5, and his witness to Christ also centres on the interpretation of scriptural texts (Ps 15:8–11; 109:1; 132:11). This recourse to Scripture appears to be a necessary part of making God's new action in history meaningful, and is a prominent feature of the possible scripturalization of Luke's own narrative which I will explore in the next chapter (§4.2.3). Without this interpretation, the glossolalic speech would remain intelligible but confusing. In a similar way, Jesus' own death and resurrection is presented as requiring scriptural interpretation on the road to Emmaus.[169]

Thus, Luke presents Peter's speech as a Spirit-empowered prophetic witness to Christ which retells God's mighty acts in recent history and creates a link with established scriptural texts. The new RE of the outpouring of the Spirit opens up the possibility that human speech can communicate revelatory content in a new way, but this RE must be interpreted in relation to established scriptural texts if it is to be properly understood. Peter's inspired exegesis already begins to suggest some implications for Luke's own text, and I will begin to draw these out in the final section of this chapter as a bridge into Chapter 4.

3.4. Religious experience, inspired exegesis and revelation

In the first sections of this chapter, I argued that Luke's depiction of Pentecost is an important pivot point in the narrative of Luke-Acts that focuses on a RE which makes revelatory speech possible for those on whom the Spirit has been poured out. First, I argued that Pentecost should be read as a theophany of the Spirit (§3.1). Given that Luke intentionally alludes to the Sinai theophany, it is reasonable to conclude that he

---

[168] It is plausible to assume that Luke's summary is not altogether removed from early Christian preaching: though it will undoubtedly reflect his own theological agenda, it was most likely written for an audience conversant with Christian claims, likely within living memory of its earliest proclamation, and led by people who were there: 'At minimum, many of the speeches preserve genuine reminiscences and reflect traditions about earlier Christian preaching' (Keener, *Acts*, I:319).

[169] Cf. Jesus' revelatory 'opening' (διήνοιγεν; Luke 24:32) of Scripture to the disciples on the road to Emmaus (24:13–35). In opening the Scriptures, 'what does the resurrected Christ reveal? From Luke's point of view he reveals the past' (Robert G. Hall, *Revealed Histories: Techniques for Ancient Jewish and Christian Historiography* (Sheffield: JSOT, 1991), 174).

is presenting this RE as a phenomenon which could convince those who experienced it that the God of Israel was active again in their midst in a new and decisive way. If Luke was writing in the 70s, it would be reasonable to assume that this reflected at least the interpretation of his sources, some of whom would likely be eyewitnesses. However, even if he is writing later, it is possible that the emphases in Luke's text reflect presuppositions present in his source material. Regardless, the narrative as it stands certainly reflects his own theological understanding and, consequently, his intentions for his own writing.

Given the apparent prevalence of tongues-speech in the earliest Christian community, experiential shaping is likely present in Luke's account of the tongues-speech at Pentecost, which is presented as theophanic and thus revelatory (§3.2). It is the third phenomenon which manifests the Spirit's presence alongside the sound like wind and the appearance of tongues of fire. As the only one available to outsiders, it plays an important role in conveying revelatory content to a new audience. This is significant for Luke's narrative as it establishes the possibility that the disciples' speech can be revelatory. Further, I have argued that it suggests this can be the result of human intention on the basis that the glossalic function of the speech potentially allows the disciples' tongues-speech to convey their sense of Spirit-filling despite the speech not communicating in languages known to them.

Thus, Luke's account of tongues-speech at Pentecost opens up the possibility of intentionally revelatory human speech. I have argued that Luke's presentation of Peter's sermon as the same kind of utterance extends the range of communicative acts which can be considered revelatory to reasoned discourse (§3.3). This demonstrates that the outpouring of the Spirit offers a paradigmatic reimagination of the possibilities of human speech within Acts that underpins the disciples' witness throughout the rest of the text and raises the possibility that Luke could have understood his own work in similar terms.

In his composition of Peter's speech, Luke also offers an interpretation of Scripture in light of God's recent actions in salvation history which itself becomes a part of God's ongoing revelation. This presents a somewhat complex relationship between Scripture, RE and revelation: Scripture logically creates the initial space of expectation for new REs, but must then itself be reinterpreted in light of God's new action in history. However, God's new action in history can be understood appropriately only by reference to his existing revelation in Scripture, and this act of understanding is itself presented as something that the Spirit makes possible.

This raises the question of how Luke intended his own work to relate to established scriptural texts. Although the OT canon was not 'closed' until after the composition of Luke-Acts[170] and the status of particular texts remained fluid during the Second Temple period,[171] it is clear that certain texts and groups of texts were treated as

---

[170] For a recent summary of the discussion, cf. Timothy H. Lim, *Formation of the Jewish Canon* (New Haven, CT: Yale University, 2013), 178–88.

[171] Cf. e.g. Eva Mroczek's argument that a 'Book of Psalms' was a later phenomenon preceded by an amorphous Psalm tradition of diverse collections determined by genre ('The Hegemony of the Biblical in the Study of Second Temple Literature', *JAJ* 6 (2015): 2–35).

authoritative long before that point.¹⁷² The apparently unambiguous NT references to 'written' sources, similarly to the 'authority of Scripture' formula in the OT ('it is written', cf. e.g. Josh 1:8; 23:6; 1 Kgs 2:3),¹⁷³ already emphasizes the importance of written texts. This is made particularly explicit in Luke's *Doppelwerk*: Luke 24:27 refers to Jesus' interpretation of 'all the Scriptures' as 'beginning from Moses and from all the prophets'.¹⁷⁴ In Acts 26:22, Luke has Paul refer to the same categories as the basis of his gospel message to emphasize its acceptability: from this stable source, it is possible to derive authority. Luke's presentation of his own work as a narrative of fulfilment is likewise an intentional attempt to derive authority from existing scriptural resources, insofar as they provide the 'promises' which come to fruition in the Third Gospel and Acts.

However, the complex relationship between Scripture, RE and revelation in Peter's speech offers evidence that Luke aims to do something more audacious than derive authority from established Scriptures. In Peter's sermon, the scriptural citations are consistently introduced with speaking terms (Acts 2:16, 17, 25, 31, 34), the majority of which are in the present tense (2:17, 25, 34). The citation of Joel is even emended to include the assertion that 'God says' the words which are cited from the prophetic book (2:17). By emphasizing the speech of God through the prophet which stands at the head of the scriptural tradition, this way of introducing scriptural citations implies a differentiation between the 'word of God' which came to the prophet and its written deposit because it presupposes 'some form of revelation or revelatory communication initiated by God prior to what is now written'.¹⁷⁵ In light of Mroczek's portrayal of an era in which the literary imagination stretched to corpora containing divine wisdom only partially available in existing texts and open to inscription in further writings,¹⁷⁶ what makes Luke's text unusual is not necessarily its claim to scriptural status. Rather, it is the way that he intends to link his own text with God's *new activity* in the life, death, resurrection and ascension of Jesus¹⁷⁷ and the outpouring of the Spirit. In his account

---

[172] As Lim notes, 'Luke and Paul had an implied notion of authoritative Scriptures', which appears to have referred to stable emergent collections, even if these were not 'closed canons' (*Formation*, 157). Cf. Michael L. Satlow's account of canonization processes which rightly separates 'acquisition of textual authority' from 'canonization' ('Bad Prophecies: Canon and the Case of the Book of Daniel', in *When Texts Are Canonized*, ed. Timothy H. Lim (Providence: Brown, 2017), 63–81 (65–7)).

[173] Manfred Oeming, 'The Way of God: Early Canonicity and the "Nondeviation Formula"', in *When Texts Are Canonized*, ed. Timothy H. Lim (Providence, RI: Brown, 2017), 25–43 (33).

[174] On this designation, cf. S. B. Chapman, *The Law and the Prophets: A Study in Old Testament Canon Formation*, FAT (Tübingen: Mohr Siebeck, 2009).

[175] Deines, 'Scripture', 271.

[176] Cf. Eva Mroczek, *The Literary Imagination in Jewish Antiquity* (Oxford: Oxford University Press, 2016), 186.

[177] This innovation in writing a new scriptural text parallels the innovation in devotion already mapped by Hurtado. Mroczek mentions Moses, Enoch, Jacob and Ezra (*Literary Imagination*, 185–7), but Luke's claims to scriptural status focus on a figure of recent historical events on the basis of REs. It is this which sets Luke-Acts off against the broader understanding of 'the perpetually unfinished nature of writing as it seemed to some of its ancient creators' Mroczek identifies: for Luke writing is unfinished because these new REs require textualization after the model of 'the law and the prophets' if they are to achieve adequate impact.

of Pentecost, then, Luke has already begun to present his own text as a deposit of REs and consequently as standing in a special relation to texts with established authority. In the next chapter, I will argue that he understood himself to be writing a text which could convey this kind of revelation, and that he consequently intended his text to be scriptural.

4

From Experience to Writing: The Inclusion of the Gentiles and the Lukan *Doppelwerk*

In Chapters 3 and 4, I am arguing that Luke intentionally presents his own writing as scriptural on the basis of its close connection to God's action in history, noticed in various religious experiences (REs). In the previous chapter, I considered the relationship between RE and human speech in Luke's depiction of Pentecost. In that narrative, Luke presents tongues-speech as part of the theophanic manifestation of the Spirit. As a result, what the disciples say as the Spirit gives them utterance functions as revelatory speech, connecting the RE of the Spirit's outpouring and the disciples' witness to Christ. Further, Luke presents Peter's scriptural sermon as the same kind of utterance, suggesting that what is true of the unique tongues-speech recorded in Acts 2:4 is at least potentially true of the disciples' 'plain speech' witness to Christ in the remainder of the story. Thus, in his pivotal depiction of the events at Pentecost, Luke establishes the possibility that the earliest disciples could intentionally speak in a revelatory way to witness to God's activity as a result of their Spirit-filling.

I concluded Chapter 3 by suggesting that the use of established Scripture in Peter's sermon already raises the possibility that Luke intended to present his writing as scriptural on the basis of the complex relationship between Scripture, RE, revelation and Luke's own text. In this chapter, I will develop this argument by considering the inclusion of the Gentiles – focusing on the outpouring of the Spirit on the Gentiles (Acts 10), Peter's defensive retelling of that episode (11:1–18) and the Jerusalem convocation[1] (15) – and Luke's own statement of purpose in the prologue to his *Doppelwerk* (Luke 1:1–4).

Luke's retelling of the inclusion of the Gentiles is the centrepiece of the narrative of Acts (§4.1) and it begins with a collection of REs (§4.1.2). The story details how Peter comes to a theological insight on the basis of his and Cornelius's REs and subsequently witnesses to his new understanding of God in a way that becomes decisive for the

---

[1] It is widely recognized that the meeting referred to in Acts 15 is not a scriptural forerunner to an 'ecumenical council' (so rightly, e.g. Jürgen Roloff, *Die Apostelgeschichte* (Göttingen: Vandenhoeck und Ruprecht, 1981), 222; Jacob Jervell, *Die Apostelgeschichte*, KEK (Göttingen: Vandenhoeck und Ruprecht, 1998), 403 n.741; Joseph A. Fitzmyer, *The Acts of the Apostles*. AB 31 (New York: Doubleday, 1998), 543. I will follow Fitzmyer (*Acts*, 543) in using 'convocation' to denote the solemnity of the assembly while avoiding unhelpful overtones.

community. I will argue that with this development, Luke portrays a movement from RE to report (§4.2): where the theophany of the Spirit brings about a decisive shift in Acts 2, it is Peter's witness to his RE-derived understanding of God's non-partiality which prompts a communal paradigm shift in chapters 11 and 15. Further, at the Jerusalem convocation Peter's witness is interpreted in relation to Scripture in the same manner that the outpouring of the Spirit is in the sermon of Acts 2:14–36, and it informs both the communal decision-making process and the creation of the Apostolic Decree (§4.3). According to Luke, this text included an explicit claim that the decision it conveys was inspired by the Spirit (Acts 15:28), and I will argue that Luke's presentation implies that the text itself can communicate revelatory content (§4.3.3).

In the final section of the chapter (§4.4), I will bring to a conclusion my argument that Luke-Acts should be seen as an intentionally scriptural writing. In his prologue, Luke offers an account of why he has written, in which he claims a close relationship to eyewitness sources and suggests that on this basis his text can offer an authoritative witness to Christ (§4.4.1). The prominence of the process of Gentile inclusion in Luke's narrative suggests that his portrayal can inform an understanding of his own purpose. Given that it describes the process by which an authoritative written communication of revelatory content is created, I will argue that exemplary features of the narrative implicitly suggest that Luke's own text is an inspired witness to God's activity (§4.4.2). This is a significant claim, and one which I will argue demonstrates that Luke-Acts was intended as a scriptural text for its initial audience (§4.4.3).

4.1. The inclusion of the Gentiles: Acts 10–15

4.1.1. Narrative setting

Two structural features highlight the importance of Luke's narrative of the inclusion of the Gentiles. First, the climax of the narrative comes in the centre of Acts.[2] Rosner argues that this likely reflects an intentional decision to mimic established scriptural texts noting that 'the notion of a literary centre is also known in biblical literature, with which Acts has many affinities, such as 1 and 2 Chronicles'.[3] Luke intentionally uses a Septuagintal style at points, making Rosner's argument inherently plausible. This suggests that Luke carefully placed this narrative in order to make a theological point, raising its importance to any understanding of his purpose in writing.

Second, the subject is given substantial space in the narrative: the story of Peter's interaction with Cornelius is the longest in Acts.[4] Its prominence is further amplified by the fact that several features are repeated in Peter's retelling (11:1–18), a passage

---

[2] Bock counts 12,385 words in Acts 1–14 and 12,502 in 15–28 (*Acts*, BECNT (Grand Rapids, Baker Academic, 2007), 486).

[3] Brian Rosner, 'The Progress of the Word', in *Witness to the Gospel: The Theology of Acts*, ed. I. Howard Marshall and David Peterson (Grand Rapids, MI: Eerdmans, 1998), 215–33 (227).

[4] So i.a. Richard I. Pervo, *Acts*, Hermeneia (Minneapolis: Fortress, 2009), 264 n.1, counting sixty-six verses for this narrative, compared with sixty for Paul's voyage to Rome (27:1–28:16).

which is redundant in terms of advancing the plot, and again later in 15:7–11. The Apostolic Decree also bears multiple repetition (15:19–29; 16:4; 21:25), demonstrating the ongoing impact of the events narrated in these passages for the remainder of the story. The agenda for this narrative is set by Peter's and Cornelius's REs in the first half of Acts 10. In Luke's presentation, this nexus of REs both sees the 'apostolic witness move decisively to the Gentile world'[5] and ultimately prompts the writing of a significant document.

Beyond these structural features, Luke also signals the importance of the inclusion of the Gentiles to his broader story of fulfilment. First, in Acts 11:16 as part of his self-defence after he has preached to Cornelius, Peter calls to mind Jesus' programmatic pronouncement by citing the 'the word of Lord'. He quotes Acts 1:5: 'John baptized with water, but you will be baptized with the Holy Spirit'. In repeating this part of Jesus' pronouncement, the quotation also echoes further backwards in Luke's narrative, recalling John the Baptist's similar prophecy (Luke 3:16). Luke uses this layered self-reference both to present the falling of the Spirit on the Gentiles as a part of the fulfilment of Jesus' programmatic pronouncement at the beginning of Acts and to interweave it with his story in a way which reaches back to the early chapters of the Third Gospel making clear that he considers this story to be a part of God's ongoing activity.[6]

Second, this connection is strengthened when Peter explicitly refers to the events of Pentecost to interpret the experience of Cornelius and his household when they encounter the Spirit and begin speaking in tongues (Acts 10:45–7; 11:15; 15:8). The falling of the Spirit on the Gentiles is thus presented as an extension of the fulfilment of Pentecost itself: it is an instance of the gift of the Spirit being given to 'all who are far off, anyone whom the Lord our God will call' (2:39).

Finally, Luke draws on LXX Amos 9:11–12 (Acts 15:16–17) to interpret Peter's report of the Spirit's involvement in his encounter with Cornelius in James's speech at the Jerusalem convocation. Like Joel's prophecy in Peter's Pentecost sermon, this text is logically prior to the events described even though Luke only mentions it afterwards to demonstrate the legitimacy of James's understanding of what has happened: the text of Amos is open to future fulfilment, and this openness underwrites its reinterpretation. In this way, Luke's portrayal of the inclusion of the Gentiles stands in relation both to his story of fulfilment and to established Scripture.

---

[5] David Peterson, *The Acts of the Apostles*, PNTC (Grand Rapids, MI: Eerdmans, 2009), 323; similarly, Pervo, *Acts*, 264; Luke Timothy Johnson, *The Acts of the Apostles*, SP 5 (Collegeville, PA: Liturgical Press, 1992), 186. Although Philip goes to Caesarea – the setting of Acts 10 – in 8:40, this is only mentioned in passing and often taken as a redactional element intended to link with Paul's encounter with Philip in 21:8. However, Barrett points out that 'Luke does not say when Philip reached Caesarea' (*A Critical and Exegetical Commentary on the Acts of the Apostles*, 2 vols (Edinburgh: T&T Clark, 1994–98), 436). It might also be possible to argue that Luke's claim that Philip 'preached in every city *until* he came to Caesarea' (εὐηγγελίζετο τὰς πόλεις πάσας ἕως τοῦ ἐλθεῖν αὐτὸν εἰς Καισάρειαν) allows the interpretation that he *did not* preach there.

[6] Cf. similarly Stephen Fowl's argument for a 'polyvalent' interpretation of the reference to Simeon in Acts 15:14 as encompassing both Peter and Simeon's *nunc dimittis* in Luke 2 ('Simeon in Acts 15.14: Simon Peter and Echoes of Simeons Past', in *Characters and Characterization in Luke-Acts*, LNTS, ed. Frank Dicken and Julia Snyder (London: Bloomsbury, 2016), 185–98).

As with his Pentecost narrative, Luke presents his text here as a record of REs and the events which develop in response to them. As I have noted above, historicity is significant for, but not central to my argument (§2.3.4). Even if Luke's account were fabricated, it would still offer evidence of a theological understanding shared between him and his intended audience. As Twelftree notes, the plethora of literary devices used to highlight the importance of these narratives 'suggest that Luke would have carefully crafted this piece so that his readers could see how he understands such theological creativity arises'.[7] Thus, the claims made here about the role of RE in decision-making and ultimately in the production of writing must be assumed to be coherent and potentially persuasive within that historical context. Indeed, this potentially speaks in favour of the historicity of the narrative: for Luke to fabricate entirely any element – the phenomena, their importance for the decision-making process or the possibility of writing as an outcome – would risk rendering his story implausible to its intended audience and undermining its usefulness. If Luke is writing within living memory to an audience still in touch with eyewitnesses, this argument is strengthened. Even if he is not, it appears that it was plausible for Luke's readers that the scriptural interpretation of phenomena such as visions, auditions and Gentile tongues-speech could be integral to communal decision-making, and that this could issue in a written document which communicated content that was perceived to have been approved by the Spirit. For this reason, the role of RE in the construction of the narrative and its implications for Luke's presentation of his own writing deserve examination.

4.1.2. A collection of REs

In Chapter 2, I defined REs as *the felt impacts of trans-empirical realities within the culturally patterned life of an individual or group*. Luke's account of the inclusion of the Gentiles begins with several such experiences. First, Cornelius's and Peter's visions are clearly presented as falling within this category, and are identified as instances of an altered state of consciousness by Malina and Pilch.[8] Each vision includes a trans-empirical reality: Cornelius sees an angel, and Peter sees a sheet coming down from heaven while he is in 'ecstasy' (ἔκστασις; Acts 10:10). In both cases, the things they see have a strong affective impact: Cornelius 'becomes afraid' (ἔμφοβος γενόμενος; Acts 10:4), and Peter 'was greatly puzzled' (διηπόρει; 10:17).[9] In both cases, the visions are deeply intertwined with culturally patterned life. Luke introduces Cornelius as a 'God fearer',[10] to link his vision with his regular prayer (10:2–3, 30), and to present his reaction

---

[7] Graham H. Twelftree, 'Is "Holy Scripture" Christian?: A Lucan Perspective', *Theology* 116 (2013): 351–60 (356).

[8] Bruce J. Malina and John J. Pilch, *A Social-Science Commentary on the Book of Acts* (Minneapolis, MN: Fortress, 2008), 74–7.

[9] The latter term is exclusively Lukan and denotes uncomprehending astonishment in the face of God's surprising action, combining cognitive (ignorance) and affective (shock) states. Cf. Acts 2:12, where the same term denotes the puzzlement of the crowd at Pentecost, and, negatively, the responses of Herod (Luke 9:7) and the chief priests (Acts 5:24).

[10] For discussion, cf. Thomas M. Finn, 'The God-Fearers Reconsidered', *CBQ* 47 (1985): 75–84; Martin Hengel and Anna Maria Schwemer, *Paul between Damascus and Antioch: The Unknown Years* (London: SCM, 1997), 61–70.

as a properly scriptural reaction to an epiphany. Peter's vision has drastic consequences precisely because of its implications for his culturally patterned understanding of God. Beyond these initial visions, however, the Spirit speaks to Peter (10:19–20), Peter's own words (10:34–43) are received by Cornelius and those present 'in the presence of God' as the expression of 'all that the Lord has commanded' (10:33) and, ultimately, the Holy Spirit is poured out 'even on the Gentiles', resulting in tongues-speech (10:45–46).

In Acts 10, the emphasis is on revelatory experiences, that is, experiences which communicate cognitive content. Partly, the importance of RE to the narrative reflects Luke's desire to ensure the action in the story is responsive to God. This is particularly visible in the tandem conversions of Cornelius and Peter: God grants salvation to Cornelius (11:18; 15:9), while at the same time decisively altering Peter's beliefs.[11] This is in keeping with the prominence of divine grace throughout Luke's accounts of conversion.[12] Talbert highlights the possibility of 'essentially cognitive' conversions, 'which involve a shift of basic paradigms about the world'.[13] Though the more usual example of such a conversion in Acts involves a 'movement from idolatry to the worship of the living God',[14] the suggestion that Peter is undergoing a cognitive conversion serves to emphasize the role RE plays in shaping his *understanding*. Peter's witness to God's impartiality is the vital element in the process which leads to the creation of the Apostolic Decree, and Luke presents that insight as rooted in REs – both the visions of Peter and Cornelius and the outpouring of the Spirit. In this way, Luke offers here a narrative depiction of the progression from initial revelatory event to report of that event, which ultimately shapes communal theological commitments.

4.2. From religious experience to report

Luke's depiction of Peter's conversion offers a case study in how REs could crystallize in written texts, because Peter's eyewitness accounts of his experience (11:4–18; 15:7–11) communicate not just 'what happened' but also his own interpretation. It is the combination of experience and reflective interpretation which ultimately serves as evidence for the community in their decision-making process. For this reason, Luke's narrative focuses on the way Peter's thinking develops during his encounter with

---

[11] For the pairing of Cornelius's and Peter's respective narratives as 'conversions', cf. Beverly R Gaventa, *Darkness to Light: Aspects of Conversion in the New Testament*, OBT 20 (Philadelphia, PA: Fortress Press, 1986), 107–22.

[12] See Roland Deines, 'Biblical Viewpoints on Repentance, Conversion, and Turning to God', in *Acts of God in History*, WUNT I.317 (Tübingen: Mohr Siebeck, 2013), 227–61 (254–5); Fernando Mendez-Moratalla, *The Paradigm of Conversion in Luke*, JSNTSup 252 (London: T&T Clark, 2004), 217–18; Charles H. Talbert, 'Conversion in the Acts of the Apostles: Ancient Auditors' Perceptions', in *Reading Luke-Acts in its Mediterranean Milieu*, NovTSup 107 (Leiden: Brill, 2003), 135–48 (144–5).

[13] Talbert, 'Conversion', 136. Gregory E. Sterling identifies conversion in Luke as 'a turn to ethical monotheism' and locates a similar structure in Philo ('Turning to God: Conversion in Greek-Speaking Judaism and Early Christianity', in *Scripture and Traditions: Essays on Early Judaism and Christianity in Honor of Carl R. Holladay*, NovTSup 129, ed. Patrick Gray and Gail R. O'Day (Leiden: Brill, 2008), 69–95 (94, 81–8)). It is significant that Peter's RE leads to changes in both his ethical knowledge and his understanding of God.

[14] Talbert, 'Conversion', 136, citing Acts 13:4–12; 14:8–18; 17:22–31.

Cornelius. I will argue that Peter's RE prompts a theological realization which leads him into conflict with the regnant paradigm (§4.2.1). The resolution of this conflict through the Spirit falling on the Gentiles demonstrates that Peter is someone whose knowledge and speech can be trusted to convey theological insight (§4.2.2). In his defence speech in Acts 11, Peter's witness to these events gains significance in two striking ways: it is interpreted in relation to a received authoritative framework, and it provokes the kind of response reserved for actual REs earlier in the narrative (§4.2.3). On this basis, I will argue that Luke is asserting the importance of Peter's witness to his encounter with Cornelius as revelatory. This culminates in Peter's contribution to the Jerusalem convocation, where I will argue that his report is treated as a source of revelation (§4.2.4).

4.2.1. Peter's RE

Since Haenchen's provocative judgement that Luke's account of Cornelius's conversion 'virtually excludes all human decision',[15] attention has been paid to the importance of human actions.[16] This focus has highlighted especially the mutual extensions of welcome and table-fellowship,[17] and can be further applied to Peter's growing understanding which I take to be key to Luke's purpose in developing the story.

Peter's response to his initial vision – a significant RE, which Luke marks out as having occurred 'in ecstasy'[18] – is to 'puzzle over' (διενθυμουμένου; 10:19) its thrice-repeated message that 'what God has made clean, you must not call profane' (10:15–16; cf. 11:9–10). While he is thinking, the Spirit interrupts him, telling him to go with the messengers from Cornelius (10:19). At this point, Peter does not understand the deeper, theological significance of his vision and this gap between divine and human understanding is the key source of dramatic irony. By the time he arrives at Cornelius's home, however, Peter's understanding has grown. He has put together the message of the vision and the words of the Spirit, applying the content of the former to the object of the latter: 'God has shown me that I should not call *anyone* profane or unclean' (10:28).

When he hears Cornelius recount his vision (10:30–33), Peter's understanding takes another leap forward. As Gaventa notes, Peter's interpretation of his vision is initially minimalist: 'All Peter indicates is that he has understood the dream well enough to obey the Spirit's order to attend to Cornelius.'[19] After he has heard from

---

[15] Ernst Haenchen, *The Acts of the Apostles: A Commentary*, trans. B. Noble et al. (Oxford: Blackwell, 1971), 362.
[16] See e.g. Robert C. Tannehill's, *The Narrative Unity of Luke-Acts: A Literary Interpretation*, 2 vols (Minneapolis: Fortress, 1986–90), 128–45, critique of Haenchen; cf. Luke Timothy Johnson, *Scripture and Discernment: Decision Making in the Church* (Nashville, TN: Abingdon, 1983), esp. chapters 4 and 5: 'Luke is so concerned to show the *human process* of coming to recognize and affirm God's intention' (90, italics original).
[17] See e.g. Joseph M. Lear, *What Shall We Do?: Eschatology and Ethics in Luke-Acts* (Eugene, OR: Wipf and Stock, 2018), 140–1.
[18] 10:10; ἔκστασις. As a technical term for a trance state it occurs only in Acts in the NT, twice in reference to Peter's vision here (cf. 11:5) and once in reference to a vision Paul has while praying in the Jerusalem temple (22:17).
[19] Beverly Roberts Gaventa, *Acts*, ANTC (Nashville, TN: Abingdon, 2003), 168.

Cornelius, though, Peter makes a sweeping statement of theological recognition that emphasizes the fact he has come to a new conclusion: 'I truly understand (ἐπ᾽ ἀληθείας καταλαμβάνομαι) that God shows no partiality (προσωπολήμπτης)' (10:34). The language of this statement is scripturally formed, echoing a claim repeatedly used to shape Israel's treatment of the powerless and the alien.[20] However, Peter here recognizes non-partiality as a fundamental characteristic of God's activity. He innovatively raises it to a theological principle applicable across the Jew-Gentile boundary on the basis of his own RE and Cornelius's account of his vision, and against the original scriptural context of the language.[21] This, however, leads him into conflict with the regnant theological paradigm in the community. Luke's description of this conflict helps clarify the role Peter's witness to his experience plays, and he offers a detailed account of how Peter's understanding develops from his initial RE that ultimately underpins the revelatory role of Peter's report to the Jerusalem convocation in Acts 15. For this reason, it will be helpful to explore how Luke presents this development.

4.2.2. Peter's epistemological journey

Through the events of Acts 10, Peter is being taught to understand God in a new way. Luke has already portrayed Peter as a disciple whose connection with Jesus made up for a lack of education (Acts 4:13),[22] and here he is led by God through a process of discovery. Peter is actively involved in the process of learning and his insight transforms his knowledge of God and his way of life. According to Dru Johnson's analysis of biblical epistemology, which focuses on how characters are portrayed as coming to know rightly, this process is typical. Johnson argues that gaining theological knowledge means 'not just learning principles or maxims, rather, it is transformative and incommensurate with the former way of existing'.[23] This also implies that the knowledge Peter gains is not solely propositional: he already has information, but his understanding has to be transformed if he is to know rightly. Thiselton suggests that there are parallels between the importance Johnson places on transformation and Gadamer's emphasis

---

[20] Cf. Lev 19:15; Deut 10:17; 28:50; 2 Chron 9:17; Ps 82:2; Prov 18:5; Sir 35:15–16.

[21] I am unconvinced that the echo here serves to demonstrate that all are equally held accountable for sin (so e.g. Bock, *Acts*, 396, erroneously citing Barrett). Rather, as Barrett argues, the accent is positive: 'Peter recognizes that a Gentile may be as good as an Israelite, and be treated by God with equal favour; Paul is compelled against his natural wish to recognize that Jews, like Gentiles, are sinners in God's eyes' (*Acts*, 519). So similarly, Eduard Lohse, 'πρόσωπον', *TDNT* VI: 768–80 (779–80).

[22] As Luke presents it, Peter and John's overall comportment evokes the reaction in Acts 4:13. This is consistent with the kind of affective change RE can prompt in a person. Cf. Mark Wynn's argument that there can be an aesthetic dimension to conversion experiences and consequently, 'if there is a distinctively theological beauty ... it will involve, evidently, a particularly weighty aesthetic good, since this good will consist in the appropriateness of the person's demeanour, and so on, relative not simply to some creaturely context, but to God' ('On the Goods of the Religious Life: Contextualizing the Approach of Richard Swinburne', *RelS* 53 (2017): 371–85 (383)).

[23] Dru Johnson, *Biblical Knowing: A Scriptural Epistemology of Error* (Eugene, OR: Wipf and Stock, 2013), 9. Johnson argues that he has identified 'monolithic features' which apply across biblical texts (149). I cannot evaluate the breadth of that claim, but elements of his framework are useful for analysing Peter's epistemological journey.

on 'practical knowledge (*phronesis*) rather than simply theoretical knowledge'[24] and such knowledge appears to be the focus of Peter's cognitive conversion.

Both Johnson and Gadamer emphasize the role of authorities in shaping knowledge. Gadamer accepts an Enlightenment distinction between faith in authority and one's own reason, but still argues for a positive role for authorities:

> The authority of persons is ultimately based not on the subjection and abdication of reason but on an act of acknowledgement and knowledge ... acknowledging authority is always connected with the idea that what the authority says is not irrational and arbitrary but can, in principle, be discovered to be true. This is the essence of the authority claimed by the teacher, the superior, the expert.[25]

Similarly, Johnson argues that in the Bible, knowing rightly requires guidance: coming to know means submitting to authorities – 'skilled knowers' – where they have superior knowledge.[26]

This raises the question of how superior knowledge can be demonstrated. Following Polanyi, Johnson emphasizes the role paradigms shared by members of a critical community play in framing issues: the regnant paradigm 'controls the scientist's view of the evidence. ... In other words, there are schools of interpretation, even within scientific communities, and merely revisiting the facts will not change the interpretation.'[27] What is required is 'contact with reality': 'Polanyi posits a world where reality intrudes upon and reforms our knowing.'[28] Similar to the way in which new discoveries prompt the re-examination of long-held theories, Johnson suggests that 'the Scriptures argue relentlessly for a knowledge of God through accredited authorities and resolve the question of theological controversy by bringing Israel *into contact with objective historical actions* ... conflicting paradigms are definitively resolved by objective actions in the real world'.[29] For example, though competing prophets might claim to have special knowledge of God, these claims can be tested by noting whether or not what they prophesy happens (Deut 18:22; Jer 28:9). Thus, for Johnson, biblical knowing does not represent a special 'genre' of knowledge arrived at via supernatural means. Similarly, Luke's narrative carefully emphasizes the development of Peter's thought process as part of the *heilsgeschichtliche* unfolding of God's purposes: God does not simply tell Peter what to think but teaches him how to think.

---

[24] Anthony C. Thiselton, *Doubt, Faith, and Certainty* (Grand Rapids, MI: Eerdmans, 2017), 34.
[25] Hans-Georg Gadamer, *Truth and Method*, trans. Joel Weinsheimer and Donald G. Marshall, revised 2nd edn (London: Continuum, 2004), 291–2.
[26] Cf. Johnson's discussion of Lukan epistemology, focusing on the account of Jesus 'opening the disciples' eyes' on the Emmaus road (*Biblical Knowing*, 113–18). In this picture, Jesus is a skilled knower who can be trusted to bring the disciples to greater understanding.
[27] Johnson, *Biblical Knowing*, 132. Cf. Thomas S. Kuhn, *The Structure of Scientific Revolutions* (Chicago: University of Chicago, ³1996). On the relationship between Polanyi and Kuhn, cf. Struan Jacobs, 'Michael Polanyi and Thomas Kuhn: Priority and Credit', *Tradition and Discovery: The Polanyi Society* 33 (2006): 26–36.
[28] Johnson, *Biblical Knowing*, 132.
[29] Johnson, *Biblical Knowing*, 133–4; italics mine.

Peter's insight into God's non-partiality clashes with the regnant theological paradigm in his community and this creates a theological controversy: it raises the question of what is required for Gentile inclusion. For Johnson, the key difference between scientific epistemology and biblical epistemology is not in their structure, but in the *kind* of reality with which contact is required: both scientists and prophets must be 'accredited' in order to shape their respective discourses, but 'the unmissable difference pertains to the means of authentication ... [In theological discourse] the means are extraordinary, unconceivable outside of a special relation to creation'.[30] In other words, when the biblical texts record a conflict of theological paradigms it is often contact with trans-empirical reality which helps resolve the controversy and this is certainly the case in Acts.

In Luke's narrative, however, Peter plays a key role in resolving the paradigm clash regarding the Gentiles because God's action does not resolve the tension directly through an RE in which his will becomes immediately apparent to the entire community, as in the example of Korah's rebellion which Johnson cites.[31] Rather, in Acts 10–11, Luke portrays the process by which Peter gains understanding in a way that allows him later to speak authoritatively at the Jerusalem convocation. In Johnson's terms, Peter is depicted as becoming a 'skilled knower' through contact with trans-empirical reality. The revelatory REs which begin the episode do not simply provide cognitive content, but act as catalysts towards a transformed way of thinking. To learn how to think rightly, Peter must 'entertain the possibility that Jesus' *good news* may be more inclusive and transformative than [he] had previously expected' on the basis of God's immediate testimony to him and Cornelius's vision report.[32] Indeed, an interesting response evoked by the initial REs is that, as Tannehill puts it, 'each is a vision that leads its recipient to be open to a stranger's experience of God'.[33] Peter's RE leads him to recognize the unexpected insight of a Gentile centurion, which pushes him to reinterpret a scriptural view of God through a new lens.

For Peter to act as a compelling witness to this new understanding of God for the community, he has to be 'accredited' in a publically visible way. As his truth claims are thoroughly theological, their validity depends upon contact with trans-empirical reality – God's noticeable action to accredit this new paradigm.[34] It is striking, then, that in Acts 10:44 the Holy Spirit interrupts Peter's sermon, 'falling' on the Gentiles present and offering a resounding validation of Peter's realization to all present, such that 'the circumcised believers who had come with Peter were amazed' (ἐξέστησαν οἱ ἐκ περιτομῆς πιστοὶ ὅσοι συνῆλθαν τῷ Πέτρῳ; 10:45). Indeed, although God remains the author of events insofar as this episode commences with two REs,[35] the falling of

---

[30] Johnson, *Biblical Knowing*, 143.
[31] Johnson, *Biblical Knowing*, 133–4. Johnson presents Korah's rebellion (Num 16) as a conflict of paradigms concerning holiness, which God resolves when the earth swallows up Korah and his followers in the presence of the community.
[32] Johnson, *Biblical Knowing*, 5, emphasis original. Here, Johnson is commenting on the apostles receiving Barnabas's report about Saul, but the point is transferable: in both cases believers must accept counterintuitive new knowledge on the basis of remarkable testimony rooted in RE.
[33] Tannehill, *Narrative Unity*, 131.
[34] Cf. Johnson, *Biblical Knowing*, 148, cf. 141–3.
[35] So similarly, Max Turner, *Power from on High: The Spirit in Israel's Restoration and Witness in Luke-Acts* (Sheffield: Sheffield Academic, 1996), 380; John T. Squires, *The Plan of God in Luke-Acts*

the Spirit can be seen as somehow responsive: it confirms a conclusion reached by Peter through 'inspired' reasoning – reasoning which starts from and includes divinely given cognitive content.

4.2.3. Peter's defence speech (Acts 11:1–18)

The form of this resounding accreditation already suggests Peter's defensive report of what has happened to the circumcised believers in Jerusalem can be understood as having a similar status to his Pentecost sermon and Luke explicitly develops parallels between the two passages.[36] Although the Spirit initially 'fell' (ἐπέπεσεν; 10:44) rather than arriving with the sound of a wind and tongues of fire, this falling is described as the 'gift of the Holy Spirit' (ἡ δωρεὰ τοῦ ἁγίου πνεύματος) being 'poured out' on the Gentiles (ἐκκέχυται; 10:45). This language occurs only here, in Peter's defence (11:17) and at Pentecost.[37] Similarly, the effect of the Spirit's outpouring is to produce glossolalic praise – 'they were speaking in tongues and glorifying God' (λαλούντων γλώσσαις καὶ μεγαλυνόντων τὸν θεόν; 10:46) – with a further linguistic parallel between τὰ μεγαλεῖα (2:11) and μεγαλυνόντων (10:46). The order is not the same, but the apostolic kerygma is proclaimed (10:36–43) and repentance[38] and water baptism are present in both narratives (10:47; cf. 2:38). Perhaps most pertinently for Peter's defence speech, the outpourings of the Spirit at Pentecost and on Cornelius's household are both followed by critical questioning to which Peter responds, although there is a significant difference in that the criticism in Acts 11 is intra-communal rather than extra-communal. The thorough development of parallels with the Pentecost narrative demonstrates that Peter's speech in Acts 11 can be expected to fulfil a similar function to his sermon in Acts 2, which offers an authoritative scriptural interpretation of God's action to a critical audience.

With this in mind, the speeches' respective relationships to Scripture deserve scrutiny. At Pentecost, tongues-speech is interpreted as the fulfilment of Joel's prophecy, and the kerygmatic sermon develops as an exposition of three Psalms. The speech relies on Scripture to make its own authority claim while offering a radical reinterpretation of the passages it cites on the basis of new REs. In Acts 11, Luke offers a further radical reinterpretation of the received framework: Peter's interpretation of the outpouring of the Spirit on Cornelius does not cite established Scripture, but twice uses elements from Luke's own narrative. First, Peter refers back to the events of Pentecost as 'in the beginning' (ἐν ἀρχῇ; 11:15). Conzelmann argues that this is a technical term pointing to a decisive beginning in salvation history,[39] and it refers here to 'the beginning of the

---

(Cambridge: Cambridge University Press, 1993, 116–19). Cf. however, the qualifications offered in Scott Shauf, *The Divine in Acts and in Ancient Historiography* (Minneapolis, MN: Fortress, 2015), 193–6.

[36] Cf. also the differences noted by Peterson (*Acts*, 339 n.63), though these are immaterial to my point.
[37] The two elements are present separately in 2:38–39 and 2:17–18, 33, respectively.
[38] That repentance remains in view for Peter's hearers is clarified in 11:18; cf. Turner, *Power*, 384–6.
[39] Hans Conzelmann, 'Was von Anfang war', in *Neutestamentliche Studien für Rudolf Bultmann zu seinem 70. Geburtstag am 20. August 1954*, ed. Walther Eltester (Berlin: Töpelmann, 1954), 194–201 (197, n.11). Elsewhere, in the NT the term refers to creation (Matt 19:4, 8; 24:21//Mark 10:6; 13:19; John 1:1–2; Heb 1:10; 2 Pet 3:4), the 'beginning' of the gospel message (Mark 1:1; Luke 1:2; John

post-resurrection community'.[40] In this way, Peter's speech refers to 'the beginning' of the fulfilment of Jesus' programmatic pronouncement in *Luke's own text* (Acts 1:5–8) to interpret the movement of the gospel to the Gentiles. Second, Peter refers back to the words of Jesus (11:16). The reference here is to the words of the risen Lord (1:5), which themselves rework the words of John the Baptist (Luke 3:16). Thus, this composition reuses traditions which are written down earlier within Luke's own narrative[41] as part of Peter's authoritative interpretation of God's most recent action in the same way that he used OT texts in Acts 2.[42]

Nor is this an isolated incident within Luke's writing.[43] Luke also draws on John the Baptist's prophecy from his Gospel on three other occasions, using language of 'the way' in combination with 'making straight' and/or 'salvation' (Acts 13:10; 16:17; 18:24–26),[44] and this kind of 'scripturalization' of elements of his own text is coherent with his broader approach. His narrative of fulfilment is clearly intended to be read in relation to OT prophecy, but it also includes predictions, such as Jesus' programmatic pronouncement in Acts 1:5–8. Thus, Luke combines OT prophecy and predictions within his own narrative to create a framework within which God's ongoing action in history must be interpreted if it is to be rightly understood. Frein highlights this in her discussion of Luke's presentation of John the Baptist: 'John's actions … are the fulfilment of God's plans as announced not only by the OT prophet Malachi but also by the angelic messenger shortly before his birth and by

---

15:27; 16:4) and the 'beginning' of Christian life (1 John 2:7, 24; 3:11; 2 John 5, 6). Cf. Gerhard Delling, 'ἄρχω', *TDNT* I: 478–89 (esp. 481–2).

[40] Pervo, *Acts*, 287, following Conzelmann. While I take Turner's point that it is 'wildly improbable' that Luke intends to suggest that the disciples were *converted* at Pentecost (*Power*, 343 n.68, contra James D. G. Dunn, *Baptism in the Spirit: A Re-Examination of the New Testament Teaching on the Gift of the Spirit in Relation to Pentecostalism Today* (London: SCM, 1970), 52), his claim that taking Pentecost as the 'beginning' of Christian experience is also arbitrary' goes too far. Assuming an original outpouring of the Spirit, it is in fact hard to understand how this would *not* be seen as inaugurating a new post-ascension era, in which God is present differently from the period of Jesus' personal presence.

[41] Hengel rightly points to the authority Luke discerns in his sources 'who were witnesses to the acts of Jesus "from the beginning" … [and] empowered missionary proclaimers of the new message' ('The Lukan Prologue and Its Eyewitnesses: The Apostles, Peter, and the Women', in *Earliest Christian History: History, Literature, and Theology*, ed. Michael F. Bird and Jason Maston (Tübingen: Mohr Siebeck, 2012), 548). Nonetheless, it remains the case that the saying referred to found stability as it is *transcribed within Luke's own text*.

[42] One potential counterargument is that Luke does not speak here about things 'written'. This is not actually problematic because Luke consistently uses verbs of speech to introduce scriptural citations in Peter's speeches, referring to 'what was *spoken* by the prophet Joel' (2:16), what 'David *says*' (2:25), what 'David *spoke*' (2:31) and what David 'himself *says*' (2:34) in his Pentecost sermon. Cf. further in this chapter, esp. notes 68–9.

[43] The citation of material included in Luke 10:7 as Scripture in 1 Tim 5:18 is also suggestive. Though it is a minority position, if this letter was in fact written by Paul it might imply the presence of stable traditions of Jesus' sayings which were accorded scriptural status. In this case, Luke's intention to offer a full, trustworthy textual version of such traditions could already be seen as an intent to write something scriptural. If 1 Tim is taken as a later document, this citation nevertheless represents an explicit and relatively early witness to the scriptural status of the Jesus sayings included in Luke's writings, which is implied already in his own self-citation here.

[44] Cf. Lear, *Eschatology*, 142–3, citing Luke 3:2–17 and Acts 13:10; 16:17; 18:24–26.

his Spirit-filled father at his birth.'[45] In this example, Luke presents John's actions as a fulfilment of both OT prophecy and prophecies within his own narrative. This establishes the possibility that his own story can add to the interpretive framework he derives from Scripture. In this instance, then, Luke reuses material from his own account of the fulfilment of Israel's tradition to frame Peter's authoritative interpretation of further REs in Acts 11.[46] When he uses elements from his own text in this way, he takes up his own account of Jesus' words and the Spirit's manifestation as having scriptural authority.

In this way, Peter's defence speech scripturalizes earlier elements of Luke's narrative to give an authoritative interpretation of God's action in his encounter with Cornelius which has a similar status to his sermon at Pentecost. This is further confirmed by Luke's presentation of the speech's impact: it 'silences' (ἡσύχασαν; 11:18) those who hear it who afterwards 'praised God' (ἐδόξασαν τὸν θεόν; 11:18). In silencing a community who 'were criticising' (διεκρίνοντο; 11:2) Peter brings their behaviour into line with the instruction of the Spirit to him that he 'should not judge' (μηδὲν διακρινόμενος; 10:19; μηδὲν διακρίναντα; 11:12). That being 'silenced' (ἡσύχασαν) has the sense of ceasing criticism in the face of a challenging commitment to God's surprising will elsewhere in Luke-Acts only reinforces the point. Of particular significance is Luke 14:4, where Jesus causes the Pharisees to 'fall silent' (ἡσύχασαν).[47] However, the response of praise (ἐδόξασαν) has an even stronger association with RE. As Pervo notes, such praise 'is the appropriate response to a miracle'.[48] It is used at significant moments in the Third Gospel to denote the shepherds' praise after they have seen Jesus (Luke 2:20), and the centurion's recognition of Jesus' innocence (Luke 23:47), as well as being a frequent response to miracles.[49] This is a significant shift: earlier in Luke's work it is RE itself which results in this kind of praise, but here Peter's report is sufficient to provoke the same reaction. In his portrayal of the Jerusalem convocation, Luke develops this still further by having James interpret Peter's speech in relation to established prophetic Scripture with Peter's witness acting as a source of revelation for the community's decision-making process.

---

[45] Brigid C. Frein, 'Narrative Predictions, Old Testament Prophecies and Luke's Sense of Fulfilment', *NTS* 40 (1994): 24.

[46] Parsons's suggestion that this dominical saying may derive from a 'gospel no longer extant' (*Acts*, 161) is unnecessary, especially given the fecundity of Luke 3:2–17 as a passage which frames missionary activity in Acts. Moreover, even if Luke *has* derived it from a source, the most likely intended allusion is to the programmatic statement at the beginning of Acts itself.

[47] Cf. also Acts 21:14: Paul's travel companions 'fall silent' (ἡσυχάσαμεν) when they see that he is resolved to travel to Jerusalem 'as a captive to the Spirit' (20:22), despite prophetic warnings about what will happen to him (cf. 21:4).

[48] Pervo, *Acts*, 288.

[49] E.g. Luke 5:25–27; 7:16; 13:13; 17:15; 18:43. Elsewhere in Acts it is associated with apostolic proclamation and salvation (4:21; 13:48; 21:20), particularly in relation to the Gentiles. There are two remaining uses: Luke 4:15 and Acts 3:13. In both cases the term is applied to Jesus. This strand possibly contributes to Luke's Christology as 'the verb can also acquire the new biblical sense of "to give and to have a share in the divine δόξα"' (Gerhard Kittel, 'δοξάζω', *TDNT* II: 253–4 (254)).

4.2.4. Peter's Jerusalem contribution (Acts 15:7–11)

Peter's second report is less substantial in its content, but its special status is possibly even more pronounced. After noting 'Peter's status as one who already knows the Spirit', Fowl points out that

> Peter's testimony is in two crucial respects not *his* testimony. First, Peter's testimony is not so much about what he has done as what he has seen God doing ... This is made most clear in 15:8 when he claims that God has testified (ἐμαρτύρησεν) to the 'cleansed hearts' of the Gentiles by 'giving them the Holy Spirit'. Here God not only becomes the subject of Peter's testimony, but the primary witness to it as well. The second respect in which Peter's testimony is not strictly his testimony concerns the fact that his account is not so much about what God has done to him ... as about what God had done to others.[50]

I will address the social aspect of Peter's testimony below (§4.3.1), but Fowl's analysis draws attention first to the prominence of God in Peter's speech. This is visible even at a grammatical level, as most of the verbs in his speech have God as subject.[51] Here, Peter is acting as a skilled knower, speaking in an authoritative voice about what God has done. Whereas in his defence speech, Peter concluded with a rhetorical question which allowed a slight distance between himself and his own conclusion – 'Who was I to be able to hinder God?'; ἐγὼ τίς ἤμην δυνατὸς κωλῦσαι τὸν θεόν; 11:17 – his contribution to the Jerusalem convocation offers a committed defence of God's impartiality. Peter argues that the gift of the Holy Spirit to the Gentiles demonstrates that they have been made clean by God who 'knows hearts' (ὁ καρδιογνώστης; 15:8) and that faith is the basis of salvation for both Jew and Gentile. In this speech, Peter shows that his conversion has taken full effect by presenting the divinely accredited position as his own.

Peter's witness to his experience-derived insight now stands on its own. Rather than interpreting God's action by reference to a received framework as he does at Pentecost and in his defence speech, he draws exclusively on his own experience and is even comfortable using this to challenge the theological claims of his opponents, accusing them of 'putting God to the test' in imposing too heavy a burden on Gentile converts. In fact, Peter's report itself now appears to require interpretation in relation to a received framework. After Barnabas and Paul have provided a necessary second witness,[52] James takes up the evidence and situates it scripturally with a composite citation based on LXX Amos 9:11–12.[53]

---

[50] Stephen E. Fowl, *Engaging Scripture: A Model for Theological Interpretation* (Oxford: Blackwell, 1998), 115, 116.
[51] Cf. Parsons, *Acts*, 211.
[52] Cf. Twelftree, 'Holy Scripture', 357.
[53] Richard Bauckham argues that this 'conflated quotation' of Amos and 'related texts which refer to the building of the eschatological Temple (Hos 3:4–5; Jer 12:15–16) and the conversion of the nations (Jer 12:15–16; Zech 8:22; Isa 45:20–3) in the messianic age' was likely derived from a source close to James along with the Apostolic Decree itself ('James and the Gentiles [Acts 15:13–21]', in *History, Literature, and Society in the Book of Acts*, ed. Ben Witherington III (Cambridge: Cambridge University Press, 1996), 154–84 (165)). Cf. also Twelftree who argues that the agreement of Acts

Here, James's speech functions similarly to Peter's Pentecost sermon and self-defence: it offers an authoritative interpretation of God's action with reference to a received, scriptural framework. This implies that Peter's report of his encounter with Cornelius and the Spirit's outpouring on the Gentiles is now functioning in the same way as actual REs functioned in Acts 2 and 10. Moreover, as Johnson notes, Luke depicts Peter's report as governing the interpretive process: '[James] does not say, "This agrees with the prophets," but says, "The words of the prophets agree with this." ... As Peter had come to a new understanding of Jesus' words *because of the gift of the Spirit*, so here the Old Testament is illuminated and interpreted by *the narrative of God's activity in the present*.'[54] In this way, Peter's speech comes to function as a source of revelation for the community at the Jerusalem convocation and the role his speech plays represents an important development because it creates a role for authoritative witness which Luke can claim for his own text.

Luke's account of the events of Pentecost established the possibility that embodied human speech could be a locus of the Spirit's revelatory presence, and the development of Peter's understanding and the divine validation of his insight allows him to represent God's witness to the Gentiles. This expands the range of expressions which can have a revelatory function to include the kind of inspired insight Peter develops in his dealings with Cornelius. It also allows Luke to introduce an element of communal discernment: Peter is not the only witness to the work of the Spirit in the lives of the Gentiles, but is accompanied by several circumcised believers (10:45–6, cf. 23), and his witness has to be weighed and received by the community for it to serve its purpose. This final point is associated with the move from report to writing, which is the subject of the next sections.

4.3. From report to decision: Critical communal reception

As noted above, there is an important social aspect involved in the development from inspired insight to writing. In the initial response to the outpouring of the Spirit on the Gentiles, members of the community seek to evaluate claims about God's recent action by questioning its relation to a culturally patterned framework, focusing on the issues of table-fellowship and circumcision (11:1–3). This carries through to the Jerusalem convocation, in which 'no little dispute' (ζητήσεως οὐκ ὀλίγης; 15:2) sees a gathering of 'apostles and elders' (15:6) reach a resolution which is apparently ratified by the whole church (15:22). I will argue that this narrative development allows Peter's paradigm shift to move from being a personal conviction to impacting the whole community, thus presenting an example of the intended impact of revelatory witness (§4.3.1). Further, at the Jerusalem convocation, James makes a decision on the basis of Peter's report and suggests that it be textualized (§4.3.2). I will argue that Luke's presentation of

---

15:16 and 4Q174 1.1.21.2.12 against extant LXX texts suggests the use of a different *Vorlage* (*People of the Spirit: Exploring Luke's View of the Church* (Grand Rapids, MI: Baker Academic, 2009), 161).

[54] Johnson, *Discernment*, 104–5; italics mine.

this process makes an implicit claim that the writing should carry scriptural authority for its addressees (§4.3.3), and that this should inform our understanding of Luke's purpose for his own writing (§4.4).

4.3.1. The critical role of the community

In his encounter with Cornelius, Peter is led to the realization that God shows no partiality (10:34). That this insight challenges communal understanding is made evident by the opposition which Peter immediately faces when he arrives in Jerusalem (11:1-3). Those criticizing Peter appear to accept that the Spirit fell on the Gentiles but disagree with his understanding of its theological significance: they allow that Gentiles may have 'accepted the word of the Lord' (ἐδέξαντο τὸν λόγον τοῦ θεοῦ; 11:1), but they want to know why Peter had table-fellowship with 'uncircumcised men' (ἄνδρας ἀκροβυστίαν; 11:3). In this dispute, Peter and those criticizing him agree on the evidence: the outpouring of the Holy Spirit meant that the Gentiles had received the word of the Lord. However, they disagree on its significance: their paradigms clash. Thus, Peter's encounter with Cornelius provides not only evidence[55] but also a new paradigm for understanding God's action: not only has the Spirit fallen on the Gentiles, but Peter has come to understand God's impartiality in a new way. On Luke's account, the resolution of the dispute is particularly reliant on Peter's witness: Paul and Barnabas also testify to God's action among the Gentiles (15:12), but it is Peter who first recognizes (10:34) and consistently argues for its theological implications (11:17; 15:8–10).

As Luke presents the process of decision-making, the community plays a critical role which draws out the significance of Peter's RE, though they do this partly by being in error. This function is anticipated earlier in the *Doppelwerk*: there is a connection between the criticism Peter faces and challenges Jesus faces in the Third Gospel (Luke 5:30; 15:2; 19:7). In those passages, Jesus asserts a new understanding of Scripture against the Pharisees and teachers of the law, and Peter does something similar at Pentecost, addressing the objections raised by outsiders (Acts 2:13). In Acts 11, however, the dispute is intra-communal: whereas at Pentecost, Peter stood up 'with the eleven' to deliver his sermon in a demonstration of the unity of the believers, he is now asserting a new understanding of Scripture in the face of questioning from members of his own community. In this way, the communal discernment glossed over in the brief reference to the unity of the twelve at Pentecost is brought to the fore in this narrative.

Luke uses a wordplay on κρίνω and its cognate διακρίνω to highlight this theme. In 11:1-3, he writes that when Peter came to Jerusalem 'those of the circumcision criticised him' (διεκρίνοντο πρὸς αὐτὸν οἱ ἐκ περιτομῆς; 11:2). The term used to describe the questioning of Peter, διακρίνω, occurs only in relation to this story in the Lukan *Doppelwerk*. Twice, in references which frame the response of the circumcised believers, the Spirit gives Peter a 'no judging' rule. When Peter initially encounters the

---

[55] As Johnson notes, 'Brute evidence always requires interpretation, making the very notion of brute evidence a misnomer' (*Biblical Knowing*, 142). In Luke's account, only Peter provides this interpretation.

messengers from Cornelius, he is told that he should go with them without 'doubting' (μηδὲν διακρινόμενος; 10:20), and when he reports the events, he claims he was told 'not to discriminate' (μηδὲν διακρίναντα; 11:12) between himself and them.[56]

Johnson rightly points out that 'what the Spirit forbade Peter to do toward the Gentiles, namely "debate/ make distinctions/ doubt" (10:20), these fellow Jews are now doing toward him'.[57] However, without the critical questioning of the community Peter's vision might have been personally significant, but would not have shaped the community's judgement. Rather than subverting the role of communal judgement and asserting the primacy of sheer RE, Luke shows how Peter's insight provokes a communal journey of discovery which roughly parallels the development of his own understanding. Whereas Peter came to the conclusion that God shows no favour on the basis of ethnic origin through a process of reasoning based on RE, though, the community is guided by his reports. In both cases Luke describes a process of inspired reasoning: reflection on Spirit-revealed content.

Peter's defence speech demands a recalibration of communal judgement in line with his Spirit-validated conclusion, and this is visible in the rhetorical question the condensed *peroratio* raises: 'who was I to be able to hinder God?' (ἐγὼ τίς ἤμην δυνατὸς κωλῦσαι τὸν θεόν; 11:17).[58] Peter's RE-shaped speech thus represents a call to the community to follow him in 'being converted'. On Luke's account, the whole community responds positively: their dissent is silenced and they praise God. Thus, the reception of Peter's report offers an exemplary response for Luke's readers to consider. While Peter's claims are challenging, they are ultimately received as authoritative on the basis of their close connection to REs, and allowed to reshape the community's understanding of God. At the Jerusalem convocation, this is taken a step further with the decision to crystallize the process of reflection on Peter's revelatory witness in writing.

4.3.2. James's judgement

In Acts 15 the resolution of chapter 11 has dissolved and the question has to be revisited. However, the earlier decision-making process remains relevant. As part of his report in 15:9 Peter rephrases his understanding of God's non-partiality, claiming that God 'did not discriminate' (οὐθὲν διέκρινεν) between Jew and Gentile in pouring out the Spirit. This demonstrated that the hearts of the Gentiles had been cleansed (15:8), implying that God had accepted them in their current state.[59] As with his earlier defence speech, Peter's contribution again 'silences' his hearers (Ἐσίγησεν; 15:12). It also forms the basis for James to 'judge' (κρίνω; 15:14). Here, the wordplay which highlights the role

---

[56] Cf. Parson, *Acts*, 156: 'Luke makes full use of the polyvalence of the word.' The final use of the term in Acts 15:9 refers to the fact that the outpouring of the Spirit proves that God no longer 'distinguishes' between Jew and Gentile.
[57] Johnson, *Acts*, 197.
[58] Cf. e.g. Parsons's rhetorical analysis of this short speech (*Acts*, 157).
[59] Cf. Loren T. Stuckenbruck, 'The "Cleansing" of the Gentiles: Background for the Rationale behind the Apostles' Decree in Acts 15', in *Aposteldekret und antikes Vereinswesen*, ed. Markus Öhler (Tübingen: Mohr Siebeck, 2009), 65–90 (87).

of communal discernment comes to its ultimate fruition as James positively renders 'the judgement to which the Spirit has been pointing at least from chapter 10',[60] putting an end to doubt and discrimination.

James's speech also sets the agenda in two significant directions. First, it unifies 'the whole church' (ὅλῃ τῇ ἐκκλησίᾳ; 15:22) with 'one accord' (ὁμοθυμαδόν; 15:25). This strong unity marks the early chapters of Acts (2:46; 4:24; 5:12) and it is a feature of the pre-Pentecostal community which sets the scene for the action of the Spirit (1:14).[61] The unity of the community here highlights that this is an idealized account which should inform the reader's response to Luke's own narrative, further emphasizing the importance of this episode to an understanding of Luke's purpose. Into this unified context, James's speech secondly introduces the idea of writing. Indeed, his decision[62] is specifically 'to write to' the Gentiles (ἐπιστεῖλαι αὐτοῖς; 15:20). With this decision, the epistemological process of discovery which began with Peter and Cornelius's visions and progressed through communal discernment to James's right judgement will now crystallize in writing.

4.3.3. From decision to inspired writing: The Apostolic Decree

The writing of the Apostolic Decree textualizes an inspired insight (15:28), and this is the first such occurrence within Luke's narrative. He draws attention to the significance of this development in his linguistic choices, as 'the formal language of direct citation of Scripture returns in James' speech'[63] for the first time in the story of the inclusion of the Gentiles (15:15). This both highlights the textual nature of the Scriptures James is citing at a critical moment and provides context for 15:23, which details how 'the apostles and elders together with the whole church' (15:22) 'wrote with their own hand' (γράψαντες διὰ χειρὸς αὐτῶν; 15:23)[64] to the Gentile believers. This phrase not only attests the authenticity and trustworthiness of the letter but also serves to emphasize the physical act of writing.[65] In this sense, there is a similarity to Pentecost: there

---

[60] Fowl, *Engaging Scripture*, 111.

[61] The relevance of ὁμοθυμαδόν is likely recognized in the 'intelligent correction' of 2:1 to include the term in certain manuscripts (cf. Pervo, *Acts*, 60).

[62] The decision is made in the first person, and communal involvement is reserved until after James's decision has been communicated (grammatically, the head verb is κρίνω, which governs the two infinitives which present the positive and negative implications of James's judgement). Twelftree rightly argues that though communal assent is implied, the inspiration claimed in the letter is mediated through the discernment process and contained within James's decision (*People*, 162), though cf. also Fowl on James as representative (*Engaging Scripture*, 112).

[63] Gail R. O'Day, 'The Citation of Scripture as a Key to Characterization in Acts', in *Scripture and Traditions: Essays on Early Judaism and Christianity in Honor of Carl R. Holladay*, NovTSup 129, ed. Patrick Gray and Gail R. O'Day (Leiden: Brill, 2008), 207–21 (220).

[64] While the participle γράψαντες dangles without explicit subject, it clearly agrees with the implicit subject of 'it seemed to the apostles and to the elders' (ἔδοξεν τοῖς ἀποστόλοις καὶ τοῖς πρεσβυτέροις; so e.g. Fitzmyer, *Acts*, 564; Mikael C. Parsons and Martin Culy, *Acts: A Handbook on the Greek Text*, BHGNT (Waco, TX: Baylor, 2003), 297).

[65] The translation of διὰ χειρὸς αὐτῶν is my own contra Parsons and Culy who take it to refer to the hand of the deliverer (*Acts*, 297). If, however, the subject is supplied (see immediately above, 249 n.71), there is no reason to assume that the antecedent for the pronoun is not also that of the supplied subject doing the sending and writing. In light of the crisis concerning authorized messengers and messages which gave rise to the convocation (cf. Acts 15:1–4), Paul's repeated

tongues-speech occurred when speakers exercised their voices as the Spirit gave them utterance; here, a letter which claims to express the opinion of the Spirit (15:28) is written by the hands of the community leaders.

The written communication of the communal decision also includes reference to its support through the spoken words of the delegation bearing it: representatives have been chosen (15:25) to travel with Paul and Barnabas 'to announce the same message by word of mouth' (διὰ λόγου ἀπαγγέλλοντας τὰ αὐτά; 15:27). The letter allows the leaders themselves to communicate their decision, making them notionally present despite their physical absence – similar to how Paul communicated decisions in his own authoritative voice via letter (1 Cor 7:6, 8, 12), assuming he achieved sufficient 'spiritual presence' through his writing (1 Cor 5:3; Col 2:5) to do this.[66] Thus, despite the fact that the Apostolic Decree is also supplemented by the employment of representatives who are presented as community-validated prophets (Acts 15:32) capable of teaching those to whom the letter is addressed (15:22, 27, 32), the revelatory function established for speech at Pentecost is claimed for this writing at this point in Luke's narrative.

After the Jerusalem convocation has reached a climax with James's decision, Luke recounts the content of the Apostolic Decree. It is distilled from the foregoing narrative to particular ethical recommendations, but the letter still contextualizes these as the united response of 'the apostles and elders of the brothers' to the actions of 'those who have gone out from us' (15:24–25). This missive is clearly intended to offer an authoritative resolution to a heated dispute in Christian communities by offering guidance to Gentile believers as to how they can behave in ways which should enable ongoing table-fellowship within mixed Christian communities. However, perhaps the most striking element of the letter is that it explicitly presents itself as communicating inspired content: 'For it seemed to the Holy Spirit and us that no further burden is to be put on you than these essentials' (ἔδοξεν γὰρ τῷ πνεύματι τῷ ἁγίῳ καὶ ἡμῖν μηδὲν πλέον ἐπιτίθεσθαι ὑμῖν βάρος πλὴν τούτων τῶν ἐπάναγκες; 15:28).

The process of textualization not only clarifies the importance of a particular content but also results in the creation of a physical document. In embedding this letter within his narrative, Luke offers 'a kind of documentary "proof," an added authoritative testimony to the story he narrates'.[67] At the same time as deriving authority from the citation of documentary evidence, though, he also presents this text as an authoritative document which is related to established Scripture in two ways. First, it is related to the prophets. As I noted at the beginning of this section, James situates

---

reference to his own hand at the end of epistles is pertinent, with the connection with authenticity particularly pronounced in 2 Thess 3:17 (see also 1 Cor 16:21; Gal 6:11–12; Col 4:18).

[66] However, cf. John M. G. Barclay's argument that 'at the time they were written, letters were Paul's least effective social tool' ('The Letters of Paul and the Construction of Early Christian Networks', in *Letters and Communities: Studies in the Socio-Political Dimensions of Ancient Epistolography*, ed. Paola Ceccarelli et al. (Oxford: Oxford University Press, 2018), 289–302 (300)). Here, Barclay notes a privileging of the living voice even where it disadvantages Paul as letter writer, though he perhaps neglects the fact that Paul's letters were most likely sent with envoys who 'performed' them, and they were thus likely delivered in the living voice, albeit not Paul's own.

I will include Ephesians and Colossians alongside the seven 'undisputed' letters, where relevant, because I take them as Pauline.

[67] Parsons, *Acts*, 217.

Peter's experience scripturally by referring to what the prophets wrote, reintroducing a solemn citation formula at a significant moment. This linguistic choice is further emphasized by a comparison with Luke's tendency to introduce scriptural citations with verbs of speech,[68] which is particularly pronounced in Petrine speeches.[69] In using a verb of writing, James draws attention to the physical form of the prophetic books, and thereby to writing as a prophetic activity. This is significant within Acts, where scriptural interpretation has also become associated with prophecy.[70] Thus, James's speech not only creates a context of unity within which the activity of the Spirit can be expected but also presents a model for the form which this action could take in the inspiration of writing.

Two further observations strengthen this connection. One the one hand, affirming the disciples as a group and Peter in particular as prophets through their connection with Jesus is a literary strategy pursued throughout Luke-Acts.[71] A key element in the way this prophetic authority is constructed is in the use of scriptural citations in characters' speeches – most prominently with Peter, but similarly with James at the Jerusalem convocation itself and in the immediate context of the writing of the Apostolic Decree.[72] On the other hand, the chosen representatives of the community, Judas and Silas, are presented as being 'themselves prophets' (αὐτοὶ προφῆται; 15:32) and fulfilling that function for the community while at Antioch delivering the letter. Thus, Luke goes out of his way to present the letter as a thoroughly prophetic communication. It stands alongside prophetic activity by communally attested representatives and in continuity with the written texts of the OT prophets whose authority James claims in interpreting Peter's experience. Here, this prophetic authority is being extended both to the substance of James's decision and the means of its communication: as the textual

---

[68] Verbs of writing are used in 1:20; 7:42; 13:29, 33; 15:15; 23:5; 24:14, while verbs of speech are used in 2:16, 25, 31, 34; 3:22, 25; 4:25; 7:48; 13:22, 34, 35, 40, 47; 25:22; 28:25. In Stephen's speech, there are also multiple references to things said by God, with various scriptural citations introduced with verbs of speaking and the accent clearly on the felt impact of trans-empirical reality in the life of the original hearer: 7:3, 5, 6, 31–4. There are also others, introduced as the spoken words of actors within the biblical narrative: 7:26, 27–8, 35, 37, 40. Finally, one scriptural citation is introduced with the verb ἀναγινώσκω (8:32), with the implication that a written text is being read aloud. Cf. also the reference to what the prophet 'says' in the cited text in 8:34.

[69] Verbs of speaking are used in Petrine speeches to introduce scriptural citations in 2:16, 25, 31, 34; 3:22, 25. Further, 1:16 refers explicitly to Scripture coming 'by the mouth of David' (διὰ στόματος Δαυὶδ) as the context for the sole introduction of Scripture with a verb of writing in a Petrine speech in 1:20. Similarly, in 3:18 Peter refers to the things God 'announced beforehand by the mouth of all the prophets' (προκατήγγειλεν διὰ στόματος πάντων τῶν προφητῶν) and the same image is picked up in 3:21. The same phrase occurs in the communal prayer when Peter and John return after their examination by the chief priests and elders in 4:25 in close connection with the introduction of a scriptural citation by a verb of speaking: 'by … the mouth of David your servant saying' (διὰ … στόματος Δαυὶδ παιδός σου εἰπών).

[70] Cf. E. Earle Ellis, *Prophecy and Hermeneutic in Earliest Christianity*, WUNT II.18 (Tübingen: Mohr Siebeck, 1978), 129–34; John R. Levison, *Filled with the Spirit* (Grand Rapids, MI: Eerdmans, 2009), 347–57.

[71] So esp. e.g. Johnson, *Acts*, 12–14. Cf. Paul Minear, *To Heal and Reveal: The Prophetic Vocation According to Luke* (New York: Seabury, 1976), 148–9: Luke-Acts is 'an account of the training of apprentice seers and exorcists … a succession of prophets from Abel to Paul'.

[72] O'Day, 'Citation of Scripture', 212–20, explores Peter's characterization, but does not consider James.

crystallization of an inspired insight, the Apostolic Decree represents the first writing of the Spirit-filled community of prophets in Acts.[73]

Second, as well as being presented as a prophetic communication after the manner of the OT prophetic literature, it is possible to see the Apostolic Decree as being related to the Torah as a liturgical text. James explains his decision to write to the churches by referring to the way in which 'from ancient generations, in every city, Moses has had those who proclaim him in the synagogues, reading aloud every sabbath' (Μωϋσῆς γὰρ ἐκ γενεῶν ἀρχαίων κατὰ πόλιν τοὺς κηρύσσοντας αὐτὸν ἔχει ἐν ταῖς συναγωγαῖς κατὰ πᾶν σάββατον ἀναγινωσκόμενος; 15:21). This is often read as a comment on the connection between the content of the Apostolic Decree and the Law.[74] However, it also contains a reference to the synagogual practice of public reading of Scripture. In making this connection, Luke presents this writing as standing in continuity with the liturgical reading of the Torah. The implication is that this letter is a new text that can be read in a worship gathering to address the question of what is required of God's people in light of Peter's new insight into God's impartiality. At the least, the possible liturgical use of the letter seems to have informed Luke's depiction of what an ideal reception would look like: in 15:30–32 the Apostolic Decree is delivered to a gathered congregation and received as an exhortation alongside other prophetic speech of the kind which likely marked out the worship services of earliest Christian communities.[75]

Whether or not Luke is here reproducing a physical document in his possession and referring to its historical first reading, assuming that his depiction of this event was plausible to his intended readers means allowing the possibility that early Christian writings were read in worship gatherings and received as exhortations alongside prophetic and inspired speech in the living voice and OT Scripture – as divine revelation. The possibility of liturgical origins for the Gospels has already been suggested[76] and the likely function of Paul's epistles as communal addresses makes such a portrayal historically plausible. Colossians 3:16 potentially hints in this direction when it refers to 'the word of Christ' in the context of the worship service. Paul's own letter appears to have been intended to convey something of that word (cf. Col 1:5, 25) despite

---

[73] For this characterisation of the group, cf. Robert P. Menzies, 'The Persecuted Prophets: A Mirror Image of Luke's Spirit-Inspired Church', in *The Spirit and Christ in the New Testament and Christian Theology*, ed. I. Howard Marshall, Volker Rabens and Cornelis Bennema (Grand Rapids, MI: Eerdmans, 2012), 52–70 (esp. 52–61).

[74] So e.g. Eckhard J. Schnabel, *Acts*, ZECNT (Grand Rapids, MI: Zondervan, 2014), 646; Peterson, *Acts*, 435–6; Pervo, *Acts*, 378–9.

[75] Cf. Christopher Forbes (*Prophecy and Inspired Speech in Early Christianity and Its Hellenistic Environment* (Tübingen: Mohr, 1995), 241–50) who argues that Christian prophecy occurred exclusively in congregational settings (246) and 'was a widespread and powerful force within early Christianity for more than a century' (249).

[76] A key source in the discussion is Justin Martyr, *1 Apol.*, 67 (ANF 1:186) which confirms that by that point (c.150) when Christians gathered 'on the day called Sunday, all who live in cities or in the country gather together to one place, and the memoirs of the apostles or the writings of the prophets are read, as long as time permits'. D. Moody Smith argues that this description implies a scriptural function within the worship service for the Gospels and adds, 'Quite possibly this practice was established well before the time of Justin' ('When Did the Gospels Become Scripture?' *JBL* 119 (2000): 3–20, 5). Paul F. Bradshaw emphasizes the lack of earlier evidence (*The Search for the Origins of Christian Worship: Sources and Methods for the Study of Early Liturgy* (Oxford: Oxford University Press, 1992), 30–56). However, this does not constitute an absolute limit on what is probable.

his physical absence (Col 2:5), and was likely read in the worship service.[77] In this sense, Luke's depiction of the creation and initial reception of the Apostolic Decree is consistent with patterns of written communication visible elsewhere in the texts of the NT. On this reading, then, Luke uses James's speech to establish a connection with the prophets and with the law for the Apostolic Decree. Luke's familiarity with the grouping of the law and the prophets as a shorthand for a proto-canonical collection of authoritative texts[78] further suggests that he may have established this connection intentionally.

What Luke's narrative makes plain is that he perceives the claim that the Apostolic Decree conveys inspired content to have been initially dependent on its proximity to RE. Peter's RE-derived insight into God's impartiality gave the document both its *raison d'être* and its potential authority, though the latter is clearly dependent on communal acceptance. In the next section, I will consider the implications of the depiction of this process whereby REs crystallized in a text which Luke presents as authoritative and inspired for his own writing.

4.4. Writing about writing: Luke-Acts in light of the prologue and the inclusion of the Gentiles

Luke's account of the creation of the Apostolic Decree details the process of theological reflection which produced an early Christian document. Accordingly, his account of its creation may have implications for an understanding of his intentions for his own writing despite evident differences between the two texts.[79] As Twelftree notes, 'Luke would have carefully crafted [his portrayal of the writing of the Apostolic Decree] so that his readers could see how he understands such theological creativity arises',[80] and it is reasonable to extend this also to inspired writing. In the dual prooemium Luke reflects on his own project, and this makes his intentions in writing somewhat

---

[77] Cf. Markus Barth and Helmut Blanke, *Colossians*, trans. Astrid B. Beck, AB 34B (London: Yale University Press, 1994), 426. Though Barth and Blanke argue that this is 'a request of God to continue to allow his word to dwell also among the Colossians', it is possible that Paul considered his letter one way in which the 'word which proclaims the Messiah ... and by which the Messiah himself is received as Lord' could continue to inform his addressees, but cf. the more pessimistic evaluation of Barclay, 'Letters', 299–300.

[78] Luke 16:16; 24:27, 44; Acts 13:15; 24:14; 28:23; cf. also 'Moses and the prophets' in Luke 16:29, 31; Acts 26:22. It is unlikely the inclusion of 'writings' in Luke 24:44 refers to a closed, tripartite canon, but this formula probably refers to a collection of authoritative Scriptures, with the law being the more stable collection. Cf. Timothy H. Lim, *The Formation of the Jewish Canon* (New Haven, CT: Yale University, 2013), 156–66. This remains the case even if such stable collections were not viewed as static but open to new contributions, cf. Eva Mroczek, *The Literary Imagination in Jewish Antiquity* (Oxford: Oxford University Press), 2016.

[79] Luke's *Doppelwerk* retells the events surrounding the origins of the earliest Christian community in narrative form, apparently to address perceived shortcomings in the material available to Theophilus, whereas the Apostolic Decree offers specific ethical guidance in response to a particular question. Moreover, although Luke implies that the Apostolic Decree *claimed* scriptural authority, a key difference between the reception history of the two writings might perhaps be their ability to *achieve lasting communal acceptance* of this claim.

[80] Twelftree, 'Holy Scripture', 356.

visible. I will argue that Luke uses his prologue to situate his work in relation to both established Scripture and recent REs and that he does this in order to present his writing as a textual witness to REs which extends the story of God's interactions with his people begun in the OT (§4.4.1). This is complemented by the emphases present in the narrative of the inclusion of the Gentiles, and I will argue that the character of this narrative suggests that Luke intended to write a scriptural history (§4.4.2). Finally, I will conclude by arguing that taken together, the emphases present in the Lukan prologue and the depiction of the progression from RE to inspired writing in the narratives of Pentecost and the inclusion of the Gentiles suggest that Luke-Acts was intended to be understood as a scriptural writing whose authority claims are rooted in its connection to RE (§4.4.3).

4.4.1. The prologue (Luke 1:1-4)

The polished style of the period with which Luke begins his Gospel has long been recognized:[81] the balanced protasis and apodosis each include three parallel elements, and the unusually literary linguistic register is marked by the density of *hapax legomena* in these verses. Despite the author's apparent care, the meaning of practically every word has been contested. Nonetheless, the prologue offers a statement of intent from the author and Brown is therefore right to argue that 'unless we are to suppose a discrepancy between the author's *declared* purpose and his *real* purpose, it would seem reasonable to expect that all hypotheses concerning Luke's purpose be related somehow to what the author himself says'[82] in these verses.

The relevance of the Gospel prologue to Acts is, however, contested on two fronts: scope and function. First, it has been argued that the Gospel prologue is only intended to refer to that text. This argument is rooted in debates regarding the relationship between Luke and Acts addressed above, where I argued for the literary unity of Luke-Acts (§3.1). There, I noted Alexander's persuasive argument that literary unity could be considered established if 'the significant omission or holding over of narrative detail from the first volume to the second'[83] is visible, which appears to be the case in respect both of the gentile mission and the discussion of clean and unclean.[84] Even if the literary unity of the works is challenged, however, the backwards glance in the prologue of Acts 1:1 to 'the first word' (Τὸν μὲν πρῶτον λόγον) establishes a connection between the two works which presents Acts as deriving its purpose from that articulated at the beginning of the Third Gospel even as it signals a change in subject.

---

[81] Cf. classically, Eduard Norden, *Agnostos theos: Untersuchungen zur Formengeschichte religiöser Rede* (Leipzig: B.G. Teubner, 1913), 316.
[82] Schuyler Brown, 'The Role of the Prologues in Determining the Purpose of Luke-Acts', in *Perspectives on Luke-Acts*, ed. Charles H. Talbert (Edinburgh: T&T Clark, 1978), 99–111 (100; italics original).
[83] Loveday Alexander, 'Reading Luke-Acts from Back to Front', in *The Unity of Luke-Acts*, ed. Jos Verheyden (Leuven: Peeters, 1999), 421.
[84] So e.g. Michael Wolter, 'Die Proömien des lukanischen Doppelwerks (Lk 1,1-4 und Apg 1,1-2)', in *Die Apostelgeschichte im Kontext antiker und frühchristlicher Historiographie*, BZABR 162, ed. Jörg Frey, Clare K. Rothschild and Jens Schröter (Berlin: De Gruyter, 2009), 476–94 (481).

Second, the question of the prologue's function has been raised. This is partly a result of its literary style which is at odds with the rest of Luke's work. This has led to the suggestion of several possible types of comparative material for this kind of introduction, including histories[85] and technical or 'trade' books.[86] That the issue remains disputed speaks against allowing a tentative identification of literary function to overdetermine interpretations of the prologue as if it were entirely separable from the rest of Luke's writing. Rather, it makes better sense to read it as a stylized statement of intent from the author, an approach in keeping with Luke's tendency to deploy a variety of literary styles to serve his own purposes elsewhere. Notwithstanding these reservations, Luke's designation of his narrative as a διήγησις ('account'; Luke 1:1) likely identifies the work as historiographical, with the brevity of the prologue accounted for by the relative brevity of the work itself[87] as well as its breadth of intended audience.[88] Such an understanding allows for relative coherence between the prologue and the content of Luke-Acts,[89] and makes sense of the concern for an ordered story which can demonstrate the certainty of traditions.

Luke 1:1–4 and Acts 1:1–2 also introduce an author and an audience. Luke presents himself as someone who can be trusted to enhance the understanding of the reader and bring them to know rightly. 'Having followed everything from the beginning carefully' (παρηκολουθηκότι ἄνωθεν πᾶσιν ἀκριβῶς; 1:3), he is capable of offering a full, orderly account of the events fulfilled which can allow his reader to know 'the truth' (τὴν ἀσφάλειαν; 1:4) of what he has been taught. This authority claim at the beginning of the Gospel is made on the basis of access to 'eyewitnesses and servants of the word' (αὐτόπται καὶ ὑπηρέται γενόμενοι τοῦ λόγου; 1:2), meaning Luke's authority is derived from close acquaintance with the witness of others to their encounters with Jesus and the Spirit.[90] In this way, the prologue situates the wider work and its author in

---

[85] Classically articulated by Henry J. Cadbury, 'Commentary on the Preface of Luke', in *The Beginnings of Christianity*, ed. F. J. Foakes Jackson and Kirsopp Lake (London: Macmillan, 1922), II:489–510, and widely followed.

[86] Influentially, Loveday Alexander, *The Preface to Luke's Gospel*, SNTSMS 78 (Cambridge: Cambridge University Press, 1993).

[87] Cf. Wolter, 'Proömien', 477.

[88] This is a key insight of Alexander, *Preface*: Luke's work is presented as 'middle-brow' rather than 'high-brow'.

[89] This is a key weakness of Alexander's suggestion that the prologue is best understood as inhabiting the 'scientific tradition': the content does not fit this designation, and the prologue cannot be deemed completely separable (*Preface*); cf. David E. Aune, 'Luke 1,1-4: Historical or Scientific Prooimion?' in *Paul, Luke and the Graeco-Roman World*, JSNTSup 217, ed. Alf Christopherson et al. (Sheffield: Sheffield Academic, 2002), 138–48.

[90] An early date could aid elements of my argument by speaking in favour of the likelihood of events recognizable to his readers underlying elements of Luke's narrative and thus the experiential shaping of his text, but a late date does not undermine it. Further, Luke's intentional use of the category of individual author and designation of an initial audience means that these concepts remain useful in interrogating the communicative intention of the text itself even if the text of the *Doppelwerk* was not entirely stable (cf. Matthew D. C. Larsen, 'Accidental Publication, Unfinished Texts and the Traditional Goals of New Testament Textual Criticism', *JSNT* 39 (2017): 362–87. Consequently, Broadhead's argument that such a 'work in progress' as the Gospels represent 'is best understood through its history of tradition, which includes both its composition history and its transmission history' does not undermine my attempt to examine the representation of authorial intent embedded within the text itself (*The Gospel of Matthew on the Landscape of Antiquity*, WUNT 378 (Tübingen: Mohr Siebeck, 2017), 319).

relation to an intended audience. The narrative is presented as the fulfilment of existing Scriptures and intended to stand alongside other gospel writings, and its author is presented as someone who can accurately convey the importance of the traditions he retells.

As for the audience, Luke addresses both works to Theophilus, likely naming a wealthy patron who made the work possible.[91] More important for my argument, however, is the claim that Luke's story is one attempt among many to tell of the 'deeds fulfilled among us' (τῶν πεπληροφορημένων ἐν ἡμῖν πραγμάτων; Luke 1:1). The key concerns of the prologue – to establish the knowledge of certain truth for its audience through a careful examination of sources – are coherent with ancient historiographical aims,[92] but the reference to fulfilment immediately situates the work in relation to the OT and implies an intended audience which already understands these texts to be significant. Thus, Luke breaks with Hellenistic understandings of history even here taking the OT as his primary intertext: the events he reports are a 'fulfilment' primarily from a scripturally informed perspective. This suggests that Luke is writing for an audience who took 'the law and the prophets' as Scripture and would thus be interested in their 'fulfilment' in recent events. The recognition of other textual retellings of the events covered in Luke-Acts further suggests that Luke's intended audience is primarily Christian.[93] Indeed, the reference to other written Gospels may even suggest that Luke expected his work to be read in Christian gatherings.[94]

The dependence on established Scripture is also visible in the kind of history Luke tells. Sterling rightly argues that Luke's notion of what history is derives from the historical writings in the OT: texts like the Deuteronomistic history 'provided the author with his understanding of what history is ... [a] confessional stance towards

---

[91] Parsons argues that the name has a literary function: 'Regardless of the historical background, from a literary perspective Theophilus functions to circumscribe the reception of Acts' (*Acts*, 26). Notwithstanding Parsons's useful suggestion that the invocation of Theophilus shapes the reception of Acts as a literary work, it is more historically plausible that the name refers to a patron than an 'ideal reader' and this limits the extent to which Theophilus can be considered a literary ideal, especially if he was known to the first readers of the Gospel and Acts.

[92] The key features of the prologue which mark out Luke's narrative as historical writing include: (1) its designation as a διήγησιν ('account'); (2) the intention to write a καθεξῆς ('orderly') narrative; (3) the author's claim of personal assessment of the apparent events; (4) the concern for sources, reference to 'autopsy' and commitment to writing ἀκριβῶς ('accurately'); (5) the claim to offer τὴν ἀσφάλειαν ('the truth'). Cf. Daryl D. Schmidt's conclusion: 'The conventions reflected in Luke's preface signal the use of "historical" narrative models, without limiting the source of such models' ('Rhetorical Influences and Genre: Luke's Preface and the Rhetoric of Hellenistic Historiography', in *Jesus and the Heritage of Israel: Luke's Narrative Claim upon Israel's Legacy*, ed. David P. Moessner (Harrisburg: Trinity, 1999), 27–60 (59–60)).

[93] Cf. C. K. Barrett, *Luke the Historian in Recent Study* (London: Epworth, 1961), 63: 'No Roman official would have filtered out so much of what to him would be theological and ecclesiastical rubbish in order to reach so tiny a grain of relevant apology.' However, cf. Hengel's suggestion that Theophilus was a high-ranking 'sympathizer' ('Lukan Prologue', 537).

[94] A later date for Luke-Acts makes this more likely, given the likelihood that readings from other Gospel writings formed part of the worship service by the second century. Indeed, if Luke-Acts is dated to c. 120, this would be only around thirty years before Justin Martyr's claim that 'the memoirs of the apostles or the writings of the prophets are read' in Christian worship gatherings (*1 Apol.*, 67 (*ANF* I:186)).

the activity of God in human activities'.[95] Thus, despite the strong stylistic influence of Hellenistic rhetoric on the prologue, its content already begins to situate Luke's own writing in relation to Scripture: it crystallizes in textual form the fulfilment of the OT in the Christ-event, and this is the sum total of 'the events which have been fulfilled among us'.

In asserting such a close relationship to established Scripture, Luke comes close to an authority-claiming strategy of 'rewritten Scriptures'. As Crawford notes, texts such as Jubilees offer 'innerscriptural exegesis' which is intended to clarify the meaning of the 'authoritative base text' and claim equal status for the new work, though not as a replacement.[96] In his prologue Luke signals his intent to pick up the OT in light of God's new action, deriving a measure of authority from doing so in much the same way as characters do within his narrative.[97] A key difference between Luke and the rewritten Scripture texts at Qumran is that the impetus for Luke's writing comes self-consciously from new events in which the impact of trans-empirical reality has been felt. Consequently, Luke is not limited to reworking available Scripture. Rather, he has a responsibility to extend its story in response to new REs, and in doing so to disseminate the new understanding of God they have prompted.

At the same time, though, Moody Smith points out that Luke actually does rewrite Mark.[98] This raises the question of the status of both Luke's synoptic source material and his own writing for the community: 'But how was Mark by then actually functioning? ... Arguably, both Matthew and Luke rewrite, augment, and re-present the Markan narrative to produce documents better suited to function as Scripture for Christian audiences generally.'[99] By taking up existing material from other gospel writings, it is possible that Luke has 'canonized' his source and 'sacralized' his own writing in a similar manner to rewritten Scriptures at Qumran.[100] Larsen's argument that the early understanding of Mark as a 'rough draft' makes it possible to imagine later gospel writings as an extension of a fluid textual tradition[101] could also point in a similar direction, given the early emergence of authoritative Jesus-traditions. Indeed, Luke attempts to situate his work in a positive relation to other gospel writings, as a text which can clarify the truth of what Theophilus has been taught. He does this on the basis of his being able to accurately convey both the events which have occurred and their significance thanks to his careful investigation of them. In his prologue, then, Luke presents his *Doppelwerk* as a 'scriptural history'. This is not intended as an

---

[95] Gregory E. Sterling, *Historiography and Self-Definition: Josephos, Luke-Acts, and Apologetic Historiography* (Leiden: Brill, 1992), 358.
[96] Cf. Sidnie White Crawford, *Rewriting Scripture in Second Temple Times* (Grand Rapids, MI: Eerdmans, 2008), 145–9.
[97] Cf. O'Day, 'Characterization', on Peter. Similarly, Levison (*Filled*, 347–57) reads scriptural interpretation as a mark of Spirit-filling in Acts, and Ellis (*Prophecy and Hermeneutic*, 130–8) reads it as a prophetic act.
[98] Moody Smith, 'Gospels Become Scripture', 10.
[99] Moody Smith, 'Gospels Become Scripture', 10.
[100] Cf. George J. Brooke, 'Between Authority and Canon: The Significance of Reworking the Bible for Understanding the Canonical Process', in *Reworking the Bible: Apocryphal and Related Texts at Qumran*, ed. Esther Chazon, Devorah Dimant and Ruth Anne Clements (Leiden: Brill, 2005).
[101] Larsen, 'Accidental Publication', 377–80.

alternative generic designation for Luke-Acts, but as a label to capture Luke's intention to offer an authoritative account of God's dealings with his people which extends the OT story into the present and details the origins of the new community Luke is a part of. These emphases come to the fore in the narrative of the inclusion of the Gentiles, suggesting that it is an exemplary episode within Luke's wider work that can illuminate my discussion of Luke's self-understanding in writing his text.

4.4.2. The inclusion of the Gentiles as exemplar

In retelling the 'events fulfilled among us' in Jesus' life, death, resurrection and ongoing impact for a Christian audience, Luke starts 'from the beginning' (ἀπ' ἀρχῆς; 1:2). This lends intuitive support to Marguerat's designation of Luke-Acts as a whole as a 'narrative of beginnings' – a biblically derived category which speaks to the text's function rather than its genre.[102] This is particularly the case when it comes to the inclusion of the Gentiles. In Acts 10–11 and 15, Luke details the spread of the Gospel beyond the Jew-Gentile boundary, and consequently the beginning of a new kind of community.

There are also linguistic and conceptual echoes between the prologue and this narrative which strengthen the connection.[103] The most superficial are repeated references to the 'beginning' (ἀρχή; Luke 1:2; Acts 10:11; 11:5, 15) and to 'handing over' (παραδίδωμι; Luke 1:2; Acts 15:28). There are linguistic connections here, but the thought is different: the 'beginnings' refer to the appearance of Christ and the outpouring of the Spirit, respectively; the prologue speaks of the handing over of tradition, whereas the Apostolic Decree refers to people who have 'handed over' their lives.

More suggestively, there are also conceptual echoes with less secure linguistic connections. First, Luke uses the *hapax legomenon* αὐτόπται to describe the 'eyewitnesses' who, together with the servants of the word, have handed on tradition (Luke 1:2), and Peter's eyewitness reports of the Spirit falling on the Gentiles clearly hold great importance throughout that episode and particularly at the Jerusalem convocation. Further, Luke uses the verbal form 'to see' (ἰδεῖν; Acts 15:6) to describe the activity of the apostles and elders in discussing the matter: Peter's 'eyewitness' brings his interlocutors to 'see' the matter correctly. Second, Luke sets himself in the context of 'many [who] have undertaken to write an account' (πολλοὶ ἐπεχείρησαν ἀνατάξασθαι διήγησιν; Luke 1:1) in the prologue and places Peter's report in the context of 'much seeking' (Πολλῆς δὲ ζητήσεως; Acts 15:7) into the question at issue. Both are intended to bring clarity over contested theological issues.

Most important, however, are the connections between the prologue and the narrative of Gentile inclusion which are both verbal and conceptual. The most straightforward is the description of Peter's initial defence of his conduct as 'orderly'

---

[102] Daniel Marguerat, *The First Christian Historian: Writing the 'Acts of the Apostles'*, SNTSMS 121 (Cambridge: Cambridge University Press, 2002), 31–4.

[103] Cf. also the analysis of Peter's speech in Acts 11 as a recapitulation of the key points of Luke-Acts in Gerhard Schneider, *Die* Apostelgeschichte, 2 vols, HThK (Freiburg: Herder, 1980), II:72.

(καθεξῆς; Acts 11:4). Luke claims this quality for his own narrative (Luke 1:3) and the term is peculiarly Lukan in the NT, occurring elsewhere only to describe temporal or geographical order (Luke 8:1; Acts 3:24; 18:23). A more intriguing connection, however, is Luke's presentation of his decision to write with the phrase 'it seemed to me' (ἔδοξεν κἀμοί; Luke 1:3). While the verb occurs nine further times in the Gospel and eight in Acts, three of these are at the Jerusalem convocation describing the decision of the Apostles and Elders with the consent of the church (Acts 15:22, 25, 28). Most strikingly, it occurs with a first-person personal pronoun in the dative within the Apostolic Decree at the precise point at which the letter claims inspiration in 15:28: 'for it seemed to the Holy Spirit and to us' (ἔδοξεν γὰρ τῷ πνεύματι τῷ ἁγίῳ καὶ ἡμῖν). Brown picks up on this connection to suggest a possible 'canonical intent' on Luke's part.[104] Sterling rejects Brown's suggestion, but on the basis of too slender a connection bearing too great a weight.[105] Indeed, individually any of the echoes I have identified could justifiably be questioned. However, their cumulative weight answers Sterling's objection and supports Brown's initial suggestion. Given that the narrative of Gentile inclusion thus appears closely tied to Luke's own expression of purpose to the extent that it can even be taken as expressing canonical intent, I will now analyse the narrative itself, arguing that it is offered as an episode in scriptural history.

As a part of Luke's story of fulfilment, the narrative details an important stage in the outworking of Jesus' programmatic pronouncement. At the same time, however, it also retells the establishment of a local community in Caesarea. Partly as a result of the prominence of the location in the story, it has been suggested that Peter's encounter with Cornelius can be read as a 'founding myth' for this local community,[106] and Wilson argues that it can consequently be read in comparison with similar Hellenistic material. He identifies eight points of confluence between Acts 10 and local 'origin stories' prevalent in contemporary Hellenistic culture: (1) the story begins with conflict in an original native city which results in a community being cast out; (2) the community must transition through a liminal space to a new home; (3) group formation is sacralized, often through divine action; (4) divine interventions are experienced as ambiguous and unexpected; (5) divine presence with the community secures its new space; (6) foundation stories are told within the foundation story; (7) community formation is concerned with the integration of outsiders; (8) the final scene is always the validation of decisions made by the founder.[107] Perhaps the most important point of basic confluence, however, is that these kinds of origin stories are intended to offer a legitimizing account of their particular communities.[108] In this respect, Luke's account

---

[104] Brown, 'Role of the Prologues', 104.
[105] Sterling, Self-Definition, 363 n.270.
[106] Cf. Richard S. Ascough, 'Greco-Roman Philosophic, Religious, and Voluntary Associations', in *Community Formation in the Early Church and in the Church Today*, ed. Richard N. Longenecker (Peabody, MA: Hendrickson, 2002), 3–19.
[107] Walter T. Wilson, 'Urban Legends: Acts 10:1–11:18 and the Strategies of Greco-Roman Foundation Narratives', *JBL* 120 (2001): 77–99. Wilson points to Virgil's Aeneid as one example, but Marianne Palmer Bonz offers a different comparison between Virgil and Luke here (*The Past as Legacy: Luke-Acts and Ancient Epic* (Minneapolis: Augsburg Fortress, 2000), 160–2).
[108] Wilson, 'Urban Legends', 80.

is certainly comparable: it is clearly intended to offer such an authoritative story of origins.

On the other hand, though Wilson's analysis offers some helpful insights, it is not clear that that it uncovers Luke's intention. In particular, there are two important points of discontinuity between Acts and Hellenistic foundation myths which relate primarily to the role played by RE in the formation of Luke's narrative. First, Luke's narrative describes events from the recent past, ostensibly on the basis of first-hand and eyewitness accounts – this, at least, is the claim explicit in his prologue and implicit in the 'we-passages' – and with the intention of offering a plausible historical version of events. This is not the case in the comparative material Wilson cites,[109] and is a significant difference. Unlike Hellenistic founding narratives, Acts is presented as a historical account of events: it claims to be a history rather than a myth.[110] In this respect, Acts falls substantially closer to its key intertext, the OT, than to possible Hellenistic sources, as Rosner clarifies: 'In setting out to report the events of the past to provide a foundation for the faith and its extension Acts is reminiscent of the books of Samuel and Kings and of the Chronicles which reflect upon sacred history for the benefit of their respective communities.'[111]

This view of history leads to a second point of divergence: Luke's story is primarily presented as God's plan. The inclusion of the Gentiles is a part of the broader narrative of fulfilment, which is situated as an extension of Israel's story. While it is true, as Wilson notes, that the believers disperse as a result of opposition,[112] this dispersion is understood more broadly in reference to the fulfilment of Jesus' pronouncement in Acts 1:8, and the figurative reading of Babel. Indeed, the locus of divine power in Luke's narrative is markedly external to Peter, who Wilson identifies as a parallel to divinely appointed founder figures. In Luke's story of Gentile inclusion, the first trans-empirical impact is with Cornelius, and it is his household on which the Spirit falls. Further, although the Spirit is intimately involved in guiding his actions, Peter is invited to Caesarea not by the Spirit but by Cornelius. This is because Luke's focus is not actually on the founding of a local community, but on the unfolding of God's purposes in history.

This is not to say that there are no points of comparison with local founding narratives: Wilson's categories tend towards the generic and are applicable to certain features of the story.[113] However, these points of comparison exist primarily because Luke claims to be offering an authoritative account of the impact of trans-empirical realities in the relatively recent past. This is why the events occur in a particular location: the validity of the narrative rests on the faithfulness of its historical

---

[109] Wilson, 'Urban Legends', 81–7.
[110] Cf. Sterling, *Self-Definition*, 379 (italics original): 'Luke-Acts argues *de rigeur* that Christianity has taken its rightful place *in history*. It must, therefore, be defined not only in relation to itself, but in relation to the larger world in which it exists.'
[111] Brian S. Rosner, 'Acts and Biblical History', in *The Book of Acts in Its Ancient Literary Setting*, ed. B. W. Winter and A. D. Clarke (Grand Rapids, MI: Eerdmans, 1993), 65–82 (82).
[112] Acts 8:4, cf. 11:19; Wilson, 'Urban Legends', 88.
[113] Cf. Loveday Alexander's similar critique of comparisons with epic poetry (*Acts in its Ancient Literary Context*, LNTS 298 (Oxford: Bloomsbury, 2007), 165–82).

testimony to Cornelius's and Peter's REs – at least as they exist in communal memory.[114] For these reasons, this narrative seems to be better read primarily as a scriptural history.[115] Indeed, the biblical narrative itself offers resources with which to shape an authoritative account of origins, and Luke draws heavily upon them.[116] In both form and content Luke-Acts seeks to present itself as a continuation of the OT narrative which records the fulfilment of its promises, with the implication that it is not too great a stretch to claim that it 'represents *sacred narrative*'.[117] Indeed, given that Luke appears to have 'canonized' earlier elements of his own text by drawing on them to 'sacralize' later passages, it is even plausible to suggest that he shared this evaluation.

So far, I have argued that the narrative of the inclusion of the Gentiles is both a vital component in Acts and characteristic of Luke's broader approach throughout the *Doppelwerk*. This is similarly the case in its intended impact. With his detailed portrayal of Peter's conversion and the subsequent communal reorientation it affects, Luke offers his audience an exemplary account of theological decision-making. In the same way that Peter's RE reshapes the community's understanding of God through his witness and inspired insight, Luke's writing intends to bring its audience to a new understanding of God.[118] Here, as throughout the *Doppelwerk*, Luke combines theology and history in a manner consistent with his OT influences, retelling the story of God's mighty acts in history for the sake of shaping his audience's understanding and response. Indeed, Hengel argues that 'Christian teaching for Luke, and for virtually the entire early church, is *Heilsgeschichte*, and thus is told through story and functions as a sequel to the Old Testament historical narrative'.[119] In the next section, I will conclude by arguing that this paradigmatic exploration of the way RE-derived insights could crystallize in a text which claimed inspiration can be read in conjunction with Luke's Pentecost narrative and statement of purpose as implying that he intended his own text as a scriptural witness to God's new revelation.

---

[114] Cf. Hengel on the importance of eyewitnesses ('Lukan Prologue', 558). Their teaching was passed on among Luke's audience and Luke explicitly communicates his intent to interact with this communal memory in the prologue. For a theoretical overview, see Barry Schwartz, 'Where There's Smoke, There's Fire: Memory and History', in *Memory and Identity in Ancient Judaism and Early Christianity*, SemeiaSt 78, ed. Tom Thatcher (Atlanta: SBL, 2014), 7–40. These points hold regardless of the date of Luke-Acts, though an early date potentially strengthens the argument.

[115] It is important to note that Wilson's thesis is that Luke is here drawing on the literary resources of Hellenistic founding narratives to shape a 'biblical history' in a way which makes it instantly intelligible and accessible to a Gentile audience.

[116] Cf. e.g. Samson Uytanlet's argument that Luke's succession narrative follows a 'deuteronomic precedent' (*Luke-Acts and Jewish Historiography: A Study on the Theology, Literature and Ideology of Luke-Acts* (Tübingen: Mohr Siebeck, 2014), 153–5); and Daryl D. Schmidt's argument that Luke's historiographical style matches that of the Deuteronomistic history ('The Historiography of Acts: Deuteronomistic or Hellenistic?' in *Society of Biblical Literature 1985 Seminar Papers*, ed. Ken Harold Richards (Atlanta, GA: Scholars, 1985), 417–27).

[117] Sterling, *Self-Definition*, 363; italics original. Cf. Rosner, 'Biblical History', 80–2, and W. Ward Gasque, 'A Fruitful Field: Recent Study of the Acts of the Apostles', *Int* 42 (1988): 117–31 (120–1).

[118] Cf. Acts 18:25–6 where Priscilla and Aquila's performance of the same function for Apollos is couched in terms closely connected to the expression of intent in Luke's prologue.

[119] Hengel, 'Lukan Prologue', 537.

4.4.3. Luke-Acts as Scripture

Though it is not altogether unheard of to suggest that Luke saw himself as writing Scripture, these claims are generally rooted in Luke's intentionally close relationship to the OT. For example, Evans suggests, 'Simply put, Luke may have thought that Luke-Acts belongs in the *Old Testament*, not some sort of *New* Testament.'[120] This remains a potent argument which has not yet been refuted, although the general assumption that canonical authority was a later theological development has meant that it has not had the impact it deserves.[121] It can be supplemented and strengthened by the possible reference to the liturgical use of early Christian texts in James's reasoning for the Apostolic Decree. If Luke's own text was ritualized in this manner, it would have connoted communal authority, a key element in the recognition of any text as Scripture.[122] However, what has not previously been explored in this respect is the relation of Luke-Acts to new REs.

This is perhaps odd given that Luke's two volumes are explicitly presented as a narrative of 'the events which have been fulfilled among us', reliant on eyewitness testimony.[123] This designation of the content of Luke's narrative is striking. As is widely recognized, these events comprise the life, ministry, death, resurrection and ongoing impact of the Christ-event. However, witnessing to these events is not a mundane task, as Strathmann notes: 'Witness cannot be borne to these facts unless their significance is also indicated and an emphatic appeal is made for their recognition in faith.'[124] It is for precisely this task that Luke presents the disciples as being empowered by the outpouring of the Spirit (Acts 1:5-8; cf. Luke 24:44-9). Further, on Luke's account any adequate retelling of the story will include a demonstration of its character as a fulfilment of the OT: this is an integral part of the significance of the events. This is visible in the outpouring of the Spirit at Pentecost, which is made manifest in the *Sprachwunder* of the overcomprehensible proclamation of 'God's mighty deeds' (τὰ μεγαλεῖα τοῦ θεοῦ) in a variety of languages. At this point, human speech becomes revelatory precisely in the inspired retelling of the story of God's action in history on

---

[120] Craig A. Evans, 'Luke and the Rewritten Bible: Aspects of Lukan Hagiography', in *The Pseudepigrapha and Early Biblical Interpretation*, JSPSup 14, ed. James H. Charlesworth and Craig A. Evans (Sheffield: JSOT, 1993), 170–201 (201 n.73); italics original. Cf. similarly Rosner, 'Biblical History'.

[121] Cf. the analysis and critique of Michael J. Kruger, *The Question of Canon: Challenging the Status Quo in the New Testament Debate* (Nottingham: Apollos, 2013), 47–78.

[122] So e.g. Brevard S. Childs, *Introduction to the Old Testament as Scripture* (Philadelphia, PA: Fortress, 1979), 41: 'It is constitutive of Israel's history that the literature formed the identity of the religious community which in turn shaped the literature.'

[123] Cf. Alexander, *Preface*, 34–41; Alexander, *Literary Context*, 133–63, on the relationship between autopsy and investigative travel. Nonetheless, it is telling that autopsy is a *hapax legomenon* and entirely replaced in Luke's narrative by the category of witness. For Luke, the category of witness seems to be primary, whereas the reference to *autoptai* likely represents a rhetorically inflected choice of vocabulary in line with historical writings.

[124] H. Strathmann, 'μάρτυς', *TDNT* IV: 474–514 (492). Cf. William James's argument that meaning can be inherent to experience (*The Varieties of Religious Experience: A Study in Human Nature* (New York: Longmans, Green & Co, 1902, repr. Abingdon: Routledge, 2008), 21), retrieved in Jason N. Blum, 'Retrieving Phenomenology of Religion as a Method for Religious Studies', *JAAR* 80 (2012): 1025–48.

behalf of his people. As Peter's sermon immediately demonstrates, this coincides for Luke with the story of 'the events which have been fulfilled among us': the story of God's mighty deeds now tells of his fulfilment of the OT in the Christ-event. This story, which Luke tells in his own text, is one which he presents as revealed and inspired: it is a story rooted in experiences of trans-empirical realities which cannot be adequately retold except in the power of the Spirit.

Beyond the RE at Pentecost and its scriptural interpretation, Peter's RE-derived insight into God's impartiality in Acts 10 becomes a revelation for the community. Through his encounter with Cornelius and the REs which mark that episode, Peter learns to witness to the ongoing μεγαλεῖα τοῦ θεοῦ by welcoming the Gentiles. Partly through their reticence to accept Peter's insight, the community plays a critical role in demonstrating the significance of this new understanding. Ultimately, this process leads to the creation of the Apostolic Decree, which conveys a decision which has been ratified by the Spirit. This claim implicitly reflects on the status of the writing itself, suggesting that the document should be seen at least in part as a product of the Spirit's involvement and, in this sense, as inspired.

As an exemplary narrative, the story of Gentile inclusion illuminates Luke's own text and this holds for its account of the production of a text which implicitly lays claim to inspiration. Luke self-consciously claims reliance on 'eyewitnesses and servants of the word' like Peter,[125] and offers a written text which is intended to address apparent weaknesses in the tradition which has been handed on to Theophilus. In this way, Luke claims that his text can offer an authoritative account of Christian origins. Although Luke presents an extensive narrative rather than a short epistle, then, his work appears to be intended to be able to resolve theological disputes in much the same way that the Apostolic Decree is presented as settling the issue of Jew-Gentile relations in mixed Christian communities. Thus, the two writings share a distinctive similarity as Luke presents them: they both represent the crystallization of revelatory, Spirit-empowered witness in writing for the purpose of resolving communal confusion.

For these reasons, it is fair to say that Luke intentionally, though implicitly, presents his *Doppelwerk* as a scriptural writing. It stands in continuity with OT Scripture which itself sets a precedent for inspired writings. It is closest to historical books like Chronicles and, like these, does not make any explicit claim to inspiration. It is in the narrative itself, and its claim to be an accurate account of God's interactions with his people, that the community is invited to recognize revelatory content. Luke-Acts textualizes Luke's witness to the words and deeds of Jesus and his ongoing impact through the disciples who are empowered by his Spirit and in this way, the connection with RE is vital to the authority claims it makes.

At the most basic level, Luke claims to write about the felt impact of trans-empirical realities within real people's lives and there is evidence that his text has been shaped by the REs he describes – even if not necessarily by his own. Beyond this, though, Luke

---

[125] Cf. Hengel, 'Lukan Prologue', 548: 'The two groups are identical.' This represents scholarly consensus (cf. similarly Joel B. Green, *The Gospel According to Luke*, NICNT (Grand Rapids, MI: Eerdmans, 1997), 41; John Nolland, *Luke 1:1-9:20*, WBC 35A (Waco, TX: Thomas Nelson, 1989), I:7) against attempts to identify two groups – and possibly two generations – in this reference.

depicts RE as establishing the possibility of revelatory human speech and writing in ways which reflect on his own work. He derives authority from the closeness of his source material to these original REs and, in presenting himself as a writer capable of conveying the 'truth' derived from these REs to his intended audience, he presents his textual narrative as the crystallization of inspired witness in a trustworthy and well-ordered written retelling of God's mighty acts. Ultimately, then, Luke lays claim to the same kind of status as his key intertext, the OT: he consistently, if implicitly, presents his writing as a scriptural text made necessary by the new activity of the God of Israel perceived in the life, death, resurrection and ascension of Jesus and the outpouring of the Spirit on the disciples.

5

From Experience to Epistle: Paul's Letter to the Galatians

In this chapter I will take up the connection I have identified between religious experience (RE) and the intentional production of a scriptural text in Luke-Acts to claim that Paul's[1] argument in Galatians is rooted in RE and that its presentation suggests he intended this writing to serve a scriptural function for its readers. First, I will suggest that Paul relies on reference to a pattern of REs which he assumes is shared between his addressees and himself to make his case. He offers an authoritative account of his own 'revelatory beginning' (1:11–12, 15–16; §5.2.1), before claiming that it has led to a participatory mode of life (2:19–20; §5.3.1). He then asserts that the same pattern can be discerned in the Galatians' experience, though it has not been fully effective: they encountered Christ in Paul's own ministry (3:1-5; 4:14; §5.2.2), received the Spirit (3:1-5; 4:6) and were baptized into Christ (3:27-8), but remain in need of Christ-formation (4:19; §5.3.2). In the closing chapters, Paul's focus turns towards the future and he offers advice regarding Spirit-guided life (5:13–26), aiming to shape the ongoing impact of these earlier REs (§5.4). Thus, I will argue that Paul's argument in Galatians is fundamentally reliant on RE: he argues from REs in order to shape the Galatians' ongoing lived experience, aiming to stop people being 'cut off from Christ' (5:4) by re-calling them to a defining relationship with him (1:6; 4:19).

I will then argue that the presentation of RE in the letter can illuminate Paul's understanding of his own act of writing (§5.5). In creating this letter, Paul aims to re-present his gospel to his addressees. Consequently, Galatians itself can be understood as a textualization of Paul's embodied evangelistic practice (§5.5.1). For this reason, the claims that Paul makes about his gospel message and its rootedness in his own RE can also be applied to the letter, suggesting that Paul understood what he was writing to include revelatory content (§5.5.2). Further, the prominence of themes present in Galatians in Paul's other writings suggests that the material which crystallized here resonated beyond the immediate context of the Galatian conflict (§5.5.3). On this

---

[1] That Galatians is an authentically Pauline literary unity is not seriously contested, though recent research has rightly raised the question of how 'authorship' can best be understood; see e.g. Nijay Gupta, 'What Is in a Name? The Hermeneutics of Authorship Analysis Concerning Colossians', *CurBR* 11 (2013): 196–217. See §5.5.

basis, I will argue that Paul intended this letter to be read as scriptural at least partly on the basis of its close connection to his RE (§5.5.4).

5.1. Religious experience in Galatians

In his commentary, Fee states that 'because of the major role the Spirit plays in the argument of this letter ... Paul here opens the windows to give a rather full-orbed view of life in the Spirit in his experience and understanding'.[2] This is true not only of the Spirit but also of RE more broadly. Paul's autobiographical self-defence refers in unparalleled detail to his reception of the gospel (1:11–12), his encounter with Christ and attendant call (1:15–16) and its reorienting impact in his Christocentric mode of life (2:19–20).[3] However, it is not only Paul's experience which comes into relatively sharp relief but also that of the Galatians. Paul points to their beginning with the Spirit (3:1–5), the apparently shared experience of the Spirit's Abba cry 'in our hearts' (4:1–7) and the possibility of 'living by the Spirit' (5:16–26).

In his discussion of Paul's RE, Engberg-Pedersen argues against the 'idealist fallacy' that Paul's language is more or less entirely abstract, figurative or theological,[4] and this must be equally applied to his descriptions of the Galatians' experience. The letter cannot offer a first-person account of their experience in the same way it does of Paul's own, but it is clearly intended to persuade the Galatians.[5] It is completely implausible to assume, for example, that Paul describes how God has sent 'his Spirit into our hearts crying "Abba! Father!"' (4:6) in a bid to convince congregations in which no one would recognize that experience. Consequently, his descriptions of the Galatians' experiences should be seen as plausible and accurate to their perception. Lyons even notes that in 3:1–5 'Paul asked them to validate the source of their Christian experience based on their own experience'.[6] Consequently, the survival of the letter and its incorporation first into collections of Paul's epistles and later into the NT canon is one strong indication that its initial recipients, and even later believers, did recognize their experiences in Paul's description.

At the same time, it is important to note the limitations of this claim. Paul does not offer an objective or impartial account of these REs. In fact, he contests the

---

[2] Gordon D. Fee, *Galatians*, PCS (Blandford Forum: Deo, 2011), 7.
[3] On Paul's 'in Christ' language as suggestive of RE, cf. Rollin A. Ramsaran, '"In Christ" and "Christ in" as Expressions of Religious Experience: Testing the Waters in Galatians', in *Experientia II: Linking Text and Experience*, ed. Colleen Shantz and Rodney A. Werline (Williston, ND: Society of Biblical Literature, 2012), 161–80.
[4] Troels Engberg-Pedersen, 'The Construction of Religious Experience in Paul', in *Experientia I: Inquiry for Religious Experience in Early Judaism and Christianity*, ed. Frances Flannery, Colleen Shantz and Rodney A. Werline (Atlanta, GA: SBL, 2008), 147–58 (150).
[5] Cf. Philip H. Kern, *Rhetoric and Galatians: Assessing an Approach to Paul's Epistle*, SNTSMS 101 (Cambridge: Cambridge University Press, 1998). Kern argues that Paul's writing does not conform to rhetorical handbook usage, but is more broadly intended to be persuasive. Such an aim would explain the presence of rhetorical devices, even though the letter does not fit to a 'macrorhetoric' outline (so Craig S. Keener, *Galatians*, NCBC (Cambridge: Cambridge University Press, 2018), 22–4; contra Hans Dieter Betz, *Galatians*, Hermeneia (Philadelphia, PA: Fortress Press, 1979), 14–26).
[6] George Lyons, *Galatians*, NBBC (Kansas: Beacon Hill, 2012), 174; cf. similarly Betz, *Galatians*, 132.

interpretation of the Galatians' experience throughout the letter – contending against his opponents that the Galatians' beginning with the Spirit precludes certain later actions (3:1–5) and that the witness of the Spirit to their sonship implies a certain relationship to the law (4:1–31). This suggests three points: (1) these REs were never 'uninterpreted' and their significance was at least partially culturally constructed and thus contestable; (2) these REs exceeded complete linguistic description and had a sufficiently distinctive character that they could resist certain interpretations; (3) an initial RE alone cannot be considered a 'complete' encounter with the gospel, but it can irreducibly contribute to faith formation. Further, I will argue that these REs contributed to the shape of Galatians: in this letter, Paul intends to convey his revealed gospel message, and in so doing to write an authoritative text for the community.

5.1.1. Patterns of RE in Galatians

Amid the range of REs described in Galatians, it is possible to discern three foci: (1) revelatory beginnings; (2) participatory lives; (3) ethical empowerment. Although this categorization does not necessarily provide an interpretive grid which includes every RE mentioned in the letter (e.g. the negative experience of enslavement to non-gods; 4:8), I will use it as a heuristic aid to focus my discussion on prominent elements which contribute to Paul's text.

First, Paul writes in unprecedented detail about his own initial encounter with Christ (1:11–12, 15–16) and speaks about the Galatians' initial evangelisation (3:1–5). In each case Paul describes a transformative originary encounter with trans-empirical reality – a revelatory beginning. This is the most important element from both literary and historical perspectives, because it forms the foundation of both Paul's argument and of the later REs he describes. Second, Paul presents his own mode of life as Christocentric to the point of co-crucifixion at the climax of his self-defence (2:19–20); for the Galatians, he describes the ideal result of their encounter with the gospel as Christ-formation (4:19) after his own example (4:12). This suggests an ongoing pattern of lived experience focused on Christ and rooted in their initial encounters. Finally, as Paul's horizon extends into the future, he points to the importance of the Spirit as the provider of eschatological hope (5:5) which empowers ethical life in opposition to the flesh (5:13–26). This discussion is rooted in the theological opposition between flesh and Spirit, but includes an affective valence. In all three cases, Paul writes about the felt impact of trans-empirical realities within the culturally patterned lives of individuals and, indeed, the whole community of the Galatians.

There is significant overlap between the three categories in Paul's thinking: it is the revelation of Christ which makes his Christocentric mode of life possible, and this in turn is basically synonymous with 'Spirit-led life'. Nonetheless, the categorization highlights parallels Paul develops between his own RE and the Galatians'. Both encounter Christ, both are (ideally) transformed and both are ethically empowered by the Spirit. It appears that Paul intends or expects the Galatians' encounter with 'his gospel' (Gal 1:8, 11) to follow a similar pattern to his own. This could support the argument that Paul's autobiographical comments are intended to be paradigmatic.[7] However, the similarity more likely reflects his expectations regarding the impact of the gospel: the consistency is derived from God's revelation in Christ rather than any particular quality in Paul's experience.[8] To elucidate the parallel pattern and its significance for Paul's argument, I will consider his and the Galatians' REs alongside each other under my three categories. Doing this will allow me to demonstrate both the importance of REs in shaping the content of the letter, and to suggest the impact of this on Paul's self-understanding as he was writing it.

5.2. Revelatory beginnings

In depicting his and the Galatians' initial encounters with Christ, Paul speaks about REs which combine cognitive content with a transformative impact which reaches beyond assent to propositions. Such experiences may be profitably understood with reference to the models of affective understanding introduced in Chapter 2, and I will argue that God's revelation of Christ in Paul can be described as an affectively toned perception, which Paul sought to manifest to the Galatians in their initial evangelization. On this account, the experience of encountering Christ qualitatively altered Paul's understanding, contributing irreducibly to his message and shaping his perception of what would constitute an adequate acceptance of this gospel.[9]

5.2.1. God's revelation of the gospel of Jesus Christ to Paul

In Galatians 1 Paul describes his own revelatory beginning as a RE in which he received knowledge both about and of Christ. In 1:11b-12, he writes that 'the gospel that was proclaimed by me is not of human origin; for I did not receive it from a human source, nor was I taught it, but I received it through a revelation of Jesus Christ (δι' ἀποκαλύψεως Ἰησοῦ Χριστοῦ)'. In 1:15-16 he adds, 'But when God, who had set me apart before I was born and called me through his grace, was pleased to reveal his Son

---

[7] Cf. George Lyons, *Pauline Autobiography: Toward a New Understanding*, SBLDS 73 (Atlanta, GA: Scholars, 1985); Beverly R. Gaventa, 'Galatians 1 and 2: Autobiography as Paradigm', *NovT* 28 (1986): 309-26. Cf. also Paula Fredriksen's comments on the conscious shaping of conversion narratives in support of this position ('Paul and Augustine: Conversion Narratives, Orthodox Traditions and the Retrospective Self', *JTS* 37 (1986): 3-34).

[8] Cf. John M. G. Barclay, 'Paul's Story: Theology as Testimony', in *Narrative Dynamics in Paul: A Critical Assessment*, ed. B. W. Longenecker (Louisville, KY: Westminster John Knox, 2002), 133-56 (155): 'For Paul, the believer is not simply the follower after Jesus who takes inspiration from Christ ... Rather, the crucifixion of Jesus is a *present* reality for Paul, present not only in the single act of baptism [n.b., a ritually mediated RE] but also in the continuing experiences and sufferings of life.'

[9] Cf. Rabens's similar construal of Paul's description of an encounter with the gospel in 2 Cor 3: '"unveiling" in 3:18 has two aspects. On the one hand there is a cognitive aspect: by means of unveiling the minds of people the Spirit provides proper understanding of the gospel ... On the other hand, Paul associates unveiling with personal closeness and immediacy' (*The Holy Spirit and Ethics in Paul: Transformation and Empowering for Religious-Ethical Life*, 2nd edn (Tübingen: Mohr Siebeck, [2]2013), 177).

to me (ἀποκαλύψαι τὸν υἱὸν αὐτοῦ ἐν ἐμοί), so that I might proclaim him among the Gentiles (ἐν τοῖς ἔθνεσιν), I did not confer with any human being.'

Though the relationship between these passages and the Acts accounts of Saul's Damascus Road experience has been questioned,[10] it is reasonable to assume that in these verses, Paul is referring to the events which prompted his decisive shift from persecutor to preacher.[11] I will consider in turn (a) the felt impact of Paul's interpersonal encounter with Christ; (b) the cognitive content of the experience; and (c) its impact on Paul's culturally patterned life in his depiction of his call. I will argue that viewing Paul's initial encounter with Christ as an affectively toned perception can bring clarity to the question of how his experience came to shape his life and thought by focusing on the contribution of the RE to his new religious beliefs and consequent writings.

(a) Felt impact: God's revelation of Christ in Paul

Paul's apostleship, call and gospel message are rooted in God's decision 'to reveal his son **in me**' (ἀποκαλύψαι τὸν υἱὸν αὐτοῦ **ἐν ἐμοί**; 1:16). While the use of 'to reveal' (ἀποκαλύψαι) with God as the subject deemphasizes Paul's own experience, his comments here offer unparalleled first-hand access to an encounter with Christ which he presents as the decisive influence on his later life, thought and work. What exactly it means to claim that Christ was revealed ἐν ἐμοί is debated. It has been taken as suggesting that Paul perceived the experience itself to be 'subjective' or 'interior' in some sense.[12] However Betz argues that 'apparently for [Paul] the two forms of visions (external and internal) are not as distinct as they may be for some commentators'.[13] In fact, the evidence of 1 Corinthians 15 even suggests that Paul perceived his encounter with Christ as having a certain objectivity,[14] supporting Witherington's argument that 'if such terms had to be used, [Paul] probably would have insisted that his encounter on Damascus Road was both objective and subjective'.[15]

The grammatically awkward use of the preposition ἐν offers a range of possible meanings, the three most relevant being 'to me', 'by means of me' and 'in me'.[16] First,

---

[10] Cf. e.g. Betz, *Galatians*, 63.

[11] The notion that the reference is exclusively to the 'various revelations' of 2 Corinthians 12 (I. E. Bosworth, 'The Influence of the Damascus Vision upon Paul's Theology', BS 56 (1899): 278–300 (291)) finds little support today. Cf. William Baird, 'Visions, Revelation, and Ministry: Reflections on 2 Cor 12:1–5 and Gal 1:11–17', *JBL* 104 (1985): 651–62 (652 n.2).

[12] See e.g. F. F. Bruce, *The Epistle of Paul to the Galatians: A Commentary on the Greek Text*, NIGTC (Exeter: Paternoster, 1982), 93; Ronald Y. K. Fung, *The Epistle to the Galatians*, NICNT (Grand Rapids, MI: Eerdmans, 1995), 64. Identification of Paul's experience as internal is particularly prevalent where parallels are sought with Merkabah mysticism (see e.g. J. W. Bowker, '"Merkabah" Visions and the Visions of Paul', *JSS* 16 (1971): 157–73).

[13] Betz, *Galatians*, 71.

[14] Cf. Richard H. Bell, 'The Resurrection Appearances in 1 Corinthians 15', in *Epiphanies of the Divine in the Septuagint and the New Testament*, ed. Roland Deines and Mark Wreford (Tübingen: Mohr Siebeck, forthcoming).

[15] Ben Witherington III, *Grace in Galatia: A Commentary on Paul's Letter to the Galatians* (Grand Rapids, MI: Eerdmans, 1998), 107.

[16] Martinus C. De Boer's suggestion of 'in my previous life' ('Paul, Theologian of God's Apocalypse', *Int* 56 (2002): 21–33 (31)) has not found favour, in part because his argument does nothing to problematize the 'most natural reading' of 'within me' (so Martinus C. de Boer, *Galatians: A*

it is possible that the dative here simply denotes the indirect object – Paul as recipient of the revelation. However, Harmon notes that this 'is a rare construction; there are only eight comparable examples in the LXX and NT combined ... in none of these places does ἐν function to indicate the person to whom a revelation is given'.[17] Harmon identifies temporal (Num 24:4; Dan 2:19; 1 Pet 1:5), locative (Judg 5:2; 1 Sam 2:27; Prov 11:13) and instrumental uses (Ezek 16:36; 22:10). Of the twelve other uses of 'to reveal' (ἀποκαλύπτω) in the Pauline corpus, four use a dative noun or pronoun (1 Cor 2:10; 14:30; Eph 3:5; Phil 3:15), three have no object (Gal 3:23; 2 Thess 2:3, 8), Romans 1:18 uses ἐπὶ with an accusative noun, Romans 8:18 uses εἰς with an accusative pronoun and 2 Thessalonians 2:6 is a passive with an accusative object. Romans 1:17 and 1 Corinthians 3:13 both use ἐν with an instrumental dative to refer to the means by which something is revealed and I will consider this more fully below. In the first instance, though, it is worth noting with Das that 'Paul regularly employs with this verb a substantive or pronoun in the dative case – but no preposition – to indicate the indirect object. In other words, Galatians 1:16 with its prepositional phrase employs a construction Paul does *not* use elsewhere'[18] to convey the sense 'to me'. This makes it unlikely, despite the popularity of the reading.[19]

The usage in Romans 1:17 and 1 Corinthians 3:13 supports the grammatical possibility that the phrase should be read here as 'by means of' me. However, the thoughts are quite different: in Romans, Paul refers to the revelation of righteousness *by the gospel*; in 1 Corinthians, to the eschatological revealing of the value of a person's deeds *by fire*. Nevertheless, in Galatians, Paul's revelation is immediately qualified with a purpose clause describing his missionary activity. The close parallelism between ἐν ἐμοί and ἐν τοῖς ἔθνεσιν ('among the nations') within 1:16 emphasizes the sense 'by means of',[20] and Paul's later claim that Christ was publicly exhibited as crucified to the Galatians in his own ministry also supports the idea.[21]

On the other hand, Das argues that the change of tense from aorist to present between the clauses demonstrates that the purpose clause specifies a consequence of God's revelation, and that a reading of ἐν ἐμοί only as 'by means of' would render the purpose clause superfluous.[22] The prominent connection between Paul's description of the revelation of Christ ἐν ἐμοί and his description of his mode of life in Galatians 2:19–20[23] speaks in favour of Das's argument. Rather than simply expressing the

---

Commentary, NT (Louisville, KY: Westminster John Knox, 2011), 92). Indeed, it is not clear how the two readings would materially differ, given that Paul's previous life was lived by him.

[17] Cf. Matthew S. Harmon, *She Must and Shall Go Free: Paul's Isaianic Gospel in Galatians*, BZNW 168 (Berlin: De Gruyter, 2010), 82.

[18] A. Andrew Das, *Galatians*, CCSS (St. Louis, MO: Concordia, 2014), 132; italics original. Cf. already James D. G. Dunn, *Galatians*, BNTC (London: Black, 1993), 64.

[19] Cf. i.a. Thomas Schreiner, *Galatians*, ZECNT (Grand Rapids, MI: Zondervan, 2010), 100–1; Peter Oakes, *Galatians*, Paideia (Grand Rapids, MI: Baker Academic, 2015), 57.

[20] So e.g. Beverly R. Gaventa, *Darkness to Light: Aspects of Conversion in the New Testament* (Philadelphia, PA: Fortress Press, 1986), 27; Markus Bockmuehl, *Revelation and Mystery in Ancient Judaism and Pauline Christianity*, WUNT II.36 (Tübingen: Mohr Siebeck, 1990), 136 n.19.

[21] See §5.2.2.

[22] Das, *Galatians*, 132.

[23] Noted by e.g. Richard N. Longenecker, *Galatians*, WBC 41 (Waco, TX: Word, 1990), 32; Dunn, *Galatians*, 64.

thought that Christ was revealed 'by means of' him, Paul here reports the beginning of a new knowledge of God and Christ marked by a 'peculiarly personal intensity':[24] he claims to have come into contact with trans-empirical reality, encountering Christ in a way which radically altered his knowledge of God. When God revealed Christ in Paul it brought about a dramatic transformation, such that he came to perceive Christ as his life source.

Nevertheless, the second and third senses, 'by means of' and 'in,' are also closely connected, as already noted by Lightfoot who renders the similar expression in 2 Corinthians 13:3: 'You seek proof of the Christ who is speaking through me [ἐν ἐμοί].'[25] Similarly, Eastman notes that 'the churches in Judea glorify God "in" Paul [Gal 1:24] because they hear of the power of the gospel displayed "in" his life'.[26] Accordingly, the ambiguity of the formulation is fertile, and possibly intentional: the revelation of Christ to the Gentiles 'by means of' Paul's ministry (1:16) reflects his attempts to bring people into contact with the same revelation which he sees as having consumed and transformed his own identity (2:20).

Turning to the verb ἀποκαλύψαι ('to reveal'), it is important to note its visual connotations – strengthened by Paul's reference to the same event in 1 Corinthians 15[27] where he uses the theophanic term ὤφθη ('appeared')[28] to describe Christ's appearance to him – as they suggest that Paul's revelation was not simply propositional. In fact, his multifaceted description of the revelation of Christ ἐν ἐμοί is suggestive of an affectively toned perception. As noted above (§2.2.1), Jonathan Edwards's description of 'that idea which the saint has of the loveliness of God, and that sensation, that kind of delight he has in that view'[29] offers an example of an affectively toned perception. Wynn argues that Edwards's description combines an affective impact with cognitive content: the *idea* of God represents an imaginative construction which would not be possible without the *sense* of God's loveliness. If this intuitive grasp of trans-empirical reality was lacking, it would qualitatively alter the idea itself. Thus, as Tomlin notes, what Edwards describes here is 'a new form of perception. Both believers and unbelievers have notions of God, however only believers grasp the "divine excellency", and this is not just a different way of interpreting experience, but a completely new ability to perceive the divine glory, holiness or beauty'.[30] Although the experiences are different,

---

[24] G. B. Caird, *Paul's Letters from Prison* (Oxford: Oxford University Press, 1976), 137.

[25] J. B. Lightfoot, *Saint Paul's Epistle to the Galatians* (London: Macmillan, 1865), 82–3. Cf. the similar connection made by Chrysostom, *NPNF1* 13:11 (Edwards): 'But why does he say, "to reveal His Son in me," and not "to me?" It is to signify, that he had not only been instructed in the faith by words, but that he was richly endowed with the Spirit; that the revelation had enlightened his whole soul, and that he had Christ speaking within him.'

[26] Susan G. Eastman, *Recovering Paul's Mother Tongue: Language and Theology in Galatians* (Grand Rapids, MI: Eerdmans, 2007), 35 n.28.

[27] So e.g. Lyons, *Galatians*, 83; Betz, *Galatians*, 70–1. Cf. Twelftree who links these visionary experiences – among others – with Paul's prophetic proclamation of the 'word of the Lord' (*Paul and the Miraculous: A Historical Reconstruction* (Grand Rapids, MI: Baylor Academic, 2013), 62 n.5).

[28] Cf. Eberhard Bons, 'The Evolution of the Vocabulary of Epiphanic Revelation from the Septuagint to the New Testament and Early Christian Literature', in *Epiphanies of the Divine in the Septuagint and the New Testament*, ed. Roland Deines and Mark Wreford (Tübingen: Mohr Siebeck, forthcoming).

[29] Jonathan Edwards, *The Religious Affections* (1746 repr., New York: Dover, 2013), 136.

[30] Graham Tomlin, 'Life in the Spirit: Identity, Vocation and the Cross of Christ', in *The Holy Spirit in the World Today*, ed. Jane Williams (London: St Paul's, 2011), 72–85 (79).

there is an important similarity between Edwards's description and Paul's presentation of his own RE. Paul appears to have felt a distinctive sense of God's glory as strength in weakness centred on the distinctive content of Christ, through which he came to a new understanding of God which was emphatically not derived from a human source (cf. 1:10–12). Thus, although Paul is not writing about love for God in Galatians 1:11–12, 15–16, he describes a striking perception of trans-empirical reality which fused a radical, non-conceptual grasp of God's revelation with a culturally patterned understanding of Jesus Christ (cf. 1 Cor 15:1–8)[31] to produce a new understanding[32] which ultimately resulted in him 'denying his own role as the acting "subject" of his own life and claiming that he has been supplanted in this capacity by Christ'.[33] In this sense, Paul perceives the person of Christ as having been 'imprinted' on him; the content of his message has become the central reality of his life.[34] Moreover, he suggests that this was given to him by God through revelation, and was emphatically not available from human sources.

There are similar emphases in Paul's description of the way in which his ministry of the new covenant (2 Cor 3:6) resulted in the Corinthians 'with unveiled faces seeing the glory of the Lord' (ἀνακεκαλυμμένῳ προσώπῳ τὴν δόξαν κυρίου κατοπτριζόμενοι; 2 Cor 3:18). As Rabens notes, Paul's description suggests that 'deeper understanding of the gospel ... should not be reduced to the reception of *cognitive* knowledge. Understanding the gospel more deeply is for Paul not divorced from knowing Christ more intimately.'[35]

(b) Cognitive content: Paul's gospel message

There are two points to consider regarding the cognitive content of Paul's revelation: its source and its character. Paul deals first with the source and his first comment about his

---

[31] Betz emphasizes the difference between Paul's claims that his gospel was based on tradition in 1 Cor 15 and revelation in Gal 1 (*Galatians*, 65), but it is implausible that Paul was unaware of Christian beliefs before his encounter with Christ. As Lyons argues, 'If Paul was ignorant of the Christian story before his encounter with the risen Christ, there is no explanation for his persecution ... [Paul's revelation] revealed that what he had considered a blasphemous Christian claim – that the crucified Jesus was the Messiah of Israel – was actually true' (*Galatians*, 72). It is also possible that an affectively toned perception could irreducibly underpin the kind of subsequent development of thought John Barclay suggests was the case for Paul: 'It is unlikely that this interpretation of the Christ-gift came to Paul fully formed in his Damascus-experience: he reconstructs this connection after many years alongside Gentile converts, whom he found gifted with the Spirit despite their failure to observe the Torah ... his Gentile mission not only embodied but also shaped his thought' (*Paul and the Gift* (Grand Rapids: Eerdmans, 2015), 361).

[32] Cf. Mark Wynn, *Emotional Experience and Religious Understanding* (Cambridge: Cambridge University Press, 2005), 96: 'While primal affects in this case no longer offer a direct (concept-independent) awareness of the character of the world, nonetheless the resulting state of mind depends for its content (depends for its sense of what the world is like) on the contribution of a primal, affectively toned sensitivity.'

[33] Richard B. Hays, *The Faith of Jesus Christ: An Investigation of the Narrative Substructure of Galatians 3:1–4:11*, SBLDS 56 (Chico, CA: Scholars, 1983), 168.

[34] Cf. Richard B. Hays, 'Christology and Ethics in Galatians: The Law of Christ', *CBQ* 49 (1987): 268–90 (280–1): 'Paul means to imply in 1:16 that Christ is revealed not only through Paul's *proclamation* but also in his *person*.'

[35] Rabens, *Holy Spirit*, 182.

gospel in 1:11 develops an opposition between 'human origin' (κατὰ ἄνθρωπον) and Christ and God as authoritative sources. This opposition is introduced in 1:1, repeated in verse 10 with reference to his apostleship and echoed again in the double denial of verse 12: 'For I did not receive it from a human, nor was I taught but …' (οὐδὲ γὰρ ἐγὼ παρὰ ἀνθρώπου παρέλαβον αὐτὸ οὔτε ἐδιδάχθην ἀλλὰ …).[36] The close connection with the preceding verses implied by the connective γάρ[37] heightens the contrast between the source of Paul's gospel and even other trans-empirical sources, such as angels (1:8). As Dunn notes, 'This was no slight alternative to put forward': angels were prominent authority figures in Jewish apocalyptic literature giving 'the stamp of heavenly authority to the message', and were even associated with the giving of the law.[38] It is also possible that Paul is contrasting himself with opponents who were claiming revelations from angels,[39] something potentially supported by the reference to the στοιχεῖα τοῦ κόσμου ('elements of the world') in 4:3, 9.[40] Against such claims Paul argues that his own message comes from the highest possible source. Though the genitive ἀποκαλύψεως ('revelation') could conceivably be either subjective (a revelation whose author is Christ) or objective (a revelation whose content is Christ), the further detail added in 1:15-16 clarifies the issue in favour of the objective reading: it is God the Father who revealed Christ in Paul. Though Paul implicitly recognizes such claims are contestable when he refers to 'another gospel' (1:6-7), it would be difficult for the Galatians – as people who had heard Paul's gospel message and been converted – to simply dismiss the claim that his RE validates it.

Oakes rightly warns against seeing this revelation as 'only a piece of information',[41] but does not fully recognize the epistemological implications of Paul's emphasis on the trans-empirical source of his revelation. With Γνωρίζω γὰρ ὑμῖν ('For I want you to know'), Paul transitions from the opening statement of astonishment (1:6-10) into autobiographical self-defence (1:11-2:21).[42] Schreiner characterizes the phrase as 'a disclosure formula [that] indicates the fundamental nature of what follows',[43] but as a verb of knowing it also highlights the epistemological conflict Paul is engaged in. It is significant, then, that this formula is also associated with the unveiling of knowledge of heavenly origin.[44] Paul is claiming that the 'gospel that was gospeled by me' (τὸ

---

[36] Cf. Longenecker, *Galatians*, 23.
[37] Despite text-critical reservations, this is likely the original reading; cf. Moisés Silva, *Interpreting Galatians Explorations in Exegetical Method* (Grand Rapids, MI: Baker Academic, 2001), 44-9.
[38] Dunn, *Galatians*, 45. Cf. also Betz, *Galatians*, 62 n.68.
[39] So e.g. Betz, *Galatians*, 53; J. Louis Martyn, *Galatians*, AB33A (New Haven, CT: Yale University, 1997), 113.
[40] So E. Earle Ellis, *Prophecy and Hermeneutic in Earliest Christianity* (Tübingen: Mohr Siebeck, 1978), 111; contra Oakes, who argues that the overall trajectory of Paul's argument suggests that his opponents 'claimed their authority based on commissioning and teaching from authoritative human sources' (*Galatians*, 45).
[41] Oakes, *Galatians*, 52.
[42] Commentators structure the first two chapters differently, but a transition is generally noted in 1:11 (cf. e.g. Oakes, *Galatians*, 51; Schreiner, *Galatians*, 95; Betz, *Galatians*, 58-62), though the use of a connective rather than adversative particle has been taken by some to imply a closer connection with 1:10 (e.g. Lyons, *Galatians*, 71; Martyn, *Galatians*, 136).
[43] Schreiner, *Galatians*, 96.
[44] Dan 2:23, 28-30, 45; 5:7-8, 15, 17; 1QpHab VII.4-5; 1QH XII.27-8; XV.27. Cf. Bockmuehl, *Revelation and Mystery*, 135-7.

εὐαγγέλιον τὸ εὐαγγελισθὲν ὑπ' ἐμοῦ; 1:11) should resolve any conflict of paradigms because of its close connection with trans-empirical reality. This is made more striking by the fact that, unlike in the similar passage in 1 Corinthians 15:3, he does not limit this claim to the message he proclaimed to this particular set of addressees: rather, it applies to Paul's preaching 'not just in Galatia, but everywhere'.[45] Although the emphasis on the content of Paul's gospel over against the agent of its proclamation in 1:8 demonstrates that Paul recognizes the inherent contestability of appeals to trans-empirical reality, his assertion of the divine source of his message is clearly an important element in securing both the truth of his paradigm-shifting proclamation and, consequently, his status as an Apostle.

Second, after he has argued that his gospel had a divine source, Paul describes the character of the revelation of Christ in him in two undeveloped references: it was 'of Jesus Christ' (1:12) and of 'God's Son' (1:16). Galatians includes several short narrative segments concerning Jesus' identity as Christ (1:3–5; 2:19b–20; 3:13–14; 4:4–7), which seems to function as a title here,[46] and the designation of Jesus as the Son of God is not widespread in Paul, but occurs at significant points and consistently in relation to Paul's gospel message.[47] In Galatians in particular, it recurs in 2:19–20 and twice in 4:4–7. In 4:4–7, Paul writes about God sending his Son (4:4) in the fullness of time 'to redeem those under the law' (ἵνα **τοὺς ὑπὸ νόμον ἐξαγοράσῃ**; 4:5), with the consequence that the 'Spirit of his Son' (τὸ πνεῦμα τοῦ υἱοῦ αὐτοῦ; 4:6) was sent into their hearts. Here, then, the theme of redemption from the law introduced in the brief reference to 'Christ who redeemed us from the curse of the law' (Χριστὸς ἡμᾶς **ἐξηγόρασεν ἐκ** τῆς κατάρας **τοῦ νόμου**; 3:13–14) is related to his divine sonship. Similarly, in 2:20, Paul writes about the life he lives in faith in 'the Son of God who loved me and gave himself for me' (τοῦ υἱοῦ τοῦ θεοῦ τοῦ ἀγαπήσαντός με καὶ **παραδόντος ἑαυτὸν ὑπὲρ ἐμοῦ**), echoing the claim of 1:4 that Jesus 'gave himself for our sins (τοῦ **δόντος ἑαυτὸν ὑπὲρ τῶν ἁμαρτιῶν ἡμῶν**) to set us free from the present evil age'. Thus, the short summaries of Jesus' identity in Galatians revolve to a significant degree around his identification as Son of God, a title which 'expresses Jesus' unique standing and intimate favour with God, and God's direct involvement in Jesus' redemptive work'[48] in Paul's letters.

Further, both the apparent reference to Christ's pre-existence as God's Son who was 'sent to be born of a woman' (4:4) and the prominence of Christ in the allusion to baptismal liturgy (3:27) which suggests an already established pattern of dyadic devotion support the suggestion that this title reflects a 'high Christology' which presupposes the divinity of Jesus.[49] This coheres with the close connection Paul

---

[45] Fee, *Galatians*, 35.
[46] Cf. e.g. N.T. Wright, *The Climax of the Covenant: Christ and the Law in Pauline Theology* (London: SPCK, 1992), 41–55; contra e.g. Dunn, *Galatians*, 26–7.
[47] There are seventeen occurrences (Rom 1:3, 4, 9; 5:10; 8:3, 29, 32; 1 Cor 1:9; 15:28; 2 Cor 1:19; Gal 1:16; 2:20; 4:4, 6; Eph 4:13; Col 1:13; 1 Thess 1:10), and the term is closely associated with Jesus' atoning work; cf. Martin Hengel, *The Son of God: The Origin of Christology and the History of Jewish-Hellenistic Religion* (Philadelphia, PA: Fortress, 1976), 8–9.
[48] Larry W. Hurtado, *Lord Jesus Christ: Devotion to Jesus in Earliest Christianity* (Grand Rapids, MI: Eerdmans, 2003), 104; cf. the discussion in 101–8.
[49] Cf. Hurtado, *Lord Jesus Christ*, 118–26; contra e.g. James D. G. Dunn, *The Theology of Paul the Apostle* (London: T&T Clark, 1998), 252–60, 266–93. For a critique of Hurtado, cf. Crispin Fletcher-Louis,

draws between Jesus Christ and God the Father in the first verses of the letter (1:1, 3), where Christ is placed firmly on the divine side of a divine/human dichotomy,[50] and is subsequently distinguished from 'an angel from heaven' (1:8). It is probable, then, that Paul's revelation was an encounter with the raised, glorified Christ,[51] perhaps in the presence of God's glory.[52] However, Paul's claim that he 'carries the marks of Jesus branded on his body' (τὰ στίγματα τοῦ Ἰησοῦ ἐν τῷ σώματί μου βαστάζω; 6:17) emphasizes that the Jesus Paul saw bore the marks of his suffering, a theme present in other post-resurrection vision accounts (John 20:20, 24-29; cf. Luke 24:40; Rev 5:6). Though this remains a speculative reconstruction, such a vision could plausibly have impressed on Paul that the claims of those he was persecuting were true precisely by evidencing the divine vindication of Jesus' resurrection.

Paul also makes clear that he considers it vital that the gospel message deriving from his revelation remains intact: to say anything else is to attempt to 'pervert' (μεταστρέψαι) Christ's story (Gal 1:7).[53] That Paul's opponents only 'want' (θέλοντες; 1:7) to do this suggests that Paul's revelation did not consist merely of information: it can, apparently of its own accord, resist perversion.[54] This supports the suggestion that in Paul's revelation, sense and idea were inseparable: his encounter with Christ involved a non-conceptual grasp of reality which consequently could not simply be altered by argument. It also supports the suggestion that Paul's argument assumes that the Galatians' RE had a sufficiently distinctive character to resist certain interpretations and support others: the same was apparently true of the gospel God revealed to him.

(c) Culturally patterned expression: Paul's Christocentric vocation

The revelation of Christ 'in Paul' not only altered his knowledge of God and formed the basis of his gospel message, it also changed Paul's perception of himself. The emphasis

---

'A New Explanation of Christological Origins: A Review of the Work of Larry W. Hurtado', *TynBul* 60 (2009): 161-205.

[50] So e.g. Schreiner, *Galatians*, 74; de Boer, *Galatians*, 24. Cf. the similar interpretation of Marius Victorinus, *Ep. Gal.* 1.1.11 (Edwards).

[51] So e.g. Hurtado, 'Revelatory Experiences and Religious Innovation in Earliest Christianity', *ExpTim* 125 (2014): 476; Seyoon Kim, *The Origin of Paul's Gospel* (1980 repr., Eugene: Wipf and Stock, 2007), 55-6; Martin Hengel, *Studies in Early Christology* (Edinburgh: T&T Clark, 1995), 172-5.

[52] Cf. Bert Jan Lietaert Peerbolte, 'Paul's Rapture: 2 Corinthians 12:2-4 and the Language of the Mystics', in *Experientia I: Sites for Inquiry for Religious Experience in Early Judaism and Christianity*, ed. Frances Flannery, Colleen Shantz and Rodney A. Werline (Atlanta, GA: Society of Biblical Literature, 2008), 159-76. Peerbolte notes the ambiguity of the use of κύριος in 2 Cor 12:1 and argues that 'if we take the description of Paul's rapture experience as formulated against the background of apocalyptic language of heavenly journeys, and consider Paul's visit to the third heaven, to paradise, as a visit to God's glory, Paul rhetorically positions this as an ascent to Christ'. Cf. also Ezek 1:26, where God's glory has an appearance 'like a human form' (מראה כמראה אדם): for Paul, this human form appears to have been Jesus Christ. However, cf. e.g. Martha Himmelfarb, *Ascent to Heaven in Jewish and Christian Apocalypses* (Oxford: Oxford University Press, 1993), as an example of studies which argue apocalyptic literature does *not* draw on visionary experience. Even if Himmelfarb is correct it would not prevent that literature serving to shape Paul's RE. Cf. Andrew T. Lincoln, *Paradise Now and Not Yet*, SNTSMS 43 (Cambridge: Cambridge University Press, 1981), 72, for a defence of Paul's apocalyptic language as experiential.

[53] Cf. Martyn, *Galatians*, 46, on the meaning of μεταστρέψαι.

[54] Cf. Oakes, *Galatians*, 45.

on the trans-empirical source of his knowledge which forms the first line of his self-defence also creates a frame within which Paul can narrate his own paradigm shift.[55] This he does in the autobiographical section which runs throughout the rest of the first two chapters, and begins with a brief reminder of his convictions, conduct and community affiliation prior to this event (1:13–14).[56]

Despite the fact that proto-Christianity was in an early stage of development at this point, Paul presents his RE as the basis of a holistic Christocentric reorientation making it possible to speak here of a cognitive conversion. As Segal notes, it demanded a communal realignment: 'Paul was a Pharisaic Jew who converted to a new apocalyptic, Jewish sect … a decisive and deliberate change in religious community.'[57] Further, Paul's changed convictions regarding Christ prompted a re-evaluation of his conduct. As Barclay notes, he now considers that 'his conduct "in Judaism" set him directly against, not for, God'.[58] Having Christ revealed to him reshaped Paul's 'comprehensive and pre-reflective understanding of reality', which acts as the 'map of fact and value for a person, legitimating all roles, priorities, and institutions by situating them in the context of the broadest horizon of reference'.[59] On Paul's account, his previous social capital was radically revalued (1:14; cf. Phil 3:2–11), and 'what happened next was *not* another stage in his development within "Judaism", a further step in his progress of zeal'.[60]

As a consequence of the far-reaching implications of his revelation, Paul was forced to renegotiate his relationship to 'the traditions of his fathers' (τῶν πατρικῶν μου παραδόσεων; 1:14). Whereas before he may plausibly have looked up to Elijah, Phineas or Mattathias as exemplary figures on whom to model his zeal,[61] his new RE situated him in a different relation to Scripture. Specifically, Paul speaks of God as the one who 'set me apart from my mother's womb and called me through his grace' (ὁ ἀφορίσας με ἐκ κοιλίας μητρός μου καὶ καλέσας διὰ τῆς χάριτος αὐτοῦ),[62] alluding to the call accounts of Jeremiah (1:5) and the Servant of YHWH (Isa 49:5), to situate himself in relation to God's revelation of his Son.

Paul not only presents the Christ-event as having a decisive, apocalyptic impact but, in evoking these passages, also consciously locates himself within a scriptural framework of interpretation of RE: he includes elements of a call narrative.[63] In doing

---

[55] Cf. Terence L. Donaldson, *Paul and the Gentiles: Remapping the Apostle's Convictional World* (Minneapolis: Fortress, 1997), who uses Kuhn's account of paradigm shifts (3–28) to analyse alterations in Paul's thought (51ff.).

[56] Cf. Michael J. Gorman, *Apostle of the Crucified Lord: A Theological Introduction to Paul and his Letters*, 2nd edn (Grand Rapids, MI: Eerdmans, ²2017), 71–2, for these categories.

[57] Alan F. Segal, *Paul the Convert* (New Haven, CT: Yale, 1990), 6–7.

[58] John M. G Barclay, *Paul and the Gift* (Grand Rapids, MI: Eerdmans, 2015), 357; italics original.

[59] Walter T. Wilson, *The Hope of Glory: Education and Exhortation in the Epistle to the Colossians*, NovTSup 88 (Leiden: Brill, 1997), 100.

[60] Barclay, *Gift*, 358; italics original.

[61] So e.g. N. T. Wright, *Paul and the Faithfulness of God* (London: SPCK, 2013), 80–9; Das, *Galatians*, 125–9.

[62] Cf. Frank J. Matera, *Galatians*, SP (Collegeville, PA: Liturgical Press, 2007), 63: 'The choice of *aphorizein* ("to set apart") is significant because it is often used in the OT in reference to someone or something set aside for consecrated service.'

[63] See esp. Baird, who argues that Paul's autobiographical comments share six elements with call accounts: divine confrontation, introductory word, commission, objection, reassurance and sign

so, the decisive discontinuity Paul sees with his previous life 'in Judaism' is nuanced as that period is brought within the frame of God's action in his life.[64] On the one hand, the God who called Paul is the same one he had previously sought to serve; on the other, it is an example of God's incongruous grace that Paul was called before his birth, despite the fact that his conduct in Judaism would set him against God.[65] In this way, his rehearsal of his own testimony is intended not simply as a recounting of mundane facts but as a retelling of recent salvation history, a testimony of the inbreaking of God's grace to Paul's life in the revelation of Christ.[66]

Paul alludes to OT prophetic writings to articulate the impact of God's revelation of Christ to him, and Martyn recognizes the force of this self-identification when he distinguishes between (auto)biographical and prophetic modes of speaking:

> Paul does not speak, then, in a biographical fashion, as though it were his intention to say, 'Let me tell you about my life and experiences!' He speaks, rather, in a prophetic fashion, concentrating in the first instance on God … Paul is thus conscious of standing in continuity with the prophetic traditions.[67]

Here, Martyn recognizes that Paul aligns himself with the OT prophets in such a way that his own revelatory encounter with Christ forms a part of his message. This brings his new RE into the foreground of his argument and 'transforms the category of biography into a theological witness focused on *God's* activity in the gospel'.[68] The link with OT prophets Paul develops here is suggestive, insofar as the person and work of Isaiah's suffering servant are similarly knitted together. Commenting on this connection, Karl-Wilhelm Niebuhr equates Paul's actions with (deutero-)Isaiah's: 'God, who through the prophet (Deutero-) Isaiah promised the inclusion of the Gentiles into his will for salvation, sends the apostle Paul to proclaim the dawn of this salvation in

---

('Visions', 656–7). That Paul's account does not share the *form* of a call narrative is perhaps due in part to his relativization of its importance: as de Boer notes, it is remarkable 'that a subordinate temporal clause rather than the main clause contains Paul's elaboration of his conversion and call' (*Galatians*, 89).

[64] Cf. Eastman, *Mother Tongue*, 36: 'This double view of the past means that the apostle's "former life in Judaism" was not simply an instance of "the present evil age" but was rather an "interruption" encompassed by the gracious action of God.'

[65] Cf. Barclay, 'Paul's Story', 144: 'The observance of the Mosaic law (keeping the traditions of the ancestors) was something of an interlude, which was not meaningless within a wider perspective but also not the bearer of grace'; Barclay, *Gift*, 356–61.

[66] Cf. David G. Horrell, 'Paul's Narratives or Narrative Substructures?: The Significance of "Paul's Story"', in *Narrative Dynamics in Paul: A Critical Assessment*, ed. B. W. Longenecker (Louisville, KY: Westminster John Knox, 2002), 157–71 (162–3):

> Paul places the Christ event within – although as the climax and culmination of – the story of God's saving purposes and their enactment in history … Paul does not have to think of the story as a simple 'line', nor as one that reflects a 'gradual maturation', in order to see the coming of Christ as something that is to be comprehended within an account of God's dealings with Israel and the world.

[67] Martyn, *Galatians*, 157.

[68] Martyn, *Galatians*, 157 n.191; italics original. Cf. similarly, Barclay, 'Paul's Story'; contra Lyons's narrower argument that Paul contrasts 'his conversion from Judaism to Christianity with the Galatians' inverted conversion' (*Pauline Autobiography*, 150).

the Christ-event.' Paul's life and ministry extend the universal project announced in that of the suffering servant.[69] In claiming this prophetic role, Paul establishes himself as one who can witness authoritatively to God's ongoing action in history – indeed, this is the purpose of referring to the revelation of Christ to him for his argument in Galatians.

Moreover, by alluding particularly to Jeremiah – a named OT prophet with a text attributed to him – he presents himself as someone who can do so in lasting, written form: 'To understand Paul's self-presentation as a prophetic figure like Jeremiah or Isaiah and teacher who is heir to Moses [cf. 2 Corinthians 3] is thus to cast him also as one, perhaps through the commitment of his disciples, who leaves a written legacy as well that will survive him.'[70] This is particularly pertinent for Paul's writing in Galatians both because it is here that Paul articulates most clearly his own understanding of his prophetic vocation and because in this letter he is attempting to re-call people to his gospel and in this way to retain a legacy in these congregations. This is an aim which he elsewhere characterizes by transposing verbs of writing to refer to the Corinthians as a 'letter of Christ prepared by [Paul and his co-workers] written not with ink, but with the Spirit of the living God' (ὅτι ἐστὲ ἐπιστολὴ Χριστοῦ διακονηθεῖσα ὑφ' ἡμῶν, ἐγγεγραμμένη οὐ μέλανι ἀλλὰ πνεύματι θεοῦ ζῶντος; 2 Cor 3:3a). In serving this aim, Paul's letter already points towards an intended authority which exceeds its initial context. This is rooted in his self-identification as someone capable of conveying God's message in the manner of an OT prophet on the basis of God's revelation to him, and I will explore the significance of this self-perception in greater detail below (§5.5.2).

5.2.2. The Galatians' beginning with the Spirit

In Galatians 3:1–5, Paul turns from his narration of the impact of God's revelation of Christ in him to the initial evangelization of the Galatians. On his account, Jesus Christ was 'publicly exhibited as crucified before their eyes' (κατ' ὀφθαλμοὺς Ἰησοῦς Χριστὸς προεγράφη ἐσταυρωμένος; 3:1), prompting a response of faith which resulted in a reception of the Spirit (3:2). As with Paul, I will consider in turn (a) the felt impact of the REs which marked the Galatians' conversion; (b) the cognitive content

---

[69] Karl-Wilhelm Niebuhr, *Heidenapostel aus Israel: Die jüdische Identität des Paulus nach ihrer Darstellung in seinen Briefen*, WUNT I.62 (Tübingen: Mohr Siebeck, 1992), 76. German original: 'Gott, der durch den Propheten (Deutero-)Jesaja den Einschluß der Heiden in seinen Heilswillen verheißen hat, sendet den Apostel Paulus zur Verkündigung des Anbruchs dieses Heils im Christusgeschehen.' Cf. also Alan F. Segal, 'The Afterlife as Mirror of the Self', in *Experientia I: Sites for Inquiry for Religious Experience in Early Judaism and Christianity*, ed. Frances Flannery, Colleen Shantz and Rodney A. Werline (Atlanta, GA: Society of Biblical Literature, 2008), 19–40 (23): 'Paul uses a prophetic anthropology to explain his spiritual body [in 2 Cor 13]. God gives the prophet his spirit and the spiritual body participates in the resurrection', ultimately becoming visible in Paul's eschatological comments in 1 Cor 15. In Gal 1, Paul is describing the experience which prompted him to think this way about his own life.

[70] Judith H. Newman, 'Speech and Spirit: Paul and the Maskil as Inspired Interpreters of Scripture', in *The Holy Spirit, Inspiration, and the Cultures of Antiquity*, ed. Jörg Frey and John R. Levison, Ekstasis 5 (Berlin: De Gruyter, 2014), 241–64 (262, cf. 259–61). That Paul dictated most of Galatians (6:11) even raises the possibility one of Paul's companions acted as a 'scribe' like Baruch did for Jeremiah, which may offer a way of understanding deutero-Pauline material.

of the 'public exhibition of Christ'; and (c) the contest over the relationship of their experiences to cultural patterns.

(a) Felt impact: Beginning with the Spirit

On Paul's account, the Galatians' initial evangelisation was marked by both mediated and immediate REs. On the one hand, God's revelation of Christ came to the Galatians through Paul's 'public exhibition'.[71] On the other they experienced the Spirit themselves. In the first instance, Paul reminds his addressees of their past experience of his own ministry: he claims that he previously brought the Galatians into contact with the revelation of Christ. For Paul to characterize his ministry in this way in such a charged context, he must have been able to count on a sympathetic hearing, and the section ultimately turns from theological argumentation to appeal 'to the strong ties which once united him and the Galatians'.[72]

In this context, Paul speaks of the Galatians' reception of him 'as an angel of God ... as Christ Jesus' (ὡς ἄγγελον θεοῦ ... ὡς Χριστὸν Ἰησοῦν; 4:14). Though it is not entirely clear whether Paul is referring to 'an angel' or 'the angel of the Lord'[73] and whether or not the double ὡς is intended as appositive or ascensive,[74] Paul is suggesting that the Galatians discerned a trans-empirical impact in their dealings with him. Indeed, their reception of him as an agent of Christ despite the possibly malignant implications of his ailing appearance[75] represents an insight which 'Paul can explicate only by referring to Christ. For only in Christ are people given the power to perceive strength in weakness.'[76] For this reason, Paul's depiction of events strengthens the possibility that the Galatians discerned in his message a positive trans-empirical impact: they encountered Christ in his message despite his affliction, and were consequently able to discern in his weakness the sufferings of Christ.[77] It also re-emphasizes Paul's own self-identification with Christ in a manner that suggests the Galatians were already aware of it and had previously accepted it.[78] The cumulative weight of these elements suggests Paul was successful in communicating something of his revelation when he initially evangelized the Galatians.

---

[71] Cf. however Troels Engberg-Pedersen's suggestion that Paul's proclamation prompted an instance of direct revelation (*Paul and the Stoics* (Louisville, KY: Westminster John Knox, 2000), 143–4).

[72] Matera, *Galatians*, 162.

[73] I take the reference to be generic, rather than a Septuagintal allusion (with Schreiner, *Galatians*, 287; contra Keener, *Galatians*, 203–4; Das, *Galatians*, 463–4) on the basis of the other references to angels (1:8; 3:19).

[74] I take it to be ascensive (contra Keener, *Galatians*, 204); the appositive reading sees here a designation of Christ as 'the angel of the Lord'. Cf. the discussion in Fee, *Galatians*, 165–6.

[75] In noting that the Galatians did not 'spit him out' (ἐξεπτύσατε) Paul raises the possibility that his ailment could have been interpreted as a sign that he possessed the evil eye; cf. John H. Elliott, *Beware the Evil Eye: The Evil Eye in the Bible and the Ancient World III* (Eugene, OR: Wipf and Stock, 2016), 212–64.

[76] Martyn, *Galatians*, 421. Cf. similarly, Bruce W. Longenecker, 'Until Christ Is Formed in You: Suprahuman Forces and Moral Character in Galatians', *CBQ* 61 (1999): 92–108 (102).

[77] Contra Witherington, Paul depicts the encounter as entirely Christocentric, making it unlikely that he intends to point positively to behaviour motivated by pagan concepts surrounding the appearances of gods on earth (*Grace*, 311).

[78] Contra Oakes, *Galatians*, 148, this is not a hyperbolic reading.

It is likely that Paul's gospel was received this way in part because it was attended by other, immediate REs. When they responded to his message with 'faith from what they heard' (ἐξ ἀκοῆς πίστεως; 3:2, 5), Paul claims the Galatians 'received the Spirit' (τὸ πνεῦμα ἐλάβετε; 3:2) and 'began by the Spirit' (ἐναρξάμενοι πνεύματι; 3:3), adding that God 'supplies the Spirit to you and works deeds of power among you' (ἐπιχορηγῶν ὑμῖν τὸ πνεῦμα καὶ ἐνεργῶν δυνάμεις ἐν ὑμῖν; 3:5). Especially given that this letter was seemingly composed in the midst of friction between Paul and the Galatians, 'Paul would not have appealed to mighty works accomplished by the power of the Spirit and experienced by the Galatians if in fact they had experienced nothing of the kind'.[79] The present tense of the final elements is particularly striking in this respect. Paul not only suggests that he expects his addressees to be able to recognize their own *past* experience in his description to verify his claims but even argues that it is *still ongoing*.[80] Moreover, as Twelftree notes, the use of 'therefore' (οὖν) to introduce the final question demonstrates that Paul is drawing a conclusion which implies agreement: 'Paul is concluding that if, as must be agreed, God acted among them initially on the basis of faith, then his ongoing action among them will have the same basis.'[81]

The Spirit's prominence in this description is conspicuous, as 3:1–5 contains the first two of fifteen references in the letter.[82] Assuming that 'works of power' (ἐνεργῶν δυνάμεις) refers to more external/objective miracles,[83] these seem to have been somehow of secondary importance to the internal/subjective reception of the Spirit for Paul: they are mentioned only once, whereas the Spirit is a prominent feature of the letter as a whole, with the emphasis lying on ethical empowerment (5:13–26) in the absence of any discussion of charismata. Indeed, Paul even refers to 'how much' the Galatians have 'experienced' (τοσαῦτα ἐπάθετε; 3:4)[84] before mentioning the ἐνεργῶν

---

[79] Bruce, *Galatians*, 151; cf. similarly Betz, *Galatians*, 130; Dunn, *Galatians*, 158. Dunn sees here a 'firsthand ... testimony to "miracles" in earliest Christianity'.

[80] Cf. Bruce, *Galatians*, 151; cf. 2 Thess 2:9.

[81] Twelftree, *Miraculous*, 189.

[82] For references which have a connection to the Galatians' initial evangelisation, see 3:2, 5, 14; 4:6. Remaining references occur in connection with the oppositions between Spirit and flesh/works of the law and grace/slavery and promise (4:29; 5:16–18; 6:8) and ethical empowerment (5:5, 16–18, 22, 25; 6:1, 8) as well as in the closing benediction (6:18). Cf. also Rabens on the close connection Paul draws between the work of the Spirit and encountering Christ in the gospel message in 2 Cor 3–4 (*Holy Spirit*, 190–203).

[83] De Boer, *Galatians*, 182–3, lists three views on the meaning of ἐνεργῶν δυνάμεις: (1) miracles performed by the Galatians; (2) miracles performed by Paul when he was with the Galatians; (3) the diverse manifestations of the Spirit within the Galatians. To me, 1 seems to me the likeliest option: the present tense of the participle and the logic of the argument seems to preclude 2; and 3 would seem essentially superfluous in the midst of other references to the work of the Spirit, though it remains possible. Cf. Twelftree, *Miraculous*, 190–1.

[84] The meaning of πάσχω in this context is disputed: on the one hand, it uniformly denotes suffering elsewhere in Paul (see 1 Cor 12:26; 2 Cor 1:6; Phil 1:29; 1 Thess 2:14; 2 Thess 1:5; cf. 2 Tim 1:12), the NT and the LXX. On the other, neutral experience is within its semantic range (cf. LSJ 1347; Josephus, *Ant.* 3.15.1). Douglas J. Moo opts for the first sense, arguing for a reference to the Galatians' persecution (*Galatians*, BECNT (Grand Rapids, MI: Baker Academic, 2013), 185–6). However, this is not a prominent topic in the letter, and that sense would go against the flow of Paul's argument (cf. Das, *Galatians*, 296; Matera, *Galatians*, 113). On the other hand, Paul's own RE is paradigmatically shaped by Christ's crucifixion and Shantz argues for a close connection between Paul's suffering and his ecstatic experience with his RE providing a framework within which his suffering can be understood and in turn inform the development of his theology (see 'The Confluence of Trauma

δυνάμεις. This suggests both that the Galatians received the Spirit in a way which was noticeable apart from particular miracles and that Paul perceived the most important recognizable elements in the reception of the Spirit to be in these less 'spectacular' experiences.

Though these REs are less easily externally identified or verified, there is no more reason to doubt their reality. Paul's argument rests heavily on them, even though he cannot entirely govern his addressees' interpretation of them. While it is clearly possible for him to contest their significance and relationship to culturally patterned frameworks, it is not possible for him to alter entirely their qualitative character in the minds of those who had them. By analogy with the qualitative experience of taste, Paul 'cannot cause the subject to have the total experience s/he has of' the Spirit,[85] nor indeed decisively alter individual or communal memory, especially if not much time has passed since the events themselves occurred.[86]

Paul also writes about a particular experience of the Spirit in more detail in relation to the Abba cry. Though in Romans the Spirit of adoption co-witnesses with the believers' spirits, in Galatians the link is drawn more closely with conversion (4:4–5) and the language is of an invasive, personal action: 'Because you are sons, God has sent forth the Spirit of his Son into our hearts, crying "Abba! Father!"' (4:6). Given the prominence of the Spirit in Paul's description of the Galatians' revelatory beginning, it is possible this reminder is an important element of his attempt to recall them to it. There are overtones here of the incongruous grace evident in Paul's account of his revelation: Paul presents the Galatians' adoption as a part of God's work on a wider horizon beyond their control (4:4; cf. 1:15), implying a decisive shift from slave to child in which God's loving salvific action became present to them through the Spirit of adoption in a noticeable way.[87] As Rabens puts it, these verses 'demonstrate that the filial intimacy with God that believers come to experience through the Spirit of adoption as sons has become the fundamental formative source in the believers' lives'.[88]

Paul also presents the Galatians' experience as one which they share with him: though the subordinate clause qualifying the recipients of the Spirit in 4:6 employs a verb in the second person ("Οτι δέ **έστε** υἱοί; 'And because **you are** sons'), he uses a first-person plural pronoun to qualify the hearts into which the Spirit has been sent (τὰς καρδίας **ἡμῶν**; '**our** hearts'). That 'hearts' is here in the plural also emphasizes

---

and Transcendence in the Pauline Corpus', in *Experientia I: Sites for Inquiry for Religious Experience in Early Judaism and Christianity*, ed. Frances Flannery, Colleen Shantz and Rodney A. Werline (Atlanta, GA: Society of Biblical Literature, 2008), 193–205; Colleen Shantz, *Paul in Ecstasy: The Neurobiology of the Apostle's Life and Thought* (Cambridge: Cambridge University Press, 2009), 131–3, 140–2). Oakes observes that viewing the use of πάσχω as a hint towards early suffering understood through this paradigm 'would fit quite well and offer a further strand to Paul's case in 3:2–5' (*Galatians*, 104), and Dunn even suggests the possibility of 'ecstatic experiences which involved some suffering' (*Galatians*, 156).

[85] Sallie B. King, 'Two Epistemological Models for the Interpretation of Mysticism', *JAAR* 56 (1988): 264: the quote is originally about the power of the 'coffee tradition' to define experiences of tasting coffee.

[86] Cf. 1:6: Paul refers to the Galatians' deserting his gospel ταχέως ('so quickly'). Whatever date is assumed, it is likely the interval is not more than three years.

[87] Cf. Wreford, 'Diagnosing Religious Experience in Romans 8', *TynBul* 68 (2017): 217.

[88] Rabens, *Holy Spirit*, 235.

that this experience is a personal one for each individual included in the community. In rehearsing these REs, Paul is trying to recall to the Galatians what they felt when they encountered Christ in Paul's preaching and received the Spirit which convinced them of their adoption.

(b) Cognitive content: The public exhibition of Christ

When he proclaimed the gospel to them, Paul claims that the Galatians received 'faith from what they heard' (ἐξ ἀκοῆς πίστεως; 3:2, 5). The double repetition of the formula serves to emphasize its importance, but its meaning is ambiguous. Sprinkle summarizes the interpretive options as follows: 'ἀκοῆς can mean: (1) act of hearing; or (2) that which is heard, a report. Πίστεως can mean: (1) act of believing; or (2) that which is believed.'[89] In this context where Paul is referring to what the Galatians witnessed during their initial evangelization, it is most likely that he is referring to the report (2) which caused them to believe (1).[90] The close connection with Romans 10:16–17 supports this reading of ἀκοῆς: there Paul draws on Isaiah's question regarding his own prophetic message, 'Lord, who has believed our message?' (τῇ ἀκοῇ ἡμῶν; Isa 53:1), to argue that 'faith comes from what is heard (πίστις ἐξ ἀκοῆς); what is heard, from the word of Christ'.[91] Given the Christocentric identification of Paul's own message already demonstrated in Galatians, it seems reasonable to take the expanded formula in Romans as consistent with the way that Paul intends to present his practice in Galatians. In hearing Paul proclaim the gospel, then, the Galatians – or at least those who converted – heard 'the word of Christ'. In encountering Christ through Paul's evangelization, the Galatians came to faith.[92]

Though the connection between Paul's ministry and the Galatians' encounter with Christ is relatively well established,[93] it is not clear precisely how the verb προεγράφη ('publicly exhibited', NRSV) should be understood. There are various options,[94] but three are particularly important. First, and predominantly, it has been taken to refer to the rhetorical efficacy of Paul's initial proclamation in 'painting word pictures'.[95] Second, it has been read as a reference to the 'impact of the cross on [Paul] himself',[96] with his ministry construed as the holistic manifestation of this impact to other people

---

[89] Preston Sprinkle, 'Πίστις Χριστοῦ as an Eschatological Event', in *The Faith of Jesus Christ: The Pistis Christou Debate*, ed. Michael F. Bird and Preston M. Sprinkle (Milton Keynes: Paternoster, 2009), 165–84 (176–7).

[90] So similarly Das, *Galatians*, 292; Keener, *Galatians*, 123.

[91] Similarly, of fifty occurrences of ἀκοῆς in the LXX the majority have the sense 'report' or 'message', and this is far the most prevalent sense in the prophetic literature.

[92] It is not possible to engage the '*pistis Christou* debate' in greater detail here. For an overview, cf. Michael F. Bird, 'Introduction: Problems and Prospects for a New Testament Debate', in *The Faith of Jesus Christ: The Pistis Christou Debate*, ed. Michael F. Bird and Preston M. Sprinkle (Milton Keynes: Paternoster, 2009), 1–15.

[93] Cf. indicatively, G. Walter Hansen, *Galatians*, IVPNTC (Downers Grove, IL: IVP, 1994), 78–9; Lyons, *Galatians*, 173; Schreiner, *Galatians*, 181.

[94] Cf. the discussion in Basil S. Davis, 'The Meaning of ΠΡΟΕΓΡΑΦΗ in the Context of Galatians 3.1', *NTS* 45 (1999): 194–212.

[95] So e.g. Betz, *Galatians*, 131; Hansen, *Galatians*, 78.

[96] Dunn, *Galatians*, 152; Davis, 'Meaning'.

in word and deed. Third, it has been seen as a reference to the use of texts in Paul's ministry.[97] In particular, Wendt has recently argued that Paul used textual prophecies as a key part of his proclamation, on the basis of the literal meaning of the verb as 'written beforehand' in Romans 15:4. On her reading, the Galatians' experience with the Spirit was taken by Paul as having allowed them special insight into his teaching from revealed prophecy.[98]

Wendt's proposal has the twin strengths of taking seriously the use of a verb of writing and emphasizing Paul's role as an inspired interpreter of Scripture.[99] However, as she herself recognizes, it works against the grammatical flow of Paul's argument[100] making it difficult to sustain. In 2 Corinthians 3, however, Paul transposes verbs of writing in the context of describing the Corinthians as a letter 'written on our hearts'. In that context, Paul is also presenting himself as an authoritative, prophetic teacher,[101] and it might be possible to see a similar transposition here: Paul's life acts as a living placard for Christ who determines his life (Gal 2:20) and whose Spirit has been sent 'into our hearts' (4:6). Although Davis rejects the suggestion that Paul – like OT prophets – 'theatrically enacted' his message on the basis that 'prophets did not re-enact past events',[102] this is both too restrictive[103] and fails to take into account the ongoing significance of the Christ-event for Paul. Muir's argument that 'Paul characterized his message as a vivid experience'[104] moves in the right direction, but unnecessarily restricts the focus to Paul's 'performance' of his gospel on specific occasions. Rather, in his every action – including every expression of ministry, and even his writing – Paul embodies the new perception gained through God's revelation of Christ in him. This is visible in the Galatians' initial interaction with Paul. He accepted their hospitality (4:15–16), and their initial evangelization involved extended contact with him, including acquaintance with his sufferings. During this time, the Apostle exhibited the one he had been crucified with in his mode of life. After all, Paul presents his gospel message as Christ himself (1:11–12), who is revealed in the Apostle (1:15–16) and has become the 'acting subject' of Paul's identity (2:19–20).[105] As Twelftree puts it, 'Paul sees not only his own experience, but also his ministry as the expression and, therefore for his converts, the experience of Jesus at work.'[106]

---

[97] As Bruce notes, classical usage suggests the possibility of a literal 'placard' (*Galatians*, 148).
[98] Heidi Wendt, 'Galatians 3:1 as Allusion to Textual Prophecy', *JBL* 135 (2016): 369–89.
[99] Wendt refers to 'Judean literature', as a way of acknowledging the fluidity of collections of texts in this period. It must be assumed, however, that texts included in the OT were at least predominant, given the density of allusions to this literature in comparison to other corpora. Moreover, the texts interpreted by Paul in Wendt's account must have already been accorded a certain religious authority for their interpretation to be significant in the first place.
[100] Wendt assumes that κατ' ὀφθαλμοὺς modifies an 'elided verb of showing' ('Allusion,' 380), arguing that this is consistent with other examples where 'Paul's syntax does not fully match his flow of thought' (n. 41).
[101] Cf. Newman, 'Speech and Spirit', 259–62.
[102] Davis, 'Meaning', 198.
[103] Cf. Steven Muir, 'Vivid Imagery in Galatians 3:1 – Roman Rhetoric, Street Announcing, Graffiti, and Crucifixions', *BTB* 44 (2014): 76–86 (78).
[104] Muir, 'Vivid Imagery', 85, citing the use of προεγράφη in magical papyri (78).
[105] Cf. Rabens's similar conclusion regarding the holistic character of Paul's ministry to the Corinthians (*Holy Spirit*, 190).
[106] Twelftree, *Miraculous*, 137.

In hearing his message, then, Paul claims that the Galatians encountered the same revelation that he did, albeit mediated through him. His ministry to the Galatians extends the reach of God's revelation of Christ 'in him' to the 'public exhibition' (προεγράφη) of Christ 'by means of him'. Indeed, the strong sense of identification Paul displays with Christ's crucifixion in his unusual use of συνεσταυρόω in 2:19b ('crucified with') must have been intended to inform his claims in 3:1 that Christ was shown crucified (ἐσταυρωμένος; 3:1) to the Galatians.[107] Thus, in seeing Christ in him, Paul claims that the Galatians came to know God in a transformative way, which constituted them as new people (3:26) and a new community (3:28) living in a new way (3:11). They were converted, with the intention that, like Paul, they would come to see themselves as living 'in Christ' (3:26; 5:6), though it is not clear that Paul considers this to have occurred (4:19).

(c) Culturally patterned expression: The contest over the Galatians' RE

Whereas Paul can assert the relationship of his own RE to his culturally patterned life, his account of the Galatians' RE is more obviously contested. In part, this is because he believes his opponents have already contested it: they have taught the Galatians that further religious observance is necessary, depicting their 'beginning with the Spirit' as a first step in covenant relationship which requires further practices – which Paul characterizes as 'works of the law' (ἔργων νόμου; 3:2, 5) – if it is to be obediently outworked.[108] Against this, Paul argues that further religious observance actually marks a deviation from the Galatians' 'beginning with the Spirit' and is a result of someone having 'bewitched' (ἐβάσκανεν; 3:1) them: to require further religious observance is to reject the revelation of Christ. This is why the Galatians' foolishness is not an issue with their intelligence, but with their spiritual discernment.

A *hapax legomenon*, the meaning of ἐβάσκανεν (3:1) is disputed. In particular, it has been suggested that Paul is using the term 'figuratively'.[109] However, as Oakes notes, 'asking whether it is figurative or literal is probably the wrong question. The pervasiveness of ancient apotropaia ... [means] it would be hard to find bewitch-type uses of *baskaino* that were truly figurative.'[110] Rather, the accusation makes best sense in the context of what Neyrey terms a 'witchcraft society', wherein what Paul perceives

---

[107] Paul does not use σταυρόω and its cognates particularly frequently (twenty occurrences of seventy-nine in the NT), but it occurs seven times in Galatians (2:19; 3:1; 5:11, 24; 6:13x2), more than any other letter (one in Rom 6:6; six in 1 Cor 1:13, 17, 18, 23; 2:2, 8; one in 2 Cor 13:4; two in Phil 2:8; 3:18; two in Col 1:20; 2:14). The compound συνεσταυρόω occurs only in Gal 2:19 and Rom 6:6, where it refers to co-crucifixion in baptism.

[108] Cf. e.g. de Boer, *Galatians*, 179: 'The new preachers in Galatia could thus conceivably have said to Paul's Galatian converts: by undertaking the rite of circumcision, you will not only enter the covenant community; you will also be enabled to achieve a form of perfection, in your living (walking) according to the law of God.'

[109] Cf. de Boer, *Galatians*, 170; Betz, *Galatians*, 130–1.

[110] Oakes, *Galatians*, 101. Likewise, the depiction of Paul in Acts puts him in contact with others who are presented as harnessing power from negative trans-empirical sources (e.g. Acts 13:9–11; 16:16–18). Twelftree, *Miraculous*, 244–8, is dubious regarding the historicity of the first example, but sees in the second 'an authentic contribution to the historical Paul' (252–5).

as prompting deviation from the goal of righteousness can be characterized as the influence of a negative spiritual force.[111] Indeed, the *inclusio* of references to conduct associated with the evil eye (3:1; 4:12–20) could suggest that Paul is here attempting to rebut an *ad hominem* attack – that he himself was an invalid interloper who had caused the Galatians harm – by critiquing the conduct and motives of his accusers. In his defence, Paul points out that the Galatians had not 'spat him out' (ἐξεπτύσατε; 4:14) – referring to spitting, a common response to encountering someone cursed with the evil eye – but welcomed him. Rather it is his envious, boastful opponents (4:17–18) who had put the evil eye on the Galatians.[112] However, Paul's rhetoric need not be read solely sociologically as an othering device. The further references to the oppressive spiritual force of the στοιχεῖα τοῦ κόσμου ('elements of the world'; 4:3, 9)[113] and angels (1:7; 3:13) reinforce the possibility that Paul actually saw malevolent spiritual forces at work in their deviation from his gospel.

Against his opponents' negative spiritual influence, Paul attempts to situate the Galatians' revelatory beginning in relation to his own and thereby to reassert its higher trans-empirical source. Paul argues that in turning to 'a different gospel' the Galatians have abandoned the one who 'called them in grace' (καλέσαντος ὑμᾶς ἐν χάριτι; 1:6). This reads most naturally as a reference to the Apostle himself,[114] but in 1:15 Paul refers to the way that he himself was 'called by [God's] grace' (καλέσας διὰ τῆς χάριτος αὐτοῦ). As McFarland notes, 'Nowhere else does Paul use the verb [καλέσας] with himself as subject; furthermore, in 1 Thess 5:24 "the one who calls" becomes a title of sorts for God.'[115] The implication is that the Galatians *should* see in their original RE an encounter with God-in-Christ which is utterly transformative: 'Both [Paul and the Galatians] were called and thus reconstituted as new creation in the Christ-event.'[116] For Paul, the counterargument to his opponents rests on recalling the Galatians to their original RE because it is here that they themselves recognized God's grace in Christ. It appears that Paul considers his addressees to have deviated from this foundational understanding of his gospel, making the letter to them necessary. Consequently, Paul clarifies the impact of his own encounter with Christ and invites the Galatians to imitate him. In the next section, I will argue that the role RE plays in the Apostle's articulation of his identity and his recommendations for the Galatians should inform our perception of his writing.

---

[111] See Jerome H. Neyrey, *Paul in Other Words: A Cultural Reading of His Letters* (Louisville, KY: Westminster John Knox, 1990), 181–206 (esp. 203–6).
[112] Cf. Elliott, *Beware*, 216–64.
[113] Cf. Richard H. Bell's emphasis on the oppressive role of spiritual forces in enslaving the Galatians (*Deliver Us from Evil: Interpreting the Redemption from the Power of Satan in New Testament Theology*, WUNT II.216 (Tübingen: Mohr Siebeck, 2007), 235–7). Guy Williams also argues for a cosmological interpretation: 'Paul understood the elements of the world to be material and physical substances which exert a demonic or hostile control over human life' (*The Spirit World in the Letters of Paul the Apostle: A Critical Examination of the Role of Spiritual Beings in the Authentic Pauline Epistles* (Göttingen: Vandenhoeck und Ruprecht, 2009), 171).
[114] See e.g. Oakes, *Galatians*, 43; Lyons, *Galatians*, 61.
[115] Orrey McFarland, '"The One Who Calls in Grace": Paul's Rhetorical and Theological Identification with the Galatians', *HBT* 35 (2013): 151–65 (153 n.6).
[116] McFarland, 'Calls in Grace', 164.

5.3. Participatory lives

Having recalled his and his addresees' foundational revelatory REs, Paul addresses the appropriate impact of these initial experiences. He sees himself as doing nothing other than attempting to recall the Galatians to his and their initial RE – which are one and the same insofar as they are encounters with God-in-Christ – in order that it may continue to shape their lives. Thus, Paul's argument is not only rooted in RE but also aims to affect ongoing REs. He does this by describing first his own Christocentric mode of life (2:19–20; §5.3.1), and then arguing that this is an appropriate mode of life for the Galatians (4:12, 20; §5.3.2) before ultimately arguing for a Spirit-led life within an eschatological horizon (5:5, 13–26; §5.4).

5.3.1. Paul's Christ-life

In one of the most striking lines in Galatians, Paul claims, 'I have been crucified with Christ; I live no longer "I", but Christ lives in me' (Χριστῷ συνεσταύρωμαι· ζῶ δὲ οὐκέτι ἐγώ, ζῇ δὲ ἐν ἐμοὶ Χριστός; 2:19–20). Here Paul makes explicit the implications of Christ's revelation 'in him': his mode of life is now no longer lived in a 'fleshly' pattern of existence even though Paul himself remains 'in the flesh'. Rather, he now 'lives by faith in the Son of God' (ἐν πίστει ζῶ τῇ τοῦ υἱοῦ τοῦ θεοῦ; 2:20). The key question for my study is whether, and in what way, this should be seen as a description of RE, because Paul appears to articulate here his core understanding of the ongoing impact of the revelation of Christ to him. This self-understanding, then, is close to the heart of his gospel message, apostolic ministry and consequent letter-writing practice, and should be seen as informing his own perception of what he is doing when he writes to the Galatians.

A wide variety of approaches to Paul's language of 'in Christ/Christ in' has been suggested.[117] The early-twentieth-century discussion of Paul's 'mysticism' by Deissman and Schweitzer[118] as a unique form within a Hellenistic context gave way to Bultmann's argument that Hellenistic mystery language was here being pressed into the service of an ecclesiological understanding.[119] Against Bultmann, Sanders argued that Paul's religion was a 'participationist eschatology'. Intriguingly, at the same time as Sanders

---

[117] Cf. *Forschungeschichten* in Kevin J. Vanhoozer, 'From "Blessed in Christ" to "Being in Christ": The State of Union and the Place of Participation in Paul's Discourse, New Testament Exegesis, and Systematic Theology Today', in *'In Christ' in Paul*, WUNT II.384, ed. Michael J. Thate, Kevin J. Vanhoozer and Constantine R. Campbell (Tübingen: Mohr Siebeck, 2014), 3–33; Grant Macaskill, *Union with Christ in the New Testament* (Oxford: Oxford University Press, 2013), 17–41; Constantine R. Campbell, *Paul and Union with Christ: An Exegetical and Theological Study* (Grand Rapids, MI: Zondervan, 2012), Kindle edition, loc. 669–1243.

[118] See §1.1.1. Cf. also in this period Wilhelm Bousset's definition of Paul's 'Christ piety' as 'the intense feeling of personal belonging and of spiritual relationship with the exalted Lord' (*Kyrios Christos: A History of Belief in Christ from the Beginnings of Christianity to Irenaeus* (1913 repr., Nashville, TN: Abingdon, 1970), 153).

[119] Cf. Rudolf Bultmann, *Theology of the New Testament* (London: SCM, 1952), 298, 311 (italics original): 'Paul *describes Christ's death in analogy with the death of a divinity of the mystery religions* … "In Christ", far from being a formula or mystic union, is primarily an *ecclesiological* formula.'

stressed the 'reality' of Paul's participation, he recognized a theoretical gap in his understanding: 'We seem to lack a category of "reality" – real participation in Christ, real possession of the Spirit – which lies between naive cosmological speculation and belief in magical transference on one hand and a revised self-understanding on the other'.[120]

Since Sanders, there have been various attempts to elucidate the importance of 'real participation'. One prominent example is Hays's articulation of 'narrative participation'. He argues that 'the identification of community members with the protagonist may be so comprehensive that it can be spoken of as "participation" in the protagonist's destiny'.[121] It is not clear, however, that this represents a different *mode* of perception, so much as it maps a change in self-understanding in the form of a transition between competing narratives. On the other hand, Martyn's 'apocalyptic' account of Paul's participation in Christ's crucifixion as 'the form of the death Paul has already experienced as the paradigmatic eschatological *anthropos*'[122] seems to move beyond human experience into a discussion of ontological reality. Although both readings can contribute to an understanding of Paul's theology, they obscure the decisive contribution of Paul's RE because they focus on theological reality at the expense of lived experience. In part, this possibly reflects the underlying theological influence of Barth: although in his *Church Dogmatics*, he takes 'union with Christ' to refer to the 'subjective' element of participation, he insists that this cannot be connected with 'psychological experience'.[123]

Though less prominent, ideas closer to 'magical transference' have also been defended. For example, Ashton argues that Paul's language can be understood by analogy with Shamanic practice and that Paul sees himself as having been 'spirit-possessed' by Christ.[124] The distinctive Christocentricity of Paul's thought makes it difficult to sustain the analogy: Paul's experience appears to have reoriented people away from established patterns of religious thought whereas the Shamanic experience Ashton considers is confirmatory, not innovative.[125]

More recently, both narrative and apocalyptic theological approaches to the NT texts have been employed to offer accounts of how the revelation of Christ might bring about the kind of holistic reorientation of the believer Paul describes. Gorman argues that for Paul, participation means coming to understand one's own narrative identity entirely in light of Christ's with the result that one materially participates in

---

[120] E. P. Sanders, *Paul and Palestinian Judaism: A Comparison of Patterns of Religion* (London: SCM, 1977), 522–3.
[121] Hays, *Faith of Jesus Christ*, 214.
[122] Martyn, *Galatians*, 280.
[123] Karl Barth, *Church Dogmatics* IV/3.2: *The Doctrine of Reconciliation* (Edinburgh: T&T Clark, 1962), 536. Hays's account of 'narrative' draws inspiration from Hans W. Frei (*The Eclipse of Biblical Narrative: A Study in Eighteenth and Nineteenth Century Hermeneutics* (New Haven, CT: Yale, 1974)), who is himself inspired by Barth (vii–viii); Barth's influence is visible in Martyn, *Galatians*, 95–7.
[124] John Ashton, *The Religion of Paul the Apostle* (New Haven, CT: Yale, 2000), 230–3.
[125] Ashton, *Religion*, 235: tribes receiving shamans 'incorporated them without difficulty into the structures of their own religion'. Paul's gospel, however, was exceptional in its iconoclasm in the syncretistic environment of Asia Minor in the first century. Cf. Larry W. Hurtado, *Destroyer of the Gods: Early Christian Distinctiveness in the Roman World* (Waco, TX: Baylor, 2016).

his crucifixion and experiences theosis: 'Thus God's declaration now of "justified!" ... effects by the Spirit, a real, existential process of transformation, which is nothing like a legal fiction'.[126] Similarly, Campbell has argued that participation implies the reception of an entirely new cognitive framework which brings about a new understanding of every situation and includes ethical and affective valences: 'It seems that Christian faith is largely coterminous for Paul with Christian thinking as a whole, whether about the nature of God and of Christ – these being captured by its confessional aspects – or appropriate ethical behavior and ministry, but including fundamental Christian moods and postures like joy, peace, and hope.'[127] Both Gorman and Campbell draw on theological resources, but they do not offer a phenomenological account of how such a change in perception might be linked to a revelation of Christ.

At issue in Paul's description of Christ living 'in him' is a grasp of the world which reaches beyond '(self-)understanding' to feeling, but whose complexity is irreducible to 'belief in magical transference'. I suggest that God's revelation of Christ in Paul could be understood as an affectively toned perception: Paul had a distinctive sense of God's glory as strength in weakness centred on the distinctive content of God's glory in Christ, and this fusion of a non-conceptual grasp of trans-empirical reality and culturally-patterned concept decisively altered his perception. On this account, Paul's claim that Christ lives 'in him' could be understood as referring at least in part to the ongoing impact of the qualitative alteration of his perception through the revelation of Christ in him, and reflecting the kind of 'change in nature' such a perception could work. Having come to perceive everything differently, Paul understood God's revelation of Christ in him to have displaced 'Paul' as his vital existential centre. This was both a theological and an experiential reality, and Eastman notes that something similar is true from a relational perspective: 'The reconstitution of the self has both corporate and individual dimensions.'[128]

My 'experiential' reading of Paul's claim that Christ lives in him offers an account of how his perception was altered that can reconcile different theological readings of the text. On the one hand, the radical alteration of perception supports Campbell's identification of faith as a new mode of 'thinking' inaccessible to the non-believer. On the other, the change occurs within Paul's culturally patterned life and is brought about by a narrative relocation 'into' Christ (cf. 3:26), which coheres with Gorman's identification of justification with co-crucifixion. Central to this process is the 'intrinsic intentionality' of Paul's initial RE: Paul's intuitive grasp of God's glory in Christ represents a new understanding of God which he claims was received from God – or 'revealed'.

Paul came to see himself differently in light of this revelatory RE, such that his gospel message became the central reality of his life. That his experience was an

---

[126] Michael J. Gorman, *Inhabiting the Cruciform God: Kenosis, Justification, and Theosis in Paul's Narrative Soteriology* (Grand Rapids, MI: Eerdmans, 2009), 101.

[127] Douglas A. Campbell, 'Participation and Faith in Paul', in *'In Christ' in Paul*, WUNT II.384, ed. Michael J. Thate, Kevin J. Vanhoozer and Constantine R. Campbell (Tübingen: Mohr Siebeck, 2014), 37–60 (44).

[128] Cf. Susan G. Eastman, *Paul and the Person: Reframing Paul's Anthropology* (Grand Rapids, MI: Eerdmans, 2017), 170.

encounter with the crucified and resurrected Christ would support Matthew Malcolm's claim that Paul is here expressing a '*kerygmatic* identity'.[129] By this, Malcolm means to refer to the employment of an 'experience-formed cultural conceptualization',[130] which construes the gospel as a norm for ongoing life. This category grows out of Malcolm's analysis of Paul's argument in 1 Corinthians, which he takes to be a paradigmatic example of a 'new type of epistolary rhetoric … [in which] the conceptual imagery of the kerygma influences the arrangement and formulation of Christian communication for a liturgical context'.[131] This fits with Paul's allusion to prophetic call narratives to express the impact of God's revelation of Christ to him, insofar as it suggests that his letter is a textualization of a more usually embodied ministry which seeks to convey a revelatory message. Below, I will develop this argument by suggesting that Paul's written expression in Galatians derives from his revealed gospel, and is intended to communicate that content in authoritative form (§5.5.2).

5.3.2. The Galatians' Christ-formation

Thus far, I have argued that one of Paul's central aims in writing to the Galatians is to recall them to their original encounter with Christ: through his 'public exhibition' of Christ, the Galatians were able to see a mediated version of God's revelation of Christ in Paul which he considers should have radically altered their perception of God, themselves and the world. However, it appears that Paul considers the Galatians' 'beginning with the Spirit' not to have come to complete fruition. In 3:27–8 he argues that the RE of their baptism confirmed them in a new identity, but in 4:12 he writes that he wishes they would 'become as I' (Γίνεσθε ὡς ἐγώ), adding in 4:19 that he is 'again suffering birth pangs for them until Christ is formed in them' (οὓς πάλιν ὠδίνω μέχρις οὗ μορφωθῇ Χριστὸς ἐν ὑμῖν). Paul initially presented Christ to them but argues that their turn away from his gospel (1:6–8) means that he must now seek to form Christ in them again.

In recalling their baptism, Paul reminds the Galatians of a ritually mediated RE[132] which functioned as a social boundary marker and situated them as participants in Christ's death. He argues that his addressees were 'baptised into Christ' (εἰς Χριστὸν ἐβαπτίσθητε; 3:27) with the implication that Christ was 'ritually imprinted' on them: 'Christian baptism not only signalled passage from one population to another but generated a new form of identity.'[133] So effective was the association of the

---

[129] Matthew R. Malcolm, '*Kerygmatic Rhetoric* in New Testament Epistles', in *Horizons in Hermeneutics*, ed. Stanley E. Porter and Matthew R. Malcolm (Grand Rapids, MI: Eerdmans, 2013), 69–89. For this designation of Galatians, see 81.
[130] Malcolm, '*Kerygmatic Rhetoric*', 79.
[131] Malcolm, '*Kerygmatic Rhetoric*', 74.
[132] Cf. Catherine Bell's argument that 'formality, fixity, and repetition', combined with 'differentiation from other forms of practice', are key elements in 'producing ritualized acts' (*Ritual Theory Ritual Practice* (Oxford: Oxford University Press, 1992), 92). Baptism fits these criteria, and 'produces nuanced relationships of power' (196) by mediating participation in Christ, which I have already argued should be seen as referring, at least partly, to RE.
[133] Luke Timothy Johnson, *Religious Experience in Earliest Christianity: A Missing Dimension in New Testament Studies* (Minneapolis, MN: Fortress Press, 1998), 77.

participant with Christ that Paul can argue that it trumps other basic categories of social identity: race, status and gender. As Johnson notes, this argument hinges on 'the adequacy of the experience of God in Christ through baptism'.[134]

This is hardly surprising given the close association which Paul makes between baptism and living in Christ: not only have the Galatians been baptized into Christ, but Paul writes that those 'of Christ have crucified the flesh' (οἱ δὲ τοῦ Χριστοῦ τὴν σάρκα ἐσταύρωσαν; 5:24). In Romans 6:5–6, Paul goes so far as to refer to baptism as a 'co-crucifixion' (συνεσταυρώθη; 6:6), using a term which occurs elsewhere only in Galatians 2:19, where it emphasizes the closeness of Paul's participation in Christ's death. Eastman argues that the putting to death of σάρξ,[135] which is clearly associated with baptism, represents the death of 'socially constructed selves' with the positive counterpart that 'the movement of God in Christ into embodied, socially enmeshed existence inaugurates a newly constructed self-in-relation "in Christ"'.[136]

On this account, Paul's mimetic language is closely connected with this new baptismal identity and rooted in his own newly constituted relation to Christ. As Eastman puts it,

> While the mingling of temporal and relational language in Paul's preaching to his converts suggests that the staying power of the gospel is mediated through the relationship he shares with them, the mingling of personal and cosmological language further suggests that this relationship has both human and divine participants. The resultant communal life that Paul envisions with his converts is to display the profoundly transformed and transformative 'mimetic' relationship that Christ has established with humanity ... in which Christ is the fixed element who is imitated but never equalled.[137]

Despite the importance with which Paul treats baptism, it does not appear to have been entirely effectual in this instance. In 3:28 Paul asserts the *idea* of the Galatians' new identity in Christ, but in 4:8–12 he appears to suggest that the *sense* might be missing: if the Galatians had truly come to know God – if they truly grasped God's revelation, and their perception was transformed – then they would recognize weak and impoverished elements (4:9) for what they are, and would not want to be enslaved. The implication is that the Galatians have not fully perceived what Paul publicly exhibited to them.

Apparently with deep feeling (4:20), Paul exhorts his addressees to 'become as I' (Γίνεσθε ὡς ἐγώ; 4:12), arguing that this is the appropriate present expression of their baptism. This is clarified in 4:19, where Paul echoes his claims that Christ was revealed ἐν ἐμοί (1:16) and lives ἐν ἐμοί (2:20) by referring to his pain until 'Christ is formed **in** you' (μορφωθῇ Χριστὸς **ἐν** ὑμῖν). The exhortation to imitation is not rare in Paul.[138] Thus, this exhortation may perhaps be an example of this letter textualizing

---

[134] Johnson, *Experience*, 101.
[135] Though it often is, this need not be a negative term: Paul writes about the life he lives 'in the flesh' by faith in Christ (2:20).
[136] Eastman, *Person*, 168.
[137] Eastman, *Mother Tongue*, 60.
[138] See 1 Cor 4:16, 11:1; Phil 3:17; 1 Thess 1:6–7; 2:14; 2 Thess 3:7–9; Eph 5:1.

Paul's embodied kerygmatic rhetoric which 'aims to effect the adoption of a new mindset and code of conduct by proclaiming the died-and-risen Messiah'.[139] This could have included exhortations to 'become as I am', living in the flesh through faith in Christ. Such an encouragement would perhaps make more sense assuming Paul was present with the people he was addressing. It would also suggest that Paul perceived his ministry holistically, as the living out of his newly cruciform life with those who received him.

Further, it can hardly be accidental that this exhortation is intertwined with the closing of the *inclusio* of references to the evil eye.[140] Against the suggestions of his opponents, Paul hopes to bring the Galatians to a 'true' (4:16) understanding of their relationship to Christ. Rather than being 'bewitched' (3:1) into slavery to malevolent spiritual forces, the Galatians should accept the implications of the new Christ-nature they have put on (3:27). This means having Christ formed in them (4:19), which entails living with the same (self-)understanding as Paul (4:12). Indeed, this is why Paul can draw on his own experience as paradigmatic: God's revelation of Christ in him transformed his perception in such a manner that he expected it to do the same to everyone else who encountered it. Insofar as Paul manifests Christ in his bodily existence he even subverts any distinction between divine and human agency, meaning that he himself can act as an adequate model for the Galatians and can even bring them 'to birth' in this new reality.[141] Moreover, the implication is that the text of this letter itself can usefully serve this purpose because it can recall the Galatians to their initial gospel encounter and enable them to be re-formed as a result.

5.4. Ethical empowerment

In addressing the formation of Christ in the Galatians, Paul points to specific impacts of their RE which extend beyond attitude to socially embodied praxis[142] – to their life lived 'in the flesh' (2:20). They are to live as 'one in Christ', abrogating all previous identities (3:28).[143] Towards the close of the letter, his focus turns towards the future and he refers to a shared waiting with hope in the power of the Spirit (5:5). Returning to the distinctive Spirit-terminology which differentiates the account of the Galatians' conversion from the Christocentric vocabulary of his own testimony, Paul exhorts his

---

[139] Malcolm, '*Kerygmatic Rhetoric*', 75.
[140] Cf. Elliott, *Beware*, 216–18.
[141] Contra Beverly R. Gaventa's argument that Paul refers here *primarily* to 'apocalyptic' birth pains rather than his own ('The Maternity of Paul', in *The Conversation Continues: Studies in Paul and John in Honor of J. Louis Martyn*, ed. Robert T. Fortna and Beverly R. Gaventa (Nashville, TN: Abingdon, 1990), 189–201): this assumes a separation between Christ and Paul which Gal 2:20 subverts.
[142] Paul notably 'slips into addressing the individual directly' in 6:3–6 and 7b–8 (Ramsaran, 'Religious Experience', 173) and this must stand in constructive tension with his focus on 'the community of the new creation' (Barclay, *Gift*, 423; cf. 3:28).
[143] For this reason, Esler is wrong to look for 'something else, and something more related to practice, rather than messianic belief' as the cause for offence in the Pauline gospel (Philip F. Esler, *Galatians*, NTR (London: Routledge, 1998), 123). To do so presupposes a divide between theology and ethics problematized by my construal of God's revelation of Christ in Paul as an affectively toned perception.

recipients: 'Live by the Spirit … and do not gratify the desires of the flesh' (5:16). As Barclay notes, this is to be a form of life 'inscribed in all manner of bodily habits and expectations'.[144] Thus, Paul is arguing for a model of human agency transformed by the Spirit, in which the Galatians 'are poised for action in a new way'[145] on the basis of their REs. Here, Paul's argument reaches beyond cognitive content into the lived experience of the Galatians on the broadest horizon.

As Zahl notes, Paul focuses on desire (5:16–17) presenting life in the Spirit 'in the simple, affective terms of a struggle between competing desires, those of the flesh and those of the Spirit. Right desiring is seen here to be in some sense more fundamental than right knowing'.[146] This offers a way to understand the tension between the assertion that those led by the Spirit will not gratify the desires of the flesh (5:16) and the exhortation to 'be guided by the Spirit' (5:25). The former implies what Dunn terms an 'overmastering compulsion',[147] whereas the latter could be taken as suggesting that control over the process is centred in the individual.[148] For Zahl, Paul offers in 5:16–25 descriptions of 'feelings, dispositions, and events that tend to happen in human lives, and that the Galatians can expect to happen in their lives, in order to give them some kind of map or guide or interpretive key with which to make sense of their own particular experiences'.[149] On this account, the list of the fruit of the Spirit (5:22–23) offers the Galatians a normative example against which they could examine their actions for evidence of the Spirit's activity. In other words, for Paul, these specific actions, moods and postures offer a tangible, embodied manifestation of the Spirit, in a similar way to how he 'takes the occurrence of miracles as evidence of God's activity' in 3:1–5.[150]

This coheres with an understanding of Paul's revelation as an affectively toned perception. Wynn argues that the kind of transformation suggested 'is not simply a matter of their having qualitatively new experiences or ideas. Their behaviour is also changed, corresponding to their new principle of activity'.[151] On this account it is possible to understand Paul's claim that certain actions are the 'fruit of the Spirit' – that they seem to result more from the activity of the Spirit within the believer than from the imposition of the believer's self-understanding – and fits with the way that affective perceptions can include bodily dispositions.[152] The apprehension of God-in-Christ is a complex perception, but the principle holds: God-in-Christ has been revealed to the Galatians and become their existential centre and Paul suggests that this can be

---

[144] Barclay, *Gift*, 507.
[145] Peter Goldie, *The Emotions: A Philosophical Exploration* (Oxford: Oxford University Press, 2000), 61.
[146] Simeon Zahl, 'The Drama of Agency: Affective Augustinianism and Galatians', in *Galatians and Christian Theology: Justification, the Gospel, and Ethics in Paul's Letter*, ed. Mark W. Elliott et al. (Grand Rapids, MI: Baker Academic, 2014), 335–52 (336).
[147] Dunn, *Galatians*, 300–1.
[148] Cf. e.g. Fee, *Galatians*, 208–10, who presents the issue as one of individual choice between one's own instincts and a new way of life in the Spirit. This obscures the lived experience of the Spirit's power.
[149] Zahl, 'Drama of Agency', 348.
[150] Twelftree, *Miraculous*, 191.
[151] Wynn, *Emotional Experience*, 130.
[152] Cf. §2.1; Wreford, 'Diagnosing', 212–13.

expected to manifest itself in 'a way of life that is quite distinct from anything that the natural person can achieve'.[153] This reflects the reconstitution of their personhood away from all previous identities, towards a new reality. However, while it does make certain actions more likely it does not remove agency, reflecting the tension present in Paul's own thought (in e.g. Phil 2:12–13).

At the heart of this shift is an encounter with Christ. Paul diminishes the terminological gap between God's revelation of Christ in him and the Spirit-governed experience of the Galatians themselves by closely associating Christ and the Spirit: what constitutes successful life in/led by the Spirit similarly fulfils the 'law of Christ' (Gal 6:2, cf. 5:14). In 5:22–6, for example, possession of the fruit of the Spirit (22–3) is a mark of belonging to Christ (24) and of being led by the Spirit (25).[154] Thus, the marks of the Spirit's work should both be visible in the Galatians, and give them cause for confidence as they 'wait' (5:5): it is not necessary to be circumcised because they already embody the impact of trans-empirical reality. In extending the temporal horizon of his comments, Paul also attempts to secure an ongoing relevance for both his gospel message and, more immediately, his letter, by situating the Galatians as actors within an eschatological horizon.[155] This hints already at the authoritative status intended for the letter: it aims to embed its readers in a kerygmatic identity, shaping any future RE on the basis of the fundamental RE of an encounter with God in Christ.

5.4.1. Summary

In this section, I have suggested that the argument of Galatians is rooted in a double pattern of RE: Paul argues that he and the Galatians both had revelatory beginnings, that these – at least should – lead to participatory lives and that they now live in the power of the Spirit. At the root of this argument is God's revelation of Christ in Paul, which I have argued can be understood as an affectively toned perception. This experiential reading of Paul's initial encounter offers a coherent explanation of the connection between his theological understanding and lived reality which can contribute to the discussion of what it means to speak about Paul's 'union with Christ', a mode of life which he presents as decisively different from any other and accessible only to believers, but in which the Galatians are insecure. In the final section of the letter, Paul also considers the way in which this decisive reorientation should manifest in ongoing embodied everyday existence. At every point, Paul's intent is to bring people into contact with the revelation of Christ 'in him'. Ultimately, then, Paul is attempting to portray Christ crucified again before the Galatians' eyes in this letter, and to bring them to an understanding which reshapes their lives. Accordingly, the written expression of his argument in Galatians is decisively shaped by the impact of

---

[153] Wynn, *Emotional Experience*, 131.
[154] The terminological closeness of Christ and the Spirit in this verse is representative of a trend in the letter as a whole and particularly of this section (5:2–6:10). Cf. also 3:13–14, 4:6 and 5:4–6; cf. Fee, *Galatians*, 226.
[155] Cf. Eastman, *Person*, 175: 'Human personhood, as intersubjectively constituted in relationship with Christ, belongs to the future, not to the past.' Cf. Zahl, 'Drama of Agency', 346–9.

God's revelation of Christ to him,[156] as is his purpose in writing: he intends to convey the revelatory impact of his RE in an authoritative text.

5.5. Religious experience and the creation of Galatians

The argument of Galatians is rooted in RE, but the act of writing itself requires further examination. In this section, I will argue that this act can be usefully interpreted within the same framework of RE by considering Paul's purpose and the particular content of the letter. I will suggest that Paul is using the letter to make himself present to the Galatians to defend his gospel (§5.5.1). This means that the letter is intended to be authoritative, and the close connection between Paul's gospel message and the content of the letter also implies a claim of inspiration derived from its roots in the revelation of Christ in him (§5.5.2). Finally, I will argue that, although Paul's text was intended to address the Galatian conflict, there are hints – internal and external – that suggest he viewed what is written here as having a relevance which reaches beyond its immediate purpose (§5.5.3). With this last point, it becomes legitimate to argue that Paul intended the text to fulfil a scriptural function.

5.5.1. Paul's purpose in writing: Galatians as defence speech

In writing Galatians Paul appears to have been addressing a charged relational context, defending his apostleship (1:1–5, 10; 2:1–10) and gospel message (1:10–11). The lack of a thanksgiving section and the 'vehement' tone of the letter, already recognized by Chrysostom,[157] suggest that he considered attack the best form of defence. Nevertheless, the letter attempts to recall the Galatians to their initial encounter with Christ through Paul's embodied ministry (3:1–5) and draw out its implications (see e.g. 3:25–4:7; 5:16–25). Thus, Martyn rightly argues that the letter is intended to replace an oral sermon which 'would have been a reproclamation of the gospel in the form of an evangelistic argument'.[158]

Partly as a consequence, Paul's role in producing the writing becomes visible in hints that he is wrestling with the limits of the medium that support Martyn's claim. For example, the Apostle attempts to offset the distance between himself and the persona adopted by his reader in 4:20 through the inclusion of a 'stage direction' by way of a reference to his own intended tone of voice. This is in keeping with Paul's practice in other letters. For example, he uses verbs of speech to refer to comments made earlier in his letters (Phlm 21) and assumes that a performance of the letter could convey not only

---

[156] Cf. Malcolm's similar conclusion regarding 1 Corinthians: 'Paul is a figure whose experience on the Damascus Road led him to a life-altering kerygma of the Messiah who died, rose, and awaits cosmic manifestation. This kerygma, it seems, went on to shape the ways in which Paul adopted and adapted rhetorical resources, whether Jewish or Greco-Roman' (Matthew R. Malcolm, *Paul and the Rhetoric of Reversal in 1 Corinthians: The Impact of Paul's Gospel on his Macro-Rhetoric*, SNTSMS 155 (Cambridge: Cambridge University Press, 2013), 268).
[157] Chrysostom, *Hom. Gal.* 1.1–3 (Edwards).
[158] Martyn, *Galatians*, 22.

the written content but also his tone (2 Cor 10:1, 11). Further, in 1 Corinthians Paul assumes that the delivery and performance of his text can even make him spiritually present (1 Cor 5:3; cf. Col 2:5) to render judgements in his own authoritative voice (1 Cor 7:6, 8, 12). That Paul can refer in Galatians to his own autograph (6:11), yet still offer blessings (6:16) and curses (1:8), demonstrates that the same presuppositions regarding the function of the letter apply here: Paul assumes that his writing makes him 'spiritually present' in such a way that he can speak authoritatively to the congregation receiving it.[159] Thus, Forbes argues that 'Paul wrote letters to function as speeches',[160] and although Paul's relationship with the Galatians is strained, his emotional appeals (e.g. 4:12–20) suggest it remains sufficiently robust for his letter to receive a sufficiently sympathetic audience that it represents an effective method for him to 'reproclaim' his gospel to them.

In doing this, though, Paul takes a significant risk: he has attempted to textualize his gospel message. As I have argued above (§5.2.1), Paul's defence of his gospel message and apostleship are intimately tied up with RE, meaning that in writing he risks flattening this element of his embodied evangelistic practice and reducing the gospel to propositional content which can be conveyed in writing. The attempt to incorporate trans-empirical elements into the argument of the letter and the inclusion of blessing and curse support this argument, because they suggest that Paul is aware of this issue and attempting to demonstrate the capacity of his writing to affect spiritual realities.[161] Betz notes this and even suggests a connection between these 'magical' elements and the representation of the gospel: 'By including this dimension of magic [with an *inclusio* of conditional curse (1:8–9) and blessing (6:16)], Paul *repeats* the Galatians' initial confrontation with the gospel.'[162] Allied with the close association Paul claims with Christ, this raises the possibility that it could even be seen as a 'heavenly letter', which Betz claims may have been 'an internal reason for Paul's letter becoming Holy Scripture'.[163]

Betz's complex macrorhetorical analysis has been called into question,[164] and rhetorical[165] and epistolary[166] analyses have proved unable to produce a decisive account of the structure of Galatians.[167] In his analysis of 1 Corinthians, however,

---

[159] Glen S. Holland, '"Delivery, Delivery, Delivery": Accounting for Performance in the Rhetoric of Paul's Letters', in *Paul and Ancient Rhetoric: Theory and Practice in the Hellenistic Context*, ed. Stanley E. Porter and Bryan R. Dyer (Cambridge: Cambridge University Press, 2016), 119–40 (131), makes a similar point regarding 1 Cor 16:21–2.

[160] Christopher Forbes, 'Ancient Rhetoric and Ancient Letters: Models for Reading Paul, and Their Limits', in *Paul and Rhetoric*, ed. J. Paul Sampley and Peter Lampe (New York: T&T Clark, 2010), 143–60 (160).

[161] This attitude is also visible in the magical papyri.

[162] Betz, *Galatians*, 25; italics original. Cf. Keener, *Galatians*, 43, who argues that the language is scriptural and Betz goes too far.

[163] Betz, *Galatians*, 25.

[164] For an early critique, see Wayne Meeks, 'A review of Galatians by Hans Dieter Betz', *JBL* 100 (1984): 304–7.

[165] Most prominently, Betz, *Galatians*, 14–25.

[166] G. Walter Hansen, *Abraham in Galatians: Epistolary and Rhetorical Contexts*, JSNTSup 29 (Sheffield: Sheffield Academic, 1989), 22–44; Longenecker, *Galatians*, c–cix.

[167] Cf. Kern, *Rhetoric and Galatians*, 258–9, who concludes that the macrorhetoric of the letter does not align with any conventional structure.

Malcolm argues that Paul's ethical exhortations in chapters 5–14 draw on Jewish and Hellenistic rhetorical resources, but are shaped by a general logic rooted in union with Christ: 'Those who are brought into union with Christ in his bodily accomplishments are called to offer their bodies selflessly to God through Christ, and participate lovingly within the body of Christ.'[168] Malcolm describes this as Paul's 'kerygmatic rhetoric', and something similar appears to be true of Paul's letter to the Galatians. This epistle 'repreaches' Paul's gospel message with the aim of 'forming Christ' in its recipients (4:19). Specifically, they are called to imitate Paul (4:12), who has been 'crucified with Christ' and now lives 'by faith in the Son of God who loved me and gave himself for me' (2:19–20). Malcolm's analysis offers a different lens through which to view Betz's identification of ways in which the text attempts to highlight its relation to trans-empirical reality. Although Paul may not have intended to write a 'magical letter', he nevertheless intended to write one which could achieve a trans-empirical impact insofar as it adequately conveyed his revelatory gospel message. Thus, the suggestion that the letter's relation to trans-empirical realities may be an internal reason for its later canonization remains a helpful insight.

5.5.2. Inspired content: Paul's gospel

Betz rightly points to the importance of Paul's Christocentric identity for an understanding of the letter's status, but before the Apostle claims that Christ now lives in him (2:19–20) he allusively employs prophetic call vocabulary to depict God's revelation of Christ in him (1:15). This means that the risk Paul takes in flattening his gospel by textualizing his embodied proclamation is substantial but not unprecedented. Rather, Paul's text is situated within a tradition which can be traced back to the prophetic literature[169] and this should inform our understanding of the letter's content. Significantly, though, while Paul alludes to Jeremiah's prophetic call to situate his own ministry (Gal 1:15–16), at the same time he asserts that his gospel is a decisively new revelation from God (1:11–12). Here, then, Paul claims to stand in a new relation to Scripture on the basis of his initial RE.

In the first instance, this prompts a re-evaluation of his relationship to established Scripture. As Hays notes, 'The pharisaic Judaism from which he defected was by all accounts a way of life grounded in the conscientious interpretation and application of Israel's sacred texts, [so] Paul's turning to Jesus Christ must have entailed some fundamental reassessment of the meaning and use of these texts.'[170] Hays points to the allusion to LXX Jeremiah 38:33 in 2 Corinthians 3:2, to argue that Paul differentiates between the Corinthians as 'a breathing instantiation of the word of God' and the

---

[168] Malcolm, *Rhetoric of Reversal*, 169.
[169] So e.g. Klaus Berger, 'Apostelbrief und apostolische Rede', *ZNW* 65 (1974): 190–231. Doering argues that Berger overstates his case, downplaying the form of the letters (*Ancient Jewish Letters and the Beginnings of Christian Epistoligraphy* (Tübingen: Mohr Siebeck), 2012, 409–10). While this must nuance Berger's argument, it does not require a complete rejection as Paul self-consciously situates himself in relation to prophetic traditions.
[170] Richard B. Hays, *Echoes of Scripture in the Letters of Paul* (New Haven, CT: Yale University Press, 1989), 122.

'script' of Israel's sacred texts: 'For Paul, the Spirit is – scandalously – identified precisely with the outward and palpable, the particular human community of the new covenant, putatively transformed by God's power so as to make Christ's message visible to all. The script, however, remains abstract and dead because it is not embodied.'[171] Hays's analysis helpfully highlights the importance of the living, Spirit-empowered community as evidence of Paul's gospel. However, it risks obscuring the fact that the 'letter of Christ' Paul writes about is itself 'enabled both through the visits, but especially through the medium of Paul's written letters to the congregation which must then be read by the living voice of a trusted surrogate'.[172] Thus, Paul's presentation of his own call as prophetic raises the possibility that he understood his writing practices in prophetic terms.

It is significant, then, that the text of Jeremiah depicts the prophet writing a letter to the exiled Judeans (Jer 29:1–23 [LXX 36:1–15, 21–23])[173] that begins, 'Thus says the Lord of hosts, the God of Israel' (Jer 29:4).[174] In this sense, Jeremiah's letter appears intended to convey revelatory content which is presented as God's message to its addressees. Examining a similar connection in his discussion of 1 Thessalonians, Deines highlights the prominence of the 'word of the Lord' formula to the creation of OT prophetic writings and notes that Paul presents his own gospel as a 'word of God' (1 Thess 2:13).[175] In Galatians, then, the allusion to Jeremiah at the point at which Paul is textualizing his embodied gospel message suggests that he may have understood his own writing practices in prophetic terms in light of this connection. As Newman puts it, 'Just as Jeremiah used a scribe to transmit his oracular pronouncements and promises (Jer 31 [sic]) so must Paul communicate in writing when his own living voice is unable to reach his audience.'[176]

Further, Newman adds that Paul's willingness to depict himself in prophetic terms suggests that he operated with 'an understanding of scripture as a living matrix of text requiring constant engagement … that is, an un-canonized set of growing scriptures'.[177] On her account, the Apostle's own letters were written to extend this growing corpus, with Paul intending them to be added to the ranks of prophetic interpretations of the Torah. Newman's depiction of an authoritative set of texts whose boundaries

---

[171] Hays, *Echoes*, 131.
[172] Newman, 'Speech and Spirit', 260. Cf. Jeffrey W. Aernie, *Is Paul also Among the Prophets?*, LNTS 467 (London: T&T Clark, 2012), 162 n.175: 'The import of the two rhetorical questions in 2 Cor. 3.1 is not to condemn the practice of writing letters of recommendation … [Paul] would be discrediting his own practice.'
[173] Jer 29:24–32 also details an exchange of letters between Shemaiah of Nehelam and Jeremiah which, in the current ordering, immediately precedes the word of the Lord to Jeremiah to write his prophetic oracles in a book (30:1–3). Doering also notes that this passage 'has become formative for a number of texts associated with Jeremiah or his companion Baruch' (*Jewish Letters*, 104).
[174] In the MT, the phrase is לארשי יהלא תואבצ הוהי רמא הכ. The LXX has Οὕτως εἶπεν κύριος ὁ θεὸς Ισραηλ.
[175] See Deines, 'Paul's Letters', 304–6.
[176] Newman, 'Speech and Spirit', 262. The comparison is strengthened if Paul's use of 'secretaries' is taken into account; cf. E. Randolph Richards, *Paul and First-Century Letter Writing: Secretaries, Composition and Collection* (London: SPCK, 2005).
[177] Newman, 'Speech and Spirit', 262–3. Cf. Eva Mroczek, *The Literary Imagination in Jewish Antiquity* (Oxford: Oxford University Press, 2016).

nevertheless remained fluid during the period Paul was active is likely correct, but is not clear that Paul's focus is primarily on textual interpretation.[178] Rather, Paul's approach is closer to Jeremiah's: he retells in authoritative voice God's new actions in his own and the Galatians' lives.

In this sense, Paul's writing is closer in intent to OT prophetic literature than the rewritten Scriptures of the Second Temple period. While there are similarities with attempts to draw out the significance of Scripture,[179] Paul's writing is emphatically *not* a rewritten Scripture drawing out the significance of Israel's sacred texts in a new context. Rather, it is a response to his new affectively toned perception of God-in-Christ. Accordingly, it is presented as a part of the manifestation of Christ in him to others and part of the expression of his prophetic vocation. In textualizing Paul's embodied performance of the gospel, Galatians is intended to offer an adequate reminder of his 'public exhibition' of Christ crucified, standing in for a 'reproclamation' in the living voice. Indeed, the letter as a whole shares the character of Paul's embodied ministry and autobiography: it acquires authority by witnessing to the impact of Christ. For this reason, the claims Paul makes about his gospel – about its source, its content and its culturally patterned impact – apply to his letter as well.

This approach to writing coheres with the manner in which God's revelation of Christ in Paul led him to recount his own experience in prophetic mode as a witness to God's activity. In this way, his RE opened up a new religious horizon for Paul, giving him a revelatory new message which he felt compelled to share. Like Peter in Acts, Paul asserts that his witness can be trusted because he is accredited as a 'skilled knower' – an apostle – by contact with trans-empirical reality (1:11–12, 15–16; 2:6–9) which he and the Galatians share (3:1–5; 4:6). This extends the story of God's interaction with his people into the present, though now in light of the decisive intervention of the Christ-event in a similar manner to the way that Luke-Acts recounts a scriptural history of fulfilment.[180] Paul's letter was intended to offer an authoritative (1:20) retelling of recent salvation history in the shape of his and the Galatians' initial encounters with Christ, and a normative account of its ongoing impact through the ethical empowerment of the Spirit (5:13–26). In this sense, it is intended to fulfil a scriptural function for its addressees.

5.5.3. Galatians' wider relevance

In this chapter I have argued that in Galatians Paul is trying to call his addressees back to a gospel message rooted in an affectively toned perception of God-in-Christ. This means that the letter crystallizes in textual form elements of Paul's revealed gospel message, implying that the content of the letter should itself be seen in the same light.

---

[178] Contra Wendt, 'Textual Prophecy'.

[179] Cf. Crawford, who identifies an important impulse underlying the scribal task of rewriting Scripture as the need 'to make the text of Scripture adaptable and relevant to the contemporary situation' (*Rewriting Scripture in Second Temple Times* (Grand Rapids, MI: Eerdmans, 2008), 3). Cf. also John J. Collins, 'Uses of Torah in the Second Temple Period', in *When Texts Are Canonized*, ed. Timothy H. Lim (Providence, RI: Brown, 2017), 44–62 (52–61).

[180] Cf. Horrell, 'Paul's Narratives', 162–3.

Further, there are internal and external indicators that Paul's articulation of his gospel here has a relevance beyond its immediate contribution to the dialogue between him and his addressees.

Taking the internal elements first, when Paul refers to the 'gospel which I gospelled' (1:11), this is not limited as it is in the parallel passage in 1 Corinthians 15:3. There, Paul refers to what he preached to one particular group, using the dative plural to designate the recipients of his letter. Here, however, no mention is made of a specific audience.[181] Moreover, in light of the wider 'ecumenical' dispute which Paul goes on to detail in Galatians 2:1–15, it makes sense to see this as a reference to the very essence of his gospel message: Paul is referring to the core of the revelatory gospel given to him by God (Gal 1:10–11; cf. 1:1–5) and which was central to his understanding of his apostleship. Indeed, the consistency of his gospel message is a key element of what he is defending here.[182]

Later in Galatians, Paul's passing reference to an ongoing waiting (5:5) also extends the temporal horizon of the letter beyond the present moment. Though Paul clearly perceives the Christ-event to have had decisive historical relevance, his intention is at least partially to secure his congregation as a legacy which can outlast his immediate influence,[183] and the postures he associates with Spirit-empowered life are intended to be normative throughout that time, however long it lasts.

Second, beyond these internal hints, the articulation of the gospel in Galatians appears to have been a resource which Paul returned to in writing his later letters.[184] It is well recognized that Galatians is unusual among Paul's letters in its appeal to God's revelation of Christ to Paul in defence of his apostleship. It is telling, then, that it shares significant similarities with Romans, wherein Paul offers the most systematic exploration of his gospel message for the benefit of addressees he likely is not yet personally acquainted with.[185] A striking common feature in the setting of these two letters is the prominence of Paul's gospel, with their similarity likely resulting from this thematic link rather than a chronological one: in both, Paul is spelling out in authoritative voice what he sees as significant elements and implications of his gospel. That there are similarities with the different context of the Corinthian correspondence reinforces the apparent centrality of the material developed in Galatians to Paul's thought. Specifically, it reinforces the likelihood that Paul is here articulating the core of his missionary message in textual form.

Though it is beyond the scope of this study to offer a comprehensive account of the debate surrounding the destination and date of Galatians,[186] the weakness of

---

[181] So similarly Fee, *Galatians*, 35.
[182] Cf. Simon Gathercole, 'E pluribus unum? Apostolic Unity and Early Christian Literature', in *The Enduring Authority of the Christian Scriptures*, ed. D. A. Carson (London: Apollos, 2016), 407–55.
[183] Cf. Newman, 'Speech and Spirit', 262.
[184] Cf. Richards's argument that Paul likely kept copies of his important letters (*Letter Writing*, 158–9). It is possible that such a collection could underlie early moves towards canonization. That collections of Paul's writings were viewed as authoritative as early as the end of the first century is visible in *First Clement* and the writings of Ignatius of Antioch and Polycarp of Smyrna.
[185] Cf. the discussion in Richard N. Longenecker, *Introducing Romans: Critical Issues in Paul's Most Famous Letter* (Grand Rapids, MI: Eerdmans, 2011), 92–166. That Romans represents an exposition of the gospel is suggested by the *propositio* itself (Rom 1:16–17).
[186] For an overview, cf. Das, *Galatians*, 19–47; Witherington, *Grace*, 1–20.

terminological arguments[187] and the lack of evidence from Acts for north Galatian detours in areas lacking Roman roads[188] makes it more likely that south Galatians are the intended recipients of the letter – specifically those in the churches planted in the cities of Psidian Antioch, Iconium, Lystra and Derbe. If Paul is writing to south Galatian churches, this opens up the possibility that the letter is one of his earliest. The significance of this for my argument lies in the strong 'family resemblances'[189] between Galatians and Romans[190] and elements of the Corinthian correspondence.[191] Though these are occasionally cited as internal evidence which favours a late date for the letter on the basis of the apparent trajectory of the development of Paul's thought,[192] if their dates were in fact separated by a number of years it could be taken as evidence that Paul's articulation of his theology in this letter had a lasting relevance which exceeded its application here. The point holds, though perhaps less strongly, even if a later date is assumed. The similarities between these letters which each address very different contexts suggest that the core of Paul's gospel message remained stable throughout his ministry and that his defence of it in this context can legitimately be seen as having had a resonance beyond its immediate application.

5.5.4. Galatians as Scripture

The internal and external suggestions that Galatians was intended to have a lasting relevance are significant insofar as they illuminate the intended function of the text. In this defensive letter Paul offers his most explicit reference to his own revelatory beginning, and situates both this and the Galatians' initial evangelization in relation to established Scripture. His own RE issued in a revealed message and prophetic call, and he rebuts alternate scriptural interpretations of the Galatians' revelatory beginning. In writing Galatians, then, the Apostle offers instead *his own* witness to the significance of these REs for the purpose of enabling the Galatians to understand

---

[187] Hemer has demonstrated that the moniker 'Galatian' can be applied to mixed-ethnicity inhabitants of the south of the province (*The Book of Acts in the Setting of Hellenistic History* (Tübingen: Mohr Siebeck, 1989), 299-305) against the earlier suggestion that it would have been impolite at best (so e.g. Martyn, *Galatians*, 16; cf. BDAG 186-7). Similarly, the argument that Paul consistently prefers to speak geographically about Roman provinces has also been problematized (Cf. Werner G. Kümmel, *Introduction to the New Testament* (London: SCM, 1966), 192-3).

[188] Any north Galatian travel would have to be located in the slender references to Galatia in Acts 16:6 and 18:23 and be deemed to have left sufficiently little trace as to have no impact in the reports.

[189] Cf. Timothy H. Lim, 'An Indicative Definition of the Canon', in *When Texts Are Canonized*, ed. Timothy H. Lim (Providence, RI: Brown, 2017), 1-24. Lim argues that 'biblical texts have affinities one with another as a family of texts, and they coincidentally resemble books that were not included in the canon'. Within the Pauline corpus, this kind of logic is often used to define which books are 'close' (genuine) and 'distant' (deutero-Pauline) relatives.

[190] Cf. already Lightfoot, *Galatians*, 49. The list of similarities (45-8) remains useful; for a recent restatement, cf. Moo, *Galatians*, 17-18.

[191] Cf. Ulrich Borse, *Der Standort des Galaterbriefes*, BBB 41 (Cologne: Peter Hanstein, 1972), 84-119; for a recent restatement cf. Fee, *Galatians*, 4-6.

[192] So e.g. Fee, *Galatians*, 4-5. The theory that Paul's theology developed sufficiently during his letter-writing career that late writings are distinguishable from earlier ones is undermined by the fact that seventeen years of reflection and missionary activity likely already lay behind him by the time he wrote even his earliest extant letter.

rightly and be formed by them – that is, he offers *a new Scripture*. The preservation of the letter implies that its initial addressees similarly viewed it as sufficiently important to ensure its survival. As a textual articulation of Paul's dynamic, embodied gospel it easily acquired authoritative status, to the extent that it possibly started to function as Scripture within his own lifetime. That his argument here appears to have a wider relevance even within the Pauline corpus suggests that this letter began to function in this way for Paul himself.

Consequently, Paul's letter was not only intended to communicate revealed content but also to function as Scripture. It achieved this aim primarily by witnessing to REs in which God's activity was discerned. In this sense, Paul's letter to the Galatians shares important similarities with Luke's *Doppelwerk*. In each case, the author intended to produce a document witnessing to the new, surprising action of the God of Israel who had become active again in Jesus Christ and consequently within the experience of the first disciples and those to whom Paul made this experience evident in his own proclamation of the gospel. In short, the similarity between the very different texts Luke and Paul wrote is that they were each intended as Scripture.

Conclusion: Religious Experience and the Creation of Scripture

In this study, I have argued that religious experience (RE) was influential in the production of NT writings which were intended as scriptural by their authors, outlining a pattern in Luke-Acts which is also discernible in Paul's letter to the Galatians despite the evident differences between the two texts. In this conclusion, I will summarize the central findings of each chapter and bring the threads together. In Section 1, I considered RE as a topic in NT research. Chapter 1 situated the work in relation to a *Forschungsgeschichte*, which began with a short comment on the broad theological trends which provided the historical context for the *religionsgeschichtliche* focus on lived experience of the Spirit that began with Gunkel. This demonstrated the contested theological nature of the topic, an insight reinforced by the lacuna in research on RE between c.1930 and Dunn's *Baptism in the Spirit* in 1970, during which time dialectical theology was a dominant theological movement. Despite the recovery of interest since Dunn, I noted four theoretical issues which had not been satisfactorily resolved: the linguistic turn raised the question of the accessibility of subjective experience through texts; constructivist accounts of RE raised the question of whether it could have innovative force; taking RE seriously raises questions concerning the nature of reality presupposed in historical reconstruction; and an inductive definition of RE remained a desideratum.

In Chapter 2, I addressed these unresolved issues. I first defended Dunn's argument that a 'sensitive reading' of the texts could allow insight into the experiences which shaped them. Next, I argued that Hurtado's account of the innovative role REs can play in theological development demands a reworking of presuppositions regarding RE. I engaged religious studies resources to argue that phenomenology of religion offered an approach to the texts which would allow the impact of REs to be foregrounded, and supplemented this general approach with Wynn's specific models comparing emotional and religious experience. To address the questions raised by RE for regnant historiographical presuppositions, I argued that the resources of theological historiography could more effectively enable an analysis of the worldviews of the authors of the texts which is nevertheless uncommitted to their truth claims. I then offered a heuristic definition of RE as *the felt impacts of trans-empirical realities within the culturally patterned life of an individual or group.*

In the remainder of Chapter 2, I considered the category of Scripture. In conversation with Deines, I outlined an account of how Scripture arises, arguing that a text is intended as scriptural if it claims an authoritative religious role on the basis that it conveys revelatory content. Though reception by a faith community is a key part of the process by which a scriptural text might become canonical, I have focused on the role of RE in shaping claims to scriptural status.

In Section 2, I applied this approach to Luke-Acts and Galatians, arguing that Luke's account of Christian origins outlines a pattern for the role of RE in shaping NT writings which is also visible, though in a different way, in Paul's letter. In Chapter 3, I focused on Pentecost (Acts 2) arguing that Luke presents the outpouring of the Spirit as a theophanic episode and that this has significant implications for the disciples' tongues-speech. As part of the event of Pentecost, the disciples' tongues-speech is included within God's revelatory action. This establishes a precedent which Luke immediately applies to Peter's sermon. This speech is described as the same kind of 'utterance' (Acts 2:11), as well as being the prototypical fulfilment of Jesus' promise that the disciples would be empowered to witness (1:8). Further, in Peter's sermon, Luke already begins to hint at the implications of the RE-derived status of these speech acts for his own text: like the prophetic Scriptures he uses in his construction of Peter's sermon, the text of Acts claims to record the revelatory speech of prophets empowered to speak God's words.

In Chapter 4, I took up the argument that Luke's presentation of these REs implies a claim to scriptural status on behalf of his own text by considering his portrayal of the inclusion of the Gentiles (Acts 10–11, 15). This long narrative describes the process by which Peter comes to a new understanding of God's character which challenges and ultimately reshapes his community's theological paradigm on the basis of REs. In the response to Peter's witness in Acts 11 and then at the Jerusalem convocation in Acts 15, Luke describes a communal journey of discovery which mirrors Peter's. It is striking that this process is guided primarily by Peter's witness, rather than directly by REs. Here, Luke shifts the locus of revelation from the events themselves to Peter's witness to them. Indeed, God's witness to the Gentiles in the RE of the Spirit-falling in Acts 10 is represented at the Jerusalem convocation in Peter's summary of the events and their significance. In Acts 11 and 15, Peter's speeches even evoke the kinds of reaction associated elsewhere with REs. Thus, it appears that Luke is presenting Peter's witness to his inspired insight in the same way that he presents the tongues-speech and sermon at Pentecost: as revelatory. Peter's contribution, supported by Paul and Barnabas's second witness, is interpreted by James in much the same way that Peter's scriptural sermon offers an authoritative interpretation of the Pentecost tongues-speech. James decides that the appropriate response is to write, and the ensuing document, the Apostolic Decree, crystallizes in textual form the impact of Peter's new understanding of God, extending its revelatory impact through writing. Significantly, the text makes an implicit claim to inspiration (Acts 15:28) which suggests that Luke is presenting the writing itself as revelatory in a similar way to the tongues-speech at Pentecost, and Peter's witness.

I concluded Chapter 4 by arguing that this reflects on Luke's own project. In Peter's initial self-defence to the circumcision party in Jerusalem, Luke refers to words of Jesus included in his own text, scripturalizing material textualized within his own narrative. More broadly, the connection Luke makes between Peter's revelatory witness to God's non-partiality on the basis of his and Cornelius's REs and the Apostolic Decree has similarities with the way he presents his own writing. In the prologue to the *Doppelwerk*, Luke claims that his text should function as an authoritative witness to Christ for Theophilus and, by extension, its wider audience. This suggests that Luke is making a claim to scriptural status. Accordingly, it is reasonable to conclude that Luke intentionally uses accounts of RE to establish the possibility of revelatory speech and writing, and that he presents his own text as this kind of writing.

In Chapter 5, I considered Paul's epistle to the Galatians, and argued that a similar pattern was visible in the way that this writing is situated in relation to REs. I began by arguing that Paul refers to a double pattern of RE in his and the Galatians' lives. First, both have revelatory beginnings in which they encounter Christ in a way which is depicted as tangible and transformative. Second, Paul assumes that for both, the appropriate impact is a participatory life which manifests its ongoing effects through the believers' new perception. Third, Paul offers an account of life in the Spirit which appears intended to act as a normative reference point for his addressees in the future – if they have encountered the Spirit, it should be made manifest in the felt impact that the believer is consistently disposed towards the actions, moods and attitudes listed as the fruit of the Spirit (5:22–6).

Galatians' argument is fundamentally rooted in RE, and – similarly to the way that Luke's accounts of RE reflect on his writing – Paul describes his own revelatory beginning in a way which establishes parallels between him and OT prophets which reflect on his writing. Because Galatians is intended as a proxy defence speech, it textualizes aspects of Paul's ministry which were more usually performed in the living voice. In light of the fact that Paul is attempting to re-call the Galatians to his own gospel, it is reasonable to suggest that this letter is intended to convey that content. This means that Paul is trying to get across the impact of his own affectively toned perception of Christ which has striking implications for the status of the writing: it includes that revealed content. Moreover, although Paul appeals to established Scripture to contest the interpretation of the Galatians' REs (Gal 3–4), I argued that his letter appears to have been intended to serve a similar, scriptural function insofar as it offers both an authoritative account of Paul's gospel and seeks to shape its reception (esp. Gal 5:16–23). That its relevance appears to have exceeded its initial context even for Paul himself only reinforces this point.

As I have consistently noted, Luke and Paul's intentions are only one side of a dialogue. Scripture necessarily exists in relation to a faith community which receives it as inspired. Though I have hinted at elements which suggest these texts received a favourable response – not least, their preservation and eventual inclusion in the NT canon – further research could consider the ways in which RE informed this reception. For example, Calvin's articulation of the inner witness of the Spirit suggests the possibility that scriptural texts can have their own affective impact:

> Scripture indeed is self-authenticated; hence, it is not right to subject it to proof and reasoning. And the certainty it deserves with us, it attains by the testimony

of the Spirit. For even if it wins reverence for itself by its own majesty, it seriously affects us only when it is sealed upon our hearts through the Spirit.[1]

It might be possible to examine this historically through a consideration of the early reception of NT texts, and Irenaeus of Lyons's aesthetic description of the difference between 'gnostic' and 'orthodox' readings of Scripture might suggest one avenue for exploration. He argues that Gnostic readings destroy the *beauty* of the scriptural witness to God:

> Their manner of acting is just as if one, when a beautiful image of a king has been constructed by some skilful artist out of precious jewels, should then take this likeness of the man all to pieces, should rearrange the gems, and so fit them together as to make them into the form of a dog or of a fox, and even that but poorly executed; and should then maintain and declare that this was the beautiful image of the king which the skilful artist constructed.[2]

An examination of early Christian writings in search of a consistent pattern in which NT texts are reported as having an affective or aesthetic impact – being beautiful or compelling in some way – may facilitate an approach to the question of their reception as Scripture which accounts for RE.

In this study, however, I have focused on the way in which RE appears to have played a role in the creation of the texts in the first place. In the paradigmatic example of Luke-Acts, it seems that there is a close connection between RE and claims to scriptural status which is also visible in Paul's epistle to the Galatians. I believe it is highly likely that this feature of these texts is exemplary rather than exceptional in the NT, and further research could develop this argument. For example, the Gospel of John is explicitly intended to shape the belief of its audience ('these things are written so that you may believe'; 20:30). The way that it does this is by offering a textual encounter with Jesus, in which the reader ideally gains an ever-greater understanding as they progress through the narrative. The Paraclete passages present the role of the Spirit in a similar way: by making Jesus present in his absence, this 'other Paraclete' will lead future believers into 'all truth' (John 16:13) – that is, into a deeper understanding of Jesus who is 'the way the truth and the life' (14:6). Thus, this text appears not only to crystallize its author's insights into Christ but also proactively to seek to shape its readers' understanding of Jesus by offering a mediated form of encounter. In this sense, the Gospel itself aims to do the work of the Paraclete in bringing people to an awareness of Jesus that will allow them to believe and confess that he is the Christ. This is a distinctive variation on the pattern established in my analysis of Luke-Acts and Galatians and an analysis of the NT from this perspective could be further expanded through an examination of the role of RE in the reception of the historical Jesus in the Gospels.

---

[1] John Calvin, *Institutes of the Christian Religion*, ed. John T. McNeill, trans. Ford Lewis Battles (Philadelphia, PA: Westminster, 1960), I:80 (1:7:5).

[2] Irenaeus, *Haer*, 1.8.1 (*ANF* I:326). Cf. the similar line of argument in Josephus's explanation of the Hebrew Scriptures in *Ag. Ap.* 1.37–43.

Though further research is needed to assess the importance of RE in shaping these other texts, my study is sufficient to allow the suggestion that REs played a key role for at least some NT authors in shaping their intentions when they came to write. This is perhaps not particularly surprising, given that most NT texts witness to the claim that divine reality was uniquely present in the person of Jesus of Nazareth. However, in light of this, it is reasonable to suggest that when these writers put pen to paper, they also had some idea that the texts they were writing were special. In this context, where the writers were immersed in the scriptural tradition of the OT, it is only a small leap to suggest that they intended to write Scripture. Of course, this does not mean that the writers imagined the NT canon as they worked on their documents. Rather, when Paul was creating Galatians and when Luke was crafting his *Doppelwerk*, they perceived in the REs to which they were responding God's decisive action towards his people and sought to reflect this to their readers after the model of the OT. In this sense, it is legitimate to say that REs prompted them to create new scriptural texts.

Bibliography

I. Primary sources

Biblical texts

Biblia Hebraica Stuttgartensia. Edited by Karl Elliger and Wilhelm Rudolph. Stuttgart: Deutsche Bibelgesellschaft, 1983.
Septuaginta. Edited by A. Rahlfs and R. Hanhart. Rev. edn. Stuttgart: Deutsche Bibelgesellschaft, 2006.
Novum Testamentum Graece. Edited by B. Aland, K. Aland, J. Karavidopoulos, C. M. Martini and B. M. Metzger. 28th edn. Stuttgart: Deutsche Bibelgesellschaft, 2012.

Ancient Jewish texts

Qumran
F. G. Martínez and E. J. C. Tigchelaar, eds. *The Dead Sea Scrolls Study Edition*. 2 vols. Leiden: Brill, 1997.

Josephus
Jewish Antiquities. Translated by H. St. J. Thackeray, R. Marcus, A. Wikgren and L. Feldman. 9 vols. LCL. 1930–65.
The Jewish War. The Life. Against Apion. Translated by H. St. J. Thackeray. 4 vols. LCL. 1926–8.

Philo
Translated by F. H. Colson, G. H. Whitaker and R. Marcus. 12 vols. LCL. 1929–62.

Pseudepigrapha
Old Testament Pseudepigrapha. Edited by James H. Charlesworth. 2 vols. Peabody, MA: Hendrickson, 1983.

Early Christian Texts

Augustine
St. Augustine, *Confessions*. Translated by Henry Chadwick. Oxford: Oxford University Press, 1991.

Irenaeus and Justin Martyr
Roberts, Alexander, and James Donaldson, eds. *The Ante-Nicene Fathers*. 1885–7. 10 vols. Repr., Peabody, MA: Hendrickson, 1994.

Greco-Roman literature

Apuleius
Metamorphoses (The Golden Ass). Edited and translated by J. Arthur Hanson. LCL. 2 vols. 1989–96.

Cicero
On Old Age. On Friendship. On Divination. Translated by W. A. Falconer. LCL. 1923.

Demetrius
Aristotle, Longinus, Demetrius. *Poetics. Longinus: On the Sublime. Demetrius: On Style.* Translated by Stephen Halliwell et al. Revised by Donald A. Russell. LCL. 1995.

Lucan
The Civil War (Pharsalia). Translated by J. D. Duff. LCL. 1928.

Plutarch
Moralia. Translated by Frank Cole Babbitt et al. 14 vols. LCL. 1927–67.

Polybius
The Histories, Volume II: Books 3–4. Translated by W. R. Paton. Revised by F. W. Walbank and Christian Habicht. LCL. 2010.

II. Secondary sources

Commentaries

Barrett, C. K. *A Critical and Exegetical Commentary on the Acts of the Apostles.* 2 volumes. Edinburgh: T&T Clark, 1994–8.
Barth, Markus, and Helmut Blanke. *Colossians.* Translated by Astrid B. Beck. AB 34B. London: Yale University Press, 1994.
Betz, Hans Dieter. *Galatians.* Hermeneia. Philadelphia, PA: Fortress Press, 1979.
Bock, Darrell L. *Acts.* BECNT. Grand Rapids, MI: Baker Academic, 2007.
Bruce, F. F. *The Epistle of Paul to the Galatians: A Commentary on the Greek Text.* NIGTC. Exeter: Paternoster, 1982.
Brueggemann, Walter. *Genesis.* Interpretation. Atlanta, GA: John Knox, 1982.
Conzelmann, Hans. *A Commentary on the Acts of the Apostles.* Edited by Eldon Jay Epp with Christopher R. Matthews. Translated by James Limburg et al. Hermeneia. Philadelphia, PA: Fortress, 1987.
Das, A. Andrew. *Galatians.* CCSS. St. Louis, MO: Concordia, 2014.
De Boer, Martinus C. *Galatians: A Commentary.* NTL. Louisville, KY: Westminster John Knox, 2011.
Dunn, James D. G. *Galatians.* BNTC. London: Black, 1993.
Edwards, Mark J., ed. *Galatians, Ephesians, Philippians.* ACCS. Downers Grove, IL: InterVarsity, 1999.
Esler, Philip F. *Galatians.* NTR. London: Routledge, 1998.
Fee, Gordon D. *Galatians.* PCS. Blandford Forum: Deo, 2011.
Fitzmyer, Joseph A. *The Acts of the Apostles.* AB 31. New York: Doubleday, 1998.
Fung, Ronald Y. K. *The Epistle to the Galatians.* NICNT. Grand Rapids, MI: Eerdmans, 1995.
Gaventa, Beverly Roberts. *Acts.* ANTC. Nashville, TN: Abingdon, 2003.
Green, Joel B. *The Gospel According to Luke.* NICNT. Grand Rapids, MI: Eerdmans, 1997.
Haenchen, Ernst. *The Acts of the Apostles: A Commentary.* Translated by B. Noble et al. Oxford: Blackwell, 1971.
Hansen, G. Walter. *Galatians.* IVPNTC. Downers Grove, IL: IVP, 1994.

Jervell, Jacob. *Die Apostelgeschichte*. KEK. Göttingen: Vandenhoeck und Ruprecht, 1998.
Johnson, Luke Timothy. *The Acts of the Apostles*. SP 5. Collegeville, PA: Liturgical Press, 1992.
Keener, Craig S. *Acts: An Exegetical Commentary*. 4 vols. Grand Rapids, MI: Baker Academic, 2012–15.
Keener, Craig S. *Galatians*. NCBC. Cambridge: Cambridge University Press, 2018.
Kurz, William S. *Acts of the Apostles*. CCSS. Grand Rapids, MI: Baker Academic, 2013.
Lightfoot, J. B. *Saint Paul's Epistle to the Galatians*. London: Macmillan, 1865.
Longenecker, Richard N. *Galatians*. WBC 41. Waco, TX: Word, 1990.
Lyons, George. *Galatians*. NBBC. Kansas: Beacon Hill, 2012.
Malina, Bruce J., and John J. Pilch. *A Social-Science Commentary on the Book of Acts*. Minneapolis, MN: Fortress, 2008.
Marshall, I. Howard. *Acts*. TNTC. Nottingham: IVP, 1980.
Martin, Frances, ed. *Acts*. ACCS. Downers Grove, IL: IVP, 2006.
Martyn, J. Louis. *Galatians*. AB33A. New Haven, CT: Yale University, 1997.
Matera, Frank J. *Galatians*. SP. Collegeville, PA: Liturgical Press, 2007.
Moo, Douglas J. *Galatians*. BECNT. Grand Rapids, MI: Baker Academic, 2013.
Nolland, John. *Luke 1:1-9:20*. WBC 35A. Waco, TX: Thomas Nelson, 1989.
Oakes, Peter. *Galatians*. Paideia. Grand Rapids, MI: Baker Academic, 2015.
Parsons, Mikael C. *Acts*. PCNT. Grand Rapids, MI: Baker Academic, 2008.
Parsons, Mikael C., and Martin Culy. *Acts: A Handbook on the Greek Text*. BHGNT. Waco, TX: Baylor, 2003.
Pervo, Richard I. *Acts*. Hermeneia. Minneapolis, MN: Fortress, 2009.
Pesch, Rudolf. *Die Apostelgeschichte*. EKK. Göttingen: Patmos, 2014.
Peterson, David. *The Acts of the Apostles*. PNTC. Grand Rapids, MI: Eerdmans, 2009.
Polhill, John B. *Acts*. NAC 26. Nashville, TN: Broadman, 1992.
Roloff, Jürgen. *Die Apostelgeschichte*. Göttingen: Vandenhoeck und Ruprecht, 1981.
Schnabel, Eckhard J. *Acts*. ZECNT. Grand Rapids, MI: Zondervan, 2014.
Schneider, Gerhard. *Die Apostelgeschichte*. 2 vols. HThK. Freiburg: Herder, 1980.
Schreiner, Thomas. *Galatians*. ZECNT. Grand Rapids, MI: Zondervan, 2010.
Stählin, G. *Die Apostelgeschichte*. NTD 5. Göttingen: Vandenhoeck und Ruprecht, 1962.
Stuart, Donald. *Hosea—Jonah*. WBC 31. Texas: Thomas Nelson, 1988.
Talbert, Charles H. *Reading Acts: A Literary and Theological Commentary on the Acts of the Apostles*. Macon, GA: Smyth & Helwys, 2005.
Thiselton, Anthony C. *The First Epistle to the Corinthians*. NIGTC. Grand Rapids, MI: Eerdmans, 2000.
Wenham, Gordon J. *Genesis 1-15*. WBC 1. Waco, TX: Thomas Nelson, 1987.
Witherington III, Ben. *The Acts of the Apostles: A Socio-Rhetorical Commentary*. Grand Rapids, MI: Eerdmans, 1998.
Witherington III, Ben. *Grace in Galatia: A commentary on Paul's Letter to the Galatians*. Grand Rapids, MI: Eerdmans, 1998.

Other secondary literature

Adams, Samuel V. *The Reality of God and Historical Method: Apocalyptic Theology in Conversation with N. T. Wright*. Downers Grove, IL: IVP, 2015.

Adams, Sean A. *The Genre of Acts and Collected Biography*. Cambridge: Cambridge University Press, 2013.
Aernie, Jeffrey W. *Is Paul Also among the Prophets?* London: T&T Clark, 2012.
Alexander, Loveday. *The Preface to Luke's Gospel*. Cambridge: Cambridge University Press, 1993.
Alexander, Loveday. 'Reading Luke-Acts from Back to Front'. Pages 419–46 in *The Unity of Luke-Acts*. Edited by Jos Verheyden. Leuven: Peeters, 1999.
Alexander, Loveday. *Acts in Its Ancient Literary Context*. Oxford: Bloomsbury, 2007.
Alston, William P. 'Religious Experience'. Pages 250–5 in *Routledge Encyclopedia of Philosophy* 8. Edited by Edward Craig. London: Routledge, 1998.
Ascough, Richard S. 'Greco-Roman Philosophic, Religious, and Voluntary Associations'. Pages 3–19 in *Community Formation in the Early Church and in the Church Today*. Edited by Richard N. Longenecker. Peabody, MA: Hendrickson, 2002.
Ashton, John. *The Religion of Paul the Apostle*. New Haven, CT: Yale, 2000.
Atkinson, William P. *Baptism in the Spirit: Luke-Acts and the Dunn Debate*. Eugene, OR: Pickwick, 2011.
Aune, David E. 'Luke 1:1-4: Historical or Scientific Prooimion?' Pages 138–48 in *Paul, Luke and the Graeco-Roman World*. Sheffield: Sheffield Academic, 2002.
Austin, J. L. *How to Do Things with Words*. Oxford: Oxford University Press, 1962.
Baird, William. 'Visions, Revelation, and Ministry: Reflections on 2 Cor 12:1-5 and Gal 1:11-17'. *JBL* 104 (1985): 651–62.
Barclay, John M. G. 'Paul's Story: Theology as Testimony'. Pages 133–56 in *Narrative Dynamics in Paul: A Critical Assessment*. Edited by B. W. Longenecker. Louisville, KY: Westminster John Knox, 2002.
Barclay, John M. G. *Paul and the Gift*. Grand Rapids, MI: Eerdmans, 2015.
Barclay, John M. G. 'The Letters of Paul and the Construction of Early Christian Networks'. Pages 289–302 in *Letters and Communities: Studies in the Socio-Political Dimensions of Ancient Epistolography*. Edited by Paola Ceccarelli et al. Oxford: Oxford University Press, 2018.
Barrett, C. K. *Luke the Historian in Recent Study*. London: Epworth Press, 1961.
Barth, Karl. *The Epistle to the Romans*. Translated by Edwyn C. Hoskyns. London: Oxford University Press, 1933.
Barth, Karl. *Church Dogmatics IV/3.2: The Doctrine of Reconciliation*. Translated by G. W. Bromiley. Edinburgh: T&T Clark, 1962.
Barth, Karl. 'Fifteen Answers to Professor von Harnack'. Page 167 in *The Beginnings of Dialectic Theology: Volume 1*. Edited by James M. Robinson. Richmond, VA: John Knox, 1968.
Batluck, Mark. 'Religious Experience in New Testament Research'. *CurBR* 9 (2010): 339–63.
Bauckham, Richard. 'James and the Gentiles (Acts 15:13-21)'. Pages 154–84 in *History, Literature, and Society in the Book of Acts*. Edited by Ben Witherington III. Cambridge: Cambridge University Press, 1996.
Bell, Catherine. *Ritual Theory Ritual Practice*. Oxford: Oxford University Press, 1992.
Bell, Richard H. *Deliver Us from Evil: Interpreting the Redemption from the Power of Satan in New Testament Theology*. Tübingen: Mohr Siebeck, 2007.
Bell, Richard H. 'The Resurrection Appearances in 1 Corinthians 15'. In *Epiphanies of the Divine in the Septuagint and the New Testament*. Edited by Roland Deines and Mark Wreford. Tübingen: Mohr Siebeck, forthcoming.
Berger, Klaus. 'Apostelbrief und apostolische Rede'. *ZNW* 65 (1974): 190–231.

Berger, Klaus. *Identity and Experience in the New Testament*. Translated by Charles Muenchow. Minneapolis, MN: Fortress, 2003.

Biggs, Adam T., Ryan D. Kreager, et al. 'Semantic and Affective Salience: The Role of Meaning and Preference in Attentional Capture and Disengagement'. *Journal of Experimental Psychology: Human Perception and Performance* 38 (2012): 531–41.

Bird, Michael F. 'Introduction: Problems and Prospects for a New Testament Debate'. Pages 1–15 in *The Faith of Jesus Christ: The Pistou Christou Debate*. Edited by Michael F. Bird and Preston M. Sprinkle. Milton Keynes: Paternoster, 2009.

Blum, Jason N. 'Retrieving Phenomenology of Religion as a Method for Religious Studies'. *JAAR* 80 (2012): 1025–48.

Blum, Jason N. 'The Science of Consciousness and Mystical Experience: An Argument for Radical Empiricism'. *JAAR* 82 (2014): 150–73.

Blum, Jason N. *Zen and the Unspeakable God: Comparative Interpretations of Mystical Experience*. Philadelphia: Pennsylvania State University, 2015. Kindle Edition.

Bock, Darrell L. 'Scripture and the Realisation of God's Promises'. Pages 41–62 in *Witness to the Gospel: The Theology of Acts*. Edited by I. Howard Marshall and David Peterson. Grand Rapids, MI: Eerdmans, 1998.

Bock, Darrell L. *A Theology of Luke's Gospel and Acts*. Grand Rapids, MI: Zondervan, 2011.

Bockmuehl, Markus. *Revelation and Mystery in Ancient Judaism and Pauline Christianity*. Tübingen: Mohr Siebeck, 1990.

Bockmuehl, Markus. 'Why Not Let Acts Be Acts?' *JSNT* 28 (2005): 163–6.

Bons, Eberhard. 'The Evolution of the Vocabulary of Epiphanic Revelation from the Septuagint to the New Testament and Early Christian Literature'. In *Epiphanies of the Divine in the Septuagint and the New Testament*. Edited by Roland Deines and Mark Wreford. Tübingen: Mohr Siebeck, forthcoming.

Bonz, Marianne Palmer. *The Past as Legacy: Luke-Acts and Ancient Epic*. Minneapolis, MN: Augsburg Fortress, 2000.

Borse, Ulrich. *Der Standort des Galaterbriefes*. Cologne: Peter Hanstein, 1972.

Bosworth, I. E. 'The Influence of the Damascus Vision upon Paul's Theology'. *BS* 56 (1899): 278–300.

Bousset, Wilhelm. *Kyrios Christos: A History of Belief in Christ from the Beginnings of Christianity to Irenaeus*. Translated by John E. Steely. Nashville, TN: Abingdon, 1970.

Bowker, J. W. '"Merkabah" Visions and the Visions of Paul'. *JSS* 16 (1971): 157–73.

Bradshaw, Paul F. *The Search for the Origins of Christian Worship: Sources and Methods for the Study of Early Liturgy*. Oxford: Oxford University Press, 1992.

Broadhead, Edwin K. *The Gospel of Matthew on the Landscape of Antiquity*. WUNT 378. Tübingen: Mohr Siebeck, 2017.

Brooke, George J. 'Between Authority and Canon: The Significance of Reworking the Bible for Understanding the Canonical Process'. Pages 85–104 in *Reworking the Bible: Apocryphal and Related Texts at Qumran*. Edited by Esther Chazon, Devorah Dimant and Ruth Anne Clements. Leiden: Brill, 2005.

Brown, Schuyler. 'The Role of the Prologues in Determining the Purpose of Luke-Acts'. Pages 99–111 in *Perspectives on Luke-Acts*. Edited by Charles H. Talbert. Edinburgh: T&T Clark, 1978.

Büchsel, Friedrich. *Der Geist Gottes im Neuen Testament*. Gütersloh: Bertelsmann, 1926.

Bultmann, Rudolf. *Theology of the New Testament*. Translated by Kendrick Grobel. London: SCM, 1952.

Burkhardt, Helmut. 'Inspiration der Schrift durch weisheitliche Personalinspiration: Zur Inspirationslehre Philos von Alexandrien'. *TZ* 47 (1991): 214–25.

Cadbury, Henry J. 'Commentary on the Preface of Luke'. Pages 489–510 in *The Beginnings of Christianity II*. Edited by F. J. Foakes Jackson and Kirsopp Lake. London: Macmillan, 1922.
Cadbury, Henry J. *The Making of Luke-Acts*. New York: Macmillan, 1927.
Caird, G. B. *Paul's Letters from Prison*. Oxford: Oxford University Press, 1976.
Calvin, John. *Institutes of the Christian Religion*. Edited by John T. McNeill. Translated by Ford Lewis Battles. Philadelphia, PA: Westminster, 1960.
Campbell, Constantine R. *Paul and Union with Christ: An Exegetical and Theological Study*. Grand Rapids, MI: Zondervan, 2012. Kindle edition.
Campbell, Constantine R. 'Participation and Faith in Paul'. Pages 37–60 in *'In Christ' in Paul*. Edited by Michael J. Thate, Kevin J. Vanhoozer and Constantine R. Campbell. Tübingen: Mohr Siebeck, 2014.
Carson, D. A., Leon Morris and Douglas Moo. *An Introduction to the New Testament*. Grand Rapids, MI: Zondervan, 1992.
Chapman, S. B. *The Law and the Prophets: A Study in Old Testament Canon Formation*. Tübingen: Mohr Siebeck, 2009.
Charlesworth, James H. 'A Review of Darrell L. Bock and Robert L. Webb (eds), *Key Events in the Life of the Historical Jesus*'. *JSHJ* 11 (2013): 203–23.
Charry, Ellen T. 'Experience'. Pages 413–31 in *The Oxford Handbook of Systematic Theology*. Edited by John Webster, Kathryn Tanner and Iain Torrance. Oxford: Oxford University Press, 2007.
Childs, Brevard S. *Introduction to the Old Testament as Scripture*. Philadelphia, PA: Fortress, 1979.
Clore, Gerald L., and Alexander J. Schiller. 'New Light on the Affect-Cognition Connection'. Pages 532–46 in *The Emotions Handbook*. Edited by Lisa Feldman Barrett, Michael Lewis and Jeannette M. Haviland-Jones. 4th edn. New York: Guildford Press, 2016.
Collins, John J. 'Uses of Torah in the Second Temple Period'. Pages 44–62 in *When Texts Are Canonized*. Edited by Timothy H. Lim. Providence, RI: Brown, 2017.
Conzelmann, Hans. 'Was von Anfang war'. Pages 194–201 in *Neutestamentliche Studien für Rudolf Bultmann zu seinem 70. Geburtstag am 20. August 1954*. Edited by Walther Eltester. Berlin: Töpelmann, 1954.
Crawford, Sidnie White. *Rewriting Scripture in Second Temple Times*. Grand Rapids, MI: Eerdmans, 2008.
Danker, Frederick W., Walter Bauer, William F. Arndt and F. Wilbur Gingrich. *Greek-English Lexicon of the New Testament and Other Early Christian Literature*. 3rd edn. Chicago: University of Chicago Press, 2000 (Danker-Bauer-Arndt-Gingrich).
Davies, Douglas. 'Social Groups, Liturgy and Glossolalia'. *Churchman* 90 (1976): 193–205.
Davis, Basil S. 'The Meaning of ΠΡΟΕΓΡΑΦΗ in the Context of Galatians 3.1'. *NTS* 45 (1999): 194–212.
Davis, Stephen T. 'An Ontology of the Spirit'. Pages 54–65 in *The Testimony of the Spirit*. Edited by R. Douglas Geivett and Paul K. Moser. Oxford: Oxford University Press, 2017.
De Boer, Martinus C. 'Paul, Theologian of God's Apocalypse'. *Int* 56 (2002): 21–33.
Deigh, John. 'Cognitivism in the Theory of Emotions'. *Ethics* 104 (1994): 824–54.
Deines, Roland. 'The Term and Concept of Scripture'. Pages 235–81 in *What Is Bible?* Edited by Karin Finsterbusch and Armin Lange. Leuven: Peeters, 2012.
Deines, Roland. 'Did Matthew Know He Was Writing Scripture?' *EJT* 22 (2013): 101–9.

Deines, Roland. 'God's Role in History as a Methodological Problem for Exegesis'. Pages 1–26 in *Acts of God in History*. Edited by Christoph Ochs and Peter Watts. Tübingen: Mohr Siebeck, 2013.
Deines, Roland. 'The Apostolic Decree: Halakhah for Gentile Christians or Christian Concession to Jewish Taboos?' Pages 121–88 in *Acts of God in History*. Edited by Christoph Ochs and Peter Watts. Tübingen: Mohr Siebeck, 2013.
Deines, Roland. 'Biblical Viewpoints on Repentance, Conversion, and Turning to God'. Pages 227–61 in *Acts of God in History*. Tübingen: Mohr Siebeck, 2013.
Deines, Roland. 'Jesus and Scripture: Scripture and the Self-Understanding of Jesus'. Pages 39–70 in *All That the Prophets Have Declared*. Edited by Matthew Malcolm. Milton Keynes: Paternoster, 2015.
Deines, Roland. 'Revelatory Experiences as the Beginning of Scripture: Paul's Letters and the Prophets in the Hebrew Bible'. Pages 275–307 in *From Author to Copyist: Essays on the Composition, Redaction, and Transmission of the Hebrew Bible*. Edited by Cana Werman. Winona Lake, IN: Eisenbrauns, 2015.
Deines, Roland. *Jakobus: Im Schatten Des Großeren*. Leipzig: Evangelische Verlagsanstalt, 2017.
Deines, Roland, and Mark Wreford. 'Epiphanies of the Divine in the Septuagint and the New Testament: Mutual Perspectives'. In *Epiphanies of the Divine in the Septuagint and the New Testament*. Edited by Roland Deines and Mark Wreford. Tübingen: Mohr Siebeck, forthcoming.
Deissmann, Adolf. *Paul: A Study in Social and Religious History*. New York: Harper & Bros, 1911.
Deissmann, Adolf. *The Religion of Jesus and the Faith of Paul*. London: Hodder & Stoughton, 1923.
Dempster, Stephen G. 'The Old Testament Canon, Josephus, and Cognitive Environment'. Pages 321–61 in *The Enduring Authority of the Christian Scriptures*. Edited by D. A. Carson. London: Apollos, 2016.
Dennett, Daniel C. 'Quining Qualia'. Pages 42–78 in *Consciousness in Modern Science*. Edited by A. Marcel and E. Bisiach. Oxford: Oxford University Press, 1988.
Depraz, Natalie. 'The Philosophical Challenge'. Pages 169–203 in *On Becoming Aware: A Pragmatics of Experiencing*. Edited by Natalie Depraz, Francisco J. Varela and Pierre Vermersch. Amsterdam: John Benjamins, 2002.
Derrida, Jacques. 'Signature Event Context'. Pages 309–30 in *Margins of Philosophy*. Translated by Alan Bass. Chicago: University of Chicago, 1982.
Dittenberger, Wilhelm, ed. *Sylloge Inscriptionum Graecarum*. 4 vols. 3rd edn. Leipzig: Hirzel, 1915–24.
Doering, Lutz. *Ancient Jewish Letters and the Beginnings of Christian Epistolography*. Tübingen: Mohr Siebeck, 2012.
Donaldson, Terence L. *Paul and the Gentiles: Remapping the Apostle's Convictional World*. Minneapolis, MN: Fortress Press, 1997.
Dunn, James D. G. *Baptism in the Spirit: A Re-Examination of the New Testament Teaching on the Gift of the Spirit in Relation to Pentecostalism Today*. London: SCM, 1970.
Dunn, James D. G. *Jesus and the Spirit: A Study of the Religious and Charismatic Experience of Jesus and the First Christians as Reflected in the New Testament*. London: SCM, 1975.
Dunn, James D. G. *The Theology of Paul the Apostle*. London: T&T Clark, 1998.
Dunson, Ben C. 'The Individual and Community in Twentieth- and Twenty-First-Century Pauline Scholarship'. *CurBR* 9 (2010): 63–97.

Eastman, Susan G. *Recovering Paul's Mother Tongue: Language and Theology in Galatians*. Grand Rapids, MI: Eerdmans, 2007.

Eastman, Susan G. *Paul and the Person: Reframing Paul's Anthropology*. Grand Rapids, MI: Eerdmans, 2017.

Edwards, Jonathan. *The Religious Affections*. 1746. Repr., New York: Dover, 2013.

Ekman, Paul. 'An Argument for Basic Emotions'. *Cognition and Emotion* 6 (1992): 169–200.

Eliade, Mircea. *Patterns in Comparative Religion*. London: Sheed and Ward, 1958.

Eliade, Mircea. *The Sacred and the Profane: The Nature of Religion*. Translated by Willard R. Trask. San Diego, CA: Harcourt Brace, 1959.

Elliott, John H. *Beware the Evil Eye: The Evil Eye in the Bible and the Ancient World III*. Eugene, OR: Wipf and Stock, 2016.

Ellis, E. Earle. *Prophecy and Hermeneutic in Earliest Christianity*. Tübingen: Mohr Siebeck, 1978.

Engberg-Pedersen, Troels. *Paul and the Stoics*. Louisville, KY: Westminster John Knox, 2000.

Engberg-Pedersen, Troels. 'The Construction of Religious Experience in Paul'. Pages 147–58 in *Experientia I: Inquiry for Religious Experience in Early Judaism and Christianity*. Edited by Frances Flannery, Colleen Shantz and Rodney A. Werline. Atlanta, GA: SBL, 2008.

Engberg-Pedersen, Troels. *Cosmology and Self in the Apostle Paul: The Material Spirit*. Oxford: Oxford University Press, 2010.

Estrada, Nelson P. *From Followers to Leaders: The Apostles in the Ritual of Status Transformation in Acts 1-2*. London: T&T Clark, 2004.

Evans, Craig A. 'The Prophetic Setting of the Pentecost Sermon'. Pages 212–24 in *Luke and Scripture: The Function of Sacred Tradition in Luke-Acts*. Edited by Craig A. Evans and James A. Sanders. Minneapolis, MN: Fortress, 1993.

Evans, Craig A. 'Luke and the Rewritten Bible: Aspects of Lukan Hagiography'. Pages 170–201 in *The Pseudepigrapha and Early Biblical Interpretation*. Edited by James H. Charlesworth and C. A. Evans. Sheffield: JSOT Press, 1993.

Everts, Jenny. 'Tongues or Languages? Contextual Consistency in the Translation of Acts 2'. *JPT* 4 (1994): 71–80.

Ferrer, Jorge N. *Participation and the Mystery: Transpersonal Essays in Psychology, Education, and Religion*. New York: SUNY, 2017.

Fetterman, David M. 'Emic/Etic Perspective'. Page 249 in *The Sage Encyclopedia of Qualitative Research Methods: A-L*. Edited by Lisa M. Given. Newbury Park, CA: Sage, 2008.

Finn, Thomas M. 'The God-Fearers Reconsidered'. *CBQ* 47 (1985): 75–84.

Flannery, Frances, Colleen Shantz and Rodney A. Werline, eds. *Experientia I: Inquiry for Religious Experience in Early Judaism and Christianity*. Atlanta, GA: SBL, 2008.

Flannery, Frances with Nicolae Roddy, Colleen Shantz and Rodney A. Werline. 'Introduction: Religious Experience Past and Present'. Pages 1–10 in *Experientia I: Inquiry for Religious Experience in Early Judaism and Christianity*. Edited by Frances Flannery, Colleen Shantz and Rodney A. Werline. Atlanta, GA: SBL, 2008.

Fletcher-Louis, Crispin. 'A New Explanation of Christological Origins: A Review of the Work of Larry W. Hurtado'. *TynBul* 60 (2009): 161–205.

Forbes, Christopher. *Prophecy and Inspired Speech in Early Christianity and Its Hellenistic Environment*. Tübingen: Mohr, 1995.

Forbes, Christopher. 'Ancient Rhetoric and Ancient Letters: Models for Reading Paul, and Their Limits'. Pages 143-60 in *Paul and Rhetoric*. Edited by J. Paul Sampley and Peter Lampe. New York: T&T Clark, 2010.
Fowl, Stephen E. *Engaging Scripture: A Model for Theological Interpretation*. Oxford: Blackwell, 1998.
Fowl, Stephen E. 'Simeon in Acts 15.14: Simon Peter and Echoes of Simeons Past'. Pages 185-98 in *Characters and Characterization in Luke-Acts*. Edited by Frank E. Dicken and Julia A. Snyder. London: Bloomsbury, 2016.
Fox, Elaine. *Emotion Science: Cognitive and Neuroscientific Approaches to Understanding Human Emotions*. New York: Palgrave Macmillan, 2008.
Fredriksen, Paula. 'Paul and Augustine: Conversion Narratives, Orthodox Traditions and the Retrospective Self'. *JTS* 37 (1986): 3-34.
Frei, Hans W. *The Eclipse of Biblical Narrative: A Study in Eighteenth and Nineteenth Century Hermeneutics*. New Haven, CT: Yale, 1974.
Frein, Brigid C. 'Narrative Predictions, Old Testament Prophecies and Luke's Sense of Fulfilment'. *NTS* 40 (1994): 22-37.
Frey, Jörg. 'Einführung'. Pages 1-63 in *Qumran und der biblische Kanon*. Edited by Michael Becker and Jörg Frey. Neukirchen-Vluyn: Neukirchener Verlag, 2009.
Frey, Jörg, and John R. Levison. 'The Origins of Early Christian Pneumatology: On the Rediscovery and Reshaping of the History of Religions Quest'. Pages 1-38 in *The Holy Spirit, Inspiration, and the Cultures of Antiquity*. Edited by Jörg Frey and John R. Levison. Berlin: De Gruyter, 2014.
Furseth, Ingur, and Pål Repstad. *An Introduction to the Sociology of Religion*. London: Routledge, 2016.
Gäckle, Volker. 'The New Temple and New Priesthood in the New Testament: The Divine Presence in the Community of Believers'. In *Epiphanies of the Divine in the Septuagint and the New Testament*. Edited by Roland Deines and Mark Wreford. Tübingen: Mohr Siebeck, forthcoming.
Gadamer, Hans-Georg. *Truth and Method*. Translated by Joel Weinsheimer and Donald G. Marshall. Revised 2nd edn. London: Continuum, 2004. Reprinted London: Bloomsbury, 2013.
Gathercole, Simon. '*E pluribus unum?* Apostolic Unity and Early Christian Literature'. Pages 407-55 in *The Enduring Authority of the Christian Scriptures*. Edited by D. A. Carson. London: Apollos, 2016.
Gaventa, Beverly R. *Darkness to Light: Aspects of Conversion in the New Testament*. Philadelphia, PA: Fortress Press, 1986.
Gaventa, Beverly R. 'Galatians 1 and 2: Autobiography as Paradigm'. *NovT* 28 (1986): 309-26.
Gaventa, Beverly R. 'The Maternity of Paul'. Pages 189-201 in *The Conversation Continues: Studies in Paul and John in Honor of J. Louis Martyn*. Edited by Robert T. Fortna and Beverly R. Gaventa. Nashville, TN: Abingdon, 1990.
Geertz, Clifford. *The Interpretation of Cultures*. New York: Basic Books, 1973.
Geivett, R. Douglas, and Paul K. Moser, eds. *The Testimony of the Spirit: New Essays*. Oxford: Oxford University Press, 2017.
Gilbert, Gary. 'The List of Nations in Acts 2: Roman Propaganda and the Lukan Response'. *JBL* 121 (2002): 497-529.
Goldie, Peter. *The Emotions: A Philosophical Exploration*. Oxford: Oxford University Press, 2000.

Goodman, Felicitas. *Speaking in Tongues: A Cross-Cultural Study of Glossolalia.* Chicago: University of Chicago, 1972.

Gorman, Michael J. *Cruciformity: Paul's Narrative Spirituality of the Cross.* Grand Rapids, MI: Eerdmans, 2001.

Gorman, Michael J. *Inhabiting the Cruciform God: Kenosis, Justification, and Theosis in Paul's Narrative Soteriology.* Grand Rapids, MI: Eerdmans, 2009.

Gorman, Michael J. *Apostle of the Crucified Lord: A Theological Introduction to Paul and His Letters.* 2nd edn. Grand Rapids, MI: Eerdmans, 2017.

Gregory, Andrew. *The Reception of Luke and Acts in the Period before Irenaeus.* Tübingen: Mohr Siebeck, 2003.

Gregory, Andrew. 'The Reception of Luke and Acts and the Unity of Luke-Acts'. *JSNT* 29 (2007): 459–72.

Griffith-Jones, Robin. 'Transformation by a Text: The Gospel of John'. Pages 105–23 in *Experientia I: Inquiry for Religious Experience in Early Judaism and Christianity.* Edited by Frances Flannery, Colleen Shantz and Rodney A. Werline. Atlanta, GA: SBL, 2008.

Griffiths, J. Gwyn. 'Some Claims of Xenoglossy in the Ancient Languages'. *Numen* 33 (1986): 141–69.

Grudem, Wayne. '1 Cor. 14:20-25: Prophecy and Tongues as Signs of God's Attitude'. *Westminster Theological Journal* 41 (1979): 381–96.

Gunkel, Heidrun. *Der Heilige Geist bei Lukas.* Tübingen: Mohr Siebeck, 2015.

Gunkel, Heidrun, Rainer Hirsch-Luipold and John R. Levison. 'Plutarch and Pentecost: An Exploration in Interdisciplinary Collaboration'. Pages 63–94 in *The Holy Spirit, Inspiration, and the Cultures of Antiquity.* Edited by Jörg Frey and John R. Levison. Berlin: De Gruyter, 2014.

Gunkel, Hermann. *Die Wirkungen des heiligen Geistes nach der populären Anschauung der apostolischen Zeit und der Lehre des Apostels Paulus.* Göttingen: Vandenhoeck & Ruprecht, 1888. ET, *The Influence of the Holy Spirit: The Popular View of the Apostolic Age and the Teaching of the Apostle Paul.* Translated by R. A. Harrisville and R. P. Quanbeck. Philadelphia, PA: Fortress, 1979.

Gupta, Nijay. 'What Is in a Name? The Hermeneutics of Authorship Analysis Concerning Colossians'. *CurBR* 11 (2013): 196–217.

Hall, Robert G. *Revealed Histories: Techniques for Ancient Jewish and Christian Historiography.* Sheffield: JSOT, 1991.

Hansen, G. Walter. *Abraham in Galatians: Epistolary and Rhetorical Contexts.* Sheffield: Sheffield Academic, 1989.

Harner, Michael J. *The Way of the Shaman.* 2nd edn. San Francisco, CA: Harper and Row, 1990.

Hays, Richard B. *The Faith of Jesus Christ: An Investigation of the Narrative Substructure of Galatians 3:1-4:11.* Chico, CA: Scholars Press, 1983.

Hays, Richard B. 'Christology and Ethics in Galatians: The Law of Christ'. *CBQ* 49 (1987): 268–90.

Hays, Richard B. *Echoes of Scripture in the Letters of Paul.* New Haven, CT: Yale University Press, 1989.

Heinen, Sandra. 'Exegesis without Authorial Intention? On the Role of the "Author Construct" in Text Interpretation'. Pages 7–24 in *Biblical Exegesis without Authorial Intention: Interdisciplinary Approaches to Authorship and Meaning.* Edited by Clarissa Breu. Leiden: Brill, 2019.

Hemer, Colin. *The Book of Acts in the Setting of Hellenistic History.* Tübingen: Mohr Siebeck, 1989.

Hengel, Martin. *The Son of God: The Origin of Christology and the History of Jewish-Hellenistic Religion*. Translated by John Bowden. Philadelphia, PA: Fortress, 1976.
Hengel, Martin. *Acts and the History of Earliest Christianity*. Translated by John Bowden. Philadelphia, PA: Fortress, 1979.
Hengel, Martin. *Studies in Early Christology*. Translated by R. Reams et al. Edinburgh: T&T Clark, 1995.
Hengel, Martin. 'The Lukan Prologue and Its Eyewitnesses: The Apostles, Peter, and the Women'. Pages 533–88 in *Earliest Christian History: History, Literature, and Theology*. Edited by Michael F. Bird and Jason Maston. Tübingen: Mohr Siebeck, 2012.
Hengel, Martin, and Anna Maria Schwemer. *Paul between Damascus and Antioch: The Unknown Years*. Translated by John Bowden. London: SCM Press, 1997.
Heschel, Abraham J. *The Prophets*. New York: HarperPerennial, 2001.
Hilborn, David. 'Glossolalia as Communication: A Linguistic-Pragmatic Perspective'. Pages 111–46 in *Speaking in Tongues: Multi-Disciplinary Perspectives*. Edited by Mark J. Cartledge. Milton Keynes: Paternoster, 2006.
Himmelfarb, Martha. *Ascent to Heaven in Jewish and Christian Apocalypses*. Oxford: Oxford University Press, 1993.
Holland, Glen S. ' "Delivery, Delivery, Delivery": Accounting for Performance in the Rhetoric of Paul's Letters'. Pages 119–40 in *Paul and Ancient Rhetoric: Theory and Practice in the Hellenistic Context*. Edited by Stanley E. Porter and Bryan R. Dyer. Cambridge: Cambridge University Press, 2016.
Hopwood, Percy G. S. *The Religious Experience of the Primitive Church: The Period Prior to the Influence of Paul*. New York: Scribner's, 1937.
Horrell, David G. 'Paul's Narratives or Narrative Substructures?: The Significance of "Paul's Story" '. Pages 157–71 in *Narrative Dynamics in Paul: A Critical Assessment*. Edited by B. W. Longenecker. Louisville, KY: Westminster John Knox, 2002.
Horsley, Greg H. R., and Stephen Llewelyn, eds. *New Documents Illustrating Early Christianity*. North Ryde: The Ancient History Documentary Research Centre, Macquarie University, 1981–92.
Howell, Brian C. 'The Divine Voice as Metaphor and Action'. In *Epiphanies of the Divine in the Septuagint and the New Testament*. Edited by Roland Deines and Mark Wreford. Tübingen: Mohr Siebeck, forthcoming.
Howell, Brian M., and Jenell Williams Paris. *Introducing Cultural Anthropology: A Christian Perspective*. Grand Rapids, MI: Baker Academic, 2011.
Hüneburg, Martin. 'Das Matthausevangelium als heilige Schrift. Vom Anspruch eines Textes'. *Quatember* 71 (2007): 144–55.
Hurtado, Larry W. *One God, One Lord: Early Christian Devotion and Ancient Jewish Monotheism*. London: SCM, 1988.
Hurtado, Larry W. 'Religious Experience and Religious Innovation in the New Testament'. *JR* 80 (2000): 183–205.
Hurtado, Larry W. *Lord Jesus Christ: Devotion to Jesus in Earliest Christianity*. Grand Rapids, MI: Eerdmans, 2003.
Hurtado, Larry W. 'Revelatory Experiences and Religious Innovation in Earliest Christianity'. *ExpTim* 125 (2014): 469–82.
Hurtado, Larry W. *Why on Earth Did Anyone Become a Christian in the First Three Centuries?* Milwaukee, WI: Marquette University Press, 2016.
Hurtado, Larry W. *Destroyer of the Gods: Early Christian Distinctiveness in the Roman World*. Waco, TX: Baylor, 2016.

Husserl, Edmund. *Logical Investigations*. Translated by J. N. Findlay. London: Routledge, 1970.
Husserl, Edmund. *The Essential Husserl: Basic Writings in Transcendental Phenomenology*. Edited by Donn Welton. Indianapolis: Indiana University, 1999.
Jacobs, Struan. 'Michael Polanyi and Thomas Kuhn: Priority and Credit'. *Tradition and Discovery: The Polanyi Society* 33 (2006): 26–36.
James, William. *The Varieties of Religious Experience: A Study in Human Nature*. New York: Longmans, Green & Co, 1902. Reprinted Abingdon: Routledge, 2008.
Jay, Martin. *Songs of Experience: Modern American and European Variations on a Universal Theme*. Los Angeles: University of California Press, 2005.
Jervell, Jacob. *The Theology of the Acts of the Apostles*. Cambridge: Cambridge University Press, 1996.
Johanson, Bruce C. 'Tongues, a Sign for Unbelievers?: A Structural and Exegetical Study on 1 Corinthians XIV.20–25'. *NTS* 25 (1979): 180–203.
Johnson, Dru. *Biblical Knowing: A Scriptural Epistemology of Error*. Eugene, OR: Wipf and Stock, 2013.
Johnson, Luke Timothy. *Scripture and Discernment: Decision Making in the Church*. Nashville, TN: Abingdon, 1983.
Johnson, Luke Timothy. *Religious Experience in Earliest Christianity: A Missing Dimension in New Testament Studies*. Minneapolis, MN: Fortress Press, 1998.
Johnson, Luke Timothy. 'Literary Criticism of Luke-Acts: Is Reception-History Pertinent?' *JSNT* 28 (2005): 159–62.
Johnson, Luke Timothy. *Miracles: God's Presence and Power in Creation*. Louisville, KY: Westminster John Knox, 2018.
Katz, Steven T. 'The "Conservative" Character of Mysticism'. Pages 3–60 in *Mysticism and Religious Traditions*. Edited by Steven T. Katz. Oxford: Oxford University Press, 1983.
Kay, William K. 'The Mind, Behaviour and Glossolalia: A Psychological Perspective'. Pages 111–46 in *Speaking in Tongues: Multi-Disciplinary Perspectives*. Edited by Mark J. Cartledge. Milton Keynes: Paternoster, 2006.
Kay, W. K., and L. J. Francis. 'Personality, Mental Health and Glossolalia'. *Pneuma* 17 (1995): 253–63.
Keener, Craig S. *Miracles: The Credibility of the New Testament Accounts*. Grand Rapids, MI: Baker Academic, 2011.
Kern, Philip H. *Rhetoric and Galatians: Assessing an Approach to Paul's Epistle*. Cambridge: Cambridge University Press, 1998.
Kim, Seyoon. *The Origin of Paul's Gospel*. Tübingen: Mohr Siebeck, 1981. Repr., Eugene, OR: Wipf and Stock, 2007.
King, Sallie B. 'Two Epistemological Models for the Interpretation of Mysticism'. *JAAR* 56 (1988): 257–79.
Kittel, Gerhard, and Gerhard Friedrich, eds. *Theological Dictionary of the New Testament*. Translated by Geoffrey W. Bromiley. 10 vols. Grand Rapids, MI: Eerdmans, 1964–1976.
Krauter, Stefan. 'Heavenly Support in 2 Maccabees 15: Biblical Memories, a Vision, and a Sword'. In *Epiphanies of the Divine in the Septuagint and the New Testament*. Edited by Roland Deines and Mark Wreford. Tübingen: Mohr Siebeck, forthcoming.
Kruger, Michael J. *The Question of Canon: Challenging the Status Quo in the New Testament Debate*. Nottingham: Apollos, 2013.
Kugel, James L. *The Bible as It Was*. Cambridge: Belknap, 1997.
Kugel, James L. *The Great Shift: Encountering God in Biblical Times*. New York: Houghton Mifflin Harcourt, 2017.

Kuhn, Thomas S. *The Structure of Scientific Revolutions*. 3rd edn. Chicago: University of Chicago, 1996.
Kümmel, Werner G. *Introduction to the New Testament*. Translated by A. J. Mattill. London: SCM, 1966.
Kurz, William S. 'Promise and Fulfillment in Hellenistic Jewish Narrative and in Luke and Acts'. Pages 147–70 in *Jesus and the Heritage of Israel: Luke's Narrative Claim upon Israel's Legacy*. Edited by David P. Moessner. Harrisburg: Trinity Press, 1999.
Larsen, Matthew D. C. 'Accidental Publication, Unfinished Texts and the Traditional Goals of New Testament Textual Criticism'. *JSNT* 39 (2017): 362–87.
Lash, Nicholas. *Easter in Ordinary*. Notre Dame, IN: University of Notre Dame Press, 1986.
Lear, Joseph M. *What Shall We Do?: Eschatology and Ethics in Luke-Acts*. Eugene, OR: Wipf and Stock, 2018.
Leisegang, Hans. *Der heilige Geist: Das Wesen und Werden der mystisch-intuitiven Erkenntnis in der Philosophie und Religion der Griechen*. Leipzig: Teubner, 1919.
Leisegang, Hans. *Pneuma Hagion: Der Ursprung des Geistbegriffs der synoptischen Evangelien aus der griechischen Mystik*. Leipzig: Hinrichs, 1922.
Levison, Jack. *Inspired: The Holy Spirit and the Mind of Faith*. Grand Rapids, MI: Eerdmans, 2013.
Levison, John R. *The Spirit in First Century Judaism*. Leiden: Brill, 1997.
Levison, John R. *Filled with the Spirit*. Grand Rapids, MI: Eerdmans, 2009.
Liddell, Henry George, Robert Scott and Henry Stuart Jones. *A Greek-English Lexicon*. 9th edn with revised supplement. Oxford: Clarendon Press, 1996.
Lim, Timothy H. *The Formation of the Jewish Canon*. New Haven, CT: Yale University, 2013.
Lim, Timothy H. 'An Indicative Definition of the Canon'. Pages 1–24 in *When Texts Are Canonized*. Edited by Timothy H. Lim. Providence, RI: Brown, 2017.
Lincoln, Andrew T. *Paradise Now and Not Yet*. Cambridge: Cambridge University Press, 1981.
Lindemann, Andreas. 'Bultmannschule'. Pages 402–10 in *Jesus Handbuch*. Edited by J. Schröter and Christine Jacobi. Tübingen: Mohr Siebeck, 2017.
Longenecker, Bruce W. 'Until Christ Is Formed in You: Suprahuman Forces and Moral Character in Galatians'. *CBQ* 61 (1999): 92–108.
Longenecker, Richard N. *Introducing Romans: Critical Issues in Paul's Most Famous Letter*. Grand Rapids, MI: Eerdmans, 2011.
Luck, Ulrich. 'Kerygma, Tradition und Geschichte Jesu bei Lukas'. *ZTK* 57 (1960): 51–66.
Lüdemann, Gerd. *Early Christianity According to the Traditions in Acts: A Commentary*. Minneapolis, MN: Fortress, 1989.
Lüdemann, Gerd, and Alf Özen. 'Religionsgeschichtliche Schule'. Pages 618–24 in *TRE* 28. Edited by Gerhard Krause and Gerhard Müller. Berlin: de Gruyter, 1977–Present.
Luther, Martin. *Against the Heavenly Prophets in the Matter of Images and Sacraments*. Translated by Conrad Bergendorff and Bernhard Erling. Luther's Works 40. Philadelphia, PA: Muhlenberg Press, 1958.
Luz, Ulrich. 'Paul as Mystic'. Pages 131–43 in *The Holy Spirit and Christian Origins: Essays in Honour of James D. G. Dunn*. Edited by Graham N. Stanton et al. Grand Rapids, MI: Eerdmans, 2004.
Lyons, George. *Pauline Autobiography: Toward a New Understanding*. Atlanta, GA: Scholars Press, 1985.

Macaskill, Grant. *Union with Christ in the New Testament*. Oxford: Oxford University Press, 2013.

Macchia, Frank D. 'Sighs Too Deep for Words: Toward a Theology of Glossolalia'. *JPT* 1 (1992): 47–73.

Macchia, Frank D. 'Babel and the Tongues of Pentecost: Reversal or Fulfilment?' Pages 34–51 in *Speaking in Tongues: Multi-Disciplinary Perspectives*. Edited by Mark J. Cartledge. Milton Keynes: Paternoster, 2006.

Maddell, Geoffrey. 'What Music Teaches about Emotion'. *Philosophy* 71 (1996): 63–82.

Malcolm, Matthew R. ʻ*Kerygmatic Rhetoric* in New Testament Epistles'. Pages 69–89 in *Horizons in Hermeneutics*. Edited by Stanley E. Porter and Matthew R. Malcolm. Grand Rapids, MI: Eerdmans, 2013.

Malcolm, Matthew R. *Paul and the Rhetoric of Reversal in 1 Corinthians: The Impact of Paul's Gospel on His Macro-Rhetoric*. Cambridge: Cambridge University Press, 2013.

Marshall, I. Howard. 'The Significance of Pentecost'. *SJT* 30 (1977): 347–69.

Matsumoto, David, and Paul Ekman. 'Basic Emotions'. Pages 69–72 in *The Oxford Handbook to Emotion and the Affective Sciences*. Edited by David Sander and Klaus R. Scherer. Oxford: Oxford University Press, 2009.

McCutcheon, Russell T. *The Discipline of Religion: Structure, Meaning, Rhetoric*. London: Routledge, 2003.

McDonald, Lee Martin. *The Formation of the Biblical Canon*. 2 vols. London: Bloomsbury, 2017.

McFarland, Orrey. ʻ"The One Who Calls in Grace": Paul's Rhetorical and Theological Identification with the Galatians'. *HBT* 35 (2013): 151–65.

Meeks, Wayne. 'A Review of Galatians by Hans Dieter Betz'. *JBL* 100 (1984): 304–7.

Mendez-Moratalla, Fernando. *The Paradigm of Conversion in Luke*. London: T&T Clark, 2004.

Menzies, Glen. 'Pre-Lucan Occurrences of the Phrase "Tongue[s] of Fire"ʼ. *Journal for the Society of Pentecostal Studies* 22 (2000): 27–60.

Menzies, Robert P. *Empowered for Witness: The Spirit in Luke-Acts*. London: T&T Clark, 2004.

Menzies, Robert P. 'The Persecuted Prophets: A Mirror Image of Luke's Spirit-Inspired Church'. Pages 52–70 in *The Spirit and Christ in the New Testament and Christian Theology*. Edited by I. Howard Marshall, Volker Rabens and Cornelis Bennema. Grand Rapids, MI: Eerdmans, 2012.

Menzies, Robert P. *Speaking in Tongues: Jesus and the Apostolic Church as Models for the Church Today*. Cleveland, OH: CPT Press, 2016.

Minear, Paul. *To Heal and Reveal: The Prophetic Vocation According to Luke*. New York: Seabury, 1976.

Moffitt, David M. 'Atonement at the Right Hand: The Sacrificial Significance of Jesus' Exaltation in Acts'. *NTS* 62 (2016): 549–68.

Moule, Charles F. D. *The Holy Spirit*. London: Mowbray, 1978.

Mount, Christopher. ʻ"Jesus Is Lord": Religious Experience and the Religion of Paul'. Paper presented at the annual meeting of the SBL, Washington, DC, November 18, 2006.

Mroczek, Eva. 'The Hegemony of the Biblical in the Study of Second Temple Literature'. *JAJ* 6 (2015): 2–35.

Mroczek, Eva. *The Literary Imagination in Jewish Antiquity*. Oxford: Oxford University Press, 2016.

Muir, Steven. 'Vivid Imagery in Galatians 3:1 – Roman Rhetoric, Street Announcing, Graffiti, and Crucifixions'. *BTB* 44 (2014): 76–86.

Newman, Judith H. 'Speech and Spirit: Paul and the Maskil as Inspired Interpreters of Scripture'. Pages 241–64 in *The Holy Spirit, Inspiration, and the Cultures of Antiquity*. Edited by Jörg Frey and John R. Levison. Berlin: De Gruyter, 2014.

Newman, Judith H. *Before the Bible: The Liturgical Body and the Formation of Scriptures in Early Judaism*. Oxford: Oxford University Press, 2018.

Neyrey, Jerome H. *Paul in Other Words: A Cultural Reading of His Letters*. Louisville, KY: Westminster John Knox, 1990.

Niebuhr, Karl-Wilhelm. *Heidenapostel aus Israel: Die jüdische Identität des Paulus nach ihrer Darstellung in seinen Briefen*. Tübingen: Mohr Siebeck, 1992.

Nimmo, Paul T. 'Introduction to the Third Edition'. Pages ix–xiii in Friedrich D. E. Schleiermacher, *The Christian Faith*. Edinburgh: T&T Clark, 2016.

Norden, Eduard. *Agnostos theos: Untersuchungen zur Formengeschichte religiöser Rede*. Leipzig: B.G. Teubner, 1913.

O'Day, Gail R. 'The Citation of Scripture as a Key to Characterization in Acts'. Pages 207–21 in *Scripture and Traditions: Essays on Early Judaism and Christianity in Honor of Carl R. Holladay*. Edited by Patrick Gray and Gail R. O'Day. Leiden: Brill, 2008.

Oeming, Manfred. 'The Way of God: Early Canonicity and the "Nondeviation Formula"'. Pages 25–43 in *When Texts Are Canonized*. Edited by Timothy H. Lim. Providence, RI: Brown, 2017.

Otto, Rudolf. 'How Schleiermacher Rediscovered the *Sensus Numinis*'. In *Religious Essays: A Supplement to 'The Idea of the Holy'*. Translated by Brian Lunn. London: Oxford University Press, 1931.

Otto, Rudolf. *The Idea of the Holy*. 2nd edn. Oxford: Oxford University Press, 1957.

Outler, Albert C. 'The Wesleyan Quadrilateral in Wesley'. *WesTJ* 20 (1985): 7–18.

Pao, David W. *Acts and the Isaianic New Exodus*. Grand Rapids, MI: Baker Academic, 2002.

Park, Sejin. *Pentecost and Sinai. The Festival of Weeks as a Celebration of the Sinai Event*. London: T&T Clark, 2008.

Parsons, Mikeal C., and Richard I. Pervo. *Rethinking the Unity of Luke and Acts*. Minneapolis, MN: Fortress, 1990.

Patterson, Stephen J. 'Is the Christ of Faith also the Jesus of History?' Pages 447–57 in *Debating Christian Theism*. Edited by J. P. Moreland, Chad Meister and Khaldoun A. Sweis. Oxford: Oxford University Press, 2013.

Peerbolte, Bert Jan Lietaert. 'Paul's Rapture: 2 Corinthians 12:2–4 and the Language of the Mystics'. Pages 159–76 in *Experientia: Sites for Inquiry for Religious Experience in Early Judaism and Christianity*. Edited by Frances Flannery, Colleen Shantz and Rodney A. Werline. Atlanta, GA: Society of Biblical Literature, 2008.

Penner, Todd C. 'Contextualizing Acts'. Pages 1–22 in *Contextualizing Acts: Lukan Narrative and Greco-Roman Discourse*. Edited by Todd C. Penner and Caroline Vander Stichele. Leiden: Brill, 2004.

Pervo, Richard I. 'Israel's Heritage and Claims upon the Genre(s) of Luke and Acts: The Problems of a History'. Pages 127–43 in *Jesus and the Heritage of Israel: Luke's Narrative Claim upon Israel's Legacy*. Edited by David P. Moessner. Harrisburg, PA: Trinity, 1999.

Pervo, Richard I. *Dating Acts: Between the Evangelists and the Apologists*. Santa Rosa, CA: Polebridge, 2006.

Peterson, David. 'The Motif of Fulfilment and the Purpose of Luke-Acts'. Pages 83–104 in *The Book of Acts in Its Ancient Literary Setting*. Edited by Bruce W. Winter and Andrew D. Clarke. Grand Rapids, MI: Eerdmans, 1993.

Phillips, T. E. 'The Genre of Acts: Moving toward a Consensus?' *CurBR* 4 (2006): 365–96.

Plantinga, Alvin. *Warranted Christian Belief*. Oxford: Oxford University Press, 2000.
Proudfoot, Wayne. *Religious Experience*. Berkeley: University of California Press, 1985.
Proudfoot, Wayne, ed. *William James and a Science of Religions: Reexperiencing the Varieties of Religious Experience*. New York: Columbia University Press, 2004.
Quash, Ben. 'Revelation'. Pages 325–44 in *The Oxford Handbook of Systematic Theology*. Edited by John Webster, Kathryn Tanner and Iain Torrance. Oxford: Oxford University Press, 2007.
Rabens, Volker. *The Holy Spirit and Ethics in Paul: Transformation and Empowering for Religious-Ethical Life*. 2nd edn. Tübingen: Mohr Siebeck, 2013.
Ramsaran, Rollin A. ' "In Christ" and "Christ in" as Expressions of Religious Experience: Testing the Waters in Galatians'. Pages 161–80 in *Experientia II: Linking Text and Experience*. Edited by Colleen Shantz and Rodney A. Werline. Williston, ND: Society of Biblical Literature, 2012.
Rennie, Bryan, ed. *Changing Religious Worlds: The Meaning and End of Mircea Eliade*. New York: SUNY, 2001.
Richards, E. Randolph. *Paul and First-Century Letter Writing: Secretaries, Composition and Collection*. London: SPCK, 2005.
Robbins, Vernon K. 'The Claims of the Prologues and Greco-Roman Rhetoric'. Pages 63–83 in *Jesus and the Heritage of Israel: Luke's Narrative Claim upon Israel's Legacy*. Edited by David P. Moessner. Harrisburg, PA: Trinity, 1999.
Rorty, Richard, ed. *The Linguistic Turn: Recent Essays in Philosophical Method*. Chicago: University of Chicago Press, 1967.
Rosner, Brian S. 'Acts and Biblical History'. Pages 65–82 in *The Book of Acts in Its Ancient Literary Setting*. Edited by B. W. Winter and A. D. Clarke. Grand Rapids, MI: Eerdmans, 1993.
Rosner, Brian S. 'The Progress of the Word'. Pages 215–33 in *Witness to the Gospel: The Theology of Acts*. Edited by I. Howard Marshall and David Peterson. Grand Rapids, MI: Eerdmans, 1998.
Rowe, C. Kavin. 'Literary Unity and Reception History: Reading Luke-Acts as Luke and Acts'. *JSNT* 29 (2007): 449–57.
Rowe, C. Kavin, and Richard B. Hays. 'Biblical Studies'. Pages 436–55 in *The Oxford Handbook of Systematic Theology*. Edited by John Webster, Kathryn Tanner and Iain Torrance. Oxford: Oxford University Press, 2007.
Rowlands, Jonathan. *The Metaphysics of Historical Jesus Research: An Argument for Increasing the Plurality of Metaphysical Frameworks within Historical Jesus Research*. PhD Thesis, University of Nottingham, 2020.
Ruzer, Serge. 'Did the New Testament Authors Aspire to Make Their Compositions Part of Scripture? The Case of the Johannine Prologue'. Pages 347–61 in *Oriental Studies and Interfaith Dialogue*. Edited by Máté Hidvégi. Budapest: L'Harmattan, 2018.
Sanders, E. P. *Paul and Palestinian Judaism: A Comparison of Patterns of Religion*. London: SCM, 1977.
Sandnes, Karl O. 'Prophecy – a Sign for Believers (1 Cor 14,20-25)'. *Bib* 77 (1996): 1–15.
Sandys-Wunsch, J., and L. Eldredge trans. and ed. 'J. P. Gabler and the Distinction between Biblical and Dogmatic Theology: Translation, Commentary, and Discussion of his Originality'. *SJT* 33 (1980): 133–58.
Satlow, Michael L. 'Bad Prophecies: Canon and the Case of the Book of Daniel'. Pages 63–81 in *When Texts Are Canonized*. Edited by Timothy H. Lim. Providence, RI: Brown, 2017.

Schachter, Stanley, and Jerome E. Singer. 'Cognitive, Social and Physiological Determinants of Emotional State'. *Psychological Review* 69 (1962): 379-99.

Schaper, Joachim. 'God's Presence amongst the Israelites According to LXX Exodus and LXX Deuteronomy'. In *Epiphanies of the Divine in the Septuagint and the New Testament*. Edited by Roland Deines and Mark Wreford. Tübingen: Mohr Siebeck, forthcoming.

Schleiermacher, Friedrich D. E. *The Christian Faith*. Translated and edited by H. R. Mackintosh and J. S. Stewart. Edinburgh: T&T Clark, 1999.

Schmidt, Daryl D. 'Rhetorical Influences and Genre: Luke's Preface and the Rhetoric of Hellenistic Historiography'. Pages 27-60 in *Jesus and the Heritage of Israel: Luke's Narrative Claim upon Israel's Legacy*. Edited by David P. Moessner. Harrisburg, PA: Trinity, 1999.

Schmidt, Daryl D. 'The Historiography of Acts: Deuteronomistic or Hellenistic?' Pages 417-27 in *Society of Biblical Literature 1985 Seminar Papers*. Edited by Ken Harold Richards. Atlanta, GA: Scholars Press, 1985.

Schniedewind, William M. *The Word of God in Transition: From Prophet to Exegete in the Second Temple Period*. Sheffield: Sheffield Academic Press, 1995.

Schwartz, Barry. 'Where There's Smoke, There's Fire: Memory and History'. Pages 7-40 in *Memory and Identity in Ancient Judaism and Early Christianity*. Edited by Tom Thatcher. Atlanta, GA: SBL Press, 2014.

Schweitzer, Albert. *Die Mystik des Apostles Paulus*. Tübingen: Mohr Siebeck, 1930.

Scott, Ian W. *Paul's Way of Knowing: Story, Experience, and the Spirit*. Grand Rapids, MI: Baker Academic, 2009.

Scott, James M. 'Luke's Geographical Horizon'. Pages 483-544 in *The Book of Acts in Its Graeco-Roman Setting*. Edited by David W. J. Gill and Conrad Gempf. Grand Rapids, MI: Eerdmans, 1994.

Segal, Alan F. 'The Afterlife as Mirror of the Self'. Pages 19-40 in *Experientia: Sites for Inquiry for Religious Experience in Early Judaism and Christianity*. Edited by Frances Flannery, Colleen Shantz and Rodney A. Werline. Atlanta, GA: Society of Biblical Literature, 2008.

Segal, Alan F. *Paul the Convert*. New Haven, CT: Yale, 1990.

Segal, Robert. 'In Defense of Reductionism'. *JAAR* 51 (1983): 97-127.

Segal, Robert. 'Reductionism in the Study of Religion'. Pages 4-14 in *Religion and Reductionism: Essays on Eliade, Segal, and the Challenge of the Social Sciences for the Study of Religion*. Edited by Thomas A. Idinopulos and Edward A. Yonan. Leiden: Brill, 1994.

Shantz, Colleen. 'The Confluence of Trauma and Transcendence in the Pauline Corpus'. Pages 193-205 in *Experientia: Sites for Inquiry for Religious Experience in Early Judaism and Christianity*. Edited by Frances Flannery, Colleen Shantz and Rodney A. Werline. Atlanta, GA: Society of Biblical Literature, 2008.

Shantz, Colleen. *Paul in Ecstasy: The Neurobiology of the Apostle's Life and Thought*. Cambridge: Cambridge University Press, 2009.

Shantz, Colleen. 'Opening the Black Box: New Prospects for Analyzing Religious Experience'. Pages 1-15 in *Experientia II: Linking Text and Experience*. Edited by Colleen Shantz and Rodney A. Werline. Atlanta, GA: SBL, 2012.

Shantz, Colleen, and Rodney A. Werline, eds. *Experientia II: Linking Text and Experience*. Atlanta, GA: SBL, 2012.

Sharf, Robert. 'Experience'. Pages 94-116 in *Critical Terms for Religious Studies*. Edited by Mark C. Taylor. Chicago: University of Chicago, 1998.

Shauf, Scott. *The Divine in Acts and in Ancient Historiography*. Minneapolis, MN: Fortress, 2015.
Shelton, James B. 'Delphi and Jerusalem: Two Spirits or Holy Spirit? A Review of John R. Levison's *Filled with the Spirit*'. *Pneuma* 33 (2011): 47–58.
Silva, Moisés. *Interpreting Galatians: Explorations in Exegetical Method*. 2nd edn. Grand Rapids, MI: Baker Academic, 2001.
Smith, Daniel Lynwood, and Zachary Lundin Kostopoulos. 'Biography, History, and the Genre of Luke-Acts'. *NTS* 63 (2017): 390–410.
Smith, D. Moody. 'When Did the Gospels Become Scripture?' *JBL* 119 (2000): 3–20.
Smith, James K. A. 'Liberating Religion from Theology: Marion and Heidegger on the Possibility of a Phenomenology of Religion'. *International Journal for the Philosophy of Religion* 46 (1999): 17–33.
Smith, James K. A. *Thinking in Tongues: Pentecostal Contributions to Christian Theology*. Grand Rapids, MI: Eerdmans, 2010.
Smith, James K. A. *The Fall of Interpretation: Philosophical Foundations for an Incarnational Hermeneutic*. 2nd edn. Grand Rapids, MI: Baker Academic, 2012.
Smith, Jonathan Z. *Imagining Religion: From Babylon to Jamestown*. Chicago: University of Chicago, 1982.
Spanos, N. P., and E. C. Hewitt. 'Glossolalia: Test of the Trance and Psychopathology Hypotheses'. *Journal of Abnormal Psychology* 88 (1979): 427–34.
Spiro, Melford E. 'Religion: Problems of Definition and Explanation'. Pages 85–126 in *Anthropological Approaches to the Study of Religion*. Edited by Michael Banton. London: Tavistock, 1966.
Sprinkle, Preston. 'Πίστις Χριστοῦ as an Eschatological Event'. Pages 165–84 in *The Faith of Jesus Christ: The Pistou Christou Debate*. Edited by Michael F. Bird and Preston M. Sprinkle. Milton Keynes: Paternoster, 2009.
Squires, John T. *The Plan of God in Luke-Acts*. Cambridge: Cambridge University Press, 1993.
Stanton, Graham N. *Jesus of Nazareth in New Testament Preaching*. Cambridge: Cambridge University Press, 1974.
Stark, Rodney. 'A Taxonomy of Religious Experience'. *JSSR* 5 (1965): 97–116.
Stark, Rodney. 'Normal Revelations: A Rational Model of "Mystical" Experiences'. *Religion and the Social Order* 1 (1991): 239–51.
Stark, Rodney. 'A Theory of Revelations'. *JSSR* 38 (1999): 287–308.
Sterling, Gregory E. *Historiography and Self-Definition: Josephos, Luke-Acts, and Apologetic Historiography*. Leiden: Brill, 1992.
Sterling, Gregory E. 'Turning to God: Conversion in Greek-Speaking Judaism and Early Christianity'. Pages 69–95 in *Scripture and Traditions: Essays on Early Judaism and Christianity in Honor of Carl R. Holladay*. Edited by Patrick Gray and Gail R. O'Day. Leiden: Brill, 2008.
Stuckenbruck, Loren T. 'The "Cleansing" of the Gentiles: Background for the Rationale behind the Apostles' Decree in Acts 15'. Pages 65–90 in *Aposteldekret und antikes Vereinswesen*. Edited by Markus Öhler. Tübingen: Mohr Siebeck, 2009.
Talbert, Charles H. 'Promise and Fulfillment in Luke-Acts'. Pages 91–103 in *Luke-Acts: New Perspectives from the Society of Biblical Literature Seminar*. Edited by Charles H. Talbert. New York: Crossroads, 1984.
Talbert, Charles H. 'Conversion in the Acts of the Apostles: Ancient Auditors' Perceptions'. Pages 135–48 in *Reading Luke-Acts in Its Mediterranean Milieu*. Leiden: Brill, 2003.

Tannehill, Robert C. *The Narrative Unity of Luke-Acts: A Literary Interpretation*. 2 vols. Minneapolis: Fortress, 1986-90.
Taves, Ann. *Fits, Trances, and Visions: Experiencing Religion and Explaining Experience from Wesley to James*. Princeton, NJ: Princeton University Press, 1999.
Taylor, Charles. *Sources of the Self: The Making of the Modern Identity*. Cambridge: Harvard University, 1989.
Taylor, Charles. *Varieties of Religion Today: William James Revisited*. Cambridge: Harvard University Press, 2002.
Temporini, Hildegard, and Wolfgang Haase, eds. *Aufstieg und Niedergang der römischen Welt: Geschichte und Kultur Roms im Spiegel der neueren Forschung*. Part 2, *Principat*. Berlin: de Gruyter, 1972-.
Thiselton, Anthony C. *The Hermeneutics of Doctrine*. Grand Rapids, MI: Eerdmans, 2007.
Thiselton, Anthony C. *New Horizons in Hermeneutics: The Theory and Practice of Transforming Biblical Reading*. Reprinted Grand Rapids, MI: Zondervan, 2012.
Thiselton, Anthony C. *The Holy Spirit: In Biblical Teaching, through the Centuries, and Today*. London: SPCK, 2015.
Thiselton, Anthony C. *Doubt, Faith, and Certainty*. Grand Rapids, MI: Eerdmans, 2017.
Tibbs, Clint. *Religious Experience of the Pneuma: Communication with the Spirit World in 1 Corinthians 12 and 14*. Tübingen: Mohr Siebeck, 2007.
Tomlin, Graham. 'Life in the Spirit: Identity, Vocation and the Cross of Christ'. Pages 72-85 in *The Holy Spirit in the World Today*. Edited by Jane Williams. London: St Paul's, 2011.
Treier, Daniel J. *Introducing Theological Interpretation of Scripture: Recovering a Christian Practice*. Nottingham: Apollos, 2008.
Troeltsch, Ernst. 'Historical and Dogmatic Method in Theology'. Pages 11-32 in *Religion in History*. Edited by J. L. Adams and W. F. Bense. Minneapolis, MN: Fortress, 1991.
Turner, Max. *Power from on High: The Spirit in Israel's Restoration and Witness in Luke-Acts*. Sheffield: Sheffield Academic, 1996.
Turner, Max. *The Holy Spirit and Spiritual Gifts Then and Now*. Carlisle: Paternoster, 1996.
Turner, Max. 'Early Christian Experience and Theology of "Tongues": A New Testament Perspective'. Pages 1-33 in *Speaking in Tongues: Multi-Disciplinary Perspectives*. Edited by Mark J. Cartledge. Milton Keynes: Paternoster, 2006.
Twelftree, Graham H. *Jesus the Miracle Worker: A Historical and Theological Study*. Downers Grove, IL: IVP, 1999.
Twelftree, Graham H. *People of the Spirit: Exploring Luke's View of the Church*. Grand Rapids, MI: Baker Academic, 2009.
Twelftree, Graham H. *Paul and the Miraculous: A Historical Reconstruction*. Grand Rapids, MI: Baylor Academic, 2013.
Twelftree, Graham H. 'Is "Holy Scripture" Christian?: A Lucan Perspective'. *Theology* 116 (2013): 351-60.
Uytanlet, Samson. *Luke-Acts and Jewish Historiography: A Study on the Theology, Literature and Ideology of Luke-Acts*. Tübingen: Mohr Siebeck, 2014.
Van der Horst, Pieter. 'Hellenistic Parallels to the Acts of the Apostles (2.1-47)'. *JSNT* (1985): 49-60.
Vanhoozer, Kevin J. *Is There a Meaning in This Text?* Grand Rapids, MI: Zondervan, 1998.
Vanhoozer, Kevin J. 'From "Blessed in Christ" to "Being in Christ": The State of Union and the Place of Participation in Paul's Discourse, New Testament Exegesis, and Systematic Theology Today'. Pages 3-33 in *'In Christ' in Paul*. Edited by Michael J. Thate, Kevin J. Vanhoozer and Constantine R. Campbell. Tübingen: Mohr Siebeck, 2014.

Volz, Paul. *Der Geist Gottes und die verwandten Erscheinungen im Alten Testament und im anschliessenden Judentum*. Tübingen: Mohr, 1910.
Von Baer, Heinrich. *Der Heilige Geist in den Lukasschriften*. Stuttgart: Kohlhammer, 1926.
Wach, Joachim. *Sociology of Religion*. London: Kegan Paul, 1947.
Wach, Joachim. *Types of Religious Experience Christian and Non-Christian*. Chicago: University of Chicago Press, 1951.
Walters, Patricia. *The Assumed Authorial Unity of Luke and Acts: A Reassessment of the Evidence*. Cambridge: Cambridge University Press, 2009.
Walton, Steve. 'Whose Spirit? The Promise and the Promiser in Luke 12:12'. Pages 35–51 in *The Spirit and Christ in the New Testament and Christian Theology*. Edited by I. Howard Marshall, Volker Rabens and Cornelis Bennema. Grand Rapids, MI: Eerdmans, 2012.
Ward, W. R. *The Protestant Evangelical Awakening*. Cambridge: Cambridge University Press, 1992.
Watson, Francis. 'Gospel and Scripture: Rethinking Canonical Unity'. *TynBul* 52 (2001): 161–82.
Webb, Robert L. 'The Historical Enterprise and Historical Jesus Research'. Pages 9–93 in *Key Events in the Life of the Historical Jesus*. Edited by Darrell L. Bock and Robert L. Webb. Tübingen: Mohr Siebeck, 2009.
Webster, John. *Holy Scripture: A Dogmatic Sketch*. Cambridge: Cambridge University Press, 2003.
Welker, Michael. *God the Spirit*. Translated by John F. Hoffmeyer. Minneapolis: Fortress, 1994.
Wendt, Heidi. 'Galatians 3:1 as Allusion to Textual Prophecy'. *JBL* 135 (2016): 369–89.
Williams, Guy. *The Spirit World in the Letters of Paul the Apostle: A Critical Examination of the Role of Spiritual Beings in the Authentic Pauline Epistles*. Göttingen: Vandenhoeck und Ruprecht, 2009.
Wilson, Walter T. *The Hope of Glory: Education and Exhortation in the Epistle to the Colossians*. Leiden: Brill, 1997.
Wilson, Walter T. 'Urban Legends: Acts 10:1–11:18 and the Strategies of Greco-Roman Foundation Narratives'. *JBL* 120 (2001): 77–99.
Wilson-Mendenhall, Christine D., and Lawrence W. Barsalo. 'A Fundamental Role for Conceptual Processing in Emotion'. Pages 547–63 in *The Emotions Handbook*. Edited by Lisa Feldman Barrett, Michael Lewis and Jeannette M. Haviland-Jones. 4th edn. New York: Guildford Press, 2016.
Wolter, Michael. 'Die Proömien des lukanischen Doppelwerks (Lk 1,1-4 und Apg 1,1-2)'. Pages 476–94 in *Die Apostelgeschichte im Kontext antiker und frühchristlicher Historiographie*. Edited by Jörg Frey, Clare K. Rothschild and Jens Schröter. Berlin: De Gruyter, 2009.
Wolterstorff, Nicholas. *Divine Discourse: Philosophical Reflections on the Claim That God Speaks*. Cambridge: Cambridge University Press, 1995.
Wreford, Mark. 'Diagnosing Religious Experience in Romans 8'. *TynBul* 68 (2017): 203–22.
Wright, N. T. 'How Can the Bible Be Authoritative'. *Vox Evangelica* 21 (1991): 7–32.
Wright, N. T. *The Climax of the Covenant: Christ and the Law in Pauline Theology*. London: SPCK, 1992.
Wright, N. T. *Paul and the Faithfulness of God*. London: SPCK, 2013.
Wynn, Mark. *Emotional Experience and Religious Understanding*. Cambridge: Cambridge University Press, 2005.

Wynn, Mark. 'On the Goods of the Religious Life: Contextualizing the Approach of Richard Swinburne'. *Religious Studies* 53 (2017): 371–85.
Yonan, Edward A. 'Clarifying the Strengths and Limits of Reductionism in the Discipline of Religion'. Pages 43–8 in *Religion and Reductionism: Essays on Eliade, Segal, and the Challenge of the Social Sciences for the Study of Religion*. Edited by Thomas A. Idinopulos and Edward A. Yonan. Leiden: Brill, 1994.
Zahl, Simeon. 'The Drama of Agency: Affective Augustinianism and Galatians'. Pages 335–52 in *Galatians and Christian Theology: Justification, the Gospel, and Ethics in Paul's Letter*. Edited by Mark W. Elliott et al. Grand Rapids, MI: Baker Academic, 2014.
Zahl, Simeon. 'On the Affective Salience of Doctrines'. *Modern Theology* 31 (2015): 428–44.
Zahl, Simeon. 'Experience'. Pages 177–95 in *The Oxford Handbook of Nineteenth Century Christian Thought*. Edited by Joel Rasmussen, Judith Wolfe and Johannes Zachhuber. Oxford: Oxford University Press, 2017.

Index of References

Biblical texts
Genesis
  1:28 — 86
  10 — 87
  11 — 70, 86
  11:7 — 70
Exodus
  19 — 70
  19:16-19 — 73–4
Deuteronomy
  4:36 — 74
  11:2 (LXX) — 87
  18:22 — 108
Psalms
  70:19 (LXX) — 87
  75:8 — 72
Isaiah
  28:11 — 86
  40:3-5 — 80
  49:5 — 144
  53:1 — 150
  61:1-2 — 80
Jeremiah
  1:5 — 144
  28:9 — 108
  29:1-23 — 165
  29:4 — 165
  38:33 — 164
Ezekiel
  1:26 — 143
Joel
  3:1-5 (LXX) — 67, 85, 95–7
  3:3 (LXX) — 75
Amos
  9:11-12 (LXX) — 103, 113
1 Maccabees — 3, 58
2 Maccabees
  3:34 — 88
  7:17 — 88
3 Maccabees
  7:22 — 87
Sirach
  17:8 — 87
  18:4 — 87
  36:7 — 88
Matthew
  3:16 — 77
  10:19-20 — 90
Mark
  1:10 — 77
  13:11 — 90
Luke
  1:1 — 69, 122–4, 126
  1:1-4 — 122–6
  1:2 — 123, 126
  1:3 — 123, 127
  1:4 — 123
  2:20 — 112
  3:16 — 72, 103, 111
  3:21-4:21 — 80
  3:22 — 77
  4:37 — 74
  5:30 — 115
  9:51 — 68–9
  10:7 — 111
  11:15 — 69
  12:11-12 — 93
  12:12 — 90
  15:2 — 115
  19:7 — 115
  21:25 — 74
  23:47 — 112
  24:27 — 99
  24:46-49 — 67, 130
  24:49 — 66, 78
Acts
  1:1-2 — 123
  1:4 — 78
  1:5 — 103, 111
  1:5-8 — 67, 111, 130

1:8	66, 79,	10:20	116
	92–3, 128	10:28	106
1:14	117	10:30-33	106
2:1	69, 81	10:33	105
2:1-4	66, 69–79	10:34	107, 115
2:2	70, 77	10:34-43	105
2:3	70–1, 77	10:44	109–10
2:4	70–1, 79,	10:45	109–10
	81–2, 89–92	10:45-46	105
2:5-13	66	10:46	82
2:5-6	81	10:47	110
2:6	80–3	11:1-3	115
2:7	82–3, 85	11:1-18	102, 110–12
2:8	74, 82	11:2	112
2:11	87–9, 110	11:4	127
2:12	82, 85	11:4-18	105
2:13	71–3, 115	11:5	126
2:13-14	85	11:12	112, 116
2: 2:14	92–4	11:15	69, 78,
2:14-36	81		110, 126
15	72	11:16	103, 111
2:16	99	11:17	110,
2:17	72, 99		113, 115–16
2:17-21	95–6	11:18	105, 112
2:18	85	13:41	85
2:19	75, 80, 85	14:4	112
2:22-23	94	15:6	126
2:25	99	15:7	126
2:31	99	15:7-11	103,
2:32	92		105, 113–4
2:32-33	78	15:8	113, 116
2:33	80, 90, 96	15:8-10	115
2:34	99	15:9	105, 116
2:37	86, 94	15:12	115–16
2:38	110	15:14	116
2:46	117	15:15	117
3:12	85	15:16-17	103
4:13	85, 107	15:20	117
4:24	117	15:21	119–20
5:12	117	15:22	117–18, 127
7:31	85	15:23	117
10	65	15:25	117–18, 127
10:1-48	78	15:27	118
10:4	104	15:28	117–18,
10:10	104		126–7
10:11	126	15:30-32	120
10:15-16	106	15:32	119
10:19	106, 112	18:25-26	129
10:19-20	105	19:6	82

Index of References

26:1	93	1:6-8	157
26:12-21	93	1:7	143, 153
26:22	99	1:8	135, 141–3, 163
26:22-23	93		
26:25	92	1:10	141
Romans		1:10-11	162, 167
1:17	138	1:11	167
843-4		1:10-12	140
8:18-21	44	1:11-12	134–5, 136–46, 151, 164
8:23	44		
8:24-25	44	1:13-14	144
8:26	44, 84	1:14	144
10:16-17	150	1:15	149, 153, 164
15:4	151	1:15-16	134–5, 136–46, 151, 164
1 Corinthians			
3:13	138	1:20	166
5:3	118, 163	2:1-10	162
7:6	118, 163	2:1-15	167
7:8	118, 163	2:19-20	134–5, 138, 142, 151–2, 154–7, 158–9, 164
7:12	118, 163		
13:1	74		
14	83–6		
14:21-25	85–6	3:1	150–3, 159
14:22	5	3:1-5	134–5, 146–53, 160, 162
14:23	86, 93		
14:24	93	3:2	148, 150
14:25	86, 93	3:3	148
15	137, 139	3:4	148
15:1-8	140	3:5	148, 150
15:3	142, 167	3:11	152
2 Corinthians		3:13	153
3	151	3:13-14	142
3:2	164	3:25-4:7	162
3:3	146	3:26	152
3:6	140	3:27	142, 157, 159
3:18	140	3:27-28	157
5:2	44	3:28	152, 158–9
5:4	44	4:1-7	134
10:1	163	4:1-31	135
10:11	163	4:3	141, 153
12:1-4	35	4:4-5	149
13:3	139	4:4-7	142
Galatians		4:6	134, 149, 151
1:1	141, 143	4:8	135
1:1-5	162, 167	4:8-12	158
1:3	143	4:9	141, 153, 158
1:3-5	142	4:12	135, 157–9, 164
1:6	153		
1:6-7	141	4:12-20	153, 163

4:14	147, 153	4 Ezra	3, 58
4:15-16	151	14-15	58
4:16	159	Liber Antiquitatum Biblicarum	58
4:17-18	153	1 Enoch	3, 58
4:19	135, 152, 157–9, 164	104-5	58
4:20	158, 162	Qumran	
5:5	135, 159, 161, 167	Community Rule (1QS) 1-3	76
5:6	152	1QpHab	3
5:14	161	4Q174 1.1.21.2.12	114
5:13-26	135, 148	11QTemple[a]	3, 58
5:16	160	Jubilees	3, 58
5:16-17	160	1.1-2	76
5:16-25	134, 160, 162	6.17-22	76
5:22-23	160		
5:22-26	161	Josephus	
5:24	158	Against Apion	
5:25	160	1.37-43	174
6:2	161	Antiquities	
6:5-6	158	3.5.2	75-6
6:11	146, 163	3.15.1	148
6:16	163	Jewish War	
6:17	143	5:19-20	3, 58
Philippians		5:391-3	3, 58
2:12-13	161		
3:2-11	144	Philo	
Colossians		Drunkenness	
1:5	120	147	72
1:25	120	Heir	
2:5	118, 121, 163	2.264	71
3:16 120		2.264-5	90
1 Thessalonians		On the Decalogue	
1:5	55	33-46	74-5
2:13	55, 165	Special Laws	
2 Thessalonians		2.189	75
3:17	118		
1 Timothy		**Early Christian texts**	
5:18	111	Augustine	
Philemon		Confessions	12
21	162		
Hebrews		Irenaeus	
12:19	74	Heresies	
Revelation		1.8.1	174
Ancient Jewish texts		Justin Martyr	
Old Testament Pseudepigrapha		1st Apology	
Baruch	3	67	120, 124

Shepherd of Hermas 58

Greco-Roman Literature
Apuleius
Metamorphoses 90

Cicero
On Divination 90

Lucan
The Civil War 71

Plutarch
Moralia 71–3, 90

Polybius
The Histories 87

Index of Names and Subjects

Adams, Samuel V. 21
Adams, Sean A. 65
Aernie, Jeffrey W. 165
Affect 29, 39-4, 84-5, 104-5, 139-40, 154-7, 160
Alexander, Loveday 65, 122-3, 128, 130
Alston, William P. 36
Apostolic Decree 117-21, 126-7
Ascough, Richard S. 127
Ashton, John 155
Atkinson, William P. 18
Aune, David E. 123
Austin, J.L. 84

Baird, William 137, 144
Barclay, John M.G. 118, 121, 136, 140, 144-5, 159-60
Barrett, C.K. 63, 86, 103, 107, 124
Barth, Karl 16, 25, 50, 155
Barth, Markus and Helmut Blanke 121
Batluck, Mark 11, 16-17, 30
Bauckham, Richard 113
Bell, Catherine 157
Bell, Richard H. 137, 153
Berger, Klaus 35, 164
Betz, Hans Dieter 134, 137, 139-41, 148, 150, 152, 163-4
Biggs, Adam T., Ryan D. Kreager, et al 43
Bird, Michael F. 3
Blum, Jason N. 29, 34-5, 40, 45-6, 48, 51, 130
Bock, Darrell L. 65-6, 68-9, 80, 92, 94, 102, 107
Bockmuehl, Markus 138, 141
Bons, Eberhard 139
Borse, Ulrich 168
Bosworth, I.E. 137
Bousset, Wilhelm 154
Bowker, J.W. 137
Bradshaw, Paul F. 120
Broadhead, Edwin K. 33, 63, 123

Brooke, George J. 58, 125
Brown, Schuyler 122, 127
Bruce, F.F. 137, 148, 151
Brueggemann, Walter 86
Büchsel, Friedrich 15
Bultmann, Rudolf 154
Bultmann School 15-16
Burkhardt, Helmut 91

Cadbury, Henry J. 64, 123
Caird, G.B. 139
Calvin, John 173-4
Campbell, Constantine R. 154, 156
Campbell, Douglas A. 156
Carson, D.A., Leon Morris, and Douglas Moo 2
Chapman, S.B. 99
Charlesworth, James H. 47
Charry, Ellen T. 12
Childs, Brevard S. 130
Clore, Gerald L. and Alexander J. Schiller 39-40
Collins, John J. 166
Conversion 104-8, 144-50
Conzelmann, Hans 75, 80, 82, 110-11
Crawford, Sidnie White 2-3, 125, 166

Das, A. Andrew 138, 144, 147-8, 150, 167
Davies, Douglas 84
Davis, Basil S. 150-1
Davis, Stephen T. 56
De Boer, Martinus C. 137, 143, 145, 148, 152
Deines, Roland 1-2, 11-12, 47-8, 54-7, 67-9, 105, 165, 172
Deissmann, Adolf 14
Dempster, Stephen G. 57
Dennett, Daniel C. 39
Depraz, Natalie 45
Derrida, Jacques 33
Divine and human agency 89-92, 159-61

Index of Names and Subjects

Doering, Lutz 164–5
Donaldson, Terence L. 144
Dunn, James D.G. 5, 11, 16–21, 25–7, 32–6, 90, 111, 138, 141–2, 148, 149–50, 160, 171
Dunson, Ben C. 53

Ecstasy 70–3, 90–1
Edwards, Jonathan 13, 42, 139–40
Ekman, Paul 39
Eliade, Mircea 28–9, 40
Elliott, John H 147, 153, 159
Ellis, E. Earle 119, 125, 141
Emotion 28–9, 39–44
Engberg-Pedersen, Troels 21–5, 29, 39, 134, 147
Enthusiasm 13, 71–2, 91
Epistemology 47–8, 107–9
Esler, Philip F. 159
Estrada, Nelson P. 81
Evans, Craig A. 90, 130
Everts, Jenny 82

Fee, Gordon D. 134, 142, 147, 160
Feeling 13, 41–44, 154–7
  Of absolute dependence 51
  In James' definition of RE 26–7
Ferrer, Jorge N. 37
Fetterman, David M. 45
Finn, Thomas M. 104
Fitzmyer, Joseph A. 67, 94, 101, 117
Flannery, Frances 24, 32–4
Fletcher-Louis, Crispin 142
Fowl, Stephen E. 103, 113, 117
Fox, Elaine 29, 39, 51
Fredriksen, Paula 136
Frei, Hans W. 155
Frein, Brigid C. 69, 111–12
Frey, Jörg 1
Frey, Jörg, and John R. Levison 11, 16, 22, 34, 45
Fulfilment 66–9, 78–81, 110–12, 124–31
Fung, Ronald Y.K. 137
Furseth, Ingur, and Pål Repstad 37

Gabler, Johann Phillip 12
Gäckle, Volker 78
Gadamer, Hans-Georg 35, 46–7, 107–8
Galatians
  Date 149 n.86, 167–8
  Within Pauline corpus 166–9
Gasque, W.R. Ward 129
Gaventa, Beverly Roberts 105–6, 136, 138, 159
Geivett, R. Douglas and Paul K. Moser 25
Gilbert, Gary 87
God's mighty deeds 87–9
Goldie, Peter 43, 160
Goodman, Felicitas 91
Gorman, Michael J. 43, 144, 155–6
Gospel
  Paul's 136–46, 152–3
  As inspired 162–8
Green, Joel B. 69, 131
Gregory, Andrew 64–5
Griffith-Jones, Robin 33
Griffiths, J. Gwyn 82
Grudem, Wayne 86
Gunkel, Heidrun 63, 80–1
Gunkel, Heidrun, Rainer Hirsch-Luipold and John R. Levison 70–6
Gunkel, Hermann 13–15, 19–26, 32–3, 40, 171

Haenchen, Ernst 81, 90, 106
Hall, Robert G. 58, 97
Hansen, G. Walter 150, 163
Harner, Michael J. 37
Hays, Richard B. 75, 140, 155, 164–5
Hemer, Colin 168
Hengel, Martin 12, 21, 49, 111, 124, 129, 131, 142–3
Hengel, Martin and Anna Maria Schwemer 104
Heschel, Abraham J. 83
Hilborn, David 83–4
Himmelfarb, Martha 143
Holland, Glen S. 163
Holy Spirit
  As power 18–19
  Galatians' encounter with 146–53
  Outpouring at Pentecost 66–79
  Outpouring on Gentiles 102–114
  Theophany of 66–9, 76–9
Hopwood, Percy G.S. 16
Horrell, David G. 145, 166
Howell, Brian C. 76

Howell, Brian M. and Jenell Williams Paris 46
Hüneburg, Martin 1
Hurtado, Larry W. 5, 11, 16–21, 25–8, 35, 37–41, 44, 50, 55, 68, 142–3, 155, 171
Husserl, Edmund 45–6

Inspiration 55–6, 57–9, 91–4, 107–10, 113–14, 117–21, 164–6

Jacobs, Struan 108
James (Apostle) 113–14, 116–17, 118–21
James, William 17, 19, 26–7, 53, 130
Jay, Martin 11, 26–7
Jervell, Jacob 92, 101
Jerusalem Convocation 101 n.1, 113–21, 126–7
Johanson, Bruce C. 86
Johnson, Dru 47, 107–9, 115
Johnson, Luke Timothy 5, 11–12, 16–21, 25–8, 30, 32, 34–6, 40, 45–6, 50, 65, 77–8, 85, 103, 106, 114, 116, 119, 157–8

Katz, Steven T. 37–8
Kay, William K. 91
Kay, W.K. and L.J. Francis 91
Keener, Craig S. 2, 34, 49, 64, 70, 82, 95, 97, 134, 147, 150, 163
Kern, Philip H. 134, 163
Kim, Seyoon 143
King, Sallie B. 38–9, 149
Krauter, Stefan 76
Kruger, Michael J. 56–7, 68, 130
Kugel, James L. 58, 76
Kuhn, Thomas S. 108, 144
Kümmel, Werner G. 168
Kurz, William S. 63, 67–8

Larsen, Matthew 54, 63, 123, 125
Lash, Nicholas 25
Lear, Joseph M. 106
Leisegang, Hans 15, 22
Levison, John R. 21–5, 34, 70–6, 77, 85, 89–90, 92, 119, 125
Lightfoot, J.B. 139, 168
Lim, Timothy H. 57, 98–9, 121, 168
Lincoln, Andrew T. 143
Lindemann, Andreas 16
Longenecker, Bruce W. 147

Longenecker, Richard N. 138, 141, 163, 167
Luck, Ulrich 88
Lüdemann, Gerd 68
Lüdemann, Gerd, and Alf Özen 15
Luke-Acts
  Date 49, 123 n.90, 124 n.94, 129 n.114
  Narrative unity 64–6
  Reception history 64–5, 121 n.79, 124 n.91
Luther, Martin 13, 16
Luz, Ulrich 16
Lyons, George 134, 136, 139–41, 145, 150, 153

Macaskill, Grant 154
McCutcheon, Russell T. 29
McDonald, Lee Martin 1
McFarland, Orrey 153
Macchia, Frank D. 84, 87
Maddell, Geoffrey 44
Malcolm, Matthew R. 157, 159, 162–4
Malina, Bruce J. and John J. Pilch 53, 77, 79, 82, 104
Marguerat, Daniel 126
Marshall, I. Howard 76
Martyn, J. Louis 141, 143, 145, 147, 155, 162, 168
Matera, Frank J. 144, 147–8
Matsumoto, David and Paul Ekman 39
Meeks, Wayne 163
Mendez-Moratalla, Fernando 105
Menzies, Glen 77
Menzies, Robert P. 67–8, 75, 80, 85, 120
Methodology 5–7, 44–50
Minear, Paul 119
Moffitt, David M. 78
Moo, Douglas J. 146, 168
Moule, Charles F.D. 12
Mount, Christopher 20, 45
Mroczek, Eva 54–5, 57, 98–9, 121, 165
Muir, Steven 151

Newman, Judith H. 55–8, 146, 151, 165–7
Neyrey, Jerome H. 152–3
Niebuhr, Karl-Wilhelm 145–6
Nimmo, Paul T. 13
Nolland, John 77, 80, 131
Norden, Eduard 122

Index of Names and Subjects

Oakes, Peter 138, 141, 143, 147, 149, 152–3
O'Day, Gail R. 117, 119, 125
Oeming, Manfred 99
Otto, Rudolf 27–8
Outler, Albert C. 13

Pao, David W. 80
Paradigm conflict 43, 47–8, 106–10, 115–16
Park, Sejin 76
Parsons, Mikael C. 49, 77, 80, 112–13, 116, 118, 124
Parsons, Mikael C. and Martin Culy. 117
Parsons, Mikeal C. and Richard I. Pervo 64–5
Patterson, Stephen J. 47
Peerbolte, Bert Jan Lietaert 143
Penner, Todd C. 64
Pentecost 66–79
Pervo, Richard I. 49, 70, 82, 92, 94, 102–3, 112–13, 117, 120
Pesch, Rudolf 82
Peter
   And Cornelius 105–13
   Contribution to Jerusalem convocation 113–14
   Sermon in Acts 292–7
Peterson, David 63, 66, 68, 94, 96, 103, 110
Phenomenology 45–6
   Of religion 40–5, 48–9
Phillips, T.E. 65
Plantinga, Alvin 48
Polanyi, Michael 108
Polhill, John B. 82, 85
Prophetic texts
   As shaping expectation 54–5, 67–8, 96–7, 99–100, 118–21
   In relation to Paul's writing 145–6, 164–6
Proudfoot, Wayne 26, 28–9

Quash, Ben 12

Rabens, Volker 42, 136, 140, 148–9, 151
Ramsaran, Rollin A. 134, 159
Reception history 33, 55–6, 121 n.79
Religious experience
   As cultural construct 24–5, 28–9, 36–41, 134–5
   Barth on 16, 155
   Definition 20, 25–6, 51–3

Historicity 49, 66, 104
Of Tongues-speech 89–92
Paul's 136–46, 154–7
Revelatory 19, 37–8, 54–9, 79–92, 106–7, 136–53
The Galatians' 146–54, 157–9
Revelation 12, 16, 25 n.102, 70–6, 92–100, 113–14, 130–2, 156–9, 164–9
Richards, E. Randolph 165, 167
Roloff, Jürgen 69, 88, 101
Rorty, Richard 31
Rosner, Brian S. 102, 128–30
Rowe, C. Kavin 64–5
Rowe, C. Kavin and Richard B. Hays 12
Ruzer, Serge 1

Sanders, E.P. 154–5
Sandnes, Karl O. 86
Satlow, Michael L. 99
Schachter, Stanley and Jerome E. Singer 28
Schaper, Joachim 77
Schleiermacher, Friedrich D.E. 13, 27, 51
Schmidt, Daryl D. 124, 129
Schnabel, Eckhard J. 77, 81, 92, 120
Schneider, Gerhard 75, 126
Schniedewind, William M. 58
Schreiner, Thomas 138, 141, 143, 147, 150
Schwartz, Barry 129
Schweitzer, Albert 14, 154
Scott, Ian W. 47
Scott, James M. 87
Scripture
   As authoritative text 56–8, 99–100, 117–21
   Galatians as 162–9
   Luke-Acts as 122–32
Searle, John R. 38, 84
Segal, Alan F. 144, 146
Segal, Robert 19, 29
Shantz, Colleen 21–5, 28–9, 34, 37–9, 148
Sharf, Robert 28, 45
Shauf, Scott 110
Shelton, James B. 72
Silva, Moisés 141
Sinai Theophany 70–7
Smith, Daniel Lynwood and Zachary Lundin Kostopoulos 63, 65
Smith, D. Moody 1, 120, 125
Smith, James K.A. 33, 40, 84

Smith, Jonathan Z. 35
Spanos, N.P. and E.C. Hewitt. 91
Spiro, Melford E. 25
Sprinkle, Preston 150
Squires, John T. 68, 109
Stählin, G. 88
Stanton, Graham N. 93-4
Stark, Rodney 19, 37, 50, 91
Sterling, Gregory E. 105, 124-5, 127-9
Stuart, Donald 67
Stuckenbruck, Loren T. 116
Subjectivity 13-14, 20-7, 32-6, 45-6, 51, 137, 141

Talbert, Charles H. 68-9, 105
Tannehill, Robert C. 64, 106, 109
Taves, Ann 28, 38, 40
Taylor, Charles 12, 26, 53
Theological historiography 46-9
Thiselton, Anthony C. 12-13, 31, 44, 83, 86, 107-8
Tibbs, Clint 11, 16, 21-25, 86
Tomlin, Graham 139
Tongues-speech 82-92
  As speech act 83-5
Trans-empirical reality 44-5, 47-8, 50-3, 90, 109-10, 138-42, 154-7, 161-4, 166
Treier, Daniel J. 47
Troeltsch, Ernst 34, 47
Turner, Max 14, 67-9, 75-6, 78, 80-4, 109-11
Twelftree, Graham H. 2, 83, 104, 113, 117, 121, 139, 148, 151-2, 160

Uytanlet, Samson 129

Van der Horst, Pieter 70, 73
Vanhoozer, Kevin J. 33, 154
Volz, Paul 15
Von Baer, Heinrich 15

Wach, Joachim 20, 28
Walters, Patricia 64
Walton, Steve 90
Ward, W.R. 13
Watson, Francis 1
Webb, Robert L. 2, 47-8
Webster, John 55
Welker, Michael 74, 82
Wendt, Heidi 151, 166
Wenham, Gordon J. 86
Williams, Guy 52, 153
Wilson, Walter T. 127-9, 144
Wilson-Mendenhall, Christine D. and Lawrence W. Barsalo 39
Witherington III, Ben 64, 76, 80, 88, 94, 113, 137, 147, 167
Witness 32-3, 36, 49-53, 59
  Peter's 79, 82-5, 92-100, 109-10, 113-14, 130-2
  Paul's 145-6, 166-8
Wolter, Michael 122-3
Wolterstorff, Nicholas 25
Wreford, Mark 19, 30, 43, 50, 149, 160
Wright, N.T. 1, 142, 144
Writing 53-9, 117-26, 130-2, 162-9
Wynn, Mark 41-4, 107, 139-40, 160-1, 171

Yonan, Edward A. 29

Zahl, Simeon 13, 29, 160-1

www.ingramcontent.com/pod-product-compliance
Lightning Source LLC
Chambersburg PA
CBHW072234290426
44111CB00012B/2088